16 80

WHO

THE HELL

IS BOB?

The Man Behind the Magic

STEVE RUDMAN

HARA
PUBLISHING GROUP

Published by Hara Publishing
P.O. Box 19732, Seattle, WA 98109

ISBN: 1-883697-67-0 -softcover
ISBN: 1-883697-70-0 -hardcover

Library of Congress Catalog Card Number: 2001089617

Manufactured in the United States
10 9 8 7 6 5 4 3 2

Rudman, Steve.
    Who the Hell is Bob? : the man behind the magic /
Steve Rudman. -- 1st ed.
    p. cm.
    Includes index.
    LCCN 2001089617
    ISBN 1-883697-70-0

    1. Walsh, Bob--(Robert M.),--1940- 2. Promoters--
United States--Biography. 3. Statesman--United States--
Biography. 4. Internationalists--United States--
Biography. 5. Popular culture--United States--
Biography. 6. Celebrities--Miscellanea. 7. United
States--Biography.   I. Title

CT275.W2565R84 2001   973.92'092
              QBI01-700512

Editor: Vicki McCown
Cover Design: Scott Fisher
Book Design & Production: Scott and Shirley Fisher

For The Two Genes, Pfeifer and Fisher

Gaumar . . . Jos!

Cover Photographs

Front Cover
Top Row (L to R): Bob Walsh and Ronald Reagan; Ruth Walsh and Nancy Sinatra; Bob Walsh and Bill Russell; Richard Blackwell. **Second Row**: Ted Turner; Armand Hammer and Bob Walsh; Eduard Shevardnadze; Arnold Schwarzenegger. **Third Row**: Jim Baumann; Tom Jernstedt; Ruth Walsh and Lawrence Welk; Lenny Wilkens. **Fourth Row**: Jane Fonda and Bob Walsh; Gene Pfeifer; Blair Farrington; Timmy Walsh. **Fifth Row**: Jack McMillan; Sara Benveniste and Bob Walsh; Kristin Hayden; Sugar Ray Robinson. **Sixth Row**: Richard Nixon and Bob Walsh; Bob Walsh and Bruce McCaw; Rick Welts; Bob Walsh and Tracie Ruiz.

Back Cover
Left Column (Top to Bottom): Toni and Bob Walsh; Tedo Japaridze; Bob Walsh and Larry Coffman; Wally Walker; Anatoly Karpov and Bob Walsh; Dave Ross and Bob Walsh. **Right Column (Top to Bottom)**: David Gogol; Lexie Welts Schulte; Bob Walsh and Don Ellis; Jim Whittaker; Olga Korbut and Kristi Yamaguchi; Stanley Kramer.

Table Of Contents

Introduction

Whatever you can do, or dream you can, begin it. Boldness has genius, power, and magic in it.

— Johann Wolfgang von Goethe

The idea for this book came into my custody in the late fall of 1996 in the form of a loose package of notes, scribblings, and typewritten stories. "For God's sake," Bob Walsh implored, handing it over in the manner of an unwanted foundling, "please do something with this." For several weeks, I couldn't determine what that could possibly be. One of Bob's narratives had to do with a prominent Catholic Cardinal who apparently favored double shots of Jack Daniels. Another told the tale of an Imperial Wizard of the Ku Klux Klan. A third recounted Bob's role in what one newspaper had described as "arguably the greatest publicity stunt of the twentieth century." A fourth took place on Nikita Khrushchev's airplane. A fifth detailed how Bob barely escaped from a mad professor with his decency intact. Bob's package also contained a couple of weird references to The Boston Strangler and Ted Bundy.

"Is all of this true?" I asked Bob.

"Wait," he said. "There's more."

And so there was. Bob provided me with bizarre accounts about Hollywood celebrities, KGB spooks, televangelists, cosmonauts, and sexual entrappers, and even more stories which indicated that Bob had been variously mixed up with kings, Third World dictators, and Mafia warlords. It soon became clear to me that a day at the office for Bob could easily include a trip through an alligator farm, a tour of a missile factory, a ringside seat at a civil war, or a jaunt through a federal hoosegow.

"In the name of God, what do you want me to do with all this?" I asked Bob.

"Whatever you can," he replied.

For reasons I can't recall now, and it was probably a random decision, I started with Bob's relationship with Timothy Leary, proceeded to his friendship with Bill Russell, and then tackled his involvement with the Kingdom of Tonga. After that I planned to get into his recruitment of Alfred Hitchcock, his hiring of Captain Kirk, and the modeling agencies he raided on behalf of Al Capp, the cartoonist who created Li'l Abner. And when I finished with that, I would see what I could do about exploring Bob's reclamation of Regis Philbin, his dealings with Eduard Shevardnadze, and his sessions with Irene Ryan, the actress who played "Granny" in *The Beverly Hillbillies*. Bob had apparently spent some amount time plying her with buckets of scotch. That took place, as I came to find out, some years before Bob played hockey against a circus bear in Lithuania, some years after he received the key to the city of Louisville, Kentucky, and just about the time he landed on a list with Walter Cronkite and Walt Disney.

Of course, my efforts to unify Bob's strange but fascinating stories failed miserably. He had, so to speak, presented me with a series of dots I simply could not fathom how to connect. That being the case, I was left with two options: surrender for the sake of my sanity, or connect them anyway just to see what would happen.

What happened was that I ran into an observation by Ashley Montagu, the famous anthropologist who had also occupied a prominent place in Bob's peculiar universe. Montagu had said that since facts are at the mercy of any juggler, they do not always speak for themselves. But the facts about Bob's life, career, and stories all bore out, at least under my haphazard investigation of them. In a way, as I also discovered, they almost had to: Fiction would have rejected Bob Walsh out of hand.

A few particulars about Bob: Born near Boston a year before Pearl Harbor; reared in a good Protestant family; educated at a liberal arts college in Ohio; produced radio and television shows in Boston and Los Angeles; ran a professional basketball franchise in Seattle; became a sports agent, and then transformed himself into a promoter, businessman, humanitarian, back-channel ambassador, and citizen diplomat.

I had known Bob for a short while in the early 1980s during his sports agent-promoter period, unaware that he already had a long history of rainbow chasing, and oblivious to the fact that he had gone on to accumulate an even greater portfolio of windmill tilting. Other than apparently harboring an eclectic genius for doing the oddball thing that worked, there seemed little about Bob that adequately explained how he had made himself into what *Reader's Digest* used to call "a most unforgettable character." Bob had never been president or CEO of a major corporation, did not come from money, had never been elected to office, or appointed to a position of power. But he had, incongruously, done things that frankly ranked as astounding. And after a while, it occurred me that Bob's package of stories served as striking endorsements of Goethe's thought referenced above: "Boldness has genius, power, and magic in it." The unwanted foundling Bob delivered to me really amounted to a collection of object lessons about the dividends that can result from belief, action, confidence, and persistence.

Norman Cousins, the former editor of *The Saturday Review*, once remarked that "The wild dream is the first step to reality. It is the direction finder by which people locate higher goals and discover their higher selves."

Riding the wild dream is what Bob and his stories are all about. I am not here to judge them, only to connect the dots.

Seattle, Washington, June, 2001

Prologue

Only in fact can someone like Bob exist.
People like Bob do not exist in fiction.
Nobody would believe they are for real.

> – Kristin Hayden, Bob Walsh Enterprises,
> Tbilisi, Georgia

September 14, 1986

*A*s Lufthansa 342 raced nine miles a minute away from Frankfurt, Germany, finally leveling off at cruising altitude, Bob Walsh hoisted himself out of seat 3A, strode to the rear of the cabin, and stood for a long time squinting out a window. Not a single light flickered in the dark void below, a vast emptiness that left Bob with only a hyperactive imagination to conjure up the Promethean torments he was certain would greet him in Moscow, the dark heart of the Evil Empire. Bob weighed his chances of falling into the clutches of the KGB, grimlyvisualizing bold headlines that announced the mysterious disappearance of an American entrepreneur. His airborne ruminations soon kindled a remembrance of a time in Hawaii, when Bob had drafted his Last Will and Testament. The document, as

Bob knew well, included a $100,000 life insurance policy, the proceeds of which would be used to fly fifty of his closest friends to the island of Maui to party and mourn his death. Invitations had already been sent out, RSVPs received. The invitees included two Hall of Fame basketball players, a former judge, several CEOs, a communications mogul, a network sportscaster, the strangest sportswriter on nine planets, an ex-wife, and several other amiable reprobates with whom Bob had closed down saloons from Seoul to Stockholm. According to his Last Will and Testament, Bob

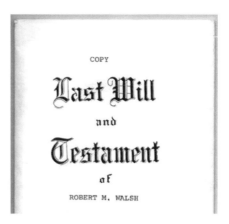

would be cremated, his ashes strewn across the Pacific, after which the revelers would get hog-faced snockered.

The pilot's voice jarred Bob from his tropical reverie: Lufthansa 342 had entered Soviet airspace, and snapping photographs through the airplane's windows constituted a security breach that would result in a confiscated camera and destroyed film. So intent were the Soviets on keeping the features and boundaries of their territory secret that Russian newspapers did not publish weather maps until the 1970s, and street maps of major cities had been published inaccurately on purpose. Moscow once even issued an edict that there would be no further mention of bridges in school textbooks, thus negating the existence of these "strategic" structures. The irony was that, while Soviet officials forbid Western tourists from snapping photos through an airplane window, American reconnaissance jets examined every last detail of their terra firma.

Bob Walsh was no tourist. A businessman from Seattle, Washington, he ventured to Moscow for a series of meetings with officials from the USSR Ministry of Sport and Ministry of Culture, and then planned to keep several appointments in Leningrad, where he would also attend the World Chess Championship between Anatoly Karpov and Gary Kasparov. But the major impetus for Bob's junket would focus on catastrophe control. Bob's principal project of the moment, the 1990 Goodwill Games, teetered on collapse. If that happened – and Goodwill Games creator Ted Turner had given Bob no reason to think otherwise — Bob's status as the major independent events producer in the Pacific Northwest would be reduced to a career scripted in the sand. Nothing else Bob had ever successfully staged, including the NCAA Men's Final Four and a hundred other events, would be worth a ruble if he couldn't deliver the Games.

Already a pariah for the manner in which he had acquired them over the objections of Seattle's parochial business cartel, Bob would be excoriated anew for falling in league with the controversial Turner and chumming with the despised Soviets. And certainly the city's newspapers would take giddy delight in pointing out how catastrophically unhinged he had been. Fortunately, the papers remained oblivious that the board of directors at Turner Broadcasting System had started to hoist a white flag on the Games because of the financial bloodbath they had absorbed in Moscow the previous July. Bob had kept a tight lid on the news, hoping he would bump into a financial miracle that would save the Games. Perhaps, he thought, there might be a way to resurrect them even if TBS declined to underwrite the cost of the event, although Bob could hardly envision how. Staging the Games would cost about $80 million and Bob had gone through most of his life with the cotton linings of both trouser pockets exposed to the world.

Bob saw two possible options if Turner's board cancelled: drop the idea of Seattle hosting the Games, or convince the Soviets that he and the Seattle Host Committee he represented could produce them without Turner and his money. This presented a daunting challenge, for as much as any American could, Turner had earned the Soviets' trust. Or, rather, they trusted his money, already having received $8.9 million of it. The Soviets had worked with Turner and his staff for nearly a year in preparation for the 1986 Goodwill Games. But they did not know Bob, nor did he know them. Bob would have to sell himself to the Soviets and do so without any knowledge of the Russian language or the Soviet way of doing business.

Worse, he would have to stand up to withering Soviet scrutiny, and do so on Russian turf, an intimidating prospect since almost everything about the Soviet Union completely overwhelmed him, starting with the sheer size of the place. Nearly nine million square miles of Soviet territory muscled their way on top of the world from the North Atlantic to the North Pacific, spanning eleven of the world's twenty-four time zones. Nearly 300 million people, representing 130 national or ethnic groups and enough religions to gag Billy Graham, occupied that amphitheater, jabbering away in eight alphabets. Bob conjured up a veritable newsreel of black-and-white stereotypes familiar to any child of the Cold War: men and women in matted coats and fur hats, punished by icy winds, trudging through thigh-deep snow, wearing a collective expression suggesting imminent banishment to Siberia; stone-faced Soviet leaders waving a stiff benediction over a panoply of military might; busts of Lenin looming over unempowered masses. Bob had no idea how he would react to Moscow, a city in his mind bathed grimly in gloom, but he had to trust, as he had so often done, that his instincts would prove correct, and that he would be able to put aside the perceptions and misconceptions that stalked his consciousness and find a way to connect with Soviet authorities.

The more Bob thought about it, the more he became struck by the extent to which happenstance had shaped and defined his career, and how his good fortune to date had often been the result of placing massive action ahead of careful planning. Mostly, Bob recognized that he was an incorrigible romantic who had a great penchant for kismet. Still, where this adventure might take him defied even a vague forecast. The Goodwill Games loomed larger in scope than any of his previous projects — bigger, bolder, and more uncertain than the Final Four or the dozens of football games, soccer matches, golf tournaments, and marathon races over which he had presided. But wherever they took him, Bob would begin to understand soon enough.

As Lufthansa 342 began its descent into Moscow, Bob Walsh, reared in a good Protestant home in the Boston suburbs by diligent, responsible, and practical parents, could not have imagined that he soon would become the international point man in an organization that would show thousands of Soviet citizens that a far different way of life exited beyond their borders. Nor could he have imagined his unlikely escapades in the mythical land of Jason and the Argonauts, or his impending involvements with bandits, presidents, and Mafia warlords. Bob did not know it then, but he had a civil war to attend, a rocket to launch, kingdoms to explore, and lives to save.

He probably would not have believed, as the distant lights ahead started to wink, that hundreds of people in the Soviet expanse below would have cheered his arrival had they known he was on the way. On the other hand, had Bob been clairvoyant, he might have gone home and yanked the sheets over his head. Two beautiful women lurked in ambush, and Bob would eventually curse himself that he had never invested in an industrial-strength padlock for the zipper on his trousers.

But those were nightmares yet to be dreamt. Right then, as Lufthansa 342's landing gears came down, Bob's ambition focused only on saving the Goodwill Games from certain extinction. What followed would become a story worthy of Forrest Gump. Only in this case, it would turn into an adventure in which reality trumped fiction.

Peace Through Pole Vaulting

Everybody knows that Bob has a lot of friends in high places. I think Bob is living proof that dynamite really does come in small packages.

> —*Ted Turner,*
>   *Vice Chairman, Time Warner,*
>   *Atlanta, Georgia*

*B*ob Walsh emerged from a private elevator on the thirty-fifth floor of the Waldorf Astoria in mid-town Manhattan one Sunday morning in the summer of 1998, fairly overwhelmed by the rich tapestries, crystal, and oils that assailed his eyes. Moving around the corner and down a hallway, Bob observed the gold lettering on the mahogany door that identified Suite 35A, whose occupant answered Bob's knock with a smile and a handshake. The man wearing tan Dockers and a green golf shirt owned a ten percent stake in Time Warner, eight ranches in New Mexico, Montana, and Wyoming, and several properties in Florida and California. *The New York Times* had reported that those holdings made him the second-largest landowner in the country behind the United States government. It was probably true. After all, what wasn't true about this once-abused maverick who had evolved into one of the leading architects of the Information Age?

It sometimes required considerable effort to remember what the world was like before 6 p.m. on June 1, 1980, the moment Ted Turner flicked the switch on his crazy dream of showering news on the world via satellite. At the time, the only players were the three broadcast networks and PBS. MTV didn't exist. The Weather Channel didn't exist. ESPN barely existed. Televangelism had yet to plague the human race. Television doled news out in distilled, half-hour helpings, served by Walter Cronkite and John Chancellor. But when Ted Turner, from the basement of a social organization's converted clubhouse, fired up Cable News Network, the world started to shrink. Before too many more years had passed, CNN's signal would leap across continents, penetrating every wall and divide political man had ever devised, giving birth to a TV universe rife with hundreds of channels.

By the time Turner escorted Bob through the kitchenette and into the sitting area of Suite 35A, they had already engaged each other in dozens of meetings, conferences, and telephone calls stretching back several years. As usual, Bob had been advised by Turner's appointment secretary that he would have a half hour with Turner, not more. Turner had a short attention span, and most people could not keep him focused beyond ten minutes. So whenever Bob visited Turner, he knew he had to get in, make his point, and get out.

One of Bob's memorable meetings with Turner had occurred five years earlier, in 1993, at CNN headquarters in Atlanta. Tucked down a long, lavishly carpeted hall on the fourteenth floor, Turner's office glittered with Oscars and Emmys and contained a veritable museum of silver sporting trophies, stuffed mallards, mounted fish, snakeskins, and oil paintings of great yachts. It also featured a velvet couch that converted conveniently into a bed. Crystal dice from Tiffanys sparkled on Turner's massive desk, near a sign that said, "Lead, Follow or Get Out Of The Way."

Accompanied by Bruce McCaw, whose family had made a fortune in cellular telephones after developing McCaw Cellular, the forerunner of AT&T Wireless, Bob had arrived to pitch Turner about the possibility of one of his networks becoming a sponsor of McCaw's IndyCar Racing Team.

2

Turner shook McCaw's hand, eyeballing the intensely private man before him.

"Bruce," he said, "I've always wanted to meet someone with more money than me. Now, what is it you two are doing?"

"A couple of things," interjected Bob. "We're looking for a sponsor for Bruce's racing team, and we're working on putting an NBA franchise in Vancouver. Bruce will be one of the major investors."

"An NBA franchise!" Turner said loudly. "I own an NBA franchise. I also own a baseball team. Wait a minute, Bruce." Turner cast his glance around the suite. "Where the hell is that magazine?"

Turner dashed into

Bob Walsh, Bruce McCaw

the office of Dee Woods, his secretary. Returning with a copy of *The Sporting News*, Turner thrust it at McCaw.

"You see this, Bruce?" Turner asked, pointing to his own photograph on the cover. "This is me, Ted Turner. See? My picture is on the front page. Me! Ted Turner! And you know what it says? It says I am the most powerful man in the world of sports. The most powerful man! Number 1 out of 100!"

Suddenly animated, Turner paced, pointing at his photo.

"The most powerful man in sports," he continued. "But you know what, Bruce? Nobody has called to congratulate me. Nobody! Can you imagine that? And do you know why? Nobody gives a shit!"

Ted tossed aside the magazine and continued to stalk the floor.

"I've always dreamed of becoming a billionaire. Always. I've worked my ass off for all these years so I could become a billionaire. And finally, the day arrived. I jumped into the car and went home. I was all excited and called my family into the living room. I said,

'Family, you know what? I've worked and waited. And today, just today, I became a billionaire.' And you know what? They didn't give a shit! But wait until you own an NBA franchise. Wait until you win the championship. Strangers will love you and players will throw champagne all over you. That, Bruce, is the only time people will give a shit."

Turner hadn't changed much since that meeting five years earlier. His hair now sported swaths of gray and the lines around his eyes seemed a little more pronounced. But Turner remained lean and well-muscled.

"So what brings you to New York?" asked Turner.

"I've got a couple of projects going in the former Soviet Union that I'd like to run by you," said Bob, who proceeded to outline them quickly lest he lose that fickle focus of Turner's.

"Sounds interesting," replied Turner. "But me? Hell, I don't have any money. No money at all. And anyway, it's about time I got going. We're heading to Central Park."

Turner had come to New York to preside over the fourth edition of the Goodwill Games, a quadrennial international athletic festival loosely patterned after the Summer Olympics, and one of his least-understood creations.

"I can't think of anything," Turner said, "I'm prouder of than the Goodwill Games. Maybe CNN, but the Games rank with CNN. God, twelve, thirteen years already. It's hard to believe."

Bob nodded, reflecting at how time had eroded so many perceptions about the man sitting opposite him. Just a dozen years earlier, Ted Turner had been in his prime as an equal-opportunity offender. He had not yet channeled his headline-making megalomania into global good causes, gone on anti-depressants, married Jane Fonda, or quit drinking, smoking, and womanizing. He had not yet evolved into the billionaire flower child who espoused world peace, funded the United Nations, or commissioned himself to mop up the mess the planet had become. Turner stood riveted in dubious prominence as the overly leveraged Captain Outrageous, the man who had spent his childhood brawling in military schools, his college years at Brown University playing the party animal (he was expelled for setting fire to a homecoming float), and much of his adulthood pricking the balloons of official pretense. He had not yet incurred the wrath of Hollywood for despoiling with color many of its classic movies, had not yet been anointed *Time's* Man of the Year, and had not yet changed, through

CNN's coverage of the Gulf War, the perception that news was something that had happened into something that *is* happening. Turner remained a decade away from presiding over a voracious media empire that would include CNN, TNT, Turner Classic Movies, CNN SI, CNN FN, CNN Interactive, CNN Newsource, CNN Airport News, The Cartoon Network, Turner Publishing, and a stake in Time Warner. He had just launched a hostile, $5.4 billion takeover of CBS, negotiated the purchase of MGM/UA's movie library for $1.6 billion, spent $64 million on the Omni shopping-hotel-office complex in Atlanta, introduced CNN Radio, and squirmed as his two moribund sports franchises, the Braves and Hawks, squatted south in the standings. Turner had been a corporate Don Quixote then with a loud drawl, his empire-building routinely overshadowed by rehashes of his turbulent days as a drunken sailor, a serial adulterer, and volcanic egomaniac given to epic boasts.

"I'd like people to look back and gasp at what I did in my lifetime," Turner had said. "I'm trying to set the all-time record for achievement by one person in a lifetime. That puts you in some pretty big company: Alexander the Great, Gandhi, Jesus Christ, Mohammed, Buddha, Washington, Roosevelt, and Churchill." Turner would have been accorded more serious attention had he been the $5 billion man he would become, or had he not caused massive eye rolling by proclaiming, "I want to be the Jiminy Cricket for America, its conscience."

He had been nowhere near that. Instead, he had carved a reputation as a multi-flavored fruit loop that flirted with bankruptcy. So when he announced he had struck a deal with the USSR State Sports Committee (Goskomsport) to organize, produce, and televise something called the Goodwill Games, the consensus was that the trap door on Turner's forehead had sprung open again, revealing yet another of the crazed cuckoos that routinely seemed to control his thoughts. Turner did not sway instant Goodwill critics much when he boasted that the Games would be "a show the likes of which the world has never seen." It had been simply understood that this and other Mars-based pronouncements gushed from the same Ted Turner who once rode an ostrich to publicize the Braves, the same Ted Turner who had said, "You think Farrah Fawcett is so great? Sleep with her five times and she'd be just like your wife."

What most everyone failed to fathom was the sea change taking place in Turner, one of those epochal shifts that guarantee things will never be the same. CNN had not yet become the video medium of record; it had barely lived down its awkward hatching as the "Chicken

5

Noodle Network," which had been accompanied by a Turner prediction of almost messianic bombast: "We won't sign off until the end of the world," he had declared. "And we'll cover that live."

It had been too early to tell whether Turner could make good on that pledge, but CNN had become available in twenty-seven foreign countries, mostly in hotels and military bases, Turner already envisioning CNN as the principal link to the geopolitical marketplace. He had, in fact, been ramping up to chisel his place in history.

"All the world leaders are going to need CNN," Turner had said after giving satellite dishes to King Juan Carlos of Spain and Italian Prime Minister Bettino Craxi. "In five years, CNN will be available in virtually every nook and cranny on this planet via satellite."

His plans to turn a bargain-basement cable network into a serious rival of the broadcast networks had roundly been viewed with bemusement. Early CNN newscasts, for example, received widespread excoriations for their lack of editing and indiscriminate story selection. But what Turner had done was nothing less than reinvent TV news. More than that, he had started to build a global communications system he hoped would one day help stop the arms race, control population, preserve the environment, and become the world leader in news and advertising.

The nexus of Turner's activism had been the Better World Society, a non-profit organization he founded to produce programs on significant issues and personalities. Turner had provided $500,000 in seed money and donated air time for Better World Society programs on Martin Luther King Jr., the Jacques Cousteau explorations, and a history of the Cuban missile crisis. He had not only planned a seven-hour video profile of the Soviet Union, he had signed an agreement of cooperation with Gosteleradio, the Soviet state committee for radio and television, for an exchange of news and entertainment programming. If that marked the beginning of Turner's strategy for using television to usher in the new millennium, his hope was that the Goodwill Games would warm the Cold War.

Turner's critics believed he had about as much chance of doing that as passing off Rocky and Bullwinkle cartoons as documentaries. The Goodwill Games, they reasoned, smacked only as a play for publicity by America's leading publicity hound, and a lame attempt to strike back at the three major networks after Turner lost the opportunity to compete for the rights to televise the Olympic Games. What especially galled the literati was not so much Turner's unfounded

6

hyperventilation that his Games would be "bigger than the Olympics," but his naïve notion that the path to peace ran through the pole vault pit, over the pommel horse, and through the motoball track.

Following the U.S. boycott of the 1980 Moscow Olympics, and Moscow's boycott of the Los Angeles Games in 1984, Turner had burst into the offices of Robert Wussler, his pin-striped aide-de-camp, and laid bare his multi-faceted dream: the two superpowers would meet on his Superstation, advancing the causes of peace and pole vaulting in a single, telegenic blow. It mattered little to Turner that athletes from the two countries had competed on hundreds of fronts since 1976, including two Winter Olympics.

Turner Broadcasting's ensuing contract with the USSR State Sports Committee, negotiated by Wussler during two dozen jaunts to Moscow, called for the inaugural Goodwill Games to be held in Moscow in July of 1986 and then four years later in an American city to be determined by TBS.

While Howard Cosell led an orchestra of objections, Turner remained glacially indifferent to what other people thought about him. Turner wanted to do the Games because he believed that no harm, and perhaps considerable good, could come if people communicated via global television, ignoring the fact many people loathe their enemies even more once they get to know them.

"All we're saying is that the Soviet Union is the Evil Empire and a bunch of bums," Turner had pontificated. "But we don't know anything about them. What are we fixin' to fight these people for? To keep from blowing ourselves up, isn't this worth a shot? Couldn't hurt."

The U.S. government thought it could. Skeptical about Mikhail Gorbachev and his embryonic reforms, *perestroika* and *glasnost*, Washington also nursed a suspicion about the private ventures of citizen diplomats operating on a grand scale in the Soviet Union, and a fear the Soviets would use such efforts for propaganda.

"We couldn't determine if Turner's deal with the Soviets was constructive or damaging," recalled Ed Salazar, who worked the Soviet desk at the State Department when Turner announced his creation of the Games. "But Turner was a major figure. We had to accommodate ourselves to that, so he wouldn't make a major blunder and we wouldn't miss an opportunity."

Turner's principal allies soon became the Soviets, who grew especially interested in a mutual sporting exchange after Gorbachev's June 11, 1985, call for sweeping political and economic reforms in Soviet society. TBS signed its contract with the USSR State Sports Committee three months later, on August 6, and three months before Reagan and Gorbachev, meeting in Geneva, agreed on a resumption of cultural and performing arts exchanges between the United States and Soviet Union. Turner got so excited over the prospect of seeking profits and preaching peace that he performed somersaults down a CNN hallway as TBS board members cringed at the boondoggle they believed he had created. Wussler tried later to put a Happy Face on it.

"Sometimes," Wussler noted, "there's a certain genius in ignoring the facts."

Deals With The Dark Side

I can't think of anybody who has ever been involved in so many different kinds of things, and on such scale. The range of Bob's activity is phenomenal.

—Gene Pfeifer, retired executive, U.S. West, Seattle, Washington

As part of its agreement with the USSR State Sports Committee, Turner Broadcasting System obligated itself to select an American city to host the 1990 Goodwill Games by the Opening Ceremony of the 1986 Games. The nearly impossible task of identifying a metropolis that would welcome Ted Turner and his ill-defined vision fell to Mike Mitchell, a TBS consultant. Mitchell, who had worked for the Los Angeles Organizing Committee during the 1984 Summer Olympics, compiled a list of twenty-seven cities and sent bid packages to each. It did not take him long to discover that few cities were interested in hosting the Games, and that, of those that were, the best candidate was Seattle, Washington.

A year earlier, Seattle had staged the most successful NCAA Final Four in the tournament's thirty-three-year history. Seattle also harbored a keen interest in Soviet affairs, the Seattle-Tashkent (Uzbekistan) Sister City pairing remaining the strongest of the original four created during the 1973 Nixon-Brezhnev summits. The first group of Soviet teenagers to visit the United States had done so through the efforts of a Bainbridge Island, Washington, organization called "Earthstewards." In addition, Seattle had hosted several extraordinary economic, cultural, and political conferences, two of which, called "Target Seattle," focused on Soviet-related issues.

Neither Bob Walsh, who had organized that Final Four, nor Jarlath Hume, the director of Seattle's Metrocenter YMCA and the instigator of the Target Seattle symposia, realized their city was under consideration to host the Goodwill Games until Mitchell telephoned Bob to ask why he had received no response to the bid packages he had dispatched to the mayor's office and Seattle City Council.

"I don't know," Bob replied. "But I'm certainly going to find out."

Bob, Jarlath, and Doug Jewett, Seattle's city prosecutor, had spent months brainstorming project ideas for the 1989 celebration of Washington's Bicentennial. But the Goodwill Games seemed more intriguing than anything they had discussed. For Bob, they rep-

Jarlath Hume

resented the opportunity to host an athletic competition considerably beyond the size or scope of any Final Four. For Hume and Jewett, both intensely interested in Russian history, they represented a chance to open a dialogue with the Soviets on issues of vital importance to the USA and USSR. Thoughtful and ambitious, Hume envisioned a companion arts festival to the Games patterned after the one the Los Angeles Organizing Committee staged during the 1984 Olympics, and believed the Games had the potential to help Washington State develop new trading relationships along the Pacific Rim.

With that in mind, Hume spoke to a banker acquaintance, convincing him to ante several thousand dollars to help finance a bid submission. Jewett then convinced the Seattle City Council to put its imprint on it, along with $12,500 in seed money, which he handled so deftly the appropriation barely caused a ripple. Only later would Hume and Jewett learn that if the city had done any kind of study, or if Mayor Charles Royer had asked his department heads if they wanted to pursue a bid for the Games, the idea would have been shouted down. But since the city studied nothing, it was seduced into endorsing the bid in blissful ignorance.

Ignorance had its price. The men who held sway over Seattle's business core quickly let it be known that they didn't want the Games, fearing first and foremost they would wind up paying for them. Neither did the University of Washington desire the Games since it would, by default, have to host a majority of Goodwill athletic events. Seattle's leading newspaper, *The Seattle Times*, opposed the Games on the grounds they would cost too much, snarl traffic, bleed taxpayers, and permit Ted Turner, who had once scandalized the yachting fraternity by raising a Frenchwoman's bra from a mast, in the door. And Turner smacked of royalty compared to the dehumanizing character of the Soviet Union, in which duplicitous men in the Kremlin masqueraded as peaceniks, a translucent sham not lost on either the thirteen million involuntary guests of the Soviet gulag or the wretched souls in Afghanistan, against whom Soviet soldiers had used, according to a United Nations report, toy bombs to kill and dismember children.

When, during a 1983 speech, Ronald Reagan described the Soviet Union as the "Evil Empire," he reflected the feelings of a majority of Americans who believed that "the only language the Soviets understand is force." So it became little wonder that a Goodwill bid failed to enthuse Seattle's downtown emperors. Walsh, Hume, and Jewett were conspiring to bring the Evil Empire right into the heart of the Emerald City.

Seattle Police Chief Patrick Fitzsimons especially worried over what might happen if Communists swooped upon his city. Too few police, he believed, enforced the law as it was; providing security for the Goodwill Games conjured up a catalog of concerns. What if Seattle won the Goodwill bid and couldn't execute? What if Turner went bankrupt? What if the Soviets pulled out? If the Games were a bargain, why weren't other U.S. cities clamoring to get them? Why hadn't

Walsh, Hume, and Jewett consulted with the people they would have to hit up for corporate support?

Bob Walsh had never been part of Seattle's business elite, even declining to join the Chamber of Commerce after its president, a cardboard character named George Duff, refused to endorse Seattle's bid for the Final Four, claiming the Chamber "doesn't want anything to do with things like that." Bob proceeded with the Final Four anyway, cementing Duff's conviction that Bob was a camel with its nose under the tent, and giving Bob the impression that if Duff couldn't see the value of the Final Four, he wouldn't see the merits of the Goodwill Games. So Bob left Duff out of any Goodwill discussions, forging ahead with the thought that establishing commercial and cultural links with a century-old enemy were compelling enough reasons to proceed. Bob figured his vision would ultimately be shared by everyone who counted. Hume and Jewett agreed. What they ignored was that Seattle, for all of its pretentions, was not disposed to embracing mega-scale international events.

Seattleites cringed at ideas they considered new or invasive and rabidly opposed any notions suggesting growth. The party line, most eloquently enunciated by *Seattle Post-Intelligencer* columnist Emmett Watson, demanded, "Keep The Bastards Out." That not only summarized the insider sentiment about the Games, it underscored the city's historic intolerance with respect to any individual who might dragoon everybody else into civic do-goodism.

In 1962, Seattle did not unanimously embrace the World's Fair, doomsayers foaming that, if built, the Space Needle would tip over. Seattle did not wholeheartedly support the construction of the Kingdome a decade later, critics carping that crowds would collapse sidewalks in Pioneer Square near the Dome. Seattle's personality worked against big, one-time projects that required consensus and teamwork, and Seattleites did not want to be part of any parade.

The Goodwill Games created objectors outside Seattle's gates. Despite Reagan's agreement with Gorbachev calling for a resumption of academic and cultural exchanges, the administration insisted the Games would not be held on U.S. soil, especially if they were awarded to Seattle. Flanked to the east by the Hanford Nuclear Reservation, to the west by the Trident Submarine Base, and housing Boeing plants to the north and south, Seattle was a closed city, strategically off limits.

The International Olympic Committee and United States Olympic Committee had their own reasons for opposing the Games, posing as they did political and financial threats to the Olympic movement.

"I thought the Games would become a lose-lose situation for everybody," recalled Jim Talbot, whose company, Pacific Marine Fisheries, had been doing business in the USSR since 1973. "And I just didn't believe Bob Walsh had the right kind of connections to generate the financial support he would need."

Bob did not belong to proper clubs where the pompous guzzled, and was not a mainstream businessman. He supported causes such as the entertaining populist movement to change the state song from "Washington, My Home" to "Louie, Louie." Where Bob's friends and colleagues saw him as adventurous, Seattle's business suits saw him as reckless. The Goodwill Games, those suits told him, amounted to just too large a burr in the civic britches.

Walsh says Seattle bid should land 1990 Games

From Page C-1

prime prospects, including New York, Chicago, Philadelphia and Los Angeles, had just about ruled themselves out earlier, although

Visualization Techniques

I've never met anyone who is such a dreamer about what could be, and in such diversity. Bob has a knack about creating a dream and then making it a reality.

—Don Nielsen, former chairman of the board,
Bob Walsh Enterprises,
Seattle, Washington

Had the Goodwill Games not found Bob Walsh, he would have found them. Bob shopped constantly for new and unusual projects. They not only defined Bob's career, to a large extent they were his life. Bob had an entrepreneurial spirit. His mind harbored an unrestricted jumble of ideas, and if he could conceive of something, it was possible. And if there was something he really wanted to do, he would find a way to make it happen. Every new project — and this was especially true of the Goodwill Games — came laced with obstacles and riddled with uncertainties. But Bob never saw impediments, only possibilities and challenges.

Each project Bob visualized became a done deal in his mind before anyone else saw square one on paper. He moved beyond blind spots while others still rubbed their eyes, beyond soft spots while others crunched numbers. He left it to bottom liners to figure out details, frequently an exasperating experience for those charged with turning his voracious visions into reality. Bob also had an entrepreneurial personality, and was always ready to gamble with no fear of being wrong. He jumped off cliffs, assuming he would enjoy a soft landing, and somehow he usually did. Many people who worked with Bob were amazed by his abandon and mesmerized by the level of risk he took when he had no idea whether one of his projects would work. The truth was, it never occurred to Bob that something wouldn't work.

George Bernard Shaw had Bob pegged perfectly: "The people who get on in this world are those who get up and look for the circumstances they want and, if they can't find them, make them." Bob had an entrepreneurial mentality, both stoked and penalized by an imagination that had no off switch. And when inspiration struck him, Bob operated as if it had already become a marketable commodity. It was his biggest asset and biggest problem.

Bob came across, in many ways, like Ted Turner, who had 100 ideas, of which ninety were crazy, another five impossible, and the last five spectacular. As a consequence, people loved to hang negative labels on Bob. As a promoter, he had done awfully well spending other people's money. As an administrator, he had never met a detail he couldn't mismanage. He made too many commitments without considering consequences. But those who knew Bob intimately saw something different — a man whose sole agenda was to accomplish something big. For whatever qualities he allegedly lacked, he compensated by surrounding himself with influential allies, astute investors, and staffers with keen eyes for detail. All of Bob's partners and investors, in their own fashion, trusted his instincts even if they didn't always understand them. They funded more than one hundred of Bob's expeditions to Moscow, Geneva, Barcelona, Stockholm, Copenhagen, London, Zurich, New York, Istanbul, Seoul, Frankfurt, and Tbilisi — just a few of the venues in Bob's global wanderings — without knowing exactly if any would ever result in economic gain.

Bob had, his investors unanimously agreed, an amazing ability to bring creative and profitable ideas to the table. Bill Russell, the basketball legend, frequently used the word "visionary" in reference to Bob; so did Ted Turner.

"Bob and I shared the dream of a more peaceful, less violent world," Turner observed after a decade of exposure to Bob. "We always had that in common."

What mainly separated Bob Walsh and Ted Turner was the fact that Bob never entertained notions about becoming a millionaire, much less a billionaire. In a lot of ways, Bob was an ordinary citizen, in many more ways he was the most extraordinary citizen imaginable. He had the wide lens to spot opportunity and the obsessive narrow-mindedness to exploit it. Unlike Turner, Bob's entrepreneurial bent generally steered him clear of the bottom line, a vast point of demarcation not only from Turner, but from Armand Hammer, the most famous — or infamous — private American entrepreneur in the seventy-year history of the Soviet Union.

Hammer operated there as a freewheeling capitalist when no one else from the West could have imagined such a thing; in a leap across the century, Bob conducted business in the former Soviet Union in a niche of his own making, recognizing, for example, the economic potential of the Republic of Georgia a half-decade before the fall of Communism and a full decade before investment bankers and oil predators swooped into the country. Hammer married a Russian woman. Bob married two. But Hammer was far more adroit at dealing with women than Bob ever was. When Hammer's wife suspected he was having an affair with an art adviser he persuaded the woman to wear a wig and change her name so his wife wouldn't find out about the romance. When Bob suspected one of his wives of having an affair, it cost him a ransom in attorney's fees. Hammer served as a benefactor to the children of Chernobyl. Bob orchestrated humanitarian efforts in Russia, Armenia, and Georgia. Until Stalin came to power, Hammer had access to Soviet leadership unmatched by professional diplomats. So did Bob. But there the similarities ended. Hammer finally left the Soviet Union with a fortune in Faberge eggs and Romanov treasures. Bob's cache included a menagerie of cats. Hammer made a killing in bourbon when prohibition ended and dabbled in cattle breeding before becoming president of Occidental Petroleum. Bob's financial pump always registered two quarts low. Hammer had a medical degree; Bob barely made it through college.

Bob belonged to a species of American — the commercial troubadour — that flourished mainly in the late nineteenth century and had pretty well died out by World War II. Some of Bob's colleagues thought of him as sort of a linear descendant of P.T. Barnum, or perhaps a Wilson Mizner, a jack-of-all trades from the 1920s. Mizner made little public impact except for his vast legacy of Miznerisms — "You're a mouse studying to be a rat" — but was, in addition, a Klondike gold seeker, Florida realtor, Broadway playwright, Hollywood screenwriter, Atlantic gambler, and prizefight manager. In some ways, the comparisons to Barnum and Mizner were unfair. While some of what Bob did qualified as circus acts — the National Aeronautics and Space Administration had a long file on one of Bob's more outrageous stunts — most of it did not. Still, the comparison with Mizner, particularly, was valid to this degree: Bob became a networker-consultant-agent-negotiator-salesman-producer-programmer-diplomat with interests in media, entertainment, athletics, real estate, banking, pharmaceuticals, dairy processing, and space technology. Unlike Barnum or Mizner, who had the unfettered run of another, extinct America, Bob operated in a world encumbered by committees, bureaucracies, and red tape. What may have separated him more than anything from the traditional entrepreneur was the fact that, at heart, Bob subscribed to Oscar Wilde's notion that any map that did not include Utopia was not worth following.

Some of Bob's ventures ended on the south side of success, but he learned important, sometimes agonizing, lessons in them. He developed a tremendous capacity for change, and a career of doing it had placed him in league with the oddest clusters of characters. He had run the table with cardinals, atheists, white segregationists, black supremacy extremists, cartoonists, chemical salvation advocates, politicians, conductors, ambassadors, murderers, ministers, conspiracy theorists, John Birchers, actors, producers, professional athletes, legal eagles, business tycoons, venture capitalists, and oil barons. But his favorite people included a woman who cut his hair, a maid, and a man who operated a dry cleaning business. Bob developed as much a sense of ease with presidents and prime ministers as he did with bellhops and parking lot attendants. Bob's critics didn't understand it. They understood only that they couldn't control him. Prominent Seattle jeweler Herb Bridge had breakfast one morning with Bob and Jarlath Hume, who wanted Bridge to chair one of the Goodwill Games committees.

"Why is it," Jarlath asked Bridge, "that this city's business leadership won't get behind Bob's projects?"

"Everybody is waiting for Bob to fail," replied Bridge. "And they're hoping he will fail."

"Fail?" asked Hume. "Why?"

"Just a natural disdain for promoters," said Bridge. "Listen, I sell things, but I don't wear blue suede shoes."

Seattle Police Chief Patrick Fitzsimons more than disdained Bob; he actively disliked him. Bob always wondered whether his arrest on a DUI charge, thrown out of court for a lack of evidence and subsequently reduced to reckless driving, stemmed from Fitzsimons' animosity towards him for pursuing the Games. True or not, Fitzsimons believed Bob to be an arrogant SOB, an opinion shared by William Gerberding, the University of Washington president, who came to resent the manner in which Bob hornswoggled the school into becoming the primary venue for the Games. Gerberding didn't understand the issues involved in the bid. He only understood that Bob did not approach his projects in a traditional, systematic way.

When Bob presented a plan, it had usually been scratched on an envelope or scribbled on a bar napkin, his financial projections often consisting only of the belief that money would turn up somewhere. Bob's operative philosophy was to roll with the punches and respond to problems as they occurred. No project had to be perfect; no project was. So Bob acted out of the box, largely ignoring committees and feasibility studies. Action, he believed, built confidence and created a bandwagon effect.

To get the Goodwill Games rolling against tides of equal parts suspicion and angst, Bob and Jarlath Hume determined that they needed a major player in their camp, someone who reached across an array of constituency groups. Hume had what he believed to be the perfect candidate. Father William J. Sullivan, a Jesuit priest, served as president of Seattle University, the Northwest's largest private college. Sullivan, who sat on the board of directors of nine organizations, soon became convinced the Games could go a long way on a non-

Rev. William F. Sullivan, Bob Walsh

political basis to improving U.S.-Soviet relations, and believed they would launch Seattle into a new era of international trade. But aware of the negative public drift, Sullivan sought out Eddie Carlson, an executive with United Airlines, and asked for advice. The architect of Seattle's 1962 World's Fair told Sullivan that chairing the Games was the right thing to do, but warned him he would get nothing but grief.

"I flat told Father Sullivan not to do it," remembered Jim Talbot, who had been doing business in the Soviet Union since 1973. "I told him the Games were a bad idea. He didn't listen."

Father Sullivan ultimately didn't listen because Hume was persuasive and because Father Sullivan had a ferocious sense of public service. Two months after Father Sullivan became chairman of the board of the Seattle Host Committee, the Turner Broadcasting System awarded Seattle the 1990 Goodwill Games in what amounted to a formality. No other U.S. city wanted anything to do with them, a fact that irked TBS Executive Vice President Bob Wussler, who thought Seattle far too much a jerkwater to host the athletic world. Wussler also wanted the Games in an Eastern Time zone that worked more favorably for television, but was forced to accept the inevitable: It was Seattle or nowhere.

Ted Turner awards the Goodwill Games to Seattle

If the selection of Seattle irked Wussler, it made Gerberding come unhinged, especially when he learned through an article in *The Seattle Post-Intelligencer* that the University of Washington would not only become the site of the Opening and Closing ceremonies, but that Goodwill athletes would commandeer the school's dormitories, turning them into an Athletes' Village. Bob understood Gerberding's resentment over having been committed without having been consulted. But Bob had no time to screw around with Gerberding or his bureaucracy, recognizing that if he had sought permission to use university facilities he would have been told no, which would have been the wrong answer. So he placed Gerberding in the position of not being able to say no.

A few days after Seattle received the bid, Wussler called the Seattle Host Committee's offices, announcing that TBS wanted to execute a letter of intent for a formal contract. A key player in the

L to R: Jarlath Hume, Bob Wussler, Father Sullivan, and Bob Walsh

formation of Cable News Network and Turner Network Television, Wussler came close to being a genius, but ingratiated himself to almost no one.

Wussler brayed condescendingly at women and made many underlings feel like remorseful dogs that had run away from home. Once, before a TBS-Seattle Host Committee dinner in Atlanta, Wussler ordered everyone where to sit. When Wussler told Shelly Yapp of the SHC staff where to plant her behind, Yapp jumped all over him.

"Bob," she snapped, "go fuck yourself. I'll sit wherever I want."

"For a minute," recollected Bernie Russi, another SHC staffer, "it shut him right up."

Gene Fisher, yet another SHC hand, did not have to resort to much of a tour de force of multi-syllabic verbosity to summarize Wussler.

"Wussler," Fisher recalled, "was a prick."

"Wussler made my skin crawl," remembered Amy Boisjolie, Bob Walsh's assistant.

"Actually," Fisher added later, "Wussler was a foppish prick."

Those ranked among the more charitable statements about Wussler, who advised the SHC that a small TBS contingent would arrive in Seattle the following Monday, with one attorney in tow. Instead, Wussler arrived with a throng of legal vultures, demanding to do a full-blown deal. The SHC quickly recruited Seattle lawyer Gordon Conger to work on a contract unlike anything any Seattle attorney had ever encountered — a four-pronged deal involving Turner Broadcasting System, the Seattle Host Committee, the USSR State Sports Committee, and Gosteleradio, the Soviet agency in charge of the USSR's radio and television agreements. TBS complicated the negotiations by refusing to allow Conger or his team to look at the

20

contract TBS had already signed with the Soviets. So Conger told his researchers to locate and read the best book ever written on this particular type of contract law.

"We found the book," recalled Hume. "It had been written by the lead attorney on the TBS negotiating team. After that, I knew we were all in big trouble."

Squirrel Politics

I felt we were watched all the time. On every floor of the Kosmos Hotel there were always two people sitting there – floor wardens. I'm sure the rooms were all bugged.

– Amy Boisjolie, former employee, Bob Walsh & Associates, Seattle, Washington

$\mathcal{E}$xcept for the opening ceremony, an extravaganza played out on the floor of Lenin Stadium by 21,000 Soviet gymnasts, jugglers, clowns, acrobats, and dancing bears, the inaugural edition of the Goodwill Games came to be judged as having laid enough eggs to feed Vladivostok through the final spasms of the Cold War. Ted Turner wanted his private Olympiad absent of politics. Instead, the Soviets refused for political reasons to permit teams from Israel, South Africa, and South Korea to compete. If not in retaliation, then in a shot at Turner, U.S. Secretary of Defense Caspar Weinberger barred a dozen members of the American military, all boxers, from participating. Turner wanted a feel-good Games to underscore U.S.-Soviet cooperation.

Instead, the Soviets got so caught up in showing off their might they loosed thousands of soldiers on Moscow, turning it into a perfect police state. Turner predicted the Games would become "the biggest non-network event in the history of television." Instead, TBS's ratings were so miniscule that one post-mortem speculated that only two Eskimos and three Coho salmon had watched. Turner's bath: $26 million, give or take a ruble.

"Money isn't every everything," Turner argued later. "Jesus Christ didn't make any money. Neither did Martin Luther King."

The Mouth of the South spent seventeen days in Moscow amid a retinue of girlfriends, playing tourist, diplomat, nuclear disarmament proponent, and public relations whirlwind. While the Soviets showered Turner with praise, and while the athletic competitions resulted in six world records, 175 U.S. media members took an almost perverse delight in spilling Turner's blood for spreading hands-across-the-sea naiveté.

The Christian Science Monitor likened Turner's Games to Celebrity Bowling. *The Los Angeles Herald-Examiner* called them a "monumental turkey." *The New York Tribune* claimed Turner was in the running for a unique medal: The Lenin Prize for Most Deaf, Dumb, and Blind Capitalist. *The New York Times* observed that if advance ballyhoo had billed the Games as a "mini" Olympics, the post mortems would emphasize the "mini." *The Baltimore Sun* argued that if Turner had entered the rifle shooting competition, he would have no toes left. And *The Chicago Sun Times* posed this question: "The Goodwill Games. Is that where a truck comes to your house and you give all your old toys to the needy?"

Turner proved cagier than his critics surmised. While TBS's ratings dipped to dismal, the network fed 129 hours of Goodwill

Ted Turner banters with U.S. athletes at the 1986 Goodwill Games

coverage via satellite to Australia, Canada, and much of Central and South America. After years of industry conversation about a fourth network, Turner had more or less created one. He had also pulled off an unprecedented three-week broadcast from the Soviet Union under difficult technical circumstances, despite having just eleven months to conceive and execute the Games. Turner had also created the first-ever business partnership between a United States company and two Soviet state agencies, Gosteleradio and Goskomsport, and done so long before *perestroika* and *glasnost* entered the popular vocabulary. He did what the Reagan administration demanded he not do, what the International Olympic Committee insisted he could not do, and what the United States Olympic Committee believed he shouldn't do. While Turner had not replicated the Olympics, he had taken the first steps toward building awareness for a product he believed had long-term merit.

As Turner left Moscow, satisfied that he had achieved something significant, the conversation focused on whether he had the resources to mount a second edition of the Games. TBS wallowed in debt, about $600 million. Turner personally languished in such financial straits that he had even agreed to dictate his autobiography for a fee of $1 million. So the inevitable speculation had it that Turner's Games appeared doomed, and it was not speculation in which Bob Walsh and the Seattle Host Committee desired to engage.

SOC and TBS officials at the 1986 Goodwill Games in Moscow

They had gone to Moscow to observe how the Soviets staged the Games, to establish relationships with the USSR's Ministry of Sport and Ministry of Culture, and had succeeded beyond their expectations. From the Ministry of Sport, the Seattle Host Committee received commitments for a series of reciprocal exchanges involving U.S. and USSR rowers, gymnasts, and figure skaters. From the Ministry of Culture, the SHC obtained a commitment to discuss American tours by the Bolshoi Ballet and Moscow Circus. Of perhaps greater importance, the SHC received a $200,000 pledge from Mike McDermott of the

Southland Corporation, which agreed to distribute 1990 Goodwill Games tickets through 78,000 of its 7-Eleven stores. The money would provide the SHC an opportunity to set in motion an emerging plan to produce a sequel to the inaugural Games that far exceeded anything Turner ever imagined.

That plan, plotted by Bob Walsh and Jarlath Hume, involved encircling the 1990 Games with a giant arts and culture festival, trade shows, business conferences, and a citizen-to-citizen exchange on a scale that had not taken place at any point in the Cold War. A broad-based Games, Bob and Jarlath reasoned, would not only make for a more meaningful event, they would provide the Seattle Host Committee with greater fund-raising potential and steer Seattle business and media thinking away from the notion that the Games were the private domain of hype artists out to plunder the public exchequer.

In the three months following the Moscow Games, Bob, Jarlath, and the Seattle Host Committee began meeting weekly to set their plan in motion. They needed to locate millions of dollars to build a world-class swimming pool, the only athletic venue Seattle lacked. They needed to establish relationships with city, state, and federal agencies, and get Washington State's Congressional delegation working on their behalf. They needed to resolve their differences with the University of Washington, and placate the White House, IOC, and USOC. To offset local misgivings about Ted Turner, the SHC invited him to Seattle to meet with business and civic leaders.

Turner accepted the invitation, and the SHC organized a reception more suited for a monarch than a maverick. But a few days before Turner's scheduled arrival, Bob Wussler called from Atlanta: Turner would be unable to attend. Bob's repeated attempts to discover why failed, leading him to the inescapable conclusion that TBS entertained second thoughts about staging another edition of the Games.

Oddball diplomacy

Turner more fun than Goodwill Games

If the Goodwill Games in Moscow were a flop, and they were as far as TV ratings are concerned, you wouldn't know it from talking to Ted Turner, the flamboyant, satellite TV guru who concocted the games as a way of promoting friendship between the superpowers.

News reports of Turner in Moscow had him toasting a Soviet official as "my Commie buddy," and coming out of Lenin's tomb with the verbal report that "He looks good. A little pale, maybe. . ."

Let's face it, Turner is a guy who knows how to have fun. And most of his lines seem to have been written for him by Woody Allen. In fact, news coverage of Ted Turner in Moscow was more entertaining than most of the athletic events of his Goodwill Games, which reportedly cost the enigmatic entrepreneur a bundle.

But why should Turner worry?

He's the guy who never met a conventional business method that couldn't be twisted to fit his own strange ways of wheeling and dealing.

However easy it is to poke fun at Turner and his methods, there's no getting around the fact that he is a success. He began with a small billboard company and a failing TV station and, at 47, has turned them into an empire that includes ownership of the Atlanta Braves, the popular cable TV channels WTBS and Cable News Network, and the MGM film library.

And there's no doubt that Turner sincerely hoped the Goodwill Games would help ease East-West tensions. Still, Turner is an oddball kind of diplomat who intersperses talk of the threat of nuclear confrontation with concern for elephants.

Elephants? Turner could write scripts for Woody Allen.

Bob had planned to return to the Soviet Union to discuss the first wave of U.S.-Soviet exchange activity and attend the World Chess Championship in Leningrad. Now his trip took on added urgency. The Soviet government had to be informed that TBS might pull the plug on the Games, and Bob had to find out if the Soviets would be willing to partner with the Seattle Host Committee in the event TBS did. Bob had no idea whether the Soviets would be receptive. But with the Games at risk and his reputation at stake, Bob flew to San Francisco and then on to Frankfurt, where as night began to fall, he boarded Lufthansa 342, bound for Moscow.

Napkin
Negotiations

*Bob's history of involvement in things
is that he takes on projects that can't
happen and they happen anyway.*

*–David Gogol, Sagamore Associates,
Washington, D.C.*

The hotel to which Bob Walsh had been assigned, Belgrad-1 at 5 Smolenskaya Street, occupied part of a bleak block not far from Red Square, where St. Basil's The Blessed rose from cobblestones in a fairytale profusion of onion domes, arches, cupolas, and spires over which Tinkerbell might have fluttered. To Bob's travel-practiced eye, Belgrad-1 offered a tourist's purgatory of threadbare carpets, dilapidated furniture, peeling wallpaper, a dank lobby polluted with smoke, showers without shower curtains, and toilet paper with the general texture of wax paper. Belgrad-1 had been slapped together in 1973 to cater to foreign businessmen, and was more or less typical of Soviet accommodations, including the fact that it featured the usual troupe of babushka women, most minus their teeth, who snooped around each floor in the manner of moles, searching for covert scraps of information.

Belgrad-1's restaurant/bar, where Bob repaired first after arriving in Moscow, extended ambience somewhat more inviting than the rest of the establishment. In addition to the several stray women who seemed to be working the room, it swarmed with a cast of characters babbling in a half dozen tongues, bent on draining Mother Russia of her vodka reserves. Bob had never been shy about killing a carafe, but Russians consumed staggering amounts of vodka, four gallons a year for every man, woman, and child, easily drinking their nearest world rivals, the Poles, straight under the table. Vodka served as Russia's ultimate elixir — a food, medicinal, and social icebreaker — and once a bottle was open, it had to be drained to the last drop. Russians made a concerted effort to get their guests forcefully drunk. If they fell on the floor or had to be carted home, well, it was all part of life.

Bob harbored no heroic notions when Belgrade-1's maitre'd escorted him to a table occupied by a man Bob judged to be in his mid-forties. He dined alone, and did not appear to be Russian. Although history has demonstrated repeatedly that talking to strangers inevitably leads to trouble, or costs money, Bob could not contain himself after ordering a bottle of wine.

"Bob Walsh," he said, extending his hand. "United States."

"Vaso Margvelashvili," the stranger replied. "From Georgia. The one on the Black Sea."

Within a matter of minutes, Bob became privy to the fact that Vaso labored on behalf of the Soviet government as director of foreign relations for Georgia State Radio and Television, that he traveled frequently, had come to Moscow on business, and was married to an Australian woman who had lived in Vancouver, British Columbia.

"I've done a lot of things there myself," Bob said. "Beautiful city."

Bob explained the nature of his business in Moscow, elaborating that he had meetings with two officials from the USSR State Sports Committee, Marat Gramov, its chairman, and Vjacheslav Gavrilin, Gramov's deputy. He had another appointment with Henrikas Yushkiavitshus, vice-chairman of Gosteleradio, a short trip to Leningrad for the World Chess Championship, and hoped to consult with Vladimir I. Litvinov in the Ministry of Culture about a U.S. tour of the Bolshoi Ballet.

"Georgia," Bob inquired. "Tell me about Georgia."

28

Vaso's story stretched well beyond two bottles of wine.

"You must come to Georgia," concluded Vaso, displaying no trace of an accent. "It's not at all like Russia."

Bob not only promised to take Vaso up on the invitation, he also agreed to meet the Georgian again before leaving Moscow.

When the two reconvened, Bob had good news. None of the Soviet officials with whom he had spoken seemed surprised that Ted Turner might cancel the Good-

Vaso Margvelashvili and Bob Walsh

will Games, and had agreed to proceed with the Seattle Host Committee in the event Turner did.

"Again," Vaso insisted, "you must come to Georgia."

But that seemed unlikely three weeks later when Bob received the shoe-dropping telephone call from Bob Wussler, who announced that TBS had decided to cancel the 1990 Goodwill Games. Unfortunately, Wussler explained, the losses in Moscow had simply been too great. And although Ted Turner had argued vehemently on behalf of continuing the Games, his board of directors wouldn't go along with him.

Bob pondered his predicament. Operating on the belief that TBS had made a firm commitment to the Games, the Seattle Host Committee had reinvented itself as the Seattle Organizing Committee, a nonprofit corporation. Since the SOC and TBS had negotiated their contract, the SOC had publicly positioned the Games not only as a Seattle event, but as a Washington State event. By getting different sectors of the state's economy involved, the SOC figured it would be in a better position to raise corporate sponsorships. In concert with that, Jarlath Hume had wrangled some money out of the Metrocenter YMCA, and the Burlington Northern Foundation had contributed $75,000 in grant funds. In addition, Father Sullivan had assembled a board of directors, and the SOC had struck a preliminary agreement with One Reel, a professional event producer, assigning it the task of preparing a plan for a performing arts festival.

Bob further winced over Wussler's telephone call in anticipation of the looming public humiliation. With the Games cancelled,

Bob would look foolish after all the controversy he had generated over the Goodwill bid. And worse, after arriving home from Moscow, Bob had called a press conference, announcing that the Bolshoi Ballet would appear in Seattle in the summer of 1990. The news had not only enthralled the city's arts community, it had elated Hume, who planned to leverage it into appearances and exhibits by other Russian artists and performers, and corporate funding for other Goodwill programs. Now Wussler's phone call changed everything.

Marat Gramov

Bob didn't tell a soul outside the SOC about his conversation with Wussler. Inside the organization, debates raged over what to do, most board members advocating a quick surrender. Without Turner's financial backing, those board members did not believe there was any chance they could raise the nearly $80 million they had estimated it would cost to stage the Games. Bob and Jarlath felt they might be able to salvage the Games, but it depended entirely on whether they could appeal to Ted Turner. If Turner could throw the SOC any kind of lifeline, perhaps the SOC could generate enough Goodwill momentum to attract corporate sponsors. The appeal would have to be made to Turner directly, not to his board, not to his lieutenants, certainly not to Wussler. And it would have to focus on the idea that the Games were Turner's personal project, that he had pulled off something remarkable in Moscow, and that it was important to keep lines of communication open between the United States and Soviet Union. But more important, a plea to Turner would have to involve a new financial proposal, one that would keep TBS involved, but wouldn't add significantly to the network's financial pressures.

The new proposal would also have to benefit the SOC. Since its credibility problem had escalated, Bob decided to ask Turner to ante up cash in the form of a broadcast rights fee to help the SOC cover its expenses over the next four years. The money wouldn't actually be a rights fee since Turner owned the Games. But calling it a rights fee seemed like a good label. The SOC would assume responsibility for organizing the Games, including raising the bulk of the funds to produce them. TBS would not incur any significant costs until television production and promotional expenses started to mount in 1990.

The scenario seemed workable to Bob, but the question remained whether Turner still had enough clout in his own company to convince the TBS board to go along with it.

When Bob arrived in Atlanta to present his plan, he found Turner pacing his office floor.

"I'm sorry, Bob," Turner said, shaking his head. "There's nothing I can do. My board has cut my arms off."

"I've got a financial proposal that I think will solve both our problems," Bob replied.

He pulled the next number out of the ozone hole over the Arctic Circle. If, Bob proposed, Turner committed $25 million, the SOC would keep the Games alive. The SOC would operate like the Los Angeles Organizing Committee had done during the 1984 Summer Olympics. Turner considered the possibility for about five seconds.

"That's a great idea," said Turner, delighted. "I never wanted to kill the Games in the first place. Okay. We're going to do this regardless of the board of directors."

Bob and Seattle attorney Doug Rogers next convened with Paul Beckham and David Raith of TBS in the lobby of the Omni Hotel, where the four of them scripted the preliminary numbers for a new agreement on a napkin. In return for what would eventually be $18 million, Turner would get his Games, amounting to eighty hours of made-for-TV programming. TBS had no idea what it had sold and Bob had no idea what he had bought, but he took the napkin back to Seattle and framed it. The date on it read November 13, 1986.

Bob and Jarlath quickly booked another trip to Moscow. Bob wanted to talk to Gavrilin about a chess tournament, and Hume had a list of things he wanted to run past Vladimir I. Litvinov at the Ministry of Culture. When they arrived in Litvinov's office, Bob couldn't help but notice the gaggle of black, rotary-dial phones on Litvinov's desk, seven in all. The Soviets had yet to figure out multiple lines, the consequence of which was that Soviet officials all had multiple telephones. The number of phones an official had indicated his level of power. Gramov, whose modest Kremlin office belied his importance in the Soviet sports hierarchy, had fifteen telephones, Yushkiavitshus nine.

Telephones almost served as status symbols, perhaps because only twenty-eight percent of the urban population and slightly less than ten percent of the rural population had them. The problem with having a telephone — aside from not knowing which one to answer — was that there was almost no access to telephone books. The most

31

recent Moscow telephone book had not been updated for fifteen years. To get a telephone number, the procedure involved a trip to an Information Bureau, providing the individual's name and year of birth, a fee, and return trip a few hours later for the number. Even with that, no guarantee could be given that telephone number would be correct. More than a third of all telephone calls reached the wrong party.

As Bob surveyed Litvinov's telephones, Hume thanked the minister for his help in procuring the Seattle appearance of the Bolshoi Ballet. As Hume spoke, Litvinov's suddenly threw up a hand.

"It's impossible for the Bolshoi to appear in the United States," said Litvinov. "The troupe will be in London."

Out of the corner of his eye, Bob observed that Litvinov's thunderbolt had turned Jarlath Hume ashen. But once the reality of what Litvinov had said sank in, Hume grew animated and argumentative.

"We've already announced it," Hume retorted. "We're counting on the ballet."

"The Bolshoi cannot appear in Seattle."

The two went on and on for twenty minutes. Finally, and probably just to get rid of Hume, Litvinov said he might be able to send the stars of the Bolshoi Ballet to Seattle in the summer of 1990. But, that meant the Soviets might send two or three people, and Hume wasn't buying it.

Hume argued so furiously that, by the end of the meeting, an exasperated Litvinov surrendered, saying he would take the matter under advisement. When Hume got outside Litvinov's office, he was as flummoxed as he was perplexed. Bob had already announced the Bolshoi's appearance. Had Bob somehow misunderstood Litvinov? Hume turned to Bob.

"Jesus Christ! What happened? I thought we had the Bolshoi."

Bob Walsh's answer astounded Jarlath Hume.

"Oh, well," Bob said, "Litvinov was a lot more positive this time than the last time."

Hume tried to digest that remark. Litvinov had told Bob the Bolshoi could not appear in Seattle in the summer of 1990. Bob had held a press conference anyway, announcing that it would. The news had been splashed all over the papers and TV.

"I couldn't imagine holding a press conference like that without having the Bolshoi securely in hand," Hume observed later. "No prudent person would have done such a thing."

No prudent person had. Bob Walsh had been pulling Bolshoi-style stunts practically all of his life.

Two Men In A Tub

I taught Bob at Marietta College. He was probably the most unusual student I ever had in more than thirty years of teaching.
  –Bernie Russi, professor of communications, Marietta College, Marietta, Ohio

*M*ost people who meandered through Bob Walsh's improbable universe had difficulty perceiving him as a man given to grandiose deeds. Physically, Bob went nose-to-nose with the average thoroughbred jockey, spoke softly, and rarely displayed animation, his expression usually ranging from disinterested to deadpan. The only public hint of emotion Bob portrayed reflected back from beneath a shock of sandy hair in those melancholy blue eyes, once described as having seen too many airport lounges and strange cities. But those eyes disguised the intrigues that percolated behind the façade. In many ways, Bob was reminiscent of a Russian *matroyska* doll: Inside the big doll reposed a smaller doll. Inside that lurked a smaller doll, and inside that a smaller one still. While Bob's muted public aura never led anyone to surmise he could affect events anywhere outside his own office, it was folly to make assumptions based on a first visual impression. Bob consistently turned soft suggestions and illusory ideas into tangible and sometimes larger-than-life projects.

Bob developed a system that more or less worked this way: He put people in a position where they were required to fill a vacuum. He would talk about a dream of his and exude unshakeable energy about it, or pose the particulars of one of his problems. Before long, everyone in Bob's sphere had become a willing participant in that project or in solving that problem. Bob's tactics prompted endless speculation over how he had developed such an innocuous but effective skill.

His lineage provides little clue. Elizabeth Walsh evicted a squalling Bob in Winthrop, Massachusetts, just about the time the German Luftwaffe transformed London into an ocean of flames. Bob's father, Matthew, wrote business articles for Fairchild Inc., which published *Women's Wear Daily*. Betty ran the advertising departments of six weekly newspapers in and around Cape Cod. In contrast to the conservative and reserved Matt, Betty had a dynamic personality, and when

Bob, Toni and Matt Walsh, 1950

people talked about the Walsh family, they invariably started with Betty. But both of Bob's parents taught him to dream and believe he could accomplish anything.

When Bob was five years old, Matt and Betty picked up the family and moved to Norwell, Massachusetts. They moved again to the Boston suburb of Kingston before settling in Scituate in a large home constructed from the remnants of a seventeenth-century pilgrim ship. Matt, Betty, Bob, and Bob's older sister, Toni, were close, strong, and Protestant, and Matt and Betty involved themselves in all of Bob's activities, particularly sports, and especially baseball. Matt attended every Little League baseball game Bob ever played and took Bob frequently to Red Sox games at Fenway Park.

By then, Bob had already become a negotiator in training wheels, one example spawned by Bob's fear that he would be bypassed as his Little League baseball team's starting second baseman. Resolving to curry favor with the manager, a fellow named Dave, Bob concocted a scheme. He told Dave that he would line him up with a beautiful young woman who was dying to go out on a date with him, although Bob had never consulted her. Bob then approached the "woman," his sister, Toni, informing her that he could hook her up with a handsome young man who was eager to romance her. Unimpressed, Toni waved Bob off. Bob deliberated over this obstacle for a few days, determining that his best approach was a frontal assault. He wheedled, argued, and cajoled until Toni capitulated, and Bob ultimately became Dave's regular second baseman.

Bob's adolescence fairly paralleled a Beaver Cleaver screenplay: No major problems at school, decent but unspectacular grades, lots of friends, considerable goofing off, occasional bursts of mischief. Later, at Silver Lake Regional High School, Bob played on the baseball team, served as president of the Key Club, and a class officer. He also had a newspaper route, worked part-time in a hardware store, and spent summers as a box boy and stock clerk at a grocery store.

The Key Club became an important outlet for the eager young Bob. Its members performed service work and involved themselves in a variety of do-good projects. Bob used his position in the club, and also as a class officer, to convince his teachers that he should be out in the community assisting the less advantaged. To that end, he spent hours conjuring up projects designed to free him from school, and a great number involved pranks.

Once, Kingston police chased Bob and several larcenous cronies after they hijacked stop signs from public thoroughfares. While not a crime wave in sufficient scope to merit prominent billing on *America's Most Wanted* today, it interested local law enforcement to the point that Bob was finally hunted down by an alert gendarme who spied him as he awkwardly attempted to cop a feel on his sweetie in the back seat of a '57 DeSoto, fashionably equipped with monster fins. When the officer ordered Bob to open the DeSoto's trunk, a stash of stop signs provided irrefutable proof of Bob's guilt.

In another spree of civil disobedience, Bob and several friends found thigh-slapping humor in decorating statues of Boston's more legendary historical figures in a variety of haberdashery, emphasizing hats and capes. Bob particularly favored the time when he cloaked the likeness of Paul Revere, which stood in a prominent public square, in a diaper.

By all accounts, Bob's most anti-social crusade involved his repeated attempts to purloin Plymouth Rock, the 1620 landing spot of the *Mayflower*. The famous rock reposes beneath a large canopy, encircled by stone columns. Bob and his thieving comrades backed up a tow truck next to the American icon and tried to make off with it. To Bob's regret, they could never budge the rock. So they resorted to misleading tourists. It went this way: The City of Plymouth employed a young man to stand in front of Plymouth Rock and spew *Mayflower* trivia. When it was time for his lunch break, a friend of Bob's presented himself as a substitute. Donning his own pilgrim hat, Bob's pal regaled tourists with the real "scoop" on the pilgrims, usually ending his spiel with little known "facts," one of which was that the female pilgrims had actually been prostitutes who used *The Mayflower* as the original *Love Boat*. Bob stood next to his buddy during these violet soliloquies, offering shocking, tabloid-style embellishments.

Since Bob exhibited a stubborn resistance to class work, he didn't bother applying to the more prestigious brain emporiums in the Boston area, recognizing that his entreaties to such institutions as Harvard would have been met with surly academic rebukes. Instead, he selected Marietta College in Marietta, Ohio, a top-notch, liberal arts school on which he had been touted by one of Matt Walsh's friends.

Marietta is situated on the north bank of the Ohio River where it greets the mouth of the Muskingum. It is the state's oldest city and named after Marie Antoinette, which never resulted in Marietta being placed on the air routes of Paris-bound jets. When Bob dropped his bags there in the fall of 1958, he found himself in environs that merged the rustic charm of a New England village — vivid fall colors, red brick streets lined with Victorian homes — with the ambience of a port city. Bob surveyed the inviting expanse of Marietta. With little mind to provide the Marietta faculty with an excuse to measure him for valedictorian robes, and being a great believer in all the known adages about letting it rip, Bob mapped a curriculum calling for him to drink beer in prodigious amounts over the next four years.

Some months after Bob arrived on campus, flirting with the notion of becoming an accounting major, and already having developed an adroitness for staring out school room windows, fogged by daydreams, he fell in league with a male professor who, without provocation or forewarning, scrubbed Bob's bare ass with a bar of soap. Since no police report was filed, the incident never made the newspapers, sparing the 15,000 residents of Marietta and the surrounding

Muskingum Valley of the sordid details of the academician's assault. Bob engineered the ensuing cover-up simply because he was too scared to talk about it.

This peculiar but significant episode in Bob's life began shortly after he received an awful sunburn. To ease his pain, Bob purchased several bottles of lotion, greasing himself liberally. Hours later, as Bob strolled aimlessly down a street, he ran into John Sandt, a Marietta professor who had been appointed Bob's academic advisor. When Sandt observed Bob's sunburn, he instructed Bob to follow him into his house, lecturing as they went that Bob needed to wash off all that lotion.

Bob did not want to enter Sandt's lair, as the owlish book-worm gave him the creeps. Although Sandt had also weaseled his way into one of the top administrative posts on campus, Dean of Men, he was not a successful individual. When soldiers returned to Marietta following World War II, Sandt had been placed in charge of Veteran Housing. Many vets frolicked by picking up Sandt and passing him along over their heads, stuffing him in hallway lockers, and occasionally attaching him by the nape of his neck to coat hooks. A 1958 Marietta faculty photograph, in which Sandt leers fiendishly in the middle of the front row, depicts an individual about five-foot-three with a gaunt face and pointed nose, accentuated by steel-rimmed glasses. Sandt had never married and lived alone, and appeared to be an early version of George McFly, with this disclaimer: Sandt today would get five to ten.

Too cowed to flee, Bob entered Sandt's house and repaired to the bathroom, where he stripped and entered the shower. It's safe to say the education Bob received next was not the one Marietta College intended to give him. He heard the bathroom door creak open and, with eyes bugging to the size of a Wimbledon trophy, watched the shower curtain part. Suddenly, a naked John Sandt seized a bar of soap and went to work. Not only did he polish Bob's rear end, the preponderance of hearsay evidence suggests that Sandt's intention was to wax it into a mega-pixel sheen. But Bob foiled Sandt's lecherous plot. Had the spotlight of history recorded the moment, it would have seen Bob leaping out of the shower, stumbling awkwardly over the bathtub, and sprawling on the floor. Without checking for injuries, Bob scrambled to his feet, grabbed his clothes, and bolted for the door. Then he burst into the street, his middle parts glaring at the world. Racing down the block, Bob abandoned plans to become an accountant, deciding in a state of complete panic and half-undress to major in radio and television instead.

Since Matt Walsh wrote for a living and Betty Walsh ran newspapers, Bob found making this new choice of majors relatively easy. Bob had taken a few classes in the Speech Department and grown fond of one of its young professors, who taught speech-related courses in radio and television. Bernie Russi was in his early twenties, not much older than Bob, and had arrived at Marietta three years earlier to launch what would become a superb thirty-two-year career at the school. Without disclosing any details of his unnerving encounter with Sandt, Bob told Bernie he was interested in studying radio and TV and asked if Bernie would consider becoming his academic advisor. Bernie agreed, handling all details of Bob's transfer to him from the predatory Sandt.

Marietta College featured a burgeoning journalism program and an excellent radio and TV department. Under Russi's tutelage, Bob worked at the school's radio station, WCMO, and wrote articles for the campus newspaper, *The Marcolian*. For a long time, WCMO was one of those tiny "wired, wireless" stations, which meant that it was connected to a transmitter that sent signals into the school's dormitories. Eventually, WCMO received a license to operate a 10-watt FM station. Although that much power barely juiced a refrigerator, Bob took to his duties as a disc jockey and station manager in a major way.

One day, attempting to goose the march of journalism, Bob informed Bernie that he wanted to attend the Kentucky Derby

Bob as a student broadcaster, Marietta College

in Louisville and file reports. Russi dismissed the idea, ticking off the reasons Bob would not be covering the Derby that year. It ranked as one of the major sports events in America, and WCMO was an insignificant campus station. The flaks at Churchill Downs would never accredit a student reporter to cover such a prestigious spectacle. The radio and TV department had no money to send Bob to Louisville, and better things to do than indulge his whim of describing the Run for the Roses. Bob pleaded that covering the Derby would become a great score for the station. As for accreditation, travel, and expenses, Bob would work those things out.

Bob and Raymond Burr

Russi's dubiousness soon turned to shock. Bob not only broadcast Venetian Way's 1960 victory on WCMO from Churchill Downs, he interviewed winning jockey Bill Hartack, and somehow wrangled an introduction to the Derby's Grand Marshal, actor Raymond Burr, then starring as Perry Mason on television. Last, and perhaps most astounding, Bob brought back to Marietta a key to the city of Louisville, awarded for a series of reports he had done promoting the place.

"I couldn't figure out how the hell Bob did it," Bernie reflected later. "I didn't want to know how the hell Bob did it. But we were probably the only 10-watt campus radio station in history to broadcast the Kentucky Derby."

Bob could not explain all the things he did, either, or what compelled him do them. One theory, espoused by Toni Walsh, suggested that Matt and Betty had been so supportive of the young and highly inquisitive Bob that he came to develop a grandiose notion that he could not only accomplish whatever he wanted, but that there were no significant downside consequences to anything he attempted. Several of Bob's colleagues shared the suspicion that his height, or lack of it, became the guiding force in his life. Bob never bought into that, but it was true that in his more imploring moments Bob had a certain waifishness about him.

When, years later, Bob forced himself into therapy to determine what accounted for his more peculiar irregularities, he advised his shrinks he could recall nothing tempestuous about his youth. While Bob recognized that his brain's repressive machinery might be too vigilant to permit an accurate assessment of what had been deposited into his primitive noodle, he nevertheless argued a case favoring childhood bliss. Despite such pleadings, Bob's head doctors rejoined that he must have blocked something out. Bob puzzled over this, never arriving at satisfactory answers. Once in a while, Bob received faint clues that seemed to illuminate his character. But Bob suspected they were merely tantalizing crumbs, spread before him for the sake of perpetuating follow-up appointments and cash flow. The fact was, the men who profited from studying Bob's head didn't do much more to help him solve the mystery of his inner self than Bob did himself. Like most people, he was a mass of conflicting impulses, obsessions, actions, and inactions; unlike most, Bob had a keen sense that his mind frequently turned inward to prey on itself.

Bob craved order, but created devilish predicaments for himself. He aspired to a conventional lifestyle, but invented the most unconventional of careers. He did not court public attention, but selected projects guaranteed to place him at the epicenter of controversy. Bob harbored a deep suspicion of news reporters, yet rarely refused to consent to an interview, and often wound up receiving a disciplinary blow in print. Illustrative of Bob's outlook was that, while he did not always seek approval from others before launching a project, he wanted it afterward. Bob had all kinds of progressive ideas but couldn't do much more with a computer than cuss at it, flailed helplessly with his answering machine, and considered his cell phone as bewildering as the Rosetta Stone. Bob did not always take care of himself physically, and occasionally wallowed in emotional mud. And yet, he wanted everyone else to be happy.

The more bizarre of Bob's problems involved his personal life, which brimmed with drama spanning the theatrical gamut, and prompted Bob to evolve into an unabridged open book, each chapter available for scanning and downloading. It did not require much experience with Bob to become acquainted with whatever demons were stalking him, and Bob's long involvement with demons in general.

But his candor made him likeable, and there were people all over the world who liked Bob and protected him. From Bob's perspective, the facts didn't seem to jive: Matt and Betty had doted over and encouraged him. But neither ever fell into the black holes of depression Bob occasionally did. Neither Matt nor Betty bequeathed to Bob his infrequent manic modes. During his sometimes unnatural highs, Bob committed himself to Herculean projects. He scraped by on four of five hours a sleep, enervated himself with caffeine, inhaled cartons of Marlboros, and was indifferent to eating and exercise. He flew all over the globe and came home burned out but bursting with ideas.

Then he toiled around the clock, making work indistinguishable from his life. Once Bob completed a project, he lapsed into his depressive mode, becoming irritable and gruff. It all filtered down to the fact that Bob's life, once independent of Matt and Betty's nest, morphed into a spectrum of serendipity, punctuated by a series of a spectacular triumphs, several narrowly missed calamities, and a few head-on wrecks.

Bernie Russi, Bob Walsh, 1961

After Bob graduated from Marietta, Russi helped him land his first job, at WTAP in Parkersburg, West Virginia, just across the Ohio River from Marietta. According to astute local wags, of which Russi was perhaps paramount, the station's call letters really stood for "Worst Television Any Place." Bob signed on as a producer-director-cameraman-janitor, essentially an all-purpose flunky. Bob did whatever needed doing around the station that the more seasoned staff members did not want to do. Although the WTAP staff was small, it more than upheld the highest traditions of journalism. The weatherman had an on-going affair with the woman who hosted the kiddy show, and the sports guy, Sam Slater, weighed 300 pounds and had a fake eye that completely rattled the audience. Bob worked nights and enjoyed major decision-making powers over what programming the residents of Parkersburg watched on any given evening.

In pre-cable days, small-market stations often carried the programming of all three networks, giving them the ability to choose which shows to televise at any given time. Such was the case at WTAP. If Bob, sitting alone in front of a console of buttons, determined that a program on NBC was dull, he simply flipped a master switch and watched ABC or CBS, the audience going with him. He did this every night for months, mainly alternating between Johnny Carson and the Big Money Movie. Frazzled WTAP viewers never knew what program they were going to watch, and the station's switchboard melted with complaints.

Bob quit WTAP before he got fired, often wondering after the invention of remote control whether he had unwittingly created channel surfing.

42

Dance With
A Wizard

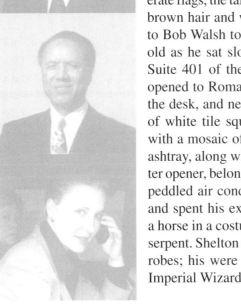

Bob had an incredible knack for finding all kinds of wackos. You never knew who he was going to bring back to the station.

– Roger Allan, former news director, WNAC (Boston), Lebanon, New Hampshire

Framed by American and Confederate flags, the tall, thin man with wavy, light brown hair and watery blue eyes appeared to Bob Walsh to be about thirty-five years old as he sat slouched behind his desk in Suite 401 of the Aston Building. A Bible opened to Romans II occupied a corner of the desk, and near it an ashtray, composed of white tile squares, had been decorated with a mosaic of red "K's." The Bible and ashtray, along with a gold, sword-sized letter opener, belonged to Robert Shelton, who peddled air conditioners from nine to five and spent his extracurricular hours astride a horse in a costume festooned with a giant serpent. Shelton eschewed traditional white robes; his were black, the signature of an Imperial Wizard of the Ku Klux Klan.

The calendar read mid-1966. Summoning what he believed to be clear evidence from genetics, anthropology, anatomy, history, and political science, Shelton, founder of United Klans of America Inc., had just gone on record with a number of hateful pronouncements, including "The Negro is a diseased animal." Shelton's spewings had galvanized Bob Walsh to action. He telephoned the titular leader of the most clandestine hooded order then operating in the American South, requesting that Shelton fly to Boston to discuss the workings of his "Invisible Empire" in a radio interview. Getting the predictable brush off, Bob waited a day before calling Shelton again. Following several unceremonious rejections, Bob flew to Shelton's hometown of Tuscaloosa, Alabama, and located the Aston Building, figuring that a personal appearance would convince the Imperial Wizard to change his mind.

Bob had returned to Boston after partying away four campaigns at Marietta College and plundering the alcoholic aquifer of Parkersburg, West Virginia, during a season at WTAP-TV. Determined to get serious about a career, Bob signed on as a twenty-three-year-old record tape librarian at WNAC-AM, a radio station whose format was sorely in need of rejuvenation. Bob's timing proved impeccable. He arrived in Boston six months before John F. Kennedy's assassination provoked America into one of the epochal social shifts of the century, and just as radio started to emerge as one of the catalysts for that change. Bob stood clueless before the impending confluence: He simply needed a job; WNAC needed help.

The station broadcast a boardinghouse stew of music and chatter that appealed mainly to an older audience and failed to cut it with

advertisers. A joke around the station even claimed that WNAC's call letters actually stood for "We Need A Commercial," which was why WNAC's parent company, RKO General, had hired Perry Ury, a veteran from WGMS – the Good Music Station – in Washington, D.C., to overhaul the format. Ury planned to make a few personnel changes and take WNAC into news and talk.

Bill Hahn's *Around Town* had long been one of the most popular

Perry Ury

44

shows on the Boston dial, and Haywood Vincent, who had once banged out news copy for Walter Cronkite at CBS in New York, anchored the afternoons. Ury kept Hahn and Vincent in their regular slots but cut loose host Bill Marlowe, a handsome Italian and notorious womanizer, and replaced Dick Applegate, a news director who hit the sauce too often, with Roger Allan, who had a roguish sense of humor and lots of innovative ideas. Ury also lured Bob Henabery away from WCBS in New York, naming him WNAC's program director. Henabery cut an imposing figure. He stood six-foot-five and proved to have a knack for spotting potential talent in others and creating an environment in which they could flourish.

When Henabery came aboard, WNAC had two major competitors, WEEI and WBZ. Both clobbered WNAC in the ratings, making Henabery's assignment fairly obvious: He had to develop a format that would attract a larger audience and more advertisers, and do it as quickly as possible. It couldn't be a music format, which Henabery believed was becoming less effective on the AM dial, and it couldn't be strictly news and public affairs. WEEI, with its heavy hit-
ter host Paul Benziquen, already
did that. So Henabery gave
WNAC a sort of happy, music-
talk slant in the mornings, and
tried to rebuild afternoon and
evening ratings through three
talk show hosts, Vincent, Palmer
Payne, and Fred Gayle.

Henabery's remake at
WNAC occurred at a time when
the radio industry's evolution
was in revolution. Top 40, which
had dominated AM through most

Haywood Vincent

of the 1950s with breathless deejays and sanitized programming, had lost a lot of audience to FM, which had less static, better fidelity, and fewer commercials. Where AM attempted to be all things to all people, FM specialized and built fantastically loyal followings. Some of the larger AM operations, such as WABC in New York, stuck to Top 40, but many stations tinkered with different formats. Some, including WNAC, tried combinations: Music/News/Talk, Music/News/Call-In, All Talk, All News. What finally distinguished

L to R: Perry Ury, John Vann, Roger Allan, and Bob Henabery

WNAC's format change was not so much its experimental nature as its radical programming.

Henabery created a series of niche shows — *Boston Kitchen, Ask Your Neighbor, Antique Auction* — that successfully addressed WNAC's needs in the mornings and on weekends by involving listeners in the exchange of recipes, practical advice, and electronic swap meets. Afternoons and evenings presented another problem. Benzequin owned the market on WEEI; WBZ, the Westinghouse station, had a great talk program hosted by Bob Kennedy and produced superbly by a young phenom, Squire Rushnell. Henabery determined that the only way to snatch ratings from Benzequin and Kennedy was to hire them, which he attempted to do, or develop shows so different in content and character they couldn't be ignored. Henabery had been in the midst of trying to figure out his next move when Hahn suggested he take a look at the twenty-three-year-old in the tape library. The kid, Hahn told Henabery, had great ideas and an intuitive genius for people skills.

Promoted to producer, and eventually given carte blanche by Henabery to program the talk shows, Bob Walsh made it his goal to either develop something in-depth and newsworthy in every program, or experiment with something off-the-wall. He became exceptionally adept at booking the unexpected, oddball, or controversial guest, starting with a series of prominent, if not infamous, extremists he knew WEEI and WBZ couldn't get.

The new format targeted listeners who had a social conscience and, unlike most contemporary talk radio, assumed intelligence on the

46

part of the audience. Although neither the station's sales reps nor RKO's corporate hierarchy in New York endorsed the format, it seemed ideal for Boston in the early 1960s. The station had access to local guests with national reputations — Kennedy family members; Henry Cabot Lodge, who had run for vice president on the Nixon ticket in 1960; state lieutenant governor Elliott Richardson, later to become Secretary of State under Richard Nixon; Tip O'Neill, future Speaker of the U.S. House of Representatives; F. Lee Bailey, a young Boston attorney who had achieved a huge reputation in the Sam Shepherd and Boston Strangler cases; and U.S. Postmaster General Larry O'Brien, later commissioner of the National Basketball Association. Bob booked all of them on WNAC's talk programs.

WNAC's signal covered Harvard, Boston College, the University of Massachusetts, Northeastern University, and MIT, giving the station access to a deep pool of expert guests on just about any topic WNAC wished to address. Bob fused those assets with a heavyweight guest list, turning WNAC into a social lubricant for debates and forums on the growing civil rights drama, school desegregation, the increasing concern over Vietnam, women's rights, and the emerging drug culture. Containing the second-largest Catholic population in the United States, Boston had also become ripe for talk about the moral and ethical considerations of the birth control pill, developed in the nearby suburb of Worcester, and the rapid changes that had taken place in the Catholic Church in the aftermath of Vatican II.

"Bob had the right idea with the way he programmed these shows," recalled Payne. "Bob went everywhere looking for guests. It was remarkable how successful he was getting them considering his age, his size, and his youthful appearance. He had an amazing sense of what worked on the air."

An unwitting discovery by a Milwaukee engineer became the pivotal event that transformed news/talk into a national medium. As Henabery described it, it occurred at WTMJ, the *Milwaukee Journal* Station, in early 1960. On a union-mandated rest break, the engineer fiddled with the take-up reel of an Ampex tape machine, idly holding the magnetic tape aloft with a pencil while slowing down the rate of movement of the tape from the "record" head to the "playback" head for seven seconds. The birth of tape-delay permitted producers control over capricious callers and led to the first significant two-way talk radio program, presciently titled *Phone Opinion*. The show aired one hour a night with a topic assigned by management and with a WTMJ staff announcer serving as host. Although not talk radio on the scale it would become, this show prompted several stations to experiment with various talk formats, and no station plunged in deeper than WNAC.

In those days, none of the elements responsible for a studio-quality signal today — satellites, fiber optics — existed, making scratchy, static-filled telephone interviews an invitation for listeners to switch stations. To keep a listener engaged, WNAC almost always required that its guests come to the station's studios, and acquiring those guests became Bob's assignment. Once Bob booked a guest, he or she would be escorted to 21 Brookline Avenue in Kenmore Square, just over the railroad tracks from the Green Monster at Fenway Park. WNAC's studios occu-

The great Jackie Robinson with Bill Hahn

pied the first three floors of the St. George Hotel, a turn-of-the-century redbrick whose lobby was festooned with crystal chandeliers and reeked of cigar and pipe smoke. Originating from the street level of the St. George, blasphemy, heresy, and occasional calumny peppered WNAC listeners, who got earfuls of, among others, Dr. Timothy Leary, a Harvard professor who had emerged as both prophet and menace for his advocacy of mind-altering drugs. Bob became the first radio man Leary allowed to camp with him at his retreat in Millbrook, New York, and his achievement of convincing Leary to submit to a series of interviews not only amazed everybody at the station, but everybody in the industry who knew about it.

"Bob was like a genie rubbing a bottle," Henabery remembered. "He'd rub his Cardinal Cushing bottle and the Cardinal would appear. He'd rub his Wizard bottle and the Wizard would appear. We just didn't get how this low-key guy could come up with all these heavy-hitter guests. He drove WEEI crazy with that stuff."

"Bob could get anybody he wanted," Payne recollected. "One of the most interesting guests he got was Bill Russell, the star center of the Boston Celtics."

To Bob, it posed a far larger but more rewarding challenge to book a reluctant guest than members of the Kennedy family, who were usually obliging, or Boston's local politicians, who were always eager. But politicians and extremists constituted only about half of Bob's headliners. He recruited celebrities such as Jimmy Durante and intellectuals on the order of Ashley Montagu, one of Bob's personal favorites. Not only had Montagu, a world-renowned specialist in anthropology, worked out the embryology of the upper jaw, which surgeons used to repair cleft palate, he published more than fifty books, including *The Elephant Man*, the basis of the film of the same name, and *The Natural Superiority of Women*, which sparked women's liberation movements. Bob brought Montagu to WNAC programs to discuss his books and banter about topical events, and maintained a steady correspondence with the anthropologist for several years.

WNAC staffers soon recognized that Bob had a rare talent for forming instant relationships with a variety of people, including the bureaucrats in Boston's political hierarchy. John A. Volpe, the governor of Massachusetts, regularly invited Bob to breakfast meetings at the Somerset Hotel, once explaining in a letter: "Realizing the great public interest in your show, I feel that it is my responsibility to make myself available to you." Bob also developed a friendship with Kenny O'Donnell, who had been John F. Kennedy's appointment secretary. O'Donnell paved the way for Bob to get into the Kennedy family compound in Hyannis Port so WNAC could conduct one of the first interviews with Rose Kennedy following JFK's assassination.

Bob's work at WNAC provided him the opportunity to hone his networking skills, which manifested themselves early in his relationship with His Eminence, Richard Cardinal Cushing, the Archbishop of Boston.

"You couldn't get much bigger than Cardinal Cushing," Hahn related later. "It was something extraordinary, something beyond belief, the way Bob seemed to hold the confidence and trust of the Cardinal."

The son of a blacksmith, Cushing was ordained in 1921, appointed Bishop of Boston in 1939, and Archbishop of the diocese in 1944. Elevated to Cardinal by Pope John XXIII in 1958, Cushing was far more than the spiritual leader of Boston's Roman Catholic community. He stood out as one of the most pervasive political and social forces in the city. In contrast to the aloof pomposity displayed by his predecessor, William Cardinal O'Connell, Cushing came off as an informal, crusty, and unpredictable cleric who had little time for abstract theology and used his pulpit as a forum to make the Church relevant to the everyday lives of ordinary people. Cushing avoided the ornate vestments of his office except when they were required for church services, and usually appeared in public in plain black garb and a straw hat. A confidant of the Kennedy family and a friend of J. Edgar Hoover, Cushing said Mass for prison inmates, accompanied groups of nuns to Red Sox games, administered the sacraments to mentally retarded children, and sliced turkey at Thanksgiving dinners for the elderly. Utterly unsubtle, Cushing had no compunction about speaking his mind, although his newspaper quotes were infrequent and his radio and TV sound bites even less so.

Tall and lean, Cushing had a rutted face, hollow cheeks, spoke in a guttural rasp, and nurtured a reputation for quick-wittedness. Those

Roger Allan with supermodel Twiggy

who spent time around Cushing knew they were in the presence of someone special, and they were. Cushing presided over the marriage of John F. Kennedy and Jacqueline Bouvier on the morning of September 12, 1953, at St. Mary's Church in Newport, R.I., involved himself in all of John's, Robert's, and Teddy's political campaigns, and became a regular at the Kennedy compound in Hyannis Port. Following the assassination of JFK, Cushing led the funeral procession, celebrating Low Mass at St. Matthew's Cathedral in Washington, D.C., before JFK's burial at Arlington National Cemetery.

"For some reason," recalled Hahn, "the Cardinal related to Bob in an astonishing way. Bob could call the Cardinal any time of the day or night because Cardinal Cushing just loved to talk to Bob Walsh."

But Cushing recoiled from most people who engaged him in cavalier conversation, and became especially irritable whenever anyone attempted to kiss his prominent ring. Once, while Bob and the Cardinal stood outside WNAC's studios, a man rushed up to Cushing, knelt down, snatched the Cardinal's hand, pursed his lips, and tried to do that which the Cardinal found most odious.

"Bob," asked the Cardinal, after the man departed, "where in the hell did you find that asshole?"

Soon after convincing Cushing to become a radio star, Bob discovered the Cardinal privately cultivated intriguing vices. He loved to gossip and enjoyed a good bottle of whiskey, favoring Jack Daniels. He smoked as many Camels in a day as he could safely sneak and had a knack for the well-placed profanity. Cushing made sure no one saw him engage in his vices, facilitating them through Bob, whom he frequently dispatched on midnight hootch runs. When Bob and the Cardinal elected to knock off an afternoon with tobacco, grog, and gab, the Cardinal would exchange his religious robes for civilian clothes and that ubiquitous straw hat, and the two would hole up in the small, quiet bar in the St. George Hotel. At Bob's prodding, Cardinal Cushing became a regular guest on WNAC's radio and television programs. It particularly annoyed WEEI and WBZ that one of the top newsmakers in Massachusetts forever after refused to appear on any program not produced or endorsed by Bob.

Although Bob and Cardinal Cushing had significant age and religious differences, they shared an ironic sense of humor. It amused more than it offended Cushing when Bob invited Madalyn Murray O'Hair, the inflammatory atheist, to discuss her unpopular views on WNAC. O'Hair had made waves by filing a lawsuit that led to the 1963 U.S. Supreme Court decision outlawing school prayer. Bob booked her on WNAC after she sued the federal government for providing tax exemptions to places

Singer Robert Goulet and Hahn

51

of public worship, and again after she sued the government to force it to remove "In God We Trust" from the currency. O'Hair and Cushing sometimes followed each other on WNAC, Cushing informing several staffers at the station that the juxtaposition constituted brilliant counter programming by Bob.

William Loeb, publisher of *The Manchester Union Leader*, New Hampshire's largest newspaper, had no use for talk radio, deeming it a medium for the unhinged. *The Union Leader* became a national force every four years when candidates for the United States Presidential election arrived in the Granite State for the first primary elections. In what political condition those candidates exited New Hampshire in large part depended on Loeb, who gutted Edmund Muskie's 1972 Presidential bid with a single editorial. Loeb derailed a lot of people, often printing his vitriolic rants in three colors with an idiosyncratic variety of typefaces. Bald with prominent eyebrows, Loeb trusted no one besides his wife, the equally eccentric Nackey Loeb. William and Nackey maintained two residences, a ranch near Reno, Nevada, and a thirty-room, neo-Tudor mansion on a 100-acre estate in Prides Crossing, Massachusetts.

It took Bob three months, countless telephone calls, numerous letters and telegrams, several floral bribes to Nackey Loeb, and eleven trips to Prides Crossing to finally coerce the fanatical voice of *The Manchester Union Leader* to appear on WNAC. Loeb ultimately became a regular on the station for one reason: He trusted Bob implicitly, eventually using his clout to help Bob line up other reluctant guests, including Barry Goldwater, the United States senator from Arizona, and George Wallace, the governor of Alabama. That the ultra-conservative Loeb volunteered to assist young, liberal Bob gain favor with Wallace, who had been ignoring Lyndon Johnson's orders to integrate Alabama schools, fascinated Hahn, took Henabery by surprise, and made Allan wonder what little hot shot Bob might come up with next.

Bob wanted Wallace on the air badly. He made repeated telephone calls to the governor, who consistently declined Bob's invitations to appear on *Boston Forum*. Wallace, Bob knew, would be an ideal guest since Boston raged with debate over school desegregation and busing. So in the late winter of 1965, Bob flew to Montgomery to see if he couldn't hook Wallace for a radio interview. After conning Wallace's secretary into setting up a meeting, Bob issued a personal invitation to Wallace to fly to Boston. Wallace again declined. But after spending an hour with Bob, who pushed and flattered, Wallace reluctantly agreed. Wallace traveled to Boston for the interview on May 11, 1966, and the show went wonderfully. The next day, Wallace sent Bob a telegram saying, "I enjoyed being on the show and we have had quite a bit of good response as a result of the program. Remember, you have a standing invitation to visit us in Alabama."

Two months after Wallace appeared on WNAC, Bob jetted to Tuscaloosa where he met Robert Shelton, the Imperial Wizard of the Ku Klux Klan. When Bob entered Shelton's wood-paneled office, The Wizard told Bob he would not fly to Boston. The Klan, he explained, could gain nothing by exposing itself to Boston radio callers, and Shelton might place himself in personal jeopardy if he agreed to go on the air and espouse Klan ideology. Besides, Shelton had no mind to travel north of the Mason-Dixon line. With that, he issued a final, irrevocable no. Two hours later, Bob had The Wizard booked for an interview.

The Imperial Wizard

Shelton actually made two trips to Boston and the newspapers snarfed it up, trumpeting both appearances for days in advance. As The Wizard feared, his arrival in Boston generated more controversy than enthusiasm. The first time he landed at Logan Airport, a fight broke out among picketers, one of whom got shoved through a plate-glass window. Shelton's second appearance at WNAC sparked nasty disturbances in Roxbury, a Boston suburb.

"Everybody wanted a peek at this weirdo," Allan recalled. "Bob always got a lot of publicity for the station because of these strange people he brought in."

"Bob was one of the earliest radio people to understand the headline, promotional, and publicity value of controversial people," remembered Hahn.

Not only did Bob understand how to cultivate publicity, he knew how to make the most of it. Bob routinely invited Boston newspaper reporters to monitor WNAC's talk shows from an adjacent studio, then made his guests available to them. To the chagrin of WEEI and WBZ, WNAC constantly hogged headlines.

The Wizard likely would not have agreed to travel north of the Mason-Dixon Line had Bob told him that he'd also booked Malcolm

X and Louis Farrakhan for appearances on WNAC. When Bob met Farrakhan, he called himself "Lewis X" and "Minister Lewis." Later head of the Nation of Islam, Farrakhan appeared on Payne's show the night he became Louis Farrakhan, announcing just before air time that the honorable Elijah Mohammad had bestowed upon him the title of "Farrakhan." Bob also did several shows with Malcolm X, whose own father had been murdered by the KKK in Lansing, Michigan. Payne had Malcolm X on twice, once before he made his famous tour of North Africa, and again after his return.

"There really wasn't a lot of positive audience reaction to either one of them," recounted Payne.

Of all the monarchs and miscreants Bob escorted through the doors at WNAC, none intrigued Payne more than Alfred Hitchcock,

Bill Hahn with The Three Stooges

who told a fabulous story on air about a woman who murdered her husband with a frozen leg of lamb. Bob had also booked The Three Stooges, Beatles manager, Brian Epstein, and Fidel Castro. The Boston Strangler, Albert DeSalvo, once came on the air from the state pen.

Bob failed to sway Ho Chi Minh. He dispatched numerous telegrams to Hanoi, hoping to wrangle an interview with the military ruler of North Vietnam, but all went unanswered. Bob also failed to cajole Richard Nixon into coming on the radio, despite spending months working on Nixon's secretary, Rosemary Woods, later responsible for the eighteen-minute gap in Nixon's Watergate tapes.

"The Castro thing was a Bobby Walsh idea," Allan remembered. "A typical Bobby Walsh method. You just got the phone number, conned some poor secretary, and called direct."

That's what Bob had done with Castro, not once, but twice.

"We didn't have Castro in studio, obviously," Allan explained later. "But most of the guests showed up at the station. Whenever Bob's guests came to town, bodyguards swarmed all over the place. Bob Walsh always had some weird person in there."

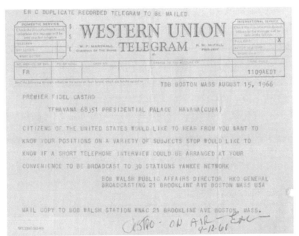

On January 13, 1967, W N A C - T V launched *The Al Capp Show*, which ran every Friday night from midnight to 1 a.m. before a live, studio audience. In addition to the

Bob booked Fidel Castro on WNAC with this telegram

famous cartoonist, *The Al Capp Show* featured people who interested Capp, mostly entertainment and theatrical types. *The Al Capp Show* also included a filmed segment titled *Al Capp At Large*, in which Capp sampled public opinion from citizens on the street. Capp's initial guests, booked by Bob, included Maureen O'Sullivan, who had played "Jane" opposite Johnny Weissmuller's "Tarzan," the comedy team of Bob & Ray, and a protest singer – because Capp loved protest singers, particularly those who followed what Capp described as the "Joan Baez school of diplomacy." Capp gave his TV show a national kickoff with an appearance on Johnny Carson's *Tonight Show*.

In the early Carson/Capp era, the success of TV talk stemmed from the lively personality of the host rather than the root of later successful talk, the emotional dysfunction of the audience. Capp became a great entertainer because he was lively and dysfunctional, which doubtless made him the crazy genius he was. For forty-three of his seventy years, Capp delighted, repelled, outraged, lauded, insulted, and satirized hundreds of people, places, attitudes, and conventions.

Capp joined the Associated Press in 1932 and drew a daily strip called *Mister Gilfeather*, which had little success. He next went to work as an assistant to Ham Fisher, creator of *Joe Palooka*. Capp could barely abide Fisher, once calling him "a veritable goldmine of swinishness," but learned a lot about the comic-strip business. In 1934, Capp pitched *Li'l Abner* to King Features, receiving a quick rejection. But United Features subsequently accepted the strip, which made its debut on August 13 that year. At the height of the strip's popularity in the 1940s, *Li'l Abner* appeared in more than a thousand newspapers. Many critics placed Capp in the company of Lewis Carroll and Mark Twain, and John Steinbeck considered Capp the greatest writer of his time. In the late 1930s, Capp's strip introduced a concept that later became a high school and college tradition, Sadie Hawkins Day, an annual event in which single women pursued single men. Capp's strip later inspired the television sitcom, *The Beverly Hillbillies*.

The Al Capp that Bob met in 1967 glared through thick horn rims and walked precariously on a wooden leg he'd worn ever since losing an encounter with a train as a teenager. Capp never appeared

Bob and Al Capp

anywhere without a cigarette in his mouth and constantly flicked ashes in all directions as he spoke. Capp fascinated Bob, both before Capp pleaded guilty to attempted adultery with a Wisconsin woman, and after he wrote a book titled *A Well-Balanced Life on a Wooden Leg*. As the show's producer, Bob booked dozens of celebrities on *The Al Capp Show*, including actress Tallulah Bankhead, actors Jack Lemmon and Van Johnson, comedians George Carlin and Fanny Flagg, and a range of personalities such as Durwood Kirby and Rudy Vallee. Bob never had trouble rounding up celebrities, because Capp was a huge celebrity himself.

Loud and profane, Capp had the annoying habit of gesturing wildly with his hands during his interviews. This so distracted both his audience and his guests that Bob devised a system to keep Capp under control. He ordered that a hole be drilled in Capp's desk on the set, looped a rope through the opening, and had the cartoonist's hands tied securely underneath the desk. Capp loathed his bondage, especially after one emotional outburst in which he gestured so mightly that he overturned the desk. The sudden rearrangement of furniture sent Capp sprawling to the studio floor in a disheveled heap.

Capp frequently ordered Bob to locate the most beautiful women in the Boston area so Capp could feature them on his show. After each of Bob's raids at the city's modeling agencies, Capp auditioned dozens of beauties, brazenly quizzing them about their sex lives as Bob listened with scarlet ears. This led to an inevitable incident in which Capp put the moves on one of the models, only to lose the support of his wooden leg as it went one way and Capp the other. Mrs. Al Capp complained regularly to Bob about her husband, saying he was one of the cheapest bastards alive, refusing to buy a new leg even though he was worth millions.

Al Capp At Large rated as Capp's zaniest feature. Once, Capp and Bob led a camera crew to Logan Airport, Capp toting a doctored version of *Life* magazine that featured a naked woman in the centerfold. Capp stopped dozens of people, explaining in mournful tones that *Life* had suffered a substantial drop in circulation, and that the magazine, in an attempt to boost sales, had made the painful decision to include a centerfold, a la *Playboy.* Capp sought opinions on this sad state of journalistic affairs, ending his interviews by unfurling the centerfold so the cameras could gauge reactions, most of which recorded the faces of men displaying the expectant air of a winner on a TV quiz show. Naturally, nearly all interviewees professed equal parts disgust, despair, and outrage that *Life* had gone the *Playboy* route. But when they departed Capp's microphone, Bob snaked furtively after them with a camera. Most scurried straight to a nearby magazine shop where they purchased a copy of *Life*.

Another time, Capp set up outside Filene's Department Store where he rang a bell and informed shoppers that he was collecting money on behalf of "the corpulent boys from Grosse Point, Michigan." Capp made it sound as if the youngsters had become embroiled in the sob story of the century when the truth was that the "corpulent boys from Grosse Point" had, according to a recent news item, the highest per-capita income in the United States. Most non-English majors Capp stopped plopped money into a bucket as Capp chortled fiendishly.

In contrast to Capp, Arthur Fiedler ranked as one of Boston's regal figures. Conductor of the Boston Pops, Fiedler inaugurated the Esplanade Concerts on the banks of Boston's Charles River and transformed standard orchestral performances by programming everything from Pachelbel to Gershwin to the Beatles. Fiedler's celebrity peaked when he conducted the Boston Pops for the American Bicentennial celebration on July 4, 1976, before an audience of 400,000.

"Bob could get Fiedler into the studio at the drop of a hat," recalled Hahn. "The only thing he had to do was buy Fielder a bottle of bourbon. Arthur would kill it during the course of a two-hour broadcast."

While Bob's ability to attract famous and offbeat guests inflated WNAC's ratings, Ury and Henabery became concerned that the rise in numbers and revenues would not satisfy RKO in New York. AM formats other than talk — especially rock — had become more popular with audiences and sales reps, and large talk audiences had evacuated to FM, whose hosts were generally antiestablishment and took strong positions against the Vietnam War and anyone representing authority. Early in 1967, Henabery realized his worst fears. Just as Bob embarked on a short sabbatical, Henabery received word that the station would switch to rock. Henabery couldn't decide whether to tell Bob about the switch, which would spoil Bob's vacation, or give Bob the bad news after he returned. Henabery finally elected to let Bob enjoy his time away and inform him about the switch in a general disclosure to WNAC employees at a later date. Henabery hated keeping Bob in the dark and was even less thrilled when it fell to him to fire the news staff.

WNAC's last talk show occurred on February 26, 1967. RKO quickly changed WNAC's call letters to WRKO-AM and moved the station out of the St. George to a new building at 7 Bullfinch Place. WRKO-AM went on to become one of Boston's great rockers.

"It was an amazing station," recollected Ury. "But it was all formula. That's when Henabery said, 'I'm gone.'"

WRKO-AM lasted as a rocker for a decade before flipping back to news/talk, reincarnating itself as "Attitude Radio." By that point, most WNAC staffers had long-since scattered, including Bob Walsh.

After his departure, the first floor of the St. George Hotel, where Cushing, Wallace, Fiedler, Capp, and The Wizard had all bent to Bob's wishes, became a pizza joint.

The Phone Lines Are Open

You can't describe Bob Walsh unless you know him. You can paint so many pictures, but you cannot paint the soul.

> – Richard (Mr.) Blackwell,
> creator of "The Worst Dressed List,"
> Beverly Hills, California

Since Bob Walsh could not conceive of a professional future in Boston after RKO trashed WNAC's talk format, he started to cast around for a new job. Bob had been mulling an offer from WTOP in Washington, D.C., for two weeks when WNAC station manager Perry Ury informed him that there might be an opening at KABC in Los Angeles. When Bob told Ury he was interested, Ury telephoned KABC's general manager, Ben Hoberman, giving Hoberman a glowing endorsement of Bob. One month and two interviews later, Bob became KABC's new production manager. KABC had been the first station in the United States to convert exclusively to talk, initiating the format in 1960. But seven years later, KABC found itself floundering in the ratings. To give them a boost, Bob determined to supplement KABC's stable of on-air personalities with a few celebrity hosts. But first he wanted to make the station the Los Angeles-area leader in community service.

If the idea at WNAC had been to showcase newsmakers who could speak authoritatively to listeners and eccentrics who could fascinate them, KABC wanted to broadly involve the audience. When Bob arrived at the station, he had all kinds of ideas knocking about in his head. He had just turned twenty-eight years old and, despite predictable butterflies, brimmed with confidence that he could get the job done. Ruth Henderson, the daughter of an Air Force commander, didn't doubt it for a minute.

Ruth had lived in the Philippines, Germany, France, and Hawaii, attending eighteen schools before she entered the ninth grade. Accomplished in ballet, tap, and acrobatic dance, she had breezed through high school and the University of South Carolina as the complete package: smart, beautiful, talented, and tenacious. In college, Ruth undertook a double major in journalism and advertising while working forty hours a week at WIS-NBC TV in Columbia, South Carolina. Somehow, she also created enough time to become a campus cheerleader, perform leading roles in *Carnival*, *My Fair Lady*, and several other productions, and win prizes in beauty contests.

One year, Ruth entered the South Carolina state finals for the Miss America pageant and swept talent, swimsuit, and evening gown competitions. The state newspaper had the layout featuring her victory all ready to roll off its press only to have to scrap it when pageant officials arbitrarily decided Ruth wasn't tall enough to have a chance in the Miss America pageant. But the next year, Ruth entered the Miss Football USA pageant. She not only won, she defeated the woman who had been first runner-up to the previous year's Miss America. By the time Ruth graduated from the University of South Carolina, she seemed headed for a career in either television or theater, and perhaps both. She made her first stop Boston, where she went to work in WNAC-TV's traffic department.

In her early twenties, Ruth had no designs on a serious relationship, much less a long-term commitment. But Bob Walsh fascinated her. He was unlike anyone Ruth had ever encountered, seemed to know every headliner in town, and had relationships with a bizarre sect of humanity that included Imperial Wizards and madcap cartoonists. Instantly mesmerized by Ruth, Bob wanted to marry her almost from the moment he spotted her. But Ruth rejected Bob's first proposal, and continued to wave off his advances, feeling she was too young and needed to give her career a chance.

Ruth maintained the charade until the night she spotted Bob at a seafood restaurant, wooing someone else. Shortly thereafter, Bob Walsh and Ruth Henderson got engaged.

The wedding took place in Columbia, South Carolina, and was one of those big, traditional ceremonies with much fuss made over the bride, bridesmaids, and their gowns, enough groomsmen to

Ruth Walsh first encountered Bob at WNAC in Boston

stock four basketball teams, and hundreds of guests, including a large contingent from Boston. Bob's father, Matt, served as his best man.

Following a honeymoon in Hawaii, Bob and Ruth returned to Boston where Bob learned that WNAC had abandoned its talk format, news that devastated him. Bob loved the characters at the station, and he and Ruth had intended to make Boston their home. Instead, after Richard Cardinal Cushing threw them a big going-away bash, they found themselves bound for Los Angeles, where they settled into an apartment near the Capitol Records building on Vista Del Mar in the Hollywood Hills.

"I didn't think we'd be in Los Angeles very long," Ruth recalled. "Bob was on a fast track. We both thought he'd wind up at ABC radio in New York. I didn't know where my own career was headed, so I went to work as a producer at KHJ."

Soon after Bob and KABC operations manager Jack Meyers began retooling the station, Bob took Kenny O'Donnell's advice and contacted Jessie Unruh, California's Speaker of the House, and arguably the state's most powerful politician not named Ronald Reagan. O'Donnell, John F. Kennedy's former appointment secretary, had told Bob that Unruh could help him establish himself in Los Angeles, and Unruh proved more than helpful. He became a regular on KABC programs and introduced Bob to Sam Yorty, Jerry Brown, and Tom Bradley, all of whom contributed to station projects.

Yorty and Bradley became especially valuable resources when Bob produced a series of public service specials titled *Day of Dialogue*. For twenty-four consecutive hours one day a month, a single

subject monopolized KABC's airwaves, including *The Generation Gap, Drug Abuse, Welfare, Crisis in the Middle East, Homosexuality, Abortion,* and *Immigration*. *Venereal Disease* offered listeners free medical examinations, attracting more than 1,000 respondents. After KABC did *Life in Red China*, *Variety* called it the "most ambitious program in radio history." KABC conducted interviews with Chinese officials in Peking, which

L.A. mayor Sam Yorty and Bob

Bob arranged during a visit to the Chinese Embassy in Ottawa, Canada, making him the first American broadcast journalist permitted in the facility. *Taxe$* broadcast the names of thousands of Southern Californians who had refunds due but had never claimed them. For *The Sexual Revolution*, Bob booked Hugh Hefner, Helen Gurley Brown, and movie producers Ross Hunter and Russ Meyer. After that special, *Variety* said, "KABC continues to offer a unique service to its community by offering for discussion the full spectrum of events in the news." In addition to its twenty-four-hour specials, KABC created dozens of public-service

Another KABC Radio 24-Hour Special

"TAXE$"

March 18, 1971

You can't avoid April 15th.
Prepare for it!

campaigns and became the first U.S. radio station to employ an ombudsman to process consumer concerns and complaints. In the first ten months of the ombudsman campaign, KABC recovered more than $75,000 for its listeners.

As a consequence of his public-service work, Bob earned a national Abe Lincoln Award from the Southern Baptist Radio and Television Commission. Reserved for a broadcaster displaying "ingenuity and excellence in promoting the moral and spiritual welfare of the nation and the world through broadcasting," the award cited Bob's work on the *Day of Dialogue* specials as well as his involvement with the Sugar Ray Robinson Youth Foundation, the Los Angeles Suicide Prevention Center, and Los Angeles law enforcement agencies. Bob joined an impressive list of previous Abe Lincoln winners, including Walter Cronkite, Bill Moyers, and Walt Disney.

Sugar Ray Robinson

After Bob added "Program Director" to his title, he made it his mission to enhance KABC's community profile. He produced KABC-sponsored concerts at the Hollywood Bowl, shows at the Shrine Auditorium starring Louie Armstrong, and involved himself in a series of off-the-wall promotions.

Bob received the Abe Lincoln Award for KABC's 24-Hour specials

One promotion focused on finding new female morning and evening traffic reporters. For air purposes, KABC christened the eventual winners, Kelly Lange and Lorri Donaldson, "Dawn O'Day" and "Eve O'Day," and then watched its ratings soar as the "Ladybirds," decked out in their sexy silver lame´ jumpsuits, became new Los Angeles celebrities.

Bob's strangest KABC promotion took its inspiration from host Ray Briem's overnight show. Briem had a semi-regular feature titled "Kooky Call," in which he made spontaneous telephone calls to random individuals all around the country. Over the course of a couple of years, Briem developed a core of about ten regulars, frequently interviewing them during his program. They became so well known to KABC's audience that Bob decided to hold a contest and allow listeners to vote

63

on their favorite. After George Naegly, a night police dispatcher from Blackstone, Virginia, was declared the winner, Bob flew Naegly and his wife to Los Angeles, where they were greeted at Los Angeles

International Airport by 2,000 KABC listeners and a full band. Then, for a week, Bob and KABC staffers escorted Naegly and his wife all over town – to Knotts Berry Farm, to an Angels baseball

"Kooky Call" winner George Naegly and wife arrive in Los Angeles

game, where Naegly threw out the first pitch, and even to the Lawrence Welk Show, where Naegly conducted the Welk orchestra on national television. That was how Bob became acquainted with Welk, and also how Ruth turned up as a dancer on his show.

Bob and Ruth Walsh with Lawrence Welk and Mr. and Mrs. George Naegly

Bob obsessed over providing KABC listeners with new reasons for tuning in, which was why he went after the Hollywood crowd. William Shatner, who played Captain Kirk on *Star Trek*, became one of Bob's first celebrity hosts. Bob also hired Jim Drury, who starred in *The Virginian,* and Robert Vaughn, co-star of *The Man From U.N.C.L.E.* Shatner, Drury, and Vaughn substituted when KABC's regular hosts went on vacation or assignment, and Vaughn was the best of the three, which was why Bob hired him to do a regular Saturday morning shift and assigned him to cover the 1972 Republican and Democratic national conventions.

Bob provided additional work to former *Bonanza* star Lorne Greene, former pro football star Merlin Olsen, Henry Gibson from *Laugh-In*, David Cassidy of *The Partridge Family*, and Ronald Reagan's daughter, Maureen Reagan, who landed a permanent show on weekends. Bob Dornan and Regis Philbin became two of Bob's more controversial hires. Known as "B-1 Bob" for his support of military spending and right-wing partisanship, Dornan railed against abortion and gay rights. After Bob lured Ruth Walsh away from KHJ, she produced Dornan's programs. Philbin had been Joey Bishop's version of Ed McMahon when Bishop had his late-night TV

Bob Walsh presents a "Great American" award to Lakers star Jerry West

talk show. One night, Philbin got into a spat with the Rat Packer and stalked off the set, after which he couldn't get a job at the La Brea tar pits. Desperate, Philbin begged Bob for a job. Hoberman recoiled at the mention of Philbin's name, but Bob hired him to work a Sunday morning shift, figuring that since nobody was listening then anyway, there wouldn't be any harm. Philbin proved successful enough that he finally talked KABC into giving him a morning TV show, which became his launching pad to *Regis and Kathy Lee*.

"Bob recognized talent in unusual places," Ruth said later. "No one thought Bill Russell would be very good, but he was wonderful. No one thought that Mr. Blackwell would be any good, but he was fabulous. Bob made KABC the talk of the town with the way he programmed the station."

Philbin occasionally joined Bob and Ruth's expanding social circle, which convened frequently during the summers at the

Huntington Sheraton Hotel in Pasadena, where Ruth worked as a Polynesian dancer when the hotel presented Hawaiian luaus.

"Bob really got into this," recalled Karl Moynes, who lived in Bob and Ruth's apartment building. "Bob started bringing all kinds of people from the station to these luaus. He brought Shatner and Drury. Mr. Blackwell came several times, and so did Philbin and Francis Gary Powers. Bob always brought Irene Ryan ("Granny" in *The Beverly Hillbillies*) to the luaus. Granny could really drink her scotch."

If Bob had gotten his way, he would have given Powers a permanent job. Shot down over the Soviet Union in 1960 and exchanged by the Soviets two years later for Russian master spy Rudolf Abel, the former U-2 pilot settled in Los Angeles, went through a divorce, and then found himself the target of broad criticism. Conservatives argued that Powers should have killed himself with a poison needle after his capture by the Soviets. Liberals felt Powers should have never been spying over the Soviet Union in the first place. By the time Bob met him, Powers had exhausted his employment options. Bob worked every angle to convince Meyers to hire Powers, and got him on the air occasionally as a fill-in talk show host. Powers later found permanent work at KNBC as its traffic reporter, becoming "The Spy in the Sky."

KABC didn't want to hire Bill Russell, either, but Bob's persistence paid off. While working at WNAC in Boston, Bob had booked Russell on Palmer Payne's show. Five years later, Bob again contacted Russell, who worked NBA telecasts on ABC with Keith Jackson, proposing that Russell host a talk show. Russell declined, and continued to decline, for more than six months. After Bob finally cajoled Russell into saying yes, KABC said no. Bob haggled with Hoberman, who objected to Russell vehemently, considering Russell an ex-jock who wouldn't be able to handle a big-time radio gig. Bob figured differently. To people not personally acquainted with Russell, he came off as intimidating and aloof. But Bob recognized that most people simply misunderstood Russell. His legendary refusal to sign autographs, for example, was not a snub at the autograph seeker but rather an affirmation of respect. Russell believed there should be more to human interaction than a hastily scribbled signature; to Russell, the gesture seemed hollow. A clue to Russell's view of the world could be found in a printed message he gave to people once he came to trust them. It said, "Our whole lives, it seems, we are only deciding how often and to whom we expose ourselves. We learn to make a shell for ourselves when we are young and then spend the rest of our lives hoping for someone to reach inside that shell and touch us. Just touch us — anything more than that would be too much for us to bear." Bob wanted to reach inside, pull Russell out, and put him on the air.

Bob knew KABC's audience would respond to Russell in a wonderful way. But after Hoberman gave a final no, Bob refused to accept it. He flew to New York to meet Bob Henabery, now running KABC's parent, ABC Radio. Bob faced a delicate situation. He didn't want to offend Hoberman, but he wanted Russell on the air and Henabery could help make that happen. Henabery did, personally leaning on Hoberman. Within five weeks, the ratings for Russell's 5 to 7 p.m. time slot shot from twenty-second in a fifty-station market to number one.

"I wasn't looking to do radio work," Russell remembered, "and there was strong resistance from Hoberman. He said white people won't listen to black people. And then half of the blacks won't listen to a black on the radio, either. But Bob and Keith Jackson kept pushing. Finally, Keith told Hoberman that if he didn't give me a shot he was going to resign as sports director. So we made a deal and Bob put together a team for me. I recognized pretty early that in terms of putting that show together and making it marketable, Bob was inspired."

One guy at the station Russell especially enjoyed was Richard Sylvan Selzer, a Depression-era slum kid from Brooklyn who had dodged his old man's fists at home and learned to survive on the streets. When the old man ran off, Selzer followed his mother to Los Angeles. One day, Selzer learned that Universal Studios was casting a series of films featuring a gang of street kids. Selzer jumped at the opportunity, earning his way into *Little Tough Guy*, which starred the original Dead End Kids and made Selzer an official member of those Hollywood legends. Three years later, Selzer reinvented himself as Dick Ellis and then, at the urging of an acquaintance, Howard Hughes, reinvented himself again as Richard Blackwell, ultimately appearing in dozens of films in minor roles. Although he never achieved stardom, he carved a unique niche in Hollywood history. Disenchanted with his screen career, Blackwell tapped a previously undiscovered gift for women's fashion. Before long, Mamie Eisenhower became a client, as did Nancy Reagan, Irene Ryan, Ann Blyth, Lily Pons, Jayne Mansfield, Jane Russell, Amanda Blake, and Goldie Hawn.

Blackwell published his first "Worst Dressed List" in 1960. By the fifth year of the list, it had become an international phenomenon. By its tenth year, critics had come to regard Blackwell's witty compilation as a cultural institution. But by the list's eleventh year, the fashion world had left Blackwell in the rear view mirror. When the hot new looks became battle fatigues, Chinese Mao uniforms, sleeveless

T-shirts, jeans, braless undershirts, and thongs, Blackwell was reduced to instant anachronism. Shortly after The Worst Dressed List marked its thirteenth anniversary, Blackwell caught a break. Sitting alone in his office one day, he received a telephone call from Bob Walsh, who inquired if Blackwell would be interested in doing one-minute commentaries on KABC.

Mr. Blackwell as a "Dead End Kid"

Bob's offer to Blackwell sent Hoberman, who considered Blackwell a weirdo, straight over the edge. But Bob believed, as did George Green in KABC's sales department, that Blackwell would attract new sponsors. Together, they convinced Hoberman to give the fashion designer a chance. Blackwell's commentaries would run ten times a day, and Blackwell would be free to stir up Los Angeles any way he wanted. And Blackwell knew exactly how he would do it. From his days of roaming the Hollywood cocktail party circuit, Blackwell realized that if he really wanted to get noticed, he should speak in a near whisper, delivered in a low purr. He knew how to manipulate pitch and tone to force the audience to hang on every word, and when Blackwell spoke, the audience dangled. Within weeks of Blackwell coming aboard, KABC's switchboard lit up with squawks of disapproval, oceans of praise, and high-minded moral indignation over his one-minute celebrity massacres.

Blackwell and KABC loved it. The only person who loathed it was Michael Jackson, one of the station's star talk show hosts and the husband of Alana Ladd, the daughter of actor Alan Ladd. Jackson had been KABC's top guy, and Blackwell had pranced in off the street, making Jackson appear as palatable as Styrofoam. Lousy with jealousy, Jackson adopted a scorched-earth policy toward Blackwell, who retaliated against Jackson's barbs by zinging his adversary in jest. During a commentary that aired during Jackson's show one morning, Blackwell pointed out that Jackson "looked like he sucked lemons and that his voice seemed to be squeezed out of him." Blackwell added, "I bet he even wears Alan Ladd's old jockey shorts, too."

Enraged that Blackwell had besmirched his reputation, Jackson demanded that KABC run Blackwell off the air. Bob responded by giving Blackwell his own talk show, sending Jackson into another dither. KABC enlarged Blackwell's mailbox to handle his fan letters, while Jackson received the occasional notice to renew his *Reader's Digest* subscription. The station did nothing else about the Blackwell-Jackson feud for a long time because Bob's instincts had proved correct. And owing to that, KABC's sales department swarmed with new accounts.

There were two Richard Blackwells. The public Blackwell presented himself as an abrasive Hollywood icon with a gargantuan ego. But if the public Blackwell skewered enemies with four-letter words that even seasoned four-letter word aficionados blanched at using, the private Blackwell kept himself light years removed from outrageous bluster. The private Blackwell visited nursing homes and prisons, provided free makeovers for poor women, and handed out money to people in need. The private Blackwell radiated compassion, but couldn't disguise his pain.

Occasionally, the two Blackwells fused. One moment the public Blackwell frothed and vented. The next minute the private Blackwell welled with tears as he recalled a life that had been a story of survival and the exorcism of personal demons. The public Blackwell did not allow many people to see the private Blackwell, but people could frequently listen to the private Blackwell on KABC, which was what both Blackwells really seemed to crave. Radio gave the former Dead End Kid the opportunity to shed the act and show everyone that the real Blackwell rose above camp, was more than a gimmick and independent from a list. And both Blackwells gravitated to Bob Walsh.

"Bob cared more for the people at the station than he did the station itself," recounted Blackwell. "Everyone on the corporate side of KABC was opposed to me going on the air. They thought all I was good for was a list of worst-dressed people. Bob saw much deeper. And I would say that if anyone started the magazine format in radio it would have been Bob. I don't think anyone else understood that you could be that varied in radio. Bob saw you could.

"Bob was the only one who would take a chance on me, the only one. And I think it's because he took the time to find out what I was all about. Bob was the most loved man at the station. Bob saved my career by letting me be who I really was. Bob was a non-gender person. He didn't threaten you with gender or with this macho crap.

He always came on just as a soul. I'm a piece of Hollywood history, and Bob protected me. I don't think I would have lasted if he hadn't. Even with his job at stake, Bob fought for me."

With Russell and Blackwell pulling huge numbers and KABC suddenly a big deal in the Los Angeles broadcasting firmament, Bob

Ruth Walsh and Nancy Sinatra

became hot stuff nationally, as Ruth always figured he would. He had won two Associated Press awards, a couple of Golden Mike awards, and several other broadcasting prizes. What happened was inevitable. One day Bob received a telephone call from ABC's Squire Rushnell, who had produced Bob Kennedy's show on WBZ in Boston. Rushnell asked Bob if he would be interested in directing a new television program in Chicago. If it worked, it would be taken to New York. If it didn't, it would be scrubbed. Happy at KABC but intrigued, Bob flew to Chicago, interviewed, and was offered the job.

But as soon as Bob arrived back in Los Angeles, he got a call from Russell. The bad news: Russell had decided to leave KABC to become coach and general manager of the Seattle SuperSonics.

"I did not want to go to Seattle — that I did not want to do," Russell explained later. "And when Sam Schulman asked me to do it I said no. But he kept asking what it would take. I finally made an outrageous proposal I knew he wouldn't accept, only he accepted it. Then I told him there was one more thing. I wanted to bring along my own assistant general manager. He didn't like it, but he agreed to it."

Russell's good news: He wanted Bob to follow him to the Pacific Northwest, placing Bob in a major quandary. He had a great job at KABC and had been offered the opportunity to produce a nationally syndicated television show for ABC. But Russell had become a close friend. After discussing it with Ruth, Bob sought out sportscaster Keith Jackson, who advised Bob to make a career switch. Jackson had launched his own career at KOMO-TV in Seattle, a city he recommended highly. Jackson also volunteered to help Ruth get a job at his old station. After thinking it over, Bob decided there was nothing left to do at KABC except more of the same. If he accepted the job in Chicago, he would be jumping into a volatile situation that may or may not work. But if he went to Seattle, he could start a new career with a man he respected deeply.

On June 11, 1973, the Associated Press carried the following news item:

Walsh Resigns KABC To Join Russell In Seattle

Radio station KABC says Bob Walsh has resigned as its program and production manager to become assistant general manager of the Seattle SuperSonics basketball team. Walsh joins Bill Russell, who recently was named coach and general manager of the National Basketball Association team. The two men have been friends for ten years. With the SuperSonics, the thirty-two-year-old Walsh will be primarily involved in administrative aspects, enabling Russell to devote more time to coaching the club.

A year after joining Russell in Seattle, Bob wondered what might have happened if he had gone to Chicago instead. The pilot show Squire Rushnell touted him on, *Good Morning Chicago*, eventually moved to New York and went into national syndication under a new name. Had Bob gone with it, he probably would have been the first executive producer of *Good Morning America*.

Shadow Of
The Needle

I had seen how Bob had put together a good organization at the radio station. When Bob said he didn't know anything about basketball, I just said, 'You don't need to know a damn thing.'

— Bill Russell, member of eleven
NBA Championship teams,
Seattle, Washington

William Felton Russell's first edition of the Seattle SuperSonics mimicked Harlem Globetrotter fodder more than it did the vintage Boston Celtics. The Sonics won only twenty-six games the season before Russell's arrival and, apart from All-Stars Spencer Haywood and Fred Brown, mainly featured an unappealing mash of journeymen — Jim Fox, Bud Stallworth, John Hummer, Dick Snyder — that inspired a stampede away from the team's ticket windows. Two other Sonics bear mention: Although a brooding psychopath who packed a gun, threatened to bludgeon opponents into an unappealing pulp, and terrified his own teammates, John Brisker possessed remarkable athletic skills. And everyone took a fast fancy to Donald "Slick" Watts, a rookie free-agent guard who festooned his bald pate with a headband, and whose innumerable nukes of the mother tongue made Yogi Berra seem like William F. Buckley.

Not long after Russell and Bob Walsh began their overhaul of the Sonic franchise, Watts barged into Bob's office and demanded an appointment with Russell, who was playing golf in Washington, D.C.

"Gotta see the coach," insisted Slick.

"Sorry," said Bob. "The boss is not around. He's 3,000 miles away."

"Well, give me the phone number so I can call him."

"I can't do that, Slick. He left me instructions that he's incommunicado."

"In communicado? Where's that?" asked the rookie. "Never mind. Just give me the phone number and I'll call him there."

Another time, Watts had been scheduled to do a personal appearance at a grade school. He showed up at the Sonics' offices beforehand decked out in sartorial finery — a new sports coat, a coordinated pair of slacks, shoes polished to a sheen, and a very hip tie.

"You look great," complimented Dave Watkins, who ran the Sonics' marketing department.

"I be lookin' good," Watts agreed.

"There's only one thing missing," Watkins said.

"Yeah?"

"How come you aren't wearing a shirt?"

Veteran Kennedy McIntosh more than matched Watts' brainlock. Shortly before the Chicago Bulls sent McIntosh to Seattle, the erratic forward had been dribbling during a game when, for no apparent reason, he stopped and stared vacantly into the stands. Coach Dick Motta yelled that the shot clock was about to expire, but McIntosh ignored him, frozen in an almost otherworldly trance. After Chicago lost possession, Motta pulled McIntosh aside.

"What the hell are you doing?" Motta was heard to say.

"I've just seen God," McIntosh responded, pointing to the cheap seats. "He's right up there."

Whirlybirds like Watts and McIntosh forced Russell into frequent getaways on the golf course. Not only did Russell inherit a team that couldn't score or play defense, his new club played most of its games against a backdrop of silence in a nearly empty Seattle Center Coliseum, a sporting galaxy far removed from Russell standards. He had been a member of two NCAA championship teams at the University of San Francisco, the star of the United States' 1956 Olympic team, and a player of indescribable importance on eleven NBA championship clubs in Boston, eight of those in unbroken succession. Russell not only reigned as the greatest team player in the history of the NBA, he had transformed the way basketball was played and revised forever how it would be taught. The conventional wisdom in the mid-1950s, and for a long time afterward, held that black players lacked intelligence. They could run and jump, but were erratic and lacked fundamentals. Supposedly, only white players possessed the brain power to understand how to play, but they couldn't run or jump like the black players. Russell brought the entire package.

Bill Russell, coaching the Seattle Supersonics, 1974

After several college coaches watched him play in the 1955 NCAA Tournament, they hastily adopted "Russell's Rules," widening the free throw lane to twelve feet and making it illegal for a player to touch the ball on its downward arc to the basket. Dartmouth coach Doggie Julian, a member of the Rules Committee, later wrote, "We weren't planning to make any changes. But after some of the coaches saw Russell play, they got scared." Russell, who had moved from Louisiana to California as a youngster, couldn't even make his Oakland high school team in his sophomore year and only rose to a third-string player as a junior. But his coordination improved, he grew to six-foot-seven, and then to six-foot-ten by the time he enrolled at the University of San Francisco. Fifty-five consecutive victories and two NCAA titles later, Russell brought a game to the NBA that his contemporaries found almost beyond imagination.

His first appearance with the Celtics occurred on December 22, 1956, against the St. Louis Hawks. Russell played just sixteen minutes but snatched twenty-one rebounds. A couple of days later, he

74

held Neil Johnston of the Philadelphia Warriors, the NBA's third-leading scorer, without a field goal for the first forty-two minutes while also pulling down eighteen rebounds. The very next evening, again playing against the Warriors, Russell grabbed thirty-four rebounds in twenty minutes.

Russell's unique gifts brought entire rows of people off their seats, and no one, with the possible exception of Red Auerbach, had expected it. No one had expected Russell to change the tempo of every game he played, but he did. No one had known what a great athlete Russell was, how refined his timing was, how incredible his anticipation was. The tape measure had failed to detect those things, much less provide a clue as to the true size of Russell's heart. Russell had arrived as something completely new, the forerunner of the kind of player who wouldn't appear en masse for two more decades. Even Wilt Chamberlain's entrance in the league couldn't detract from Russell's genius. Although Chamberlain had a three-inch height advantage and fifty pounds on Russell, Russell beat up Chamberlain in the one place Chamberlain was vulnerable: his mind. Lew Alcindor, who would become Kareem Abdul-Jabbar, watched Russell with a reverential eye as a kid growing up in New York City. Bill Walton considered Russell his all-time favorite player. Russell didn't know it, but emerging young centers all over America emulated his game, and he was idolized in places he didn't know existed.

Long before television spread through Europe and the Soviet Union, the Voice of America carried broadcasts of the 1956 Olympics and, later, Boston Celtic games. Little kids locked behind the Iron Curtain talked about and imitated Russell, fascinated by his matchups with Chamberlain and in awe of what Russell could do, which was pretty much whatever he pleased. One year, Russell traveled to Yugoslavia with a team of NBA All-Stars. The Yugoslavs had a red-haired kid who was reputed to be the best player in Europe. Before the game, Auerbach took Russell aside and told him that he didn't want Russell to score or rebound, just to stop that red-haired Yugoslav. The first time the Yugoslav came down the court, he got the ball and went up for a jumper. Russell went with him and slammed it away. After Russell stuffed the Yugoslav for the sixth consecutive time, the Yugoslav took two steps backward and heaved the ball at the basket. It hit the top of the backboard, ejecting Auerbach off his seat.

"Damn you, Russell!" Auerbach barked. "He hit the backboard!"

The next time the Yugoslav came down court, Russell blocked his shot so hard that it hit the kid in the face, nearly breaking his nose. The Yugoslav ran down the ball, kicked it into the stands, threw a tantrum, and got kicked out of the game.

Russell routinely did the same thing to NBA players, sometimes blocking three and four shots in a row from different players. He once blocked a Chamberlain fadeaway jumper. Nate Thurmond, who stood six-foot-eleven, quickly retrieved the ball and tried to jam it in the basket. Russell blocked Thurmond's shot, too. No other player matched Russell's total control over the area of the floor and sky around the opponent's basket. He had no time for anything less than an all-out commitment to team play and little use for anyone who could not make a contribution. Fourteen times in Russell's career — college, Olympics, and the NBA — it all came down to one game, and fourteen times the team with Russell won. Russell averaged eighteen points and nearly thirty rebounds in those games.

Russell dominated regular-season games, entire regular seasons, and all postseasons for more than a decade without ever having to score a basket. Because he understood positioning, angles, and movements, and all the barely visible elements of the game, he became the first player in NBA history to help generate his team's offense from his own defense. Because he studied shooters and their shots, he knew when each player was going to release, what type of shot that player had, and where he had to be to block it. And if he didn't block it, he knew where balls would come off the rim, enabling him to collect thousands of rebounds. Russell averaged 22.5 rebounds over the course of his career, many of them a direct result of his anticipation. But more than anything, Russell burned with an otherworldly desire to win that went unmatched until Michael Jordan arrived in the NBA a quarter of a century later.

In the seventh game of the 1962 NBA Finals against the Lakers, Russell scored thirty points and snatched forty rebounds, a monumental statistical achievement Russell simply ignored. After the game, Russell got dressed and went home. The next morning, he and his wife drove to Maine for a vacation. Russell hadn't looked at the box score, never saw the newspapers, and did not find out for thirty-five years that he was still the only player in league history with a thirty-point, forty-rebound playoff game, and still held the playoff record for most rebounds in a single quarter at nineteen.

"All I knew," Russell admitted later, "was that we won by two points."

As a player, Russell did not study statistics, glancing at them only once a month. He did not find them meaningful. Only pride and effort had meaning, which was why Russell became the consistent difference in transforming a series of great Boston teams into the sporting dynasty of the twentieth century.

While Russell's performances would become the stuff of legend, the Russell persona often left a glacial chill with Boston press and Celtics fans. To those who did not know him, he seemed distant and unapproachable, a man who harbored a festering anger. Cobble that to the Russell scowl and the picture developed into one of looming intimidation. But the Boston press and Celtic fans had not been called a "nigger," an "animal," a "big, black gorilla," a "black bastard," and a "baboon," as Russell had. They had not been denied seating in restaurants and admission to hotels. Russell refused to suffer fools and became adamant about protecting his sovereign privacy. In his early days in Boston, he adopted a policy of speaking only when spoken to; he would not become the bigot's stereotype of The Negro.

In his final days with the Celtics, the only interviews he gave were the mandatory ones after ball games. Otherwise, speaking for public consumption did not interest him unless he felt he had something to say. He would not subject himself to a question and answer period; that would put him in the position of saying something over which he had no control. Reporters could shade his answers to the left or the right, for or against, depending on their whim, ignorance, clumsiness, or bias. And no matter what he said, half the people would agree with him and half would disagree. Russell found it a useless exercise.

Later on, and despite having been a talk show host himself, he wouldn't appear on talk shows. They had degenerated into back-and-forth, full-volume mindlessness, and Russell would not expose himself to any situation in which people might treat him with disrespect. Nor would he willingly place himself in a situation where he would be forced to insult another person. Since he harbored a strong distaste for hero worship, he refused to sign autographs, even extending the ban to his own Celtics teammates. He made few exceptions. After doing a radio interview on Palmer Payne's show on WNAC in the mid-1960s, Russell was asked by Bob Walsh for an autograph. Russell gave him one, but after that gave no more for many years. Russell's anti-autograph and anti-interview policies became two of his least-understood convictions in a vast spectrum of behaviors comprehensible only to him.

One year, *Sports Illustrated* asked Russell if he would write an article, touching on the "quota" issue in the NBA, an unwritten rule stating that no team could carry more than two or three black players. Russell believed the rule existed; a lot of white executives argued that it did not, despite the fact that no teams ever had more than two or three black players. A Boston sportswriter finally validated Russell's belief when, discussing the Celtics' prospects for an upcoming season, he wrote, "The Celtics will not keep four Negroes. The crowds won't stand for it and neither will the owners." Another time, while Russell

and Rick Barry worked an NBA game on television, Barry made an insensitive and apparently clueless crack about Russell's "watermelon grin." Russell spent the rest of the game in stone-cold silence, and Barry couldn't figure why Russell had suddenly become a sphinx. CBS eventually fired Barry, and most observers figured Russell had been behind it. But Russell had nothing to do with Barry's firing. Some time later, Turner Broadcasting wanted to hire Russell to do some color work. After Russell made the deal, TBS informed him that it wanted to hire Barry as the play-by-play announcer. TBS asked Russell if he had any objections. He did not. He had thought long and hard about Barry, deciding that

Bob with Bill Russell, courtside, 1975

Barry was insensitive to people regardless of race, creed, or color. That being the case, TBS could hire him.

In 1968, San Jose State sociology professor Harry Edwards organized an Olympic boycott. CBS decided to do a story and compiled a list of athletes it wanted to interview, Russell prominent among them. When a CBS staffer called Russell and told him to show up at a taping at two o'clock the next day, Russell declined. The man, first of all, had invaded his privacy, and second, had given Russell an order. No one got away with that. When the man persisted, Russell hung up. Then a CBS sportscaster called and told Russell he absolutely had to do the interview. Infuriated, Russell hung up again. Fifteen minutes later, another CBS functionary called, chastising Russell for placing him in an awkward spot.

"You absolutely have to show for this interview," the CBS man said.

"Oh, really?" Russell replied. "And what makes you think you can just call me up and tell me what to do? I don't even know you. You are going to vouch for the guys who have been calling me. But who is going to vouch for you?"

Officials at the Naismith Memorial Basketball Hall of Fame in Springfield, Massachusetts, told Russell they desired to induct him into the shrine of heroes. Russell bypassed the ceremony. The Celtics advised Russell that they wanted to retire his number 6 in front of a clamoring Boston public. Russell replied that he didn't want a public tribute and made the Celtics lock the doors. He had his own reasons for what he did and didn't do, and it was nobody's business. From this side of the façade, Russell presented a fascinating amalgam: the paramount team player and quintessential lone wolf, a genius in group dynamics and the ultimate solo artist.

Following the 1959 NBA season, Russell traveled to Africa on a State Department tour to teach basketball fundamentals to any kids who wanted to learn. He got a tiny projector, rounded up 200 basketballs, bought a plane ticket, and took off. Just him. He ventured to Libya, Ethiopia, Nigeria, the Ivory Coast, Liberia, Sierra Leone, and Senegal.

"I didn't care if any of the kids spoke English," Russell observed later. "Where basketball and kids are concerned, there is no such thing as a language barrier."

Russell stopped first in Tripoli, where a press conference had been arranged. Russell had been warned to be careful. Communist writers would be present; they might try to embarrass the United States. The first question thrown at Russell came from a Communist writer.

"What is your real reason for coming to Libya?" he asked.

Russell responded that it was because he wanted to share the joy of a game he had loved since he was nine years old.

"You don't have to be great to have fun playing basketball," said Russell. "You don't even have to be good. You just have to want to play."

"What's the name of the king?" the Communist writer asked Russell.

"I don't know the king's name."

"How can you come here and say you want to be a friend of the Libyan people and you don't even know the king's name?"

"Because it doesn't interest me. I'm not here to be a politician or a diplomat. I'm here to teach basketball. And that has nothing to do with a king. And your politics I don't care about."

Russell cared mainly about friendships, which he based on trust, the linchpin in his relationship with Bob Walsh. And Russell cared about principles. When he agreed to run Sam Schulman's basketball team, he was offered a bonus based on the team's attendance figures. Russell refused, telling Schulman that increasing attendance was part of his duties and that he would accept no additional pay for doing a job he was being paid to do. Russell did not believe in incentives. He never had a single incentive clause in any of his contracts with the Celtics. Incentives for individual performance disrupted team play. If Russell needed rebounds to meet an incentive standard, the temptation would have been to position himself to get those rebounds. But that might take the Celtics out of their defensive scheme. So when Russell talked contract with Auerbach, the talk was about playing hard and winning. Nothing else mattered; people either understood it or they didn't, and most people didn't.

Neither did they understand that Russell's façade evolved into a greater piece of defensive wizardry than the tens of thousands of shots he blocked and disrupted. Behind the public mask hid a man sensitive, generous, gregarious, and intellectually curious. Bob Walsh watched Russell cry on more than one occasion. He witnessed the difficulty Russell had in getting close to people. It was, Bob felt, a shame; Russell had so much to give. He was loyal and had a prankish sense of humor.

But when Bill Russell and Bob Walsh arrived under the shadow of the Space Needle, there was no humor in the Seattle SuperSonics. Russell, whom John Wooden had called "the most important player ever to play the game," and Walsh, barely beginning to comprehend his assignment, had elected to operate a franchise that had only 350 season ticket holders, hardly a running head start for the first African-American to be given complete control of a major sports franchise. And that wasn't the worst of it. The Sonics had already deteriorated into a public relations disaster, and it would have been far worse had anybody known the extent of the drug abuse on the team. It made rich irony: The man who had personally cared only about winning as a player looked at the new team he was about to coach and immediately understood that winning was not the most important thing; the man who had publicly seemed to care nothing about image now recognized that image was everything.

"I can't tell you how many times I got called at two and three o'clock in the morning to find out the players were busted," remembered Russell. "I'd make a call to a lawyer, and I'd say, 'This is Bill Russell.' And he'd say, 'Oh, shit! Who's in jail now?' Then he'd call another lawyer and he'd go get these guys out of jail and keep it out of the newspapers. We had to keep these things out of the paper because the franchise couldn't handle it. The commissioner finally called me because I wasn't reporting these things to the league. They'd gone through a review of police records all over the country and here's this list of Sonics. The commissioner was really pissed. He said, 'I ought to fine you $25,000.' I told him that if those kinds of things got in the papers we'd have to move the franchise. One reason I went to Seattle

Bob Walsh flanked by Sonics Tommy Burleson (left) and Slick Watts

was that I thought if I didn't the franchise might have to move. The Sonics were not accepted in the community. Over the stern objections of a lot of people who were there when we arrived, we instituted a lot of programs. We held practices at the schools during the assembly period. We wanted every kid, from kindergarten through the twelfth grade, to meet the Sonics personally. I wanted those kids to go home and talk about the Sonics. We did a lot of things like that. Our second year — and this was Bob's idea — the official team photograph was with a Boeing 747. We got a lot of Boeing workers interested in the Sonics because this picture was all over the Boeing plant, and they had fifty thousand people working there. We wanted them to say, 'Hey, the Sonics are okay.' You might get one or two hundred to come to a game."

Russell's first team made a ten-game improvement to 36-46, and his second finished 43-39, making the playoffs for the first time in franchise history. Those clubs attracted customers first because they represented vast improvements over previous Sonic teams, next because of Russell's marquee status, and also because Russell endorsed the implementation of novel entertainment packages to complement the games. Bob and Dave Watkins, who handled public relations, collaborated on elaborate pre-game and halftime shows, often recruiting some of Russell's friends — Quincy Jones, Lou Rawls, Dionne Warwick, Johnny Mathis — to perform. One time, Bob brought William Shatner up from Los Angeles to recite the national anthem. Bob also tapped the local talent scene, giving such up-and-comers as saxophonist Kenny G. opportunities to play in front of a large crowd.

With Russell's blessing, Bob consulted with Philadelphia GM Pat Williams about the Sixers' wild halftime promotions, incorporating some of them into Seattle's intermission mix. The sidebar entertainment at Sonics' games evolved into the most sophisticated in the league. Given Bob's wealth of experience at KABC, he had a huge creative advantage in the promotional arena, needing all of it given Schulman's frugality. Plus, Bob had the advantage of operating both with a consummate professional in Watkins, and with Russell's stamp on his ideas. Russell had promised Schulman that the owner would get more than he had bargained for, and the big man delivered. In fact, Russell made his boss a promise after watching Sonics fans practically boo Schulman out of the Seattle Coliseum: One day those booing fans would give Schulman a standing ovation. It happened faster than Schulman ever imagined. Immediately after the Sonics clinched their first-ever playoff berth, Russell instructed team radio announcer

Bob Blackburn to take two chairs to mid-court so that he and Schulman could talk to the fans who had remained to celebrate. When Schulman got up to leave, he received the standing ovation Russell promised.

Not all of the innovations Bill Russell and Bob Walsh conjured up fell into the entertainment category, nor did they necessarily focus exclusively on the Sonics' franchise. For example, Bob once compiled a feasibility study aimed at showing that the NBA would be a far better game with a third referee. The NBA experimented with three officials during one exhibition season, but scrapped the idea during the regular season on the grounds that it was too expensive. A decade later, the NBA adopted the three-official policy. Another time, with the NBA All-Star Game slated for Seattle, Bob decided, at the urging of local civic activist Freddie Mae Gautier, to stage a special tribute to Dr. Martin Luther King, who had been assassinated six years earlier. Freddie Mae had grown up in the same Seattle neighborhood as Quincy Jones, was plugged into the Jesse Jackson, Andrew Young, Dr. Ralph Abernathy crowd, and had been acquainted with Dr. King, having served for ten years on his Southern Christian Leadership Conference Board of Directors. Freddie Mae believed that Seattle needed to honor Martin Luther King. Bob Walsh and Bill Russell agreed; the NBA did not, viewing a tribute as too controversial. With Dr. King's two sons, Marty and Dexter, in attendance, the tribute took place anyway, a full decade before Congress declared a federal holiday in honor of the slain civil rights leader.

The Sonic front office also made a concerted effort to turn the All-Star Game into a splashy affair. In those days, few teams went to any lengths to entertain fans. Most just opened the doors. The All-Star Game provided an opportunity for the Sonics to do something big, and they did. They created a festive look for the Seattle Coliseum and booked live entertainment that included singer Dionne Warwick. It marked the first time any NBA team had attempted to create a total entertainment package around a single game.

Russell also backed Bob's plan for a revised local television package. When Russell and Bob first came to the Sonics, the team's games were being telecast on a small independent station, Channel 13, that failed to reach about two-thirds of the Puget Sound region, including the swank areas of Mercer Island and the east side of Lake Washington where most of the potential season ticket holders resided. Bob proposed a switch of the Sonics' telecasts to the CBS affiliate, KIRO-TV. The move to KIRO resulted in a windfall. Local broadcast

83

revenues jumped from $120,000 a year to $800,000 a year in one fell swoop.

"What it did," Russell explained later, "was make the franchise economically viable."

Another of Bob's ideas bore fruit, but not for several years. Along with Russell, Watkins, and others in the front office, Bob believed the Sonics had outgrown the Seattle Center Coliseum. From an average crowd of about 5,000 prior to Russell's arrival, attendance had jumped to averages of 11,996, 12,797, and 13,592 over the next three seasons. Bob asked Seattle Center officials to revamp the facility so that seating could be expanded. When they declined, Bob proposed that the Sonics move to the Kingdome, where they could average as many as 17,000 fans a game. Two problems quickly surfaced. Sonics Vice President Zollie Volchok opposed a move to the Kingdome, and the Dome, designed as a baseball-football facility, had no basketball configuration. Russell, who had demanded the title of general manager precisely so he could keep individuals such as Volchok from meddling, waited for Volchok to leave town, then dispatched Bob to New Orleans to get a copy of the basketball schematic for the Louisiana Superdome. With that in hand, Bob and Kingdome manager Ted Bowsfield devised a floor location and seating plan. This not only enabled the Sonics to smash every franchise and NBA attendance record, it became the key reason the National Collegiate Athletic Association ultimately awarded Seattle three Final Fours.

"In all successful endeavors what you come up with is the relationship between people on the team," Russell remarked later. "This was our team. I had to trust Bob and he had to trust me. All I ever did with Bob from the first time he became part of my consciousness was trust him. He never came at me with any bullshit. I know what he did with the radio thing in Los Angeles, how he put it together, and that he was bound to succeed in Seattle. So I trusted him and I listened to him. All I ever wanted to do was back him up and provide him with the opportunity to let his creative ability come out."

At once the most demanding and least restrictive general manager in the NBA, Russell wanted to make the SuperSonics a first-class franchise. But he didn't want to do the general manager's daily work. So Bob did that, coordinating the activities of the front office, handling off-court player issues, pursuing sponsorships, serving as a liaison with the league and Seattle Center Coliseum.

When it came to coaching, Russell ruled all. In his final seasons in Boston, he had arguably been the greatest player-coach in sports history. Certainly no one else who managed bench strategy, while also taking a full-time role in the game's playing action, had ever contributed so heavily toward winning a championship. In his last year as a player-coach with the Celtics, 1969, Boston faced a New York Knicks team in the second round of the playoffs that had beaten the Celtics six out of seven games during the regular season. Before Game One, Russell surveyed the stats and asked himself what he had to do to change the outcome of the game. He detected a major flaw in Boston's offense, a flaw that created a flow for the New York defense. Russell made an adjustment, making it imperative that New York adjust to his adjustment. By the time the Knicks figured out what Russell had done, it was too late. Boston won the series, four games to two, and went on to claim the last championship of the Russell era.

Russell tried to teach the Sonics players all that he knew. He preached the concept of team; his players didn't always listen. Russell had an implicit, perhaps unrealistic, faith that his players would do the jobs they were hired to do. That was what he had done; that's not always what Russell received in return. Russell had so much to say, and so many ways to inspire. He kept his friends spellbound when he talked – about anything. He could spin fantastic yarns about the old days with an eerie recall of detail, and instantly cite specific situations or plays from games that had been buried in the archives for forty years. But with some of the players he inherited, Russell could not connect. He received frequent criticism for being too aloof and nurturing a poor work ethic, ironic since Russell the player had worked harder than anyone. Russell the player only had to be told once, sometimes not at all. But Russell the coach never had the luxury of coaching anyone like himself.

Russell's last two Sonic teams finished 43-39 and 40-42. An itching Sam Schulman wanted a championship; he was ready to make a change and it happened by mutual consent. It happened even though the Russell era erased the negativity that had surrounded the club since its inception. It happened despite dramatically improved attendance and significant prospects for the future. Through Russell's trades and draft choices, the Sonics stood on the verge of becoming something special. They had added a young superstar in Dennis Johnson, and were a year away from acquiring Jack Sikma, Marvin Webster, Paul Silas, and Wally Walker. Those players enabled the Sonics to reach the

NBA Finals in 1978 and win the championship in 1979. But by that time, Lenny Wilkens had taken over as coach, the Sonics averaged 19,000 fans a game in the Kingdome, and most people had forgotten all about the contributions Russell had made.

He was gone, having vanished into his own solitude.

The Five
Percent Solution

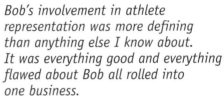

*Bob's involvement in athlete
representation was more defining
than anything else I know about.
It was everything good and everything
flawed about Bob all rolled into
one business.*

> – Rick Welts, ex-president,
> NBA Properties,
> New York City, New York

Ted Bundy's intermittent telephone calls to Bob Walsh & Associates always provoked lively office debates as to whether Bundy should be hanged, juiced, or eviscerated, with his entrails placed out for the buzzards. Bundy had located Bob Walsh through one of his misguided girlfriends, a Tacoma, Washington, woman who professed undying devotion for Bundy whenever she passed along one of his cryptic messages to Bob. Bundy had also contacted Bob through Ruth Walsh. Working for KOMO-TV, Seattle's ABC affiliate, Ruth had covered a string of Bundy murders, interviewing the serial killer several times in his Florida jail cell. For a long while, Ruth couldn't figure out what to make of Bundy. Every time she asked if he had committed all those ghastly crimes, Bundy replied murkily, "I don't think I did," or "You've investigated it, what do you think?" What gave Ruth great pause was a letter. After her mother died of cancer, Ruth received only a few expressions of sympathy – a couple of cards from professional colleagues, a two-hour phone call from Bill Russell, and a long, compassionate letter from one of America's most heinous desperados. Although genuinely touched by Bundy's words, Ruth came to believe that Bundy had committed a gruesome cache of murders, that he was not guilty of some murders he was accused of, and that he probably committed murders nobody would ever know about. In the course of her reporting and jailhouse conversations with Bundy, Ruth saw every side of the man, concluding that two entirely different people shared Bundy's mind and thoughts and provoked his actions.

Bob pushed Ruth to write a book about Bundy; he knew somebody was going to — probably several somebodies — and who better than Ruth? But after eight years of tracking the Bundy story Ruth decided against it.

"I'd reached a point where I knew too much about people who were close to Bundy," Ruth explained later. "I did not want to hurt those people."

But Bundy wanted a book anyway, and prevailed upon Bob to make it happen. He dispatched notes to that effect to Bob through the loopy Tacoma woman and called Bob frequently from Florida, where he awaited trial for the Chi Omega and Kimberly Leach murders. Bundy usually wanted to discuss how they should proceed and whether Bob would become his literary agent. Bundy sprinkled their conversations with diatribes in which he either waxed about his innocence or offered commentary on the headlines of the day. Sometimes Bundy called out the blue, looking for Ruth.

As he had with the Boston Strangler, Bob harbored a perverse fascination for Bundy, but Bob was not a literary agent and had no intention of representing a psycho. For one thing, Bob rather favored the idea of state of Florida serving up Bundy over easy. For another, Bob had all the work he could handle tending to his own clients, a burgeoning omnibus of stars and wannabes Bob assembled after snatching a loose idea and sprinting with it.

About the time Bill Russell left the Seattle SuperSonics, Lenny Wilkens joined the franchise as director of player personnel. Since Bob assumed that Lenny, who had become an instant friend, was fated to replace him, he explored a couple of other NBA opportunities, including one with Ted Turner in Atlanta. But Bob did not want to move, and Ruth had become so entrenched at KOMO — she had been promoted to evening co-anchor — that it made little sense for her to leave. The more Bob thought about it, the more he came to believe he should strike out on his own as a sports agent.

He had an excellent relationship with the Seattle SuperSonics and connections with the managements of the Seattle Seahawks and Seattle Mariners. He had negotiated dozens of basketball contracts and felt he knew how to generate endorsement opportunities for potential clients. If he could collect a 5 percent commission on some of the outlandish sports contracts that were awarded almost daily, he had the potential to put some serious coin in his pocket. And while he built a client base, Ruth now had the wherewithal to carry the financial load.

After Bob resigned as the Sonics' assistant general manager, he hooked up with Doug Baldwin, a young attorney also on the stalk for athletic flesh. They leased office space on the southern edge of downtown Seattle, going into business as Walsh-Baldwin Enterprises. The partnership didn't even last a year. Bob went into the office one day to discover that Baldwin, without explanation, had packed his own stuff and disappeared. Bob renamed the company Bob Walsh & Associates, and for a while his "associates" included a telephone, coffee pot, and a carton of Marlboros. But with typical tenacity, Bob built a stable of clients. Bruce Seals, a SuperSonics forward, became his first. Then Russell, Keith Jackson, and Wilkens signed on, followed by filmmaking genius Stanley Kramer, a recent Seattle transplant who had directed *Judgment at Nuremberg, The Defiant Ones, High Noon, It's a*

Mad, Mad, Mad, Mad World, Guess Who's Coming to Dinner, The Caine Mutiny, and *On the Beach.* Bob also recruited the Seahawks' highly popular quarterback/wide receiver combination of Jim Zorn and Steve Largent, and struck a motherlode in the 1982 senior football class at the University of Washington, landing a majority of the school's thirteen National Football League draft choices.

Steve Raible

Before long, Bob found himself representing more than 100 individuals, notably Matt Millen of the Oakland Raiders, Steve Raible of the

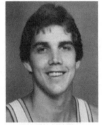

Wally Walker

89

Seahawks, Jack Sikma and Wally Walker of the SuperSonics, Dan Issel of the Denver Nuggets, Portland Trail Blazer Coach Jack Ramsay, hy-

droplane driver Chip Hanauer, synchro- nized swimmer Tracie Ruiz, football leg- end Bud Wilkinson, TV personalities Rob Weller and Merlin Olsen, and jazz singer Sarah Vaughn. But to the dismay of Rick Welts, one of Bob's first hires at BWA, some clients turned into clinkers, taking horrendous professional liberties with Bob.

"To watch how invested Bob became in these clients was hard to take," Welts observed later. "Bob was taken advantage of over and over. He

Tracie Ruiz

also made decisions that were not in his

Jim Zorn

financial interest and, for the most part, not sig- nificantly appreciated. Bob would do anything and go anywhere for his clients. He would even loan money to them."

"When I went to work for Bob," remembered Kimberly Brown, "he was representing a football player from the University of Wash- ington named Don Dow. I'd never heard of this guy. Dow had been drafted by the Seahawks. When he got cut from the team, his wife called up in tears. Bob told her that everything would be okay. The next thing I know, Dow was working in our office. I thought, who the hell is this guy?"

Rick Welts had started out as a ball boy with the SuperSonics. He subsequently became an assistant trainer, moved into the team's public relations department, and then followed Bob to BWA. Together, they not only collected clients, but collaborated on one venture after the other, some more successful than others. They produced a premier for Stanley Kramer's last and worst film, *The Runner Stumbles*; devel- oped an innovative advertising plan for the SuperSonics' SuperChannel, an early version of Direct TV; staged a series of basketball games in- volving members of the Seahawks football team; and promoted a string of basketball camps and NBA exhibition games in Alaska and Canada. Bob and Rick prowled constantly for endorsement opportunities for

BWA clients. While there was only so much they could do for Seahawk lineman Bill Dugan, who frequently practiced his blocking techniques on wide-eyed cows, they located a variety of promotional deals for Wilkens, Russell, Kramer, Ruiz, and others. Bob not only helped Russell and Kramer become *Seattle Times* guest columnists, he convinced Russell to take part in a two-character play to benefit the Seattle Children's Theater, which had been flirting with bankruptcy. The play,

The Former One-On-One Basket-ball Champion, sold out every performance and generated enough revenue to build a new theater.

Not all of Bob's efforts panned out as neatly. For Raible, a Seahawk wide receiver who rec-ommended Bob to other players on the team, and Linda Fernandez, who had won

Bill Russell clowns with the cast of The Former One-On-One Basketball Champions

TV's Superstars competition, Bob attempted to broker a deal with Nautilus, a fitness equipment company. The three of them flew to Delan, Florida, for a meeting with Arthur Jones, the Nautilus founder. Jones appeared to be in his sixties, his perky wife in her twenties. They lived in a palatial estate surrounded by pools stocked with alligators and decorated with photographs of voracious crocodiles dining ravenously on Africans. Jones commented colorfully on these repasts as he fed mice to an astonishing collection of boa constrictors.

Jones spent part of the meeting attempting to impress upon Bob, Steve, and Linda the extent of his physical prowess, doing so by jumping from the floor to his desk. Toward the end of the meeting, Jones brought out a film. Its highlight moment occurred when a large crocodile was slit open, revealing the remains of some hapless native. Bob, Steve, and Linda departed Florida without an endorsement deal.

Bob worked hard to expand the parameters of his business, agentry not being nearly enough to satisfy his appetites. In Boston, he had not been content to produce radio shows; he jetted around the country trying to locate the strangest guests imaginable. In Los Angeles, he programmed some of the most ambitious shows in that city's radio history. With the Sonics, Bob had the vision, as well as the support of Russell and Dave Watkins, to erase the distinction between sports and entertainment. Central to Bob's character was his almost genetic predisposition to make each project larger than its original definition. For example, even with 100 clients to serve, Bob spent nearly a year chasing after the idea of placing a National Basketball Association franchise in Vancouver, British Columbia.

While Bob knew that the NBA harbored plans to one day award a franchise to a Canadian city, he had no evidence that the league wished to explore Vancouver, nor did he know if anyone in Vancouver desired to own an NBA team. Undaunted, Bob became messianic about Vancouver's chances. He sounded out Ted Bowsfield, a Canadian who ran operations at Seattle's Kingdome. Bowsfield suggested that Bob talk to Grant McDonald, an attorney who represented Vancouver-based Nelson Skalbania, a rapidly emerging sports guru who had been nicknamed "The Phantom of the Franchises."

The flamboyant Skalbania had made a fortune buying and selling buildings, and his favorite trick involved the purchase of an office complex or hotel with the intent to "flip" or sell it immediately, pocketing a quick profit. Skalbania also had a flair for the unusual. He once traded his half interest in the Edmonton Oilers hockey team for a $200,000 Rolls Royce that had been used in the movie *The Great Gatsby*, a diamond ring, and some mortgages.

At his financial peak, Skalbania did an average of $200 million worth of business a week, and spent a lot of that money. He had apartments in Edmonton, Calgary, and Hawaii, a couple of mansions in Vancouver, a pair of Rolls Royces, an executive jet, a yacht docked in the Caribbean, office buildings in Alberta and British Columbia, and land holdings in Prince George, Toronto, Montreal, and California.

The Canadian impresario also immersed himself in professional sports in a significant way. He purchased the Indianapolis Racers of the World Hockey Association, ultimately pulling off the hockey equivalent of Boston's 1919 sale of Babe Ruth to the Yankees by selling eighteen-year-old Wayne Gretzky to the Edmonton Oilers.

Skalbania then bought the National Hockey League's Atlanta Flames and the North American Soccer League's Memphis Rogues for a combined $18 million and moved both to Calgary. When Bob met the Phantom of the Franchises, Skalbania had just raided nine National Football League players, including Los Angeles Rams quarterback Vince Ferragamo and the Atlanta Falcons' star kick returner Billy "White Shoes" Johnson for another of his Canadian franchises, the Montreal Alouettes.

Skalbania had so many things going on, both in and out of sports, that he often couldn't keep track of everything. Bob and Rick loitered in Skalbania's office one morning when his secretary entered and told Skalbania that movers were on the way.

"What movers?" Skalbania asked.

"We're moving out of this building," the secretary replied, "because you traded it for one down the street."

"Shit!" said Skalbania. "I forgot about that. Did we do that?"

Bob's first meeting with Skalbania lasted fifteen minutes. After Bob cavalierly informed Skalbania that an NBA franchise was practically his for the asking, Skalbania inquired if Bob really could get him in the NBA. Bob confidently declared he could.

"What does this franchise cost?" asked Skalbania.

"I don't know yet," replied Bob. "But if I'm going to act on your behalf it's going to take $25,000."

Skalbania wrote a check. Now that Bob had successfully recruited Skalbania, he figured it was time to introduce the NBA to the new Canadian owner it didn't know it had. A few days later, Bob and Rick showed up at NBA headquarters in New York, presenting themselves as sophisticated brokers who could produce a legitimate buyer for a franchise in a city, as it turned out, about as far off the NBA's radar screen as, say, Damascus, Syria.

Fortunately for Bob and Rick, they found an ally in Simon Gourdine, the NBA's deputy commissioner. Gourdine became so infatuated with Vancouver that he lobbied Commissioner Larry O'Brien and several influential owners into the view that the Canadian city was precisely the place to be. When Bob discovered what Gourdine had done, he promptly instructed Skalbania to send a $25,000 deposit to league headquarters. Just like that, Skalbania had emerged as a contender for a franchise.

By contemporary standards, the NBA of the early 1980s brimmed with rubes. The expansion committee did not think it necessary to conduct a background check on Skalbania, figuring that his finances must be in order. Newspapers, after all, carried frequent articles outlining Skalbania's tycoonish tears through the Canadian marketplace, most portraying him in terms of a high roller with cash to squander. So eight months after learning of Skalbania's interest in the NBA, league owners gathered at the Beverly Hills Hotel in Los Angeles to vote on Skalbania's application for a franchise. O'Brien congratulated Skalbania for becoming the first Canadian to own an NBA franchise. Skalbania then rose to make what everyone thought was going to be an acceptance speech. Instead, he asked how much the franchise would cost.

"Sixteen million dollars," said O'Brien.

"Is that $16 million Canadian or $16 million U.S.?"

"Sixteen million U.S."

"I'll only pay $16 million Canadian."

"The league had raised the price of the franchise above what anybody expected it to be," Welts remembered. "Dallas had sold for $12 million a few years earlier. Then the price jumped to $16 million. Skalbania considered it an insult. And he managed to insult the owners with the way he handled the situation."

After chewing on the owners, Skalbania stalked out of the room, never to be heard from again.

"We were all in shock," Welts recalled. "Bob and I left town with our tails between our legs and feeling pretty sorry for Simon Gourdine. We had no idea Skalbania wouldn't follow through or that money was any kind of issue."

The truth emerged months later. Skalbania had over extended himself, causing his financial empire to collapse. Skalbania wound up a reported $10 million in hawk to thirty creditors who could have gone after him, but instead gave him $2 million more so he could earn their money back. He did.

After the Skalbania fiasco, Bob studiously avoided any telephone calls from NBA headquarters, turning his attention to writing a series of guest columns for *The Seattle Times* and recording daily sports commentaries for KVI, a local radio station.

Bob had just arrived at the studio one day when he received a telephone call from Bruce Marr, a former KABC colleague who was looking for a new job. After checking around, Bob discovered that

94

KVI had plans to switch to an all-talk format and was hunting for a program director. Bob sought out Jim Johnson, KVI's station manager, fairly painting Marr as the best program director in the world. Johnson called Marr, who jumped on a plane for Seattle, and became KVI's program director two days later.

Bruce Marr's first major decision was an odd one, Bob thought: He cancelled Bob's commentaries and threw him off the air.

"It wasn't anything personal," Marr later mused. "I just didn't think Bob was very good."

But Bob developed a solid reputation as an agent. For two consecutive years, *Sport Magazine* polled National Football League general managers, asking them to rate the agents, and Bob finished in the top two both times. But Bob soon grew disillusioned with the business. Agentry not only did not satisfy his expanding ambitions, the sleazy aspects of it troubled him greatly. Too many college athletes drove cars their agents had purchased for them against the rules. Too many handed envelopes stuffed with cash to college prospects in hotel lobbies at bowl games. Too many dispensed drugs to potential clients, and too many athletes took advantage of the prostitutes their agents gleefully provided. Bob enjoyed representing Russell, Wilkens, Jackson, Largent, Kramer, Raible, Hanauer, and Ruiz, but found he squandered too much time acting as a baby-sitter for unappreciative athletes. So rather than nurse them and take their cash, he quit on principle.

As Bob deliberated over his next professional move, Ruth Walsh placed him on irrevocable waivers. The split shocked many of their colleagues, who considered Bob and Ruth a dream couple. They enjoyed a wide circle of friends, owned a new house in the Seattle suburb of Newport Shores, and had successful careers. Perhaps too successful. Bob had traveled constantly, first with the SuperSonics, then on behalf of his clients, finally in service to his growing consulting and event business. Ruth routinely matched Bob's marathon schedule, always spending extra hours at KOMO perfecting her pieces. As the years evaporated, Bob and Ruth sacrificed important time together, even spending six of their first nine wedding anniversaries apart. Their divorce could have been more amicable; it could have been more nightmarish. It fell somewhere in between, leaving both Bob and Ruth profoundly saddened. Bob moped for months, his emotional barrier reduced to the thickness of Saran Wrap.

Bob consoled himself with the thought that his father, Matt, didn't have to watch the breakup. Matt had been happily married to Betty Walsh for more than forty years. He'd been the best man when Bob married Ruth, and he'd always adored her. Matt had been gone for nearly four years. After his dad's retirement, Bob and Ruth had moved him and Betty out of Boston's harsh winters into a nice place in San Juan Capistrano, California. But when Matt came down with emphysema, Bob relocated his parents to New Hampshire where they could be closer to Bob's sister, Toni. Betty fell so completely apart after Matt's death that Bob moved her to Seattle. Betty felt as anguished as Bob the day he told her that he and Ruth had decided to go their separate ways.

"Overlaying Bob's genius is a complex personality," Ruth observed later. "Bob can paint incredible pictures, but has a difficult time communicating his soul. It's almost as if Bob is beyond a personal life. I was a help to Bob in many ways and I let him down in some emotional areas. Because he's always out there somewhere, it's bewildering for Bob to focus on small things. That's why it's so hard for him to deal with a personal relationship. And yet, he is a deeply caring person.

"Once, my mother became ill with cancer and went through her treatment. When she finished, I wanted to take her on a trip and spend some time with her. Bob and I had planned a trip to Hawaii. We looked forward to this Hawaii vacation because that was our time. But Bob told me to take his ticket and my mother to Hawaii. He gave up his ticket unselfishly, out of nowhere.

"Bob has a way of being able to touch people in an unexpected way. He had an enormous respect for me as a woman, and as a working woman. There was never any challenge with that in our marriage. I was in a very male-dominated profession and was the first woman to do a lot of things. I dealt with a lot of men who didn't respect women in business. It was nice to have a husband and a partner who supported my work and supported me."

Bob had no intention of dating anyone after Ruth until he encountered a saucy Frenchwoman named Nicole Preveaux. A brunette with seductive eyes and a sense of humor, Nicole worked for a travel agency that specialized in booking ship cruises to weird ports of call, such as Devil's Island. Although smitten with Nicole, Bob deferred any thought of marriage, using work as his principal therapy to deal with his divorce.

One of the oddest assignments to come Bob's way occurred soon after he started squiring around Nicole. The Seattle Visitors and Convention Bureau had held a contest aimed at providing Seattle, "The Queen City," with a new nickname. The winning entry, ironically submitted by a woman from California, turned out to be "The Emerald City." When the Visitors and Convention Bureau announced the new name with great fanfare, it was widely mocked. "The Emerald City," critics charged, conjured up images of Dorothy, Toto, and the Wicked Witch. One newspaper cartoonist depicted Tin Man, Scarecrow, and the Cowardly Lion huddled under a Seattle bridge, all dripping wet. Invisible Seattle, a group of local comics, called "The Emerald City" a "linguistic Frankenstein."

Bob Bushman, the head of the Visitors and Convention Bureau, asked Bob to come up with a plan to reverse public sentiment. It took Bob two weeks to arrive at a solution. He telephoned Keith Jackson in Los Angeles and asked if Jackson would mention "Emerald City" every time he came to Seattle to broadcast a sports event. Bob made the same request of Howard Cosell, who frequently came to town to do Monday Night Football on ABC. He pleaded with an old friend, Doug Looney, to refer to Seattle as "The Emerald City" in his pieces in *Sports Illustrated*. Bob spent weeks calling everyone he knew in Boston and Los Angeles, and at ABC, NBC, and CBS in New York. After that, almost every national broadcaster who showed up to do a game in Seattle opened his telecast by saying, "Welcome to the Emerald City." Bob reasoned that if Seattle residents heard enough outsiders refer to Seattle as "The Emerald City," it would legitimize the name. And he was right.

In the thick of Bob's campaign to legitimize Seattle's new nickname, he drew another assignment from Gene Pfeifer, a top executive at Pacific Northwest Bell, to work as a consultant for the company. The Bell System had just split apart and Pfeifer had been trying to adapt to a new world of competition. Pfeifer wanted Bob to get Pacific Northwest Bell more involved in community activities. Together, they brainstormed all sorts of ideas, then Bob had an inspiration. The movie, *Chariots of Fire*, had just been released and Bob loved the theme song. He talked it over with Pfeifer, and they created the "Emerald City Marathon," sponsored by Pacific Northwest Bell.

The Emerald City Marathon not only sealed the deal on Seattle's name change from "The Queen City" to "The Emerald City," it gave Bob the idea that Bob Walsh & Associates could create, own, and operate sports events as well as bid to host them. As Bob deliberated over the possibilities, he bumped into an opportunity that would take his career to a brand new level.

Gene Pfeifer (left) at the Emerald City Marathon

March Madness

It was Bob who dramatically expanded the concept of March Madness at the Final Four. Obviously, history will write upon Bob's name that he was a very innovative genius.

> *– Jim Host, Host Communications, Lexington, Kentucky*

Before 1984, the NCAA Men's Basketball Tournament never inspired office pools and side wagers or compelled network television to splurge billions of dollars for the privilege of providing wall-to-wall coverage. Before 1984, no such day as "Selection Sunday" existed. Nobody talked about the Sweet Sixteen and the Great Eight, much less seeds, brackets, major upsets, and PTPers. The NCAA tournament more accurately resembled a little jig than a Big Dance. Not that the tournament lacked entertainment or athletic value; it didn't. But it didn't have cities all across America stumbling over themselves to host it. It did have tournament tickets — even Final Four tickets — often going unused.

After 1984, by the time Bob Walsh got through with it, the NCAA Tournament featured a moniker known everywhere. "March Madness" had become a month of delightful athletic lunacy that would soon evolve into one of the fattest cash cows in the annals of games playing.

The idea that Seattle might bid for a Final Four did not spring from the imagination of Bob Walsh. Nor did it come from Ted Bowsfield or Bill Sears, who respectively ran the Kingdome and made certain

Bob Walsh with BWA president Kimberly Brown

that its events received suitable exposure in the public prints. The idea first dawned on a future stockbroker from Bellevue, Washington, named Mike Maruhashi, more or less a Kingdome gopher in those days working in the employ of the publicity-minded Sears. As a college basketball town, Seattle did not exactly rival Raleigh-Durham, Lexington, Lawrence, or even Tucson, but it had the only domed stadium on the West Coast that included a basketball configuration, and it could accommodate 40,000 fans, far more than most Final Four venues. Seattle not only had that selling point in its favor, the Final Four had not been played on the West Coast since 1975, the year UCLA coach John Wooden won his tenth and last national championship in San Diego.

Bowsfield, Sears, University of Washington Athletic Director Mike Lude, and Hartley Kruger of the Seattle Visitors and Convention Bureau, representing the Seattle Host Committee, made their pitch to the National Collegiate Athletic Association during Final Four site selection meetings in Salt Lake City, Utah. They hoped to land the 1983 Final Four, but were willing to settle for anything: Seattle had not hosted any NCAA Tournament games since 1952, practically another athletic age. Following their presentation, Bowsfield and Sears lounged in the coffee shop at the Hotel Utah when Tom Jernstedt, the assistant executive director of the NCAA, gave them the good news: Seattle had been awarded the 1984 Final Four. Bowsfield, Sears, and Jernstedt had no idea that the Final Four would never be the same.

100

Bowsfield and Sears, in fact, didn't even know what to do with the Final Four once they acquired it. But they knew who would know: Bob Walsh, in conjunction with Bowsfield, had developed a floor and seating configuration for Seattle SuperSonics basketball games at the Kingdome, and Bob's company had successfully executed several sports projects and promotions, including the Emerald City Marathon. When Bowsfield presented Bob with the opportunity to become involved in the Final Four, Bob recognized at once that producing all ancillary events surrounding the event would significantly enhance the profile

Bob Walsh surveys a Final Four banner

of Bob Walsh & Associates and give Seattle a chance to showcase its hospitality and special attractions.

Bob soon envisioned the biggest, most elaborate Final Four in history, a celebration to exceed all previous basketball celebrations, the most user-friendly, feel-good national championship yet created. Drawing on some of his KABC promotions, he imagined non-stop parties, boat cruises in Puget Sound, salmon barbecues, limo service for NCAA officials and VIPs. The most important VIPs would be greeted at Seattle-Tacoma International Airport with bands and cheerleaders and lavished with champagne and gifts. All VIPs would have access to a brand new Mercedes Benz or BMW, and each would be assigned a driver. A shuttle system would be

set up through a transportation committee so that other NCAA officials, media, and guests could get quickly and effortlessly to the Kingdome, around town, and back their hotels, which would feature Final Four information centers. Volunteers would be recruited to serve as guides and hosts.

Before 1984, no host city had created a local organizing committee to exploit all the possibilities attendant to a Final Four. But Bob, Sears, and Bowsfield created one to ensure that the 1984 Final Four would become a four-day festival to remember. For the first time in the event's history, a host city's downtown would be festooned with pennants, banners, and welcoming billboards. For the first time, bands and cheerleaders would be positioned strategically on city streets to add to the celebratory nature of the occasion. And Bob would add one more touch: He would adopt Sears' idea of painting a huge yellow brick road just outside the Kingdome. The CBS cameras would find "The Road To The Emerald City" irresistible.

Many of the Seattle Host Committee's ideas for the 1984 Final Four hatched from the debris left by other host cities, especially Albuquerque, site of the 1983 Final Four. Although the event concluded with one of the greatest games in NCAA Tournament history, North Carolina State's 54-52 upset of the Phi Slama Jama fraternity from the University of Houston, its extracurricular aspects had been fraught with problems. Transportation was a mess. A coaches' party in Albuquerque's Old Town featured a less than palatable menu of barbecued beans, hot dogs, and draft beer served outside in penguin weather. Albuquerque officials offered no entertainment of consequence and had nothing to keep fans and officials occupied between sessions of the tournament. Seattle Host Committee members recognized they had a great opportunity to create not only a seminal event in the history of the Final Four, but in the history of Seattle.

Bob Walsh and beauty queens, 1984 Final Four

102

Of all the people who failed to understand Bob's vision, George Duff failed to understand it the most. When Bob told the president of Seattle's Chamber of Commerce that thirty thousand Final Four visitors, loaded with cash, plastic, and enthusiasm, would pump millions of dollars into the local economy, he got a dismissive response. Duff insisted that he'd never heard of the Final Four; the Chamber did not involve itself in "that kind of activity." Determined to organize the greatest Final Four of all time without a Chamber endorsement, Bob and the Seattle Host Committee nevertheless raised and spent nearly $1 million, five times the highest previous amount ever splurged on the event. The money, effort, and ingenuity paid off.

"Bob did a marvelous job with the Final Four just as it was really beginning to take off into its major growth period," Jernstedt remarked later. "The local organizing committee he gathered was a testimony to his managerial ability. He put together a very talented group of individuals, mobilized them, and provided leadership. His organization served as a model that other cities used in following years."

"The people in Seattle literally rewrote the book on how to host the Final Four," recalled Rick Baker, who ran the 1986 Final Four in Dallas and eventually became director of the Cotton Bowl. "It was a whole new era. Without a doubt, Bob Walsh and his staff started some new things that other cities which followed had to be cognizant of or they were going to look pretty foolish."

"All at once in Seattle, the Final Four became March Madness," recalled Jim Host, who handles all broadcast rights for and performs marketing services on behalf of the NCAA. "Before Seattle, we never had billboards welcoming the Final Four into town. We never had department stores decorated, merchandize stands on the streets, parties at the hotels, or special VIP accommodations. The whole scope of what is now March Madness dramatically expanded at that Final Four in Seattle. After Seattle, everybody else who hosted a Final Four tried to copy what Seattle did. Bob Walsh was the first guy who actually went in with a local organizing committee and tried to figure out ways to make things better. And he succeeded brilliantly. People don't really understand that the Final Four did not start to take off as a national phenomenon until the event got to Seattle. But people who have been connected with it as long as I have know that's when it took off. Before 1984, the Final Four was really a non-event. Today it's a spectacle. That Final Four caused everybody I know to look at Seattle as a hugely progressive city."

"That Final Four was my first exposure to Bob," Jernstedt remembered. "From that point on I followed his career and was amazed at how he went from doing all these things nationally to all these bigger things internationally."

Bob's fish project clearly ranked among the stranger escapades.

Dream You Can

The thing to keep in mind about Bob is how many people he knows and the amazing number of lives he has touched. That's only one reason why we've been friends for such a long time.

> *– Lenny Wilkens, Basketball Hall of Fame inductee, Seattle, Washington*

*B*y the time Bob Walsh & Associates became enmeshed in the Goodwill Games, it had evolved into one of the more peculiar companies in the annals of commerce. Most BWA staffers could only mumble when asked to explain precisely what the company did, since the truth was that it brimmed with an eclectic bazaar of activity and bustle. BWA organized all ancillary activities surrounding the 1987 NBA All-Star game at the Kingdome, produced another edition of the Emerald City Marathon, promoted two golf tournaments, a hydroplane race, and a professional figure skating championship. It consulted on a major exhibition of Chinese art at the Seattle Center, conducted a food drive and anti-drug campaign, developed a bid for the 1992 Super Bowl, helped create the Washington

State Film Council — the first movie, originally backed by Steven Spielberg, told the story of a Washington State family that kept a Sasquatch for a pet — and unabashedly pitched a Salmon Derby. A lone Coho salmon, implanted with a wire tag  bearing the code C36 just aft of its left eye, swam somewhere in Puget Sound. The prize for catching it: $1 million. No one snared the elusive fish, but 7,000 stymied piscatorians collaborated to set a world record in simultaneous skunkings.

BWA also labored on the Rainier Bank Golf Classic, NCAA Division I soccer and Division III football championships, and the NCAA Women's Final Four. In addition to event planning, BWA plunged into public affairs work, took on marketing and promotional jobs, performed public relations projects, and got involved in consulting deals – whatever it took to keep the company moving and its creditors at bay.

Most BWA projects came off without a hitch. The "25th Anniversary Reunion of the 1963 Mount Everest American Expedition," an event BWA organized to celebrate Jim Whittaker's successful triumph of the mountain, drew raves from all participants. Conversely, BWA abandoned some projects for lack of cash. Bob spent a year and more than $50,000 pursuing a bid for the Winter Olympics, but had to abandon the effort when he ran out of money. BWA also spent $100,000 in staff time, travel costs, and other expenses trying to land the 1988 Republican National Convention, including $15,000 to properly fawn over and liquor up members of its Site Selection Committee. But the convention went elsewhere because of a scheduling snafu at the Kingdome.

BWA usually had six to seven employees, depending on the number and size of its projects and the ebb and flow of BWA's credit line. Most had just graduated from college and did not stay on long. Once they had sufficient experience, or once they burned out responding to the tyranny of the urgent, they moved to bigger companies for less stress and higher pay.

Gene Fisher became a notable exception. After meandering through Mississippi, Alabama, and Colorado, Fisher arrived in Seattle in the aftermath of the 1984 Final Four, knocked off a few temporary jobs, and then hooked up with BWA, where he orchestrated whatever project required attention. Older and more experienced than the majority of BWA staffers, Fisher had a meticulous eye for detail, a flair for threading his way through red tape, and thrived in an environment in which he could exercise his ingenuity. Fisher quickly became one of Bob's most trusted allies, as did Kimberly Brown, an attractive, intelligent woman with a wicked sense of humor. Like Bob, Kimberly had a radio background and precisely

BWA's Kimberly Brown and TV star Phil Donahue

the right kind of personality and disposition to deal with the diverse nature of the company's projects and the whims of its leader, Bob Walsh.

"Bob brought me in to do legwork and clean up his messes was the way I looked at it," Kimberly explained later. "Bob didn't do a lot of supervising. He let you do your own thing."

"There were times when you loved working for Bob and other times when you would get totally frustrated," recalled Amy Boisjolie, one of Bob's longtime assistants. "He came in one day and said he needed light bulbs. It turned out that he needed those big round ones that go around a bathroom mirror. I asked him how many he needed and he said he needed thirty-two. Bob had let every single bulb burn out before replacing any of them. With Bob, you just did whatever needed to be done."

In hindsight, BWA's most embarrassing project probably started to speed south from the moment Bob heard about plans for a simple lunch. Since Bob tended to imagine 10,000 bikini-clad women on a beach if he spotted a spec of sand, this simple lunch gave Bob several outlandish ideas, his main one being a black-tie extravaganza featuring 200 performers, including an entire symphony orchestra, a huge gospel choir, sundry singing acts, *Tonight Show* band leader Doc Severinsen, fifty professional football players, an elaborate video presentation, and 2,500 guests.

It all started when Bob got call from Gary Wright, the Seahawks' director of public relations, who asked Bob if he would be

Blair Farrington

interested in working on a celebration of the team's tenth anniversary. Bob had always wanted to produce a big show in Seattle, so he met with Seahawk General Manger Mike McCormack to discuss the format. McCormack quickly dashed Bob's tie-and-tails scheme, insisting he wanted a simple lunch, nothing fancy. And he most especially did not want anything that involved the use of audio-video equipment. McCormack had just attended a presentation in which the audio-video equipment had failed, and everyone involved had been embarrassed.

Bob pleaded with McCormack to reconsider the scope of the event, arguing that Seattle deserved a major celebration and the Seahawks warranted a community-wide accolade. McCormack continued to balk. But Bob jawed and mule-traded McCormack for three weeks, finally convincing McCormack to agree that a small, intimate dinner was probably more appropriate than a lunch. After all, the team had reached its tenth anniversary. But no audio-video equipment.

With those marching orders, Bob contacted Blair Farrington, a former Hollywood dancer and model who had performed with Cher, Mitzi Gaynor, Debbie Allen, Gloria Estefan, George Burns, and Charles Bronson before his career ended in injury while portraying James Bond on the sixty-third Academy Awards Show. Farrington had also choreographed a variety of television and theatrical specials, including *The Merv Griffin Show*. One of Farrington's shows called for two numbers featuring synchronized swimmers. When Farrington discovered that Bob represented Tracie Ruiz, a gold medallist at the 1984 Summer Olympics in Los Angeles, he got hold of Bob, and they worked out a deal calling for Ruiz and her Olympic partner, Candie Costie, to appear in Farrington's production.

To add an additional touch of panache to McCormack's little dinner party, Bob next contacted Gerard Schwarz, director of the Seattle Symphony, and hired his orchestra. Then Bob recruited Doc Severinsen to lead it. He made arrangements to hold McCormack's intimate soiree at the Seattle Opera House, which, of course, would seem positively empty without a 100-person, gospel-singing contingent from Seattle's Mount Zion Baptist Choir. Naturally, the highly popular Ostroms, a local singing act, had to be there. And with all these important performers in attendance, the NBC affiliate, KING TV, would have to televise the show.

The one thing Bob could not have was what he wanted most — a video presentation. To demonstrate to McCormack that the show couldn't go on without one, Bob got Michael Kostov, the best video man in Seattle, to gather and edit Seahawk tape and work it into a presentation. They played the finished product for McCormack, who was, despite his misgivings, very impressed. Bob and Farrington explained that a rear projector and a huge screen would be lowered into place at Farrington's command at the conclusion of the live performances. The highlight videos would be played, interspersed with live appearances by fifty current and former Seahawks players. McCormack reluctantly gave his approval, but only after Bob guaranteed that nothing would go wrong.

On the morning of the show, Doc Severinsen arrived from Los Angeles and Farrington flew in from Las Vegas. That afternoon, the symphony, gospel choir, the Ostroms, and Severinsen all went through rehearsals under Farrington's astute direction. About 6 p.m., Farrington announced that he wanted to test the video presentation. Each segment ran about four minutes, each had been edited to perfection, and the equipment worked perfectly — clear video, crisp audio, not a glitch.

A sellout crowd of 2,500 people, each of whom had paid up to $60 to be there, began arriving at about 7:30 p.m. for what Bob Walsh knew would be the social highlight of the season. Finally, the house lights dimmed and Farrington ordered the curtain up. Schwarz strolled on stage to thunderous applause, lifted his baton, and the Seattle Symphony played an overture that received a rousing ovation. Then a huge ovation greeted Severinsen. Now it was time to show a video recap of the Seahawks' first season. Farrington confidently directed the screen projector to be lowered and ordered the video to start.

Murphy's Law is a curious thing. It states that if anything can go wrong it will, but there is no corollary to the law that suggests everything will go all wrong all at once, and on cue, and in front of 2,500 people who had paid $60 apiece. But it did. It started with the mirrored ball that had been suspended above the performers and lit by numerous spotlights, which effectively blinded the audience to the activities on stage. The audience wouldn't have seen anything anyway: the video machine didn't work. After a few agonizing minutes, Farrington again called for the video. Again nothing happened. Audio-video whiz Michael Kostov didn't know what was wrong. Sensing that this extravaganza was suddenly collapsing under the tonnage of its own ambition, Bob wondered what the weather was like in Tonga.

A flustered Farrington ordered and reordered the video presentation to commence as the audience whispered and twittered, and McCormack squirmed in his seat. Thoroughly galled at the equipment problem, Farrington had no choice but to toss the show to Severinsen and the Ostroms.

Official Invitation to Seahawks Tenth Anniversary

When they finished, Farrington again cued the video presentation; again nothing happened. By this time Kostov stood backstage cursing, Bob was on the phone with Air India, and the emcee had been forced to explain to a bemused audience that the projector had broken down and there would be no video. A lip synch routine scheduled to feature Seahawk players also had to be scrubbed. But the second half of the show would include a variety of great entertainment, beginning with the Mount Zion Baptist Choir, which would be backed up by the Seattle Symphony under the able direction of Doc Severinsen.

As the curtain rose and house lights dimmed, Farrington got ready for the gospel choir to begin the first part of "The Battle Hymn of the Republic." Five seconds later, he issued his first command.

"Cue the choir."

Nothing happened for ten seconds.

"Cue the goddamn choir!"

Farrington waited five more seconds.

"Cue the fucking choir!"

Farrington then saw his problem: The piano player, Phyllis Byrdwell, was missing. Actually, make that two problems: The choir was also missing. What Farrington didn't know in his moment of mounting exasperation was that the Seattle Fire Department, sirens blaring, had already raced to the Opera House brandishing hoses, picks, and axes. A dozen rather ample female members of the gospel choir, including the pianist and four soloists, had gotten stuck in an elevator between the balcony and the first floor, and firefighters and unnerved ushers were frantically trying to pull them out through a hole in the top of the elevator. The singers had all gone to the balcony to watch the first half of the show. When they piled on the elevator to return to the stage level for the second half, they knocked it out of commission. With no video, no piano player, and no gospel choir, many of the 2,500 people got up to leave; those who remained laughed uncontrollably. Finally, the choir reassembled and prepared to sing. But the Opera House lights suddenly went out, obscuring McCormack's face, now a vivid maroon.

Gene Fisher knew the newspaper reviews would be bad; he just didn't know how bad. At midmorning the next day, he summoned the courage to drop a quarter in a nearby newspaper box. After he read *The Seattle Times* he approached Bob.

"It's even worse than you thought," he said, handing the paper to Bob.

The Times had described the previous evening's entertainment in terms of a lemon that had puckered shut the mouths of everyone in the Seattle Opera House. The production, *The Times* opined, ". . . had

Don't blame my friend, Bob Walsh, for Seahawks' fiasco

had all the tragi-comic élan of a dropped touchdown pass." *The Times* even went so far as to suggest, "Blair Farrington and Bob Walsh should be used as tackling dummies over at the Seahawks training camp." *The Times'* journalistic goosing sent Farrington and Walsh fleeing to the San Juan Islands, where they spent two days bolstering the economies of several watering holes.

When Bob returned to Seattle, he demanded justice. He had paid $15,000 to Doc Severinsen. It had cost another $15,000 to produce the Seahawks' highlight video, and nobody at the Opera House had seen it. He had paid $2,000 to the Mount Zion Baptist Choir and it had warbled in the dark. He had paid $32,000 to the Seattle Symphony and $2,500 to Blair Farrington. In all, he had spent $90,000, and *The Seattle Times* had written, "Most everything was horribly, unbelievably, embarrassingly awful."

Mrs. Byrdwell, the piano player, stewed for a week, finally dashing off a missive to Ewen Dingwall, the general manager of The Seattle Center, in which she complained bitterly, "The Mount Zion Baptist Church Choir was part of the celebration for the Seattle Seahawks' Tenth Anniversary in the Opera House. Twelve members of our choir had the added adventure of being trapped in the elevator as we made our way from the balcony to the backstage area, just prior to the intermission. We spent the next hour and ten minutes between the first balcony and the main floor . . . The elevator had no telephone, so there was no way of communicating with the outside. We banged on the walls of the elevator to attract attention. The alarm bell in the elevator was so faint we had trouble hearing it – let alone anybody else . . . Psychologically, it takes all your stamina to endure something like this. It was hard to breathe, with twelve people in there. I shudder to think what would have happened if one of us had a heart attack as a result of the induced stress. It has been a week since this experience and I'm still dreaming about it. I've also had trouble getting into other elevators."

Bob couldn't figure out how so many things could have gone so horrendously wrong. The video equipment failure hadn't been his fault. It hadn't been his doing that the Mount Zion Baptist Choir had decommissioned the elevator. Bob sought validation that he was not the culpable party and went looking for it at the Seattle Center, which operated the Opera House. Particularly irritated by the elevator breakdown, Bob met with the Center's deputy director, Kathy Scanlan, a woman who had a reputation for Annapolis determination.

"I think I should get something back," Bob told her.

Scanlan issued a peremptory harrumph.

"You're telling me that the elevator caused your entire event to go sideways?" Scanlan finally asked. "I don't think so."

"That's what I'm telling you," replied Bob.

"I'm not giving you a thing," said Scanlan.

To Bob, the whole situation seemed so unfair. He got up and left the meeting utterly dispirited and mumbling darkly, hoping he would have no further encounters with Kathy Scanlan.

Treasure Of The Argonauts

The mentality of your society is almost totally commercialized. To keep the character that Bob has is God's gift, really.

> – Kakha Gvelesiani, war hero,
> Tbilisi, Georgia

When Bob Walsh finally kept his appointment in Soviet Georgia with Vaso Margvelashvili, the man with whom he'd consumed half a vineyard at the Belgrad Hotel in Moscow, among the first stories Bob heard was an old one that told how the Georgians acquired their land. It went something like this: While God parceled out portions of the earth to all the people in the world, the Georgians feasted and drank wine. When they finally turned up to claim their land, God told the Georgians he was sorry, he had no more. Never mind, replied the Georgians, who then invited God to join them in a feast. God enjoyed the feast so much He gave the Georgians the last spot He had left, the one He had secretly reserved for Himself.

This special place is now part of the isthmus separating the Black and Caspian seas. It is a land whose history is measured not in centuries but in millennia, and whose culture is abundant with myths, many springing from Greek mythology.

In the 13th century B.C., Jason and the Argonauts departed Iolcos in northern Thessaly in search of the Kingdom of Colchis in what is now western Georgia. They sailed across the Aegean, through the Dardanelles, into the Sea of Marmara, through the Bosporus and across the Black Sea, finally entering the Colchian realm of King Aeetes. It was there Jason and the Argonauts wrested the Golden Fleece from the dragon that had been drugged by the sorceress Medea.

From a nearby mountain called Kazbek came another legend. It was there that Prometheus, who had stolen fire from the heavens and created man out of clay, was chained to a rock by Zeus so an eagle could dine nightly on his liver.

According to another myth, the Amazon warriors also came from Georgia. They supposedly lived somewhere near the Tergi River and, the stories say, burned off their right breasts in order that they might draw their bows more accurately. Yet another myth describes a place in southwestern Georgia called Mushki. The Mushki king, Mita, may have been Midas of the Golden Touch.

At the confluence of Georgia's Kura and Aragvi rivers, near Georgia's ancient capital Mtskheta, stands one of the most sacred of the country's 5,000 monuments, the Cathedral of Sveti-tskhoveli, built between 1010 and 1029 A.D. over the site of a much more ancient church. One column supporting the church is ringed with carved grape-vines. On the east side of the church, two carved bulls' heads protrude from the masonry, and the northern façade features an arm and a hand. The fingers clutch a bevel. According to this legend, the architect commissioned to rebuild the original fifth-century basilica succeeded so brilliantly that his jealous mentor ordered his right hand severed as punishment. An inscription near the carving says, "This is the hand of Arsukidze, servant of God. Pray for him." The Georgians claim that Sveti-tskhoveli is the second most sacred place in the Christian world, surpassed only by the Church of the Holy Sepulcher in Jerusalem.

Georgia is linked to the Holy Land through another legend. In the first century A.D., a Georgian Jew, Elias, converted to Christianity and was in Jerusalem when Jesus was nailed to the cross. Elias purchased Jesus' robe from a Roman soldier at Golgotha and brought it back to Georgia. When Elias's sister, Sidonia, seized the robe she immediately fell over dead. The robe could not be torn from her grasp, so Sidonia was buried with it. From Sidonia's grave soon grew an enormous cedar tree. Almost 300 years later, St. Nino of Cappadocia (in central Turkey), a holy slave woman, came to Georgia and cured Queen Nana of a strange illness, which apparently convinced Queen Nana's husband, King Mirian, to convert to Christianity. He chose to build Georgia's first Christian church at Sidonia's grave site. To support the church, the king ordered the enormous cedar chopped into seven columns. The seventh column had magical properties and rose in the air by itself, returning to earth only when St. Nino prayed a whole night beside it. A sacred liquid then flowed from the column, curing people of all their diseases. St. Nino — many Georgian women are still named after her — also fashioned the Georgian crucifix, making the cross from vine branches tied together with her own hair. This remains the cross of the Georgian Orthodox Church, and it partially accounts for Georgia's adoration of the grape.

It is closer to fact than mythology that Georgian soil is almost certainly the first place men cultivated grapevines. In *Vintage: The Story of Wine*, Hugh Johnson wrote, "Archaeologists accept accumulation of grape pips as evidence of winemaking. The oldest pips of cultivated vines so far discovered and carbon dated — at least to the satisfaction of their finders — were found in Georgia, and belong to the period 7000 to 5000 B.C." Even now, the icons in Georgian churches are adorned with frames that depict clusters of grapes, and grape motifs decorate Georgian tombstones. Whenever there is talk of Georgian wine, there is talk of the Georgian Horn. This is the story: Since the Georgians lived and fought for their country in the steep mountains of the Caucasus range, they relied upon, for the meat, and admired, for their strength and agility, the mountain sheep. Georgians often drank wine from sheep horns. Some of the larger and more elaborately decorated horns are now housed in Georgian museums. Inscribed on one of them is this phrase: "He who drinks me to the bottom owns me."

Situated almost where Europe and Asia fuse, Georgia is about the size of South Carolina. Its northern frontier follows the axis of the Greater Caucasus Mountains, formed at the same time as the Alps in Europe, and includes borders with the southern Russian republics of Dagestan, Chechnya, Ingushetia, North Ossetia, Kabardino-Balkaria, and Karachay-Cherkessia. Georgia abuts Azerbaijan and the vast wastes of Central Asia to the east; to the south, southeast, and southwest lie Armenia, the tableaus of Iran, and the most desolate parts of Turkey. To the west is the Black Sea, under whose bordering hills lie buried the swords of Huns who long ago brought destruction on the Roman Empire.

Civilization probably took *Georgian King Vakhtang Gorgasali* root in Georgia before it did in Mesopotamia. By the sixth century B.C., distinct kingdoms in Colchis, now west Georgia, and Kartli, now east Georgia, flourished. Because Colchis and Kartli reposed in the crosshairs of important east-west and north-south trade routes, between Europe and Asia and Russia and the Middle East, they became one of civilization's greatest battlegrounds, first ensnared in tempests between Greece and Persia that Herodotus wrote about in his *Histories*. Pompey's legions brought Colchis under Roman rule in 65 B.C. In the fourth century A.D., Kartli converted to Christianity and was made part of the Byzantine Empire, a development whose significance cannot be overestimated, turning as it did Georgia toward the West and away from the Muslim world.

Over the next dozen centuries, Georgia got pancaked, partitioned, and parceled out in collisions between the Byzantine and Persian empires, the Arabs and Ottoman Turks, and the Turks and the Mongol hordes. In the eighteenth century, the Russians commenced an annexation process that ultimately resulted in Georgia's incorporation into the Soviet Union.

Tbilisi, the capital city, often bore the brunt of the conqueror's heel. It has been left in ruins or burned to the ground anywhere from twenty-nine to forty-three times since its founding in the fourth century. To-

day, it spreads out over nineteen miles, snaking along either side of a gorge formed by the Kura. Tbilisi is neither

Tbilisi is a city that features dozens of ancient churches

entirely European nor entirely Asian, but rather a multiethnic city in which Georgians, Greeks, Jews, Armenians, Azeries, Russians, and Kurds have coexisted for centuries amid a fermentation of influences — Byzantine, Persian, French classical, Moorish, Turkish, and Soviet — that symbolize the turbulence of the region.

Experimental School No. 1, Tbilisi, Georgia

118

Often called the "Paris of the Orient," Tbilisi is an amalgam of the fourth century, the Middle Ages, the 1940s, and the late twentieth century in which the local temperament is a blend of heroism and calamity. Georgians are proud, charming, fierce, hospitable, and gregarious. Family and friends mean everything to Georgians, who believe — and this is no myth — that personal worth is judged not by worldly goods, but by the number of one's friends.

Against this backdrop, Bob Walsh arrived in Tbilisi to meet Vaso Margvelashvili, who quickly introduced Bob to the most important Georgian rituals. The Georgians, Bob discovered, reveled in food, song, wine, and hospitality, an ageless truth perhaps best symbolized by the fifty-five-foot statue of *Kartlis Deda* that looms on Sololaki Mountain above Tbilisi's Old Town. In one hand, Mother Georgia holds a sword for her enemies; in the other she offers a bowl of wine for her friends. Mother Georgia's message, imparted by all of her sons and daughters, became clear to Bob soon enough. Each Georgian meal turned into a theater in permanent performance, Georgian tables sagging beneath platter after platter of food: Flat bread the size of a trashcan lid baked fresh daily in the kilns of the Old Town, cheeses, yogurt, lamb, pork, kidney beans, dumplings, sturgeon, roasted mushrooms, spinach and walnut pates, chicken, potatoes, lavish cakes and pastries, and Borjomi mineral water, the Georgian Perrier.

The Georgian Table

Imagine a pizza that folds over on itself like an omelet, flavored with melted cheese, double the size of a Frisbee, and three times the size of an ordinary stomach. Called *khachapuri*, it is part of a

119

banquet that Georgians refer to as *supra*. Every time it is time to eat, and in Georgia it always is, the Georgians pile the table with so much food the tablecloth practically vanishes. Then the wine is poured. Every toast has to have more wine, dinner has to have more wine, and even the wine has to have more wine.

The non-Georgian is ill-equipped to deal with such revelry, but for Georgians it is part of their culture and history, and even part of their geography. In the Caucasus Mountains, twenty-six miles of interconnecting caves and tunnels have somehow been dug out — when and by whom nobody knows. The scene within almost leaps from the pages of *The Secret of Santa Vittoria*, a story of peasant Italians in World War II who hid the town's wine supply from invading Nazis. Those miles of tunnels and caves are stocked with wine, brandy, and champagne numbering in the hundreds of thousands of barrels and bottles. The belief, apparently, is that should a war break out, Georgians will repair to the caves and drink wine made from 500 varieties of grapes until the war ends. Georgians do not drink wine in the same volumes that Russians inhale vodka. Georgians respect — even revere — their wine, treating it as the gift that it is: wine fit for the saints. And maybe because of this, Georgian wine usually does not induce bestial hangovers. Hornfuls can be consumed, but because of the wine's remarkable purity there are rarely nasty consequences.

Georgia's most important wine-growing region is Kakheti, situated in the easternmost part of the country, and for centuries the entry point for foreign invasions. Each village has its own variety of wine, and villagers haggle over the advantages of their soil versus that of their neighbors. When it is harvest time, in October, a ladle is dipped into a clay amphora, buried underground where the wine ferments. Then the fruits of the harvest are tasted. In many villages, grape clusters are draped over cantilevered balconies, almost the Kakhetian equivalent of silk World Series banners. The result of Kakhetian winemaking is found in a Soviet-style building in Tbilisi. Preserved behind a padlocked door are thousands of dust-covered bottles of Georgian wine. This is the Scientific Research Institute of Horticulture, Viticulture, and Wine-Making, a tribute to nearly eight centuries of a way of life.

The most elaborate Georgian gatherings are led by a "tamada," a banquet director-orator-emcee, who proposes traditional toasts to guests, friends, ladies, family members, relatives, motherland, peace, health, and happiness. The tamada's toasts are lengthy and theatrical, and each is responded to and interpreted by table members. Georgia's most famous tamadas are eloquent and quick-witted. They make jokes, encourage everybody to laugh and drink, and do it all over again. And there is a ritual to this. It is not permissible to drink until the tamada has made his toast. Only then can others do the same. It is not proper to propose a different toast unless the tamada gives his permission. If a toast is made to a visitor, the visitor must wait to drink until everyone else has drunk. Toasts are proposed in order: a toast to peace, to the reason for the gathering, to the hostess, to parents and ancestors, to Georgia as motherland, to friends, to the memory of the deceased, to life, to children, and to each guest. After that there is a toast to the tamada, and a final toast to a safe journey home. While the more important toasts require drinking to the bottom, tradition calls for spacing out the drinking. In Georgia, it is bad form to get drunk. Most toasts end with everyone bellowing "Gaumar . . . Jos!" — the equivalent of "cheers."

Enamored with Georgian revelry, Bob made an instant decision to include the Georgians in the Goodwill Games. In addition to proposing an exchange of Tbilisi and Seattle television personnel for the purpose of creating travelogue-type documentaries, Bob came to a tentative, multifaceted agreement with those same Georgian State Television representatives: Bob would encourage tourism in Georgia and set up a business to import Georgian wine to the American market.

Since Georgia belonged to a Soviet Union still mired in the Cold War, Bob did not know whether the Georgians had the legal competency to sign a letter of intent to do a private wine deal, especially without approval from Moscow. But the Georgians happily signed the letter of intent and therefore Bob signed, even though he couldn't read the document, which had been drafted in Georgian.

And then they all drank to their new enterprise.

A One-Woman State Department

An individual really can make a positive difference in this world. Sometimes, it just takes a lot longer than you ever imagine. The journey itself is as significant as the destination and whatever you learn en route gives you the strength and determination to carry you forward to your next creation.

*– Lynne Cox, marathon swimmer,
Los Alamitos, California*

Not far from the Bering Sea, on a treeless coastal plain, Nome, Alaska, unfolds as a haphazard patchwork of unpaved streets, weathered boxy houses, and mean little joints like the Polar Bar and Bering Sea Saloon. The end of the storied Iditarod Trail, Nome is hundreds of moose-trampled miles from anywhere else, and it's hardly the remotest outpost in the territory. An hour's ride north by bush plane over Mary's Igloo and Tin City, then another six miles by snowmobile, Wales, Alaska, presents itself as little more than a few dozen sorry hillside shanties on the westernmost point of the North American continent. From Wales, it's twenty-three miles by skiff or chopper to Little Diomede Island, two square miles of sloping granite that rises 1,200 feet above sea level and serves as home to a couple of hundred Inuits who live in ramshackle shelters built on stilts. And from there, it's another three miles across the Bering Strait to Big Diomede Island, inhabited for a good part of eternity by millions of walrus and sea otters, and for most of the twentieth century by forty troops of the Soviet Red Army.

Lynne Cox first sought to swim the frigid Bering Strait in 1976

To the north of the Diomedes, the Chukchi Sea spreads into the Arctic Ocean. To the south, Norton Sound devolves into the Bering Sea, one of the most treacherous bodies of water on earth. The Bering Sea is fed a cold current from the Arctic and a warm one from the Pacific; the confluence causes heavy fogs and storms that sometimes produce waves reaching forty feet in height. Winter temperatures range from −31° to -49°; average temperatures for June, July, and August hover in the low fifties. Once an Ice Age land link, the Bering Strait is a narrow channel through which the International Dateline runs, separating today from tomorrow and Russian territory from the United States. Big Diomede is Russian, Little Diomede American.

Not much ever happened on the Diomede Islands during the Cold War. The Inuits on Little Diomede hunted walrus and got drunk; the Red Army soldiers on Big Diomede got drunk right back and glared at the Inuits through a spyglass from an observation point on a tall rock. Otherwise, life on either side of the ideological gap amounted to an ongoing exercise in survival. Inuits, meaning "Real People," on Little Diomede melted snow and ice for their personal water supply, blunted the winter winds with crude oil stoves, used honey buckets for liquid waste disposal, and burned their combustible solid debris. In Cold War days, crossing the Strait from America to Russia constituted a felonious breach of Soviet security, punishable by whatever measures Soviet soldiers deemed appropriate. Even with that threat, a few misanthropes foolishly tested the Red Army's resolve.

In April of 1986, thirty-three-year-old American John Weymouth took a serendipitous romp across the still-frozen Strait from Little Diomede to Big Diomede. A drifter from San Francisco, Weymouth became the focus of international attention after Soviet soldiers snatched and interrogated him for two weeks. Weymouth's excuse for infringing on Soviet territory: He had an apparent hanker to wander around. After negotiations between the U.S. State Department and Kremlin, Soviet authorities returned Weymouth to Little Diomede; the last anyone heard of him, he had purchased an airplane ticket to Seattle and disappeared. Two months before Weymouth wandered into the Soviet Union, a Californian and a Frenchman attempted a stroll across the Strait, the Frenchman stupidly sliding across on a sailboard. Soviet soldiers arrested both men. The Red Army even detained three Little Diomede walrus hunters for fifty-two days after they accidentally strayed into Soviet territory.

Since the breakup of the Soviet Union, a new challenge has lured to the Strait a menagerie of the world's misguided and ill-advised. They have come to walk, ride, or mush from Russia to Alaska and back, or from Alaska to Russia and back. The caveat is that the journey must be made in May, when the shifting ice of the Strait is breaking up and navigation is trickiest. A Canadian and British pair came with a plan in the Alaskan spring of 1996 to traverse the ice towing a raft. The effort failed miserably. A convoy of Italians arrived on the Russian side of the Strait with a notion, uproariously unsuccessful, to drive to Alaska in arctic trucks, while an Iowan lamely attempted to bicycle across the Strait with a Russian companion. The Inuits have always thought such thrill-seekers loco and plotted ways to extract cash out of them for rescue attempts, of which there have been many. In 1995, the Alaskan Air National Guard spent several thousand dollars plucking a disoriented Frenchman and his dog team off the ice. That same year, the cost to rescue three stranded Russians reached a quarter of a million dollars. When the Coast

Guard arrived in helicopters, the Russians had been encircled by twenty polar bears.

The oddest attempt to cross the Strait occurred on a late-summer day in 1987 when the Bering ice was in seasonal retreat and the waters in the Strait were running very cold, a day that dawned bleak and foggy with a hint of drizzle. Normally barren of civilians, Big Diomede had been transformed by abrupt command from Moscow into an encampment almost worthy of a *National Geographic* pictorial. The Soviets had set up a warming tent and two buffet tables, replete with a waiter in a white smock, ready to serve hot tea, bread, dried fish, and chocolate-covered coconut candy. One Inuit woman stood in the morning chill holding a bouquet of wildflowers; another clutched a pair of beaded Eskimo slippers. Along with perhaps thirty Soviet political and sports officials and representatives of the Soviet news agency TASS, the natives had been conscripted by the Soviet government to serve as the official greeting party for thirty-year-old Californian Lynne Cox, who was about to swim from the United States to the Soviet Union.

Arguably the world's greatest marathon swimmer, Cox specialized in long, cold-water, rough-water swims, and hers would be the longest, most treacherous cold-water swim ever attempted. The temperature in the Strait hovered at 40° – water so cold most people couldn't drink it; so frigid that if it had been a little bit colder Cox could have walked across it; so icy that each breath Cox took would make her chest heave and ache. The Inuits believed the water to be far too cold for human survival beyond thirty minutes. Cox would not only be in the water for two hours, and possibly longer, she would not be wearing a wet suit, nor would she be coated in a protective layer of lanolin that would allow her body to retain heat — by both intent and design.

Two years earlier, Cox had crossed Lake Myvatn in Iceland, where the water temperature registered 40°, without a wet suit. She had successfully completed another swim, also without a wet suit, through thin ice in Alaska's Glacier Bay, where the water was so frigid that her two accompanying boats had effectively been used as icebreakers. When Cox emerged, her core body temperature,

Cox's Swim Has Been 16 Years in the Making

Los Angeles Times Headline, 1987

normally a shade above 97°, had remarkably jumped past 99°. Despite a compelling cache of evidence that Cox was a rare physical specimen, and more suited to attempt the Bering Strait swim than any human on the planet, Little Diomede's Inuits predicted confidently that the Strait was unconquerable. Percy Milligrock, an ivory carver, blurted to *The Los Angeles Times*, "It's way too cold. I think they'll have to pull her out."

Those who research physiological exotica say that water leaches heat from the body approximately twenty-five times faster than air, so the risk of Cox lapsing into acute or "rapid-onset" hypothermia seemed substantial. Cox had never suffered hypothermia but was well acquainted with its symptoms — fingers splaying with the loss of motor control, a graying in the face, a discoloration in the feet, disorientation, the inability to distinguish sky from water — and aware, too, of what could happen if she reached a hypothermic state. When the temperature at the body's core falls below 94°, violent shivering — the body's attempt to generate heat — sets in and cardiac arrest can follow. If that happened to Cox, it would be critical to get her out of the water as quickly as possible, just one reason she would not be coated with lanolin. The combination of her weight, 180 pounds, and the body grease would make it almost impossible for rescuers to pull her to safety. The lanolin would also render useless any significant research into hypothermia, and that was part of the point of attempting the swim.

The unstable currents of the Bering Strait between Big Diomede and Little Diomede presented another danger. Because they flow in a northerly direction, Cox would actually have to swim between four and six miles to get across the nearly three-mile Strait. That's if she was lucky. If the currents ran too strong, Cox could be swept into open water toward the Chukchi Sea, and the accompanying support boats probably would be unable to help her. The local shark population posed an additional danger. The Great Pacific Shark and the Salmon Shark inhabited the area and were not known to attack humans, but who really knew?

While Cox did not feel inclined to offer herself as a snack, she had encountered danger in a variety of guises. Not only had she confronted sharks, she had wrestled poisonous jellyfish, battled hellacious currents, gulped raw sewage, negotiated her way past floating land mines, lapsed into hallucinations, fainted in water hundreds of feet deep, and become lost in fog in the middle of the night. In the curious world of Lynne Cox, a shark loomed as a scary nuisance, but it wouldn't stop her.

Enraptured by the idea of swimming across the International Dateline, plunging from today into tomorrow, Cox first entertained the notion of crossing the Bering Strait in the American Bicentennial year of 1976. No one had ever done it, and no one save Cox had the physical gifts to do it. So it would be a first and almost certainly a last. A Bering Strait swim also dovetailed perfectly into Cox's core philosophy — that the solo athlete could transcend both geographic distance and political differences. Cox designed many of her swims as symbolic gestures of goodwill and cooperation between people of different countries and cultures.

In high school, and later as a history student at the University of California at Santa Barbara, Cox wondered whether private individuals could change the world. She studied history to find out why wars and other events oc-

SWIMMER LYNNE COX BRACES FOR AN ICE WATER ORDEAL, A DIRE CROSSING IN THE BERING STRAIT

People Magazine Headline, 1987

curred, what caused change, and how individuals influenced change. The Bering Strait swim had long been her primary athletic goal and, if successful, would become her greatest achievement, because the Soviets would have to open a border that had been closed for more than forty years. On a practical level, the swim would be part cultural exchange, part scientific experiment, and part promotion — in fact, a culmination of everything Cox had ever done, and she had done some incredible things.

Along with her brother and two sisters, Cox started to swim competitively at the age of nine. Soon after, coaches introduced Cox to interval training, in which she and other members of her swim team were required to cover a series of distances. The faster they finished a given distance, the more rest they got before the next interval. Cox couldn't swim as fast as her peers, so that by the time she finished an interval, her teammates would have had about ten seconds rest. Cox would only get a couple of seconds to rest before beginning the next interval. But interval training helped Cox build stamina and aerobic power. By the time the Boston-born Cox turned twelve, she and her siblings knew they wanted to become national-caliber athletes. But Manchester, New Hampshire, where Cox lived, offered her little chance

127

to launch an international swimming career. Cox asked her parents if the family could move. Amenable, Albert and Estelle Cox gave the children their choice of California, Hawaii, or Arizona. They selected California, where the best coaches were located. The family moved to Los Alamitos, south of Los Angeles, and enlisted the assistance of Olympic swim coach Don Gambrill.

While Cox had designs on becoming an Olympian, she found the distances available to her were too short; she could not record decent times. Cox also grew bored going back and forth in pools. But Cox discovered she had a tremendous capability for long-distance swimming. A short time later, Cox heard about a swim club that took part in long-distance ocean swims and asked Gambrill if she could change directions. Gambrill agreed; in 1971, when Cox was fourteen, she entered three events — the three-mile, two-mile, and one-mile races — at an annual rough-water swim near her home. She won them all, prompting her to begin serious training with prolonged 6 a.m. swims off Seal Beach, California.

Cox made her first foray into long-distance swimming by going twenty-six miles from the California coast to Catalina Island. It took her twelve hours and four minutes. The next year, at age fifteen, she swam the twenty-seven-mile English Channel, breaking both the men's and women's world records, clocking nine hours, fifty-seven minutes. Although her record was broken a month later by Davis Hunt, an Englishman, Cox returned in 1973, reclaiming it. A year later, she shattered the men's and women's records for the swim from California to Catalina. That same year, Cox attempted her second international swim, going fifteen miles down the Nile in Egypt before quitting. She swallowed mud, slime, and sewage, negotiated her way through dead rats, and navigated past barrels that had been placed in the river to keep discarded land mines from floating away. That swim landed Cox in the hospital.

"I almost died," Cox recalled. "I got a combination of dysentery and food poisoning. The raw sewage was another reason I got so sick. The little Nile, which runs through downtown Cairo, is where all the raw sewage empties, and the big Nile is where the chemical and industrial stuff comes out. After about fifteen miles, I passed out in the water. I was seventeen years old and very upset with myself for giving up, but I couldn't go any further. It took a long time for me to realize my body has limits."

Cox then dedicated herself to swimming the world's coldest, most dangerous, and unchallenged waterways, and to making herself available to hypothermia research. In 1975, Cox became the first woman to successfully swim the eleven-mile Cook Strait between the north and south islands of New Zealand. It took her twelve hours and two minutes in currents that stretched the swim to more than twenty miles. In fact, after five hours, Cox, bobbing like a cork, found herself farther from the finish than she had been at the start. But she made it with considerable encouragement. A radio commentator covered the swim; as Cox battled tides and sun glare, listeners began calling into the radio station. Cox's support crew turned up the volume on their radio so she could hear the messages of public support. Cox also learned from the broadcast that Air New Zealand had altered its flight paths so passengers and crew could monitor her progress.

The next year, Cox became the first to swim across the Strait of Magellan in Chile. The nearly five-mile swim took only an hour, but Cox did it without a wet suit in water so cold – 42° – and so rough that at the end of her swim the boat accompanying Cox couldn't land. The Cox party had to return through the Strait in a full-blown gale. Cox later became the first to swim Oresund, a twelve-mile stretch between Denmark and Sweden, and Skagerrak, a fifteen-mile Strait between Norway and Sweden. In 1977, Cox swam the channels separating three different Aleutian Islands off Alaska. A year later, she swam ten miles around South Africa's Cape of Good Hope, a crossing during which her crew fended off sharks with spear guns. The waters were too rough for shark cages, but Cox wouldn't have used one anyway. Cox then went seven miles around Kagoshima Bay, Japan, in 1979, and in 1983 embarked on Southern Alps swims of New Zealand lakes, becoming the first to successfully navigate Ohau, Tekapo, and Pukaki on the southern end of the island where water temperatures hovered menacingly in the low forties.

In 1984, Cox performed a series of "Swims Across America" — fourteen lakes, rivers, and bays, including Lake Tahoe, the Boston Harbor, the Detroit River, and nine other of the highest, coldest, and most treacherous waterways in the country. She passed on the warm and dirty Mississippi, which contained boils where rocks formed sudden depressions that might have sucked her under. Cox's "Swims Across America" served as a prelude to her next adventure. From August through October, 1985, Cox completed a series of "Swims Around the World." In an eighty-day span, Cox did a ten-mile warm-up from the

Queen Mary in Long Beach, California, to the Seal Beach pier. She went ten miles up the Potomac River near Washington, D.C.; swam seven miles through the 40° waters of Lake Myvatn in Iceland, and twenty miles across the Strait of Gibraltar from Morocco to Gibraltar. As an encore, Cox logged four miles across the Strait of Messina between Italy and Sicily; ten miles around the island of Delos off the Greek coast; two miles across the Bosporus in Turkey; seven miles across Lake Kunming in China; a one-day ordeal across five lakes of Mount Fuji in Japan; one mile across the 38° waters of Glacier Bay, Alaska; twelve miles in San Francisco Bay from the Golden Gate Bridge to the Bay Bridge; and five miles around the Statue of Liberty.

Cox could get into water that would kill most people and come out energized. Where a fully clothed man in 40° waters has a life expectancy of twenty-five minutes, Cox could spend several nearly naked hours in it and emerge with a couple of goose bumps. So water with a temperature of 50° seemed tropical to Cox, and water in the sixties felt like a hot tub. By contrast, if someone else became immersed in 50° water, they would turn into a Popsicle before covering a mile.

Barbara Drinkwater, a research physiologist, conducted her first experiments on Cox in the late 1970s. Drinkwater discovered that Cox's body temperature routinely went up after a long-distance swim in frigid waters. Drinkwater also found that Cox had an evenly distributed fat layer that made up 30 to 35 percent of her body weight, giving her almost perfect balance between heat lost and generated. Her body acted as a natural wet suit.

That same phenomenon had saved an Icelandic fisherman in 1984. Gud Laugur Friedthorssom had been pitched from a boat when it became caught in a net and capsized. After clinging to a broken keel for forty-five minutes, Friedthorssom and two companions attempted to swim to shore in 42° waters. Friedthorssom's svelte companions disappeared within ten minutes, but Friedthorssom, who weighed 300 pounds, made it despite swimming for six hours. The insulating property of his body fat saved him.

Drinkwater made another find: Cox's body density was exactly the same as seawater, her proportion of fat and muscle so well balanced that she neither sank nor rose above the water, giving her natural buoyancy. Through treadmill testing, Drinkwater also learned that Cox had the same aerobic power as a marathon runner, enabling her to swim for long periods of time without burning much energy. She would need that aerobic power to cross the Bering Strait.

Cox had been planning the swim on and off for eleven years, rehearsing its exact moment in her mind since 1985, when she sought an exemption to a 1948 Soviet moratorium on crossing between Little Diomede and Big Diomede islands. Cox had actually received permission from a Soviet official to attempt the swim in 1976, but had backed off, the decision not entirely hers.

She could not get confirmation of approval from anyone else in the Soviet government, had little financial support, and worried about the temperature in the Strait. At that point, the coldest water she had been in was 42°, and she wondered how far she could push her body. But subsequent experiences helped convinced her she could make it, or that she at least ought to try.

"The Glacier Bay swim was one of the things that convinced me I could swim the Strait," Cox subsequently explained. "But that was just a one-mile swim. The water turned out to be 38°. Once you get below 50°, it seems as though each degree makes a big difference. Because I was able to handle 38°, I thought maybe the Strait was possible. But after Glacier Bay I was so numb that I had lost complete sensation in my hands and feet. And I thought, if Glacier Bay was one mile and the Bering Strait is 2.7, the currents, we go off course, hmmm, can we really do this? I didn't know."

But she had a mind to try. For nearly 800 days, and at a cost of more than $100,000, which came from her earnings as a free-lance writer, from her father, a radiologist, and from some limited commercial sponsorships, Cox worked on the logistical arrangements: airfare, supplies, medical testing equipment, lodging, transportation, escort boats, and equipment. At the same time, she trained six days a week, three hours a day, on Alamitos Bay, south of Los Angeles. Her principal hurdle boiled down to convincing the Soviet government to authorize the swim, an almost impossible task in the view of everyone she consulted about the project. Said Alaska Senator Ted Stevens to his aides: "There is not a chance in hell the Soviets are going to open that border." He presented a strong case: The border had been closed for more than forty years; U.S.-Soviet relations were strained; Cox had no personal contacts in the Soviet Union, and swimming the Strait seemed, in the view of a lot of people, to be an idea that sprang from a deranged hallucination. Still, Cox explored every available avenue. She contacted her congressmen and California officials. She wrote to

Elizabeth Dole, the Secretary of Transportation, which oversaw the Coast Guard. She dispatched letters to the United States Navy and contacted Nome's Convention & Visitors Bureau.

Cox's coach, Joe Coplan, phoned, faxed, and telexed everyone he could think of on both sides of the Atlantic — sports officials, medical experts, politicians, press people — who might help convince the Soviets to permit Cox to swim, receiving a modicum of support from The Athletics Congress, the U.S. Swimming Federation, and United States Olympic Committee. Alaska Senator Frank Murkowski contacted Yuri Dubinin, the Soviet ambassador in Washington, D.C., on Cox's behalf. Cox also persuaded U.S. ambassador Steven Rhinesmith to endorse the swim. William Keatinge, a University of London hypothermia expert, wrote to a Soviet colleague, pleading that he lobby Soviet medical committees to get behind a Cox swim in the interest of hypothermia research. Jacques Cousteau's people even intervened. Cousteau had an expedition boat in the area, anchored in Dutch Harbor in the Aleutian Islands. Cox had hoped that the French oceanographer would assist in her attempt. His crew offered her the use of the *Alcyon*, a 100-foot vessel, for rewarming and support, but finally had to concede it couldn't get clearance from the Soviets to cross the International Dateline. Coplan telexed Marat Gramov, chief of the USSR State Sports Committee, imploring him "in the spirit of international friendship and cooperation" to approve the swim. On June 30, Alaska Governor Steve Cowper cabled Mikhail Gorbachev, arguing that a Cox swim would be "an important contribution toward a closer relationship between our two regions."

Cox also enjoyed media backing. *People* magazine did a piece. *USA Today* ran a story, as did *The New York Times* and *The Orange County Register*. Some of the national coverage questioned Cox's motives for trying to swim the Bering Strait, labeling her attempt a "stunt" and "publicity grab." But Rich Roberts, a well-respected reporter for *The Los Angeles Times*, defended Cox in a number of articles, pointing out that Cox had struggled to raise money for the swim; that only a few sponsors — Dupont Corporation, Speedo America, Rocky Boot Company, and the Women's Sports Foundation — had tossed any money her way; that Cox sincerely desired to make a gesture of goodwill; that she intended to offer herself as a subject for hypothermia research; that her goal of swimming the Strait was, if slightly bizarre, entirely legitimate.

But misguided association complicated the issue. Before Lynne Cox, Diana Nyad had certified herself a quintessential queen of stunt. On August 15, 1978, Nyad made a widely reported attempt to swim from Cuba to Florida in a $55,000 motorized anti-shark cage. While Cox hardly shared Nyad's flair for showmanship, she still had her detractors. Pat Omiak, the mayor of Little Diomede Island, told *The Los Angeles Times*, "You know how people are. They just want to try something to make a big headline."

Cox pushed harder, finally receiving a call from Rozanne Ridgway, the U.S. Assistant Secretary of State for European and Canadian Affairs, who promised to contact the Soviet Ambassador on Cox's behalf. Ed Salazar, who worked under Ridgway, became the first federal official to really give Cox a serious listen and offer help. Salazar worked on the Soviet Desk at the State Department, where he monitored Soviet affairs and dealt with bilateral exchange activities.

"The first time I got a call from Lynne I thought she was a kook," Salazar admitted later. "But I was impressed that Lynne had very specific questions. And she followed up. I finally realized that here was someone who had a vision. So I advised her on how to communicate her interest to the Congress, the National Security Council, and the Russians."

Either insensitive to goodwill gestures or overly sensitive to security issues, the Russians refused to listen. Nobody could tell for certain because the Soviets stonewalled the subject, treating it as if it didn't exist. What was true was that the Kremlin remained red-faced over an incident involving Mathias Rust. A nineteen-year-old West German pilot, Rust had taken off on an unauthorized flight from Helsinki, Finland, the previous May 29 and flown 400 miles through Soviet airspace before landing his single-engine Cessna 172 in the middle of Red Square. Rust's headline-making breach of Soviet security so upset the Kremlin that Rust had started a four-year stay in a labor camp, leaving Soviet officials to endure a joke to the effect that Soviet border guards, instead of keeping their eyes peeled for airplanes, had been sipping vodka through straws when Rust's plane shot right over their heads.

Cox did not discover until much later that the Soviets privately viewed the whole idea of a Bering Strait swim as utter lunacy. Such a thing had never been attempted and the Soviets saw no reason to attempt it now, especially since Big Diomede contained military equipment. The Soviets also considered the project too expensive — almost a million U.S. dollars. To pull it off, the Soviets would have to galvanize a small army of people in a remote part of the country, which made no sense. A Lynne Cox swim would accomplish nothing. Therefore, she absolutely could not swim the Bering Strait.

Had Lynne Cox been privy to Soviet thinking, she may not have taken a huge leap of faith. Cox waited around as long as she could for a Soviet response. When none came, she took off for Anchorage, hoping that the Soviets would give their approval. As Cox left California, wondering what might happen next, she had no idea she was about to become one of Bob Walsh's most significant projects.

Citizen Diplomacy

Bob was never a capitalist shark. My people felt Bob did what he did for an idea, not for money. That is very dear to our Russian heart and soul.

– Helen Shiskana, resident, Moscow, Russia

Gene Fisher, the Seattle Organizing Committee's director of special projects, sat in his office drinking coffee one morning when he received word from an SOC staffer that the United States Information Agency had phoned with an inquiry: Could he help arrange for a woman named Lynne Cox to swim from the United States to the Soviet Union? Fisher blinked several times and recoiled in his chair, not certain he had heard this correctly. Some woman wanted to swim from the U.S. to the USSR? By Fisher's geographical reckoning, Lynne Cox had to be daft, a dufus, on drugs, or all of the above. Such a swim could only be attempted at the Bering Strait, a wicked stretch of sea no human had ever conquered. And even if Cox somehow had the ability to do it, which Fisher didn't believe for a second, the

Soviet government would probably have her arrested the minute she crossed the International Dateline.

Shaking off his skepticism, Fisher dutifully dispatched a telex to Bob Walsh, then en route to the Soviet Union, advising him of the USIA request. For Fisher, the timing of this incongruous assignment couldn't have been better. He had just wrapped up another curious task which, when SOC staffers first heard about it, prompted them to stare at both Gene and Bob with the kind of glazed eyes usually seen on slaughterhouse steers: an international exchange of fish. Mikhail Taratuta of Gosteleradio had implored Bob for months to investigate the possibility of rounding up a dozen live fish and transporting them to Russia for ultimate deposit in the Moscow River. Taratuta entertained a misguided notion that American fish would mate with Russian fish, somehow underscoring improving relations between the United States and Soviet Union. The fish project had landed in Fisher's lap, soon convincing him that Taratuta's request constituted ecological lunacy. But in the interest of furthering the cause of the Games, he plunged into the particulars, causing him unrelenting grief.

It had been a nightmare trying to figure out what kind of fish to acquire, where to get the goddamn fish, how to legally get the fish out of the country, and how to keep the fish alive so they could copulate their little fish brains out in the Moscow River. There had been dozens of telephone conversations with University of Washington fisheries experts, who explained to Fisher that fish, whether knocked out or frozen, would never make it to Moscow alive. Somewhere in the maze of naysayers, Fisher finally located a cooperative voice, who suggested the fish might be packed in dry ice. Since the University of Washington didn't have proper packing materials, Fisher scoured Seattle for them, eventually locating a wholesale dealer of tropical fish, who negated the dry ice theory, suggesting instead a chilled, sealed container supersaturated with oxygen, or some such chemical thing. Fisher made a command decision to go for it. After the twelve subject fish had been drugged and packed in a container bound with duct tape, Fisher handed it over to Bob for transportation to Moscow, certain the fish would survive the trip. The container, he also noticed, appeared just big enough to hold a portable nuclear weapon, explaining why Bob set off a cacophony of alarms as soon as he reached customs in Copenhagen.

Bob had no permission to bring fish into Denmark. He did not have documentation proving the contents of a container that looked like it might house an explosive device. Somehow, Bob talked his way past Copenhagen customs agents and got on an airplane bound for Moscow, fish in hand. However, when Bob arrived, customs agents there went berserk. They couldn't open the container and inspect the fish, as Bob explained, because the fish would die.

"Maybe what you've got there," one grave official told Bob, "could take out half of Red Square. We could get in big trouble for letting you through."

After a couple of well-placed telephone calls to Taratuta at Gosteleradio and Vjacheslav Gavrilin at the USSR State Sports Committee, Bob received clearance to take the fish into Moscow. Unfortunately for the archives of international romance, all the fish died in Taratuta's bathtub before they could be sent on a collective blind date in the Moscow River.

In addition to the fish, Bob carried with him one of the more intriguing telexes he had ever seen. Relayed through Fisher, the message had come from Molly Raymond of the United States Information Agency. Molly worked for a division of the USIA that had been established by Ronald Reagan to promote cultural exchanges between the United States and Soviet Union. In a mainly facilitative role, Molly assisted American citizens who wanted to interact with their Soviet counterparts.

Many of those Americans had become convinced that there had to be a way through grassroots diplomacy to break down the mistrust that had built up in the decade and a half since Richard Nixon and Leonid Brezhnev ushered in the era of detente. Current events moved in their favor; current politicians hadn't caught up. After Reagan took office, his administration banned most trade with the Soviet Union, suspended Aeroflot flights, and refused to permit cultural and scientific exchanges between the U.S. and USSR. It denied U.S. entry visas to some Soviets and intensified rhetoric about "fighting limited nuclear wars" against The Evil Empire. But as the Reagan administration gradually softened its position, the biggest convert became Reagan himself. A few days before his 1985 Geneva summit with Mikhail Gorbachev, Reagan surprised political observers with what they dubbed his "People-to-People" speech.

"Imagine," said the President, "how much good we could accomplish if more individuals and families from our respective countries could come to know each other in a personal way. The time is ripe to take bold new steps to open the way for our peoples to participate in an unprecedented way in the building of peace."

Several bold steps had already been taken, among the most dramatic a series of television space bridges that linked relatively small American audiences with audiences of 200 million at a time in the fifteen republics of the Soviet Union. Conducted via satellite, the space bridges had little impact in the United States until talk show host Phil Donahue embraced them. On December 29, 1985, a month following the Reagan-Gorbachev summit, Donahue and Soviet commentator Vladimir Pozner teamed up for *Citizen Summit*, the first TV space bridge seen by millions of Americans. *Citizen Summit* featured Donahue and Pozner discussing refuseniks, dissidents, psychiatric wards, and Andrei Sakarov. Never before had any Soviet citizen seen or heard such frank public discussion about so many taboo topics. Pozner, who spoke seven languages, received 77,000 hand-written letters from his countrymen in response to the program.

Many individuals involved in the space bridges believed that if U.S. and Soviet citizens could talk informally, the confrontational posture adopted by the governments of the two superpowers might also relax. By the time of the Donahue-Pozner space bridge, only a handful of Americans had attempted any kind of citizen diplomacy in the Soviet Union, the most prominent among them Ted Turner, who wanted to engage the Soviets in a massive athletic exchange. Turner believed the Goodwill Games could make a positive difference in U.S.-Soviet relations. The Soviets not only agreed, they believed that citizen diplomats of far less rank than Turner could help facilitate dialogue with the U.S. government.

But to top-down thinkers in official Washington, citizen diplomacy amounted to populist poppycock for tourists who thought their efforts would keep missiles in silos. Official Washington's view changed markedly when a citizen diplomat had a higher profile and might accomplish something that would expose official U.S. diplomatic policy as bankrupt. Which was why, even as Reagan encouraged the resumption of mutual cultural exchanges, his administration climbed walls when Turner ventured to Moscow for the inaugural edition of the Goodwill Games. While the administration endorsed the global responsibility and independent thinking embodied in citizen diplomats, it threw up roadblocks when the activities of citizen diplomats encroached on policy-making objectives. Turner encroached in a major way. Turner not only might accomplish something, it would be on television all around the world. In fact, what Turner really accomplished was never televised, broadcast on radio, or printed in the newspapers, and most Soviets immediately recognized what it was.

"We found," Henrikas Yushkiavitshus of Gosteleradio told Bob in the aftermath of the inaugural Goodwill Games, "that we had the same professional problems as the Americans, the same family problems. They were ordinary people like we were."

Citizen Diplomacy rooted in precisely that idea. Citizen diplomats could not create policy, negotiate treaties, or direct armies. But they could create an exchange of thought and attitude, develop projects, and get into details. As Michael Shuman of the Palo Alto-based Center for Innovative Diplomacy explained it, citizen diplomats considered themselves the Lilliputians in the story of Gulliver. Each Lilliputian would wrap a tiny thread around the huge giant. No one thread would hold the giant down, but all of those threads, the economic threads, the social threads, the cultural threads, the friendship threads, would keep the giant silent and inert.

By the summer of 1987, many Americans, many of them prominent, began entering the Soviet Union en masse. Leonard Nimoy went there to talk about saving whales. Robert De Niro, Donald Trump, John Le Carre, and Graham Greene went there to talk about movies, hotels, and books. Billy Joel, John Denver, Bonnie Raitt, James Taylor, and the Doobie Brothers went there to sing. Every American who went there had a goal to make something happen, or just make a dent. Molly Raymond heard many of their stories, spending each day talking to people who had reasonable and unreasonable plans, big ideas, and bigger dreams. And Lynne Cox had the biggest dream of all. Although Molly thought it wonderful, she had no idea what to do with it, or how it could possibly be accomplished.

So Molly issued a request to Bob Walsh via Gene Fisher, explaining that Alaska Senator Frank Murkowski had asked the USIA's assistance in helping Lynne Cox swim the Bering Strait. Bob didn't know anything about Cox, but recognized instantly that a swim by an American woman to Soviet shores would attract international attention not only to Cox, but to the Goodwill Games. Shortly after Bob arrived in Moscow, he poked around Soviet ministries to see if he could find out anything. When Bob asked Taratuta and Pavel Kuznetsov of Gosteleradio what they knew about Cox, both told him the swim wouldn't happen.

"It's too impractical," said Kuznetsov.

"The project is idiotic," added Marat Gramov, head of the USSR State Sports Committee.

"The whole idea is insane," Gramov's deputy, Vjacheslav Gavrilin, told Bob. "Besides, the KGB would never permit it. The area is thousands of miles from civilization. The woman cannot make the swim."

"Do you seriously think," Bob argued, "that this woman is going to carry a camera and photograph a military installation? If *glasnost* is for real, here's a chance to meet Cox on the Soviet side and proclaim her a heroine for peace."

Gavrilin felt uncomfortable finding himself boxed in by Bob's logic, and Bob detected Gavrilin's discomfort. He knew that most Russians were not big on innovative thinking and had a fear of being exposed as less than perfect. He also knew that if Russians didn't believe they could do anything about something, they pretended it didn't exist. And if that didn't work, they created things that didn't exist. In fact, they had been honing the public charade into high art ever since Catherine the Great entrusted one of her numerous lovers, Grigory Potemkin, with organizing the New Russia. He didn't so much organize it as he redecorated it. Catherine had been scheduled to sail down the Dnieper River to inspect development in what is now the Ukraine. In advance of her visit, Potemkin ordered the construction of special fake villages along her projected route, each consisting of rows of pretty, two-dimensional façades. To embellish the artifice, Potemkin imported all manner of peasants and slaves, dressing them in colorful country-folk garb. For all Catherine knew, her waving minions lived in prosperity.

Potemkin Villages existed wherever Russians chose to create them. Hedrick Smith recounted in *The Russians* that just before Richard Nixon's trip to Moscow in 1972, entire neighborhoods were burned down so new buildings could be constructed to impress the U.S. President. Two years after Nixon's visit, Gerald Ford visited Vladivostok in the Soviet Far East. In his extraordinary work, *Russia: Broken Idols, Solemn Dreams*, David K. Shipler described how, in advance of Ford's meeting with Brezhnev, Soviet officials spruced up Ford's route from the Vladivostok airport to the city. The Soviet government evacuated people living along the airport highway, set fire to their ramshackle homes, and cleared away the rubble. Then the Red Army marched into a nearby forest, felled hundreds of trees, hauled them to the highway, and stuck them upright in deep snow so that Ford would be greeted by lines of lovely firs on his way into the city.

Kevin Klose's story in *Russia And The Russians* illustrates the degree to which the Russians cleaned up for company. As Klose tells it, *Pravda* printed a tale about a new tractor repair factory scheduled to serve farms near Leningrad. When it came time to dedicate the factory, *Pravda* lavished praise on the officials who saw to it that the factory was built and functioning, uncharacteristically ahead of schedule. Only one problem: The factory didn't exist. What did exist was a heap of roofless buildings on a rubble-strewn industrial site. *Pravda* finally figured out what happened. From the moment work got underway, the project suffered delays. As they multiplied, construction officials papered the truth, signing off on completion reports when nothing had been completed. Soon, senior bureaucrats began praising local officials for their remarkable efforts. When officials deemed the factory ready for the machine tools that would recondition tractor engines, there was more trouble: Officials responsible for building the tools hadn't built them because they had never expected anything but delays. But the tool enterprise signed off on delivery and installation reports, and forwarded the papers to Leningrad. Now the factory was, theoretically, ready for production. Meanwhile, an old but functioning factory was torn down, the new one making it obsolete. The local environmental inspector signed off on the new factory as non-polluting. The fire inspector testified it was not a fire hazard. Later, when the truth came out, the inspectors insisted they had behaved in stellar fashion: Since the factory didn't exist, it couldn't pollute or pose a fire hazard. So thorough was the deception that the chairman of the State Committee of Agricultural Technical Means recommended medals for dozens of officials.

That factory served as a metaphor for a lot of things. Communist Party members disavowed religion but had their children baptized in the Russian Orthodox Church and were themselves baptized. The huge Moskva outdoor swimming pool had served as the site of thousands of clandestine baptisms, particularly in winter when steam rising from the water obscured illegal leaps into faith. School teachers spread Soviet doctrine in the classroom, but trashed it outside, placing students in the conflicting position of learning one thing while thinking another. Soviets took pride in their educational system, but some of the most significant elements of their history were kept from them. One year, the government cancelled all final history exams for Soviet schoolchildren after concluding that much of what had been taught was wrong, and that the official passing of lies from generation to generation had to end. Plenty had been passed in a staggering number of ways.

In Bob's early trips to Moscow, he noticed a skyline cluttered with construction cranes, but none ever moved. As Alexander Kozlovsky, a deputy at the USSR State Sports Committee, explained, the Soviet government had erected them to hoodwink the few Westerners who visited the country into assuming Moscow was a bustling metropolis. The windows at the GUM department store featured fancy imported goods that could not be purchased inside. The menus at tourist hotels ran for pages, but most of the printed fare was unavailable.

Ted Turner once found himself at the center of an amusing Potemkin-style caper. During one of his trips to the Soviet Union, Turner

 informed his Soviet hosts that he wanted to do some hunting. Although happy to accommodate Turner, they had to be sure Turner shot something. So they flew Turner and Jane Fonda to a mountainous part of Georgia, where a

Ted Turner and Jane Fonda in a game preserve

herd of cute, tiny deer pranced out of the woods as soon as Turner disembarked the helicopter and literally licked salt off his hands. The Soviets had dropped Turner in a game preserve. Turner couldn't shoot hapless little animals, so he shooed them into the woods, walked AWAY from them, then turned around to hunt them. The deer would have none of it. Instead of fleeing Turner, they chased after him.

Bob's Russian friends told him dozens of Potemkin stories, his favorite the tale of big-shot Communist Party leaders who took a fishing vacation to the Black Sea. To make sure the bosses caught fish, local Party officials arranged for scuba divers to take fish into the water, swim underneath the boats, and attach them to the hooks.

"The military would even paint the leaves greener to impress the big generals," recalled Sergei Sviridov, who worked at the USSR State Sports Committee. "Moscow was a Potemkin Village. The Soviet Union was a Potemkin Village. We were so controlled that we had to use our brains in order to maneuver."

Many Russians embraced the fresh ideas running through Soviet society. They listened to the radio, watched television, read newspapers, and learned things they had never known. It was all so intoxicating, spawning hope, aspiration, and energy. But it also spawned insecurity and misgiving. Sweeping change required a Russian that did not yet exist. It required different politics, education, and know-how, and they did not yet exist. Russians liked to talk about all kinds of questions, but felt incapable of resolving any of them. So they talked more than they acted, the reverse of the way Bob Walsh careened through life.

Understanding this, Bob determined he would resort to blandishment, flattery, and conniving. He would convince Soviets officials they could not fail if they permitted Lynne Cox to swim the Bering Strait. But more than that, Bob would convince them they would turn out to be heroes if they seized the opportunity that a Cox swim presented.

Bob thought it interesting that Russians had such a revolutionary history — they still spoke about the Great Patriotic War as though it had happened yesterday, not in the 1940s — but were deer in headlights when it came to implementing new ideas. Then again, they had difficulty implementing old ones. They had the greatest mineral wealth in the world, but couldn't exploit it. They had oil, but no profitable means of tapping it. They had the largest forests on the planet, but suffered paper shortages. The Moscow Metro, a boggling feat of engineering, had escalators among the steepest and fastest on the planet. But they frequently came to sudden halts, causing the hapless people riding them to tumble forward like dominoes. Cakes of filth adorned Moscow's buses and trolleys, but a Soviet citizen could be fined for driving a dirty car. Water trucks washed Moscow's streets during thunderstorms. A factory in the Ukraine manufactured thousands of pairs of sunglasses; the lenses were so dark it was impossible to see the sun through them even when looking directly at it.

Michael Binyon chronicled a wonderful anecdote in his book, *Life In Russia*. A freight train carried concrete beams from Moscow to Leningrad, passing on its way a freight train carrying identical

143

concrete beams from Leningrad to Moscow. Nothing ever changed because change stood at loggerheads with central planning.

Incompetence did not lard every aspect of Soviet life. Everyone had something, but no one had a lot, and everyone would have had more if not for the legendary inefficiency. Actor Peter Ustinov once described the frustration of a German general who dealt with Russians during World War II: "We were defeated by Russian inefficiency. We had the best intelligence service available to any army. I would even say that such quality was wasted on the Russians, who talked on their radiotelephones without any effort at disguising their intentions, without codes. We knew they would attack near Minsk with three divisions and air support. We knew the date, even the hour. And we were ready. But owing to Russian inefficiency those divisions never reached Minsk. Their trains ran out of fuel, and the local commander told them he had no food for them, and the best thing to do was to attack the Germans and attempt to capture supplies. As a consequence they attacked 200 kilometers away from where we were expecting them and by the time we reacted, it was too late."

Bob understood Soviet concerns about security on Big Diomede Island. But he also understood the Soviets had a penchant for secrecy exceeded only by a deeper penchant for distortion. That being the case, they usually said no to any novel proposal. So Bob worked Soviet ministries hoping to build a consensus on the swim, and did so using the kind of personal interaction so valued among Russians that nothing could happen without it. Russians loved people who laughed, told jokes, cried, fell in love, and drank too much — all reassuring features of humanity. The Russians would negotiate with Bob because he would laugh, tell jokes, cry, maybe fall in love, and drink too much. And then he would spring his scheme.

Silk Road Schemes

At the beginning of our friendship, when Bob was describing his new projects to me, I thought: Jesus Christ, he'll never be able to do all that. But he did! Now I shall not be surprised if he tells me he is going to start a project on the moon.

    – Sergei Sviridov,
        Russian Olympic Committee,
        Moscow, Russia

When Bob Walsh entered into a tentative agreement with officials from the Georgian State Committee for Radio and Television to import wine to the United States, he felt reasonably certain his new business partners had a mind to sell Soviet state property for their private enrichment. Bob harbored no moral qualms over it, but wondered what would happen if they got caught. Would they be jailed? Banished? In the Soviet Union, it didn't take much to run afoul of authorities or attract the attention of the KGB. Even such seemingly inconsequential activities as practicing martial arts, or studying extrasensory perception, had been declared punishable offenses, as had listening to foreign radio transmissions, Tedo Japaridze's crime.

Tedo grew up in a Tbilisi, Georgia, still darkened by Stalin's shadow. His maternal grandfather had been erased in the great Soviet purge of 1937, and his grandmother had been sent to prison in Siberia for several years for marrying an "enemy of the state."

"When I was a young boy," Tedo later explained, "we had an old-fashioned radio set. My father, a sports journalist, used to listen to this box. This transmission was something I did not understand. My father told me this was VOA — Voice of America. And this strange organization we kept hearing about was NBA. I thought NBA . . . CIA . . . KGB . . . FBI. Oh, my God! This could be very dangerous! To just listen to these transmissions was one of the top crimes. One could easily be arrested by the Soviet secret police, and we had to be careful as there were many informers. But forever in my memory will be the figure of my dad, almost glued to the old radio set, trying to get through this unbearable static to hear some news."

The news that most interested Tedo in the mid-1950s concerned a tall, skinny American basketball star who had almost single-handedly destroyed the Soviet national team at the 1956 Olympic Games in Melbourne, Australia. A friend of Tedo's father, an Olympic wrestler, had participated in those Games and returned to Tbilisi with enthralling stories about the American. Otar Korkiya, the captain of the 1952 Soviet national basketball team, and Nodar Dshordshikiya, another top player, had also seen the American devastate the Soviets. The American's name was Bill Russell, and he had gone on to star for the Boston Celtics.

"One day my father had his ear to this box, listening to these VOA transmissions," Tedo recalled. "My father said, 'Tedo, do you know what Bill Russell just did? He just blocked ten or twelve shots.' This was the same Bill Russell about whom Otar Korkiya and my godfather told us during some drinking session at my house. Now Bill Russell was with strange organization — NBA. I don't know what NBA is. And there were other names: Bob Cousy, Bill Sharman, John Havlicek, Red Auerbach. Bill Russell has this huge competition with Wilt Chamberlain, and he is blocking shots, jumping high, doing this and that. Georgia did not have television in those days. The first time I ever see professional game, there is movie somebody has smuggled in from United States. It's Cincinnati Royals and Oscar Robertson. But I never saw Bill Russell. So that's when I started creating with my imagination from Voice of America."

146

Tedo told all his friends about Bill Russell, and soon they swapped stories and imitated Russell on the playground.

"We created our own legends," Tedo remembered. "We talked about what Bill Russell did. And then we played and pretended we were doing the same thing. A good friend of mine once told me, 'Tedo, did you know what happened yesterday?' And my friend said Bill Russell could reach with basket his foot. I said, 'Are you crazy?' But this became one of the fairytales about Bill Russell — that he could reach with basket his foot."

Tedo's father not only taught him about Bill Russell, he introduced him to American jazz, Tedo quickly becoming a fan of Oscar Peterson and Benny Goodman. Tedo loved listening to his father talk about American entertainers such as Glenn Miller, Frank Sinatra, John Wayne, and Jimmy Stewart.

"This was also dangerous," Tedo explained later. "I remember a neighbor of mine. His father was jailed because he made public that he liked jazz. He was an active participant in daily gatherings at our house and they put him into the jail. He spent some time in Soviet prison in Siberia because he played jazz on the saxophone."

Tedo's interest in Bill Russell and jazz piqued his interest in the United States, which eventually prompted a love affair with American literature. Tedo devoured all the greats — Mark Twain, O'Henry, James Fenimore Cooper, Jack London.

"So first," Tedo reflected, "there was basketball and music, then basketball and *The Great Gatsby*. And I started looking at maps and researching facts about United States. Later, when I became a student, I joined Department of Foreign Languages and studied English, and after that I joined U.S.-Canadian Studies Institute in Moscow, the number one think tank. I started watching America more seriously. And the number one person who initiated this in me was Bill Russell. Because of Bill Russell, I started admiring America and introduced myself to American values, institutions, culture, and people. Without knowing about this crazy Georgian kid in the street who imitated him, Bill Russell influenced me to become an admirer of a wonderful country."

Tedo never got caught committing the crime of listening to foreign radio, and Bob could only hope that the Georgian wine entrepreneurs would be as fortunate. Getting the deal done did not surprise Bob as much as the speed with which it was put together. Whenever Bob did anything in Moscow, it required weeks, sometimes months.

The Georgian wine deal had taken less than a month to complete, which exacerbated Bob's concern as to whether the Georgians

Gene Pfeifer, left, Bob Walsh, and Berni Russi study the wine contract

had any right to enter into such an agreement. Were they avoiding Moscow? What did these Georgian TV guys have to do with the local wine industry? On the other hand, Bob didn't wonder too much about it. Mainly what he thought was, Hell, this is good wine.

Accompanied by Bernie Russi and Gene Pfeifer, Bob returned to Tbilisi to execute a formal contract. Russi, who had rescued Bob from John Sandt's immoral clutches at Marietta College a quarter of a century earlier, had retired from teaching, moved to Seattle, and joined the Seattle Organizing Committee as a "special assistant to the president." Pfeifer, who had spent thirty-one years at Pacific Northwest Bell, had joined the SOC as its Chief Operating Officer. Pfeifer previously had supported numerous projects of Bob's, including the Emerald City Marathon and Rainier Bank Golf Classic.

The wine deal, Bob's first commercial venture in the Soviet Union, technically involved a Bob Walsh & Associates spin-off, "Georgian Imports, Inc.," and "interested organizations of the Republic of Georgia (Georgia S.S.R.) of the Union of Soviet Socialist Republics." It gave Georgian Imports, Inc. exclusive rights to import Georgian wines, brandies, and champagnes to the United States. The two

Berni Russi, left, Bob Walsh, and Gene Pfeifer discuss the wine deal

key sentences in the contract said, "First party (Georgians) agrees that it will not grant any other right, authority, or license, exclusive or non-exclusive, to any other person,

148

government, or entity to act as its representative or agent, or to promote, sell, market, appoint distributors, or distribute its products in North America. The parties warrant that they have full authority to enter into this agreement." Georgian Imports, Inc. also agreed to host, at Seattle Organizing Committee expense, several Georgian TV personalities in Seattle for the purpose of filming a documentary on the Goodwill Games.

"We're signing this document and everything was in Georgian," recalled Pfeifer. "I was thinking, What are we signing here? But I just went with the flow."

A striking young woman about five-foot-five with light brown hair became an unexpected part of the celebratory toasts that followed. She had, she told Russi and Pfeifer, graduated from Moscow State University's Institute of Foreign Languages. In addition to her exceptional English, Nina Aksyonova appeared to be one of the most physically stunning women the Soviet Union had to offer, at least in the considered view of Bob, who felt the blood rush clear out of his head as soon as he saw her.

"She almost looked like a ballerina," recalled Pfeifer.

"Bob was breaking up with Nicole Preveaux," Russi revealed later. "One of the last things my wife, Julie, told me as I got on the plane to fly to Moscow was to not let Bob fall in love with a Russian. So we are waiting for our luggage and in walks this gorgeous female. She says, 'Mr. Walsh, the sports committee has assigned me to you.' I said, 'Oh, my God, I've screwed up already.'"

"Nina subsequently accompanied us to Tbilisi," Pfeifer explained later. "And that's when we got involved in that wine deal."

Problems plagued the deal from the start. The wine didn't "travel" well. Georgians used antiquated bottles and corks that exposed the wine to air. By the time the wine had been shipped and opened, it suffered from wine trauma and had a noxious taste.

Bob flanked by Gene Pfeifer & Vaso Margvelashvili

Georgian Imports, Inc. decided it needed to find a new way to get the wine to the United States, or different bottles and corks. But the second problem with the wine-import deal negated the first. Within a matter of weeks, Bob and his partners discovered the Georgians had executed similar "exclusive" agreements with several other groups, including some Americans.

Bob barely noticed, utterly zeroed in as he was on the dazzling Soviet translator.

Winning The Cold War

Bob Walsh did a lot of very creative things to make the Goodwill Games a special event. He was always coming up with new and great ideas.

— Rex Lardner, former executive, Turner Broadcasting System, Atlanta, Georgia

*O*n satellite imaging maps, the Diomede Islands appear to be places of no more consequence than the two cents an acre the United States paid Russia to acquire Alaska in 1867. Big Diomede is eleven square miles, its tiny outline vaguely resembling Alabama or Mississippi. Little Diomede is only four square miles; slightly tapering to a cape at its southern end, it is reminiscent of a miniature Illinois. Most regular maps don't even bother to publish images of the Diomede Islands. Although they both contain small, permanent civilizations, they are so remote and relentlessly forlorn — no public telephones on Big Diomede and only one on Little Diomede that isn't always working — it hardly seems worth the effort. Viewed from a light plane or helicopter, the Diomede Islands present an entirely different picture, inducing a completely different sensation. More often than not, nature near the Diomedes is in utter anarchy. Nasty and freakish, the weather changes every day, sometimes every hour. There is fog one minute and no fog the next. Dead calm is suddenly overwhelmed by banshee blizzards. Waves writhe and heave in the Bering Strait, breaking every which way. The gales become so deafening they turn ordinary conversations into shouting matches.

Lynne Cox, the world's most accomplished marathon swimmer, had flown to Anchorage, then to Nome, on to the village of Wales, and finally to Little Diomede Island, receiving her first glimpse of the Bering Strait not long after her helicopter swept over the York Mountains. It was a cold day in late July and the Strait greeted Cox with magnificent contempt. It appeared much rougher than any lake, bay, or river in her experience, far more menacing than either the Cape of Good Hope or the Strait of Magellan. Of all the places she'd seen, of all the waterways over which Cox had exercised temporary dominion, none came close to this. The water temperature hovered somewhere in the mid-thirties, Fahrenheit, ominous since saltwater froze at 28°. It was slightly less than three miles from Little Diomede, where Cox stood, to Big Diomede, where she hoped to swim. But the distance might as well have been a million miles.

As Cox gaped at the Strait, momentarily psyched out, she briefly convinced herself that she hadn't a chance of swimming across it. In addition to the chaos in the water, the wind had cranked up to forty knots. The vortex it created could suck a descending helicopter straight into the water or blow one right off its landing pad. Cox wondered if even a *umiak*, a thirty-foot walrus-skin boat, could get through this wicked channel. The Strait might simply inhale it whole, like a dolphin sliding down the gullet of a Great White. Perhaps the Inuits had been right. Maybe swimming the Strait was a lunatic idea. Certainly Cox would never be able to train in water like this. She would be whisked into open ocean. If she ultimately received permission from the Soviet government to swim the Strait, the weather would have to be a lot more cooperative, and then timing would be everything. Cox would have to be ready to go at a moment's notice.

Lynne wondered if she was politically naïve. The Soviet government had requested a list of names of the people who wanted to cross the Strait with her, along with their proposed route. But the Soviets had given no other indication they were going to open the border; they had barely acknowledged Cox's existence. Maybe they thought she was like all those other screwballs who had attempted to cross the Strait. And what if the Soviet government opened the border and no support boats were available? Pat Omiak, the mayor of Little Diomede Island, had talked to Joe Coplan, the project director, about a rental fee of $30,000 for *umiaks* and guides. Cox had nowhere near that kind of money. But those *umiaks* were the only boats on Little Diomede Island. Cox had asked Omiak to consider lowering the fee. He told her, without much encouragement, that he would have to discuss it with Little Diomede's walrus hunters. To make matters worse, the U.S. Navy had rejected Cox's request for collateral support, recommending that Cox contact the United States Coast Guard, which had a new cutter anchored off Nome. Cox had done that, but had heard nothing back, and the kind of safety net the Coast Guard could provide was almost mandatory. Uncertain as how to resolve the issue, Cox had called Bruce Evans, an assistant to Alaska Senator Frank Murkowski. Then she telephoned Gene Fisher at the Seattle Organizing Committee and Ed Salazar at the U.S. State Department to get their recommendations. Salazar and Fisher advised Cox they would relay her concern to their Soviet contacts, but now it seemed even their efforts had gone for naught. After so much work and so many years, the whole project seemed on the verge of unraveling. Cox found it difficult to figure out what to do next, or what could have been done differently, or more effectively. Since there didn't seem to be much, all Cox could do was wait.

Following her scouting trip to Little Diomede Island in the company of an ABC-TV camera crew, Cox returned to Nome to continue training and acclimating herself to Alaskan water temperatures. Dr. William Nyboer, a cardiologist at the University of Michigan, would arrive a week later and begin testing his medical equipment. He would be joined by his son, Dr. Jan Nyboer, Dr. William Keatinge, project director Joe Coplan, and Maria Sullivan, a longtime Cox friend. Keatinge, flying in from the University of London Medical College, specialized in the physiology and treatment of immersion hypothermia. The younger Dr. Nyboer was an ophthalmologist interested in sports medicine, a captain in the Naval Reserve in Anchorage, and a triathlete. A rental house in Nome would serve as their base of operation. When the time came, they would all fly to Wales, where they would ride the weekly mail helicopter to Little Diomede Island. It was the cheapest way to get there, and the only one

Cox could afford. But that was *if* the time came. If it didn't, Cox had done a lot of work for nothing.

Cox and her supporters had generated nearly $160,000 to cover air fare, lodging, boat rentals, medical supplies, and equipment, including everything from tents, sleeping bags, float coats, rain gear, insulated boots, hats, socks, and gloves to water bottles, cook sets, stoves, compasses, flashlights, hot packs, thermoses, and waterproof matches. They had spoken to scores of people. The project had been endorsed by Alaska Governor Steve Cowper, U.S. Ambassador Steven Rhinesmith, the U.S. State Department, several congressmen, and the people planning the Goodwill Games. A lot of media heavyweights supported her swim, if only in the interest of boosting circulation. *The Los Angeles Times* had a reporter en route to Alaska; *People* magazine had dispatched a reporter and a photographer; a documentary had been planned. After some misgivings, ABC-TV agreed to do a special on the swim. Joe Novella, an ABC-TV producer, and Randy Tolbin, his cameraman, had already shot footage, and Novella had come up with a terrific theme. He wanted to link Cox's idea of the border opening to Mikhail Gorbachev's policy of *glasnost*. But Moscow remained silent and time was running short. The Soviets knew that Cox wanted to make the swim in less than two weeks. She figured something was wrong, but didn't know what, or why. If the Soviets refused to give her permission to cross the Strait, should she go for it anyway? Or, should she go as far as the International Dateline and call it a moral victory? What were the repercussions of going all the way?

As Lynne mulled over her dilemma and options, Bob Walsh grubbed around Moscow ministries where he made a significant discovery. The key to the Cox swim might be the Soviet Peace Committee. Staffed by a number of young Soviets willing to take on innovative initiatives and argue on their behalf in the interest of improving international relations, the Peace Committee had assisted an American named Chris Senie achieve his goal of participating in a bicycle ride for peace with several Soviets and Scandinavians. In cooperation with the USSR State Sports Committee, it had supported American Cynthia Lazaroff's efforts to lead a mountaineering expedition involving U.S. and Soviet youths. Some years before, it had participated in the off-the-record Dartmouth Conferences organized by *Saturday Review* editor Norman Cousins. The Soviet Peace Committee might have supported a more sinister purpose. In addition to reported claims of covert Soviet funding of Western anti-nuclear groups, Soviet officials had acknowledged the benefits they received from the political pressure those groups brought to bear on their governments. In 1982, John McMahon, deputy director of the Central Intelligence Agency, testified before Congress that the USSR had channeled $100 million annually to the Western disarmament movement and that such funds "enabled the movement to grow beyond its own capabilities."

Bob didn't know much about the Peace Committee beyond the fact that it acted as the Soviet Union's "authorized fighters for peace," and that it had been sponsoring the travel of Soviet peace delegations to the United States for fifteen years. The Peace Committee might be helpful in securing Soviet approval for Cox to swim the Strait. So when Bob returned to Seattle, he dispatched a telex to Generikh A. Borovick, the head of the Peace Committee, and followed up his meeting with Vjacheslav Gavrilin of the USSR State Sports Committee with another one.

Telex ID# 411426 MIR SU
Generikh A. Borovick
President
Soviet Peace Committee

Dr. Mr. Borovick:

The national press in the United States is heavily following the results of the request by Mr. Joe Coplan of New York to have Lynne Cox swim the U.S. island Little Diomede to the Soviet island Big Diomede in the Bering Strait. There is daily national coverage and everyone is awaiting the answer from the Soviet side. As we discussed in our meeting last week, we want, as friends, to advise you of the tremendous interest here. Perhaps you could check on situation again. If there is any change, would appreciate your letting me know the status.

Best Regards,

Bob Walsh, CEO
Seattle 1990 Goodwill Games

Telex ID#411287 PRIZ SU
Vjacheslav Gavrilin
Vice Chairman
USSR State Sports Committee

Dr. Mr. Gavrilin:

Regarding our discussion concerning the Lynne Cox swim across the Bering Strait, there has been a tremendous amount of press in the United States as to whether permission will be granted from your side. We appeal to you to act promptly.

Best Regards,

Bob Walsh, CEO
Seattle 1990 Goodwill Games

On Bob's behalf, Gene Fisher telexed similar messages to more than a dozen Soviet officials, particularly imploring Marat Gramov, head of the USSR State Sports Committee, and Henrikas Yushkiavitshus of Gosteleradio, for quick approval. In them, Bob, via Fisher, argued that the Cox swim had become a critical component of the Goodwill Games, a natural extension of the successful exchanges that had taken place between the U.S. and USSR, and the most obvious opportunity yet to demonstrate that *glasnost* was genuine. Bob and Gene also informed Gramov and Yushkiavitshus that Cox planned to make the swim with or without their approval, although Bob had no way of knowing that because even Cox hadn't determined how far she would swim. Bob simply figured he didn't need to know. It was only important what he told the Soviets. If they prevented Cox from swimming the Strait, or made some kind of incident out of it, they would look ridiculous and *glasnost* would seem hopelessly bankrupt. For good measure, Bob pointed out that the American press remained poised in high anticipation, awaiting Soviet approval, which was not necessarily the case. Bob only intended to manufacture an issue in which Soviet honor and ingenuity would seem at stake on the one hand with urgency rising on the other. Bob had employed similar tricks several times; they nearly always worked. The break Bob hoped for came on July 23 when the USSR State Sports Committee sent him a telex at Seattle Organizing Committee headquarters. While promising nothing, it said:

Telex ID# 41128A PRIZ SU
Attention Mr. Bob Walsh
CEO
1990 Seattle Goodwill Games

USSR State Committee for Physical Culture and Sports considers now the possibility of rendering the assistance in swim attempt in view of carrying on medical experiment. Please advise urgently the following information: schedule time and route of swim; means of transportation of scientists and the accompanying persons on the route of the swim; composition of participants from the USA; data necessary for visa arrangements (surname, first name, date of birth, passport number, occupation, and route of their travel back to the USA); detailed list of services provided by the Soviet side. Waiting your urgent reply.

Best Regards,

USSR State Sports Committee

Fisher provided the information, but a week lapsed without another word from Moscow. Although Soviet silence irked and unnerved Cox, Bob Walsh found it predictable. It always took the Soviets much longer to say yes or no than the average American imagined. And if it was going to be yes, the Soviets had to do A,B,C,D,E, F, and G before nodding in the affirmative. The Soviet government often waited until the very last minute before approving anything, if it approved it at all. On July 30, with Cox clueless in Alaska, Bob received notice from Yushkiavitshus that he would speak on Cox's behalf to other ministers.

Telex ID#411287B PRIZ SU
Attention Mr. Bob Walsh
CEO
1990 Seattle Goodwill Games

Regarding the Lynne Cox/Bering Strait Swim, the proposal is being considered and we will advise definite decision later. No top sports officials had previously been aware of the project.
Best Regards,

Henrikas Yushkiavitshus,
Gosteleradio

To the contrary, all the top Soviets, including Marat Gramov, had been aware of Cox's desire to swim the Strait from the beginning. Even Mikhail Gorbachev knew about it. Gramov and Gorbachev, close personal friends, had received telexes about the Cox swim from Alaska Governor Steve Cowper a month earlier on June 30. Joe Coplan had telexed Gramov on the same subject a week before that. The Soviets had ignored the cables, hoping Cox would give up and go away, which plainly wouldn't happen as long as Bob Walsh strode the planet. He believed the swim constituted an historic first that eclipsed all previous Soviet-American exchanges, and would build a stronger base for the Goodwill Games. Despite Yushkiavitshus's more encouraging telex, Bob continued his lobbying efforts, the highlight of which was a meeting in the Kremlin, during which Bob told twenty Soviets who insisted the Cox swim was impossible for security reasons that, since this was the era of *glasnost*, they were all full of crap.

Lynne Cox worried eleven time zones removed from this loop, consoled only by her personal preparations to swim the Bering Strait. Each day, she worked out for almost two hours in the 52° to 56° swells of Norton Sound on the southern side of the Seward Peninsula, where walrus and seal preyed and migrating bowhead whales spouted plumes in the distance. Cox often complained that the water temperatures, for her at least, seemed almost tropical. When Dr. William Nyboer Sr. and Maria Sullivan arrived, they set up a tent with a cot and table where they placed their medical equipment. They had brought along an electrocardiogram machine to measure Cox's heart rate, which registered fifty-two to fifty-seven beats per minute during her training sessions and as low as forty-four beats per minute when she wasn't training. They had a rectal probe with a forty-foot chord that would trail after Cox as she swam the Strait. The physicians would use it to measure Cox's core temperature, hoping not to diagnose hypothermia. They also had a portable defibrillator in case Cox went into cardiac arrest, an infrared heat flow measuring device to gauge Cox's skin temperature, and a machine to measure Cox's electrical activity. Dr. William Nyboer had written extensively on that subject, and the development in the early 1980s of commercial instruments for quick, accurate measurement of electrical conductivity allowed him to apply his research techniques to field studies of hypothermia.

When a sudden storm overturned the tent that housed the power generator for the equipment, the Cox medical team moved the field laboratory inside the rental house. In another part of the house, where the media milled, the phone rang constantly: CNN, NBC, NHK Japanese television, CKO Canada, the BBC in Great Britain, ABC Radio,

Reuters, *The Anchorage Daily News, The Long Beach Press Telegram, The Philadelphia Enquirer, The Orange County Register, The Boston Globe, The Manchester Union Leader, The New York Times, The Chicago Sun Times.* Everybody, including Libby Riddles, the first woman to win the Iditarod Sled Dog Race and Nome's town priest and minister, wanted to talk to Cox — everyone except the Soviet officials Cox was so anxious to hear from. Cox did, however, hear from the United States Coast Guard. It would not support the project. If the swim was too dangerous, the Coast Guard wouldn't permit Cox to do it. And if the swim wasn't too dangerous, Cox didn't need the Coast Guard. Cox also heard from Pat Omiak, the mayor of Little Diomede Island. His news was more encouraging. He had agreed to drop the rental fee for the *umiaks* from $30,000 to $5,000, still way too much.

As Cox fretted about support boats, she didn't know the Soviets had good reason for not calling yet. They were still doing A,B,C,D,E,F, and G — mobilizing men and equipment, contacting doctors and interpreters, figuring out the appropriate food and gifts to transport, deploying the Soviet Navy to the Bering Strait, and arranging for the military commander on Big Diomede Island to build special ramps so the American team could land their walrus-skin boats on the island's rocky shoreline. The *umiaks* could not land without ramps; the rocks would puncture them. The Soviet government had also been busy identifying the individuals it wanted to serve on the official welcoming committee for Lynne Cox and arranging for them to fly to Siberia. Most of them, including Dr. Rita Zakharova, a sports medicine physician assigned to set up a rewarming tent for Cox on Big Diomede's beach, had never met each other. In fact, most of them had never heard of Big Diomede Island, whose Russian name was Ostrov Ratmanova. Some of the Soviets en route to Siberia tried to figure out the location of Ostrov Ratmanova, but ran into two problems: Soviet maps were hard to find; most maps excluded Ostrov Ratmanova for reasons of state security.

Cox and her delegation gathered one night at Nome's Golden Nugget Hotel to watch the ABC-TV special Joe Novella had produced. Novella had, Cox thought, created an inspiring piece. Using a film clip of Gorbachev stepping off a plane, the narrator ended the special by saying, "The question is, will Secretary General Gorbachev give Lynne Cox permission to make her swim?" Immediately after the telecast, ABC overnighted copies of the tape to Soviet Ambassador Yuri

Dubinin in Washington, D.C., and Gorbachev in the Kremlin. After the show, the Cox entourage debated over whether Cox should swim to Big Diomede in the absence of Soviet approval. The doctors, Keatinge and Nyboer Sr., argued against it; the journalists argued for it. Both Rich Roberts of *The Los Angeles Times* and Jack Kelley of *People* magazine made the case that Cox owed it to herself to go all the way. Besides, it would be a great story. And if the Soviets threw her in prison, that would be a greater story. Dr. Keatinge disagreed, pointing out that an unauthorized crossing might create an international incident, and that he did not want to participate in such a venture. That gave Cox pause for thought: If she chose to swim the breadth of the Strait, did she really want to do so without her doctors?

Still no word from Moscow. Then the weather up and down the Alaskan coast turned foul. Fog rolled in, smothering the Diomedes. In Nome, the wind blew so hard the airport had to be closed, forcing the cancellation of several flights from Anchorage. Cox and her entourage began to pack their gear for the trip to Wales, where they would be met by a helicopter pilot named Eric Pentilla who would fly them out to Little Diomede on the mail flight when conditions were right. Cox didn't know how long they would have to wait before they could fly to Wales, but she found out soon enough. Poor weather grounded her team all of Tuesday, August 4, and for a good part of Wednesday, August 5. But early on Wednesday, as the fog cleared over the western half of the Bering Strait, the Soviets left the Siberian mainland for Big Diomede Island so they could set up tents, check equipment, and off-load supplies. In the early afternoon, Cox and her team got the word: Although weather conditions weren't optimum, they were taking off for Wales.

The flight turned harrowing. Caught in crosswinds, the craft rocked across the sky, landing just as the fog rolled back in. The good news: they had made it. The bad news: Pat Omiak told Coplan he still hadn't committed to a reasonable rental fee for his flimsy boats. The better news — or was it worse news? — was that Big Diomede teemed with activity. Two Soviet vessels, almost the size of football fields, had anchored about a mile off the southern end of the island. Soviet soldiers flew transport helicopters from the decks of the vessels to the shoreline, where they had set up tents and posted guards. Omiak told *The Orange County Register* that he hadn't seen so much happening on Big Diomede Island since the Cuban missile crisis, concluding that the Soviets were preparing to blockade the Strait.

Omiak did not trust the Russians. He once had relatives on Big Diomede, and the Soviets had removed them long ago to the Siberian mainland so Big Diomede could be transformed into a military installation. He immediately radioed the Alaskan National Guard, which alerted the United States Air Force, which sent up planes to check out the situation. When the Soviets saw the U.S. jets on their radar screens, they sent up their own planes. As these fighter planes checked each other out over the Bering Strait, thousands of miles from nowhere, Cox and her team fell asleep on the floor underneath the billiard tables in the igloo-shaped Wales Community Center. Back in Seattle, Bob Walsh received the telex he had been waiting for.

Telex ID# 411287B PRIZ SU
URGENT
Attention Mr. Robert Walsh
President Seattle Organizing Committee
1990 Goodwill Games

RE: LYNNE COX BERING STRAIT SWIM

We have received and noted information on participants in the expedition. Visas are not required for this group to cross the Bering Strait. We are ready to render assistance to Lynne Cox in the swim. Your group will be met at International Dateline. Please inform where Miss Cox is at present and what day until August 12 she intends to carry out swim. We need exact Greenwich and Moscow time.

PLEASE URGENTLY ADVISE

Best Regards,

USSR State Sports Committee.

Gene Fisher promptly dispatched a telex to the USSR State Sports Committee:

Telex ID#412287 PRIZ SU
Vjacheslav Gavrilin
Vice Chairman
USSR State Sports Committee

Dear Mr. Gavrilin:

Miss Cox is in Wales, Alaska. Either she or Joe Coplan can be reached at telephone numbers 907-664-3501, 907-664-3671, or 907-664-9931. Regarding your requests on date and time, it is difficult to answer specifically. In discussions this morning with Miss Cox, weather on Strait is poor. Suggest you call directly to Cox or Coplan at above numbers for up-to-the-minute information. Understand weather conditions look good for tomorrow. We stand by ready to help and can coordinate all information if necessary. Thanks a million for your assistance. Your favorable participation will be widely noted in U.S. press.

Thank You,
Gene Fisher
Bob Walsh & Associates

The Soviets had not only become concerned with looking bad in the eyes of the world by denying Cox permission to swim; they — and "they" apparently included Mikhail Gorbachev — had been genuinely impressed, if not swayed, by the ABC-TV tape they received from the network. Novella had produced a superb piece about Cox, graphically underscoring all of Bob Walsh's verbal entreaties and harangues. The Soviets had determined to seize the moment, offering to render any assistance they could.

When Cox heard the news, she almost couldn't believe it. But the USSR State Sports Committee had sent a confirming telex to The Athletics Congress in Indianapolis and United States Swimming Inc. in Colorado Springs. Ed Salazar of the U.S. State Department, one of Cox's staunchest supporters, had confirmed it; so had Soviet Ambassador Yuri Dubinin. And on top of that, Pat Omiak had agreed to rent the Cox contingent a pair of *umiaks* and guides for just $500, a $29,500 discount off Omiak's original, gouging quote.

The Soviets had arranged to have a small flotilla of boats patrol the area around the International Dateline equipped with radar equipment. In case fog covered the Strait, the radar would detect the small motor boats accompanying Cox. While the Soviets wanted to know when Cox would begin her swim, only so they would be ready for her, her exact moment of immersion in the Strait obviously could not be determined with any kind of accuracy. It all depended on the weather. Cox told Fisher she planned to swim the following morning, or on any subsequent morning at 8 a.m. What it really came down to was that she would swim as soon as the Strait granted her permission.

There would be a signal: red and blue balloons would be released from the shoreline of Little Diomede Island. The Soviets would see them easily through binoculars from Big Diomede, provided fog did not obscure their view. But if fog developed, that could become a huge problem. Big Diomede had no public telephone service. If Cox needed to send a message three miles across the Strait, it would have to go through Moscow, eleven time zones away, or Seattle, which would then relay the information to Moscow. Moscow would then contact one of the large vessels anchored off Big Diomede Island, and the Soviet Navy would relay the message to the welcoming committee on the Big Diomede coastline. But all this depended in large degree on whether Little Diomede's telephone worked. So the synchronization of the swim effectively hinged on one telephone that tended to malfunction and the unpredictable whims of the Strait, which could throw a mean fit at any moment.

The welcoming committee on Big Diomede had completed preparations for Cox's arrival. Rita Zakharova's rewarming tent reposed on a bluff just above a snowbank where she hoped Cox would land. The military commander had made sure the wooden ramps for Cox's support boats were in place. With the weather on Big Diomede suddenly favorable, the welcoming committee simply assumed Cox had started to swim. It waited and watched, peered and wondered. The welcoming committee couldn't figure out what might be keeping her. When some of the Soviet soldiers scanned the Little Diomede shoreline through their binoculars, they saw nothing except an occasional false alarm — usually seals. The welcoming committee didn't know that Cox remained grounded in Wales, still enveloped by fog, as Cox had no way to communicate with Big Diomede directly. And for whatever reason, Fisher could not be reached to convey another change in plans to Moscow.

Later that afternoon, when the fog began to clear, Cox's helicopter pilot, Eric Pentilla, told the group to pack; they were going to Little Diomede Island. They would be shuttled out in three groups, Cox in the second one. As evening approached, Cox again stood on the beach of Little Diomede Island. The fog had lifted.

"We didn't know if it was going to be foggy or clear or where the Russians were going to meet us," Cox explained later. "There was a fear of the cold, a fear of the current. Little Diomede, like Big Diomede, basically looked like a volcano on the water. It's very rocky and misty, and no earth to really grow anything. The people pretty much survive on walrus meat. I kind of wondered why they would choose to live there. It's dark so much of the year, so cold and so windy. I wondered how they could be happy."

While Cox tried to sleep on the floor of Little Diomede's only schoolhouse, the Inuits stayed up to party. Opening a border after forty years, they reasoned, made an evening of profound merrymaking mandatory. But as they danced and sang, more bad weather moved into the Bering Strait. By the morning of August 7, it was bleak and foggy with a hint of drizzle. Up early, Cox was anxious to get started. But when she saw fog again shrouding the Strait, she had an eerie recollection of the night she had been lost in the fog while swimming near Catalina Island off the California coast. It really worried her; 45° water was not the place to get lost in the fog, and this water was not only colder than that, it was probably much colder farther out in the Strait. As frustrated as she was worried, Cox wanted to leave at 8 o'clock in the morning, but communication problems with the Soviets thwarted her. And after partying all night, the Inuits had slept late, further holding up the swim.

"The fog was getting thicker and thicker," recalled Cox. "I was doing my best not to go nuts. I asked Dr. Nyboer to see if he could move things along. In the meantime, we've told the Soviets we were going to meet them at a certain time, and that time has already passed."

When Cox learned to her dismay that she would not be able to go at 8 a.m., she readjusted her start time to 9 a.m. Dr. Nyboer told her not to get her hopes up just yet because the Inuits still weren't ready. While they got ready, Cox had an apple juice and bagel breakfast and Dr. Nyboer prepared to take some pre-swim readings. Once the swim started, Dr. Nyboer would closely monitor Cox's core temperature, skin temperature, heart rate, and vital signs, including her blood pressure. The numbers amazed Dr. Nyboer. Cox's pulse rate registered forty-four, her skin temperature 70°, and her core temperature was 100.2°, three above normal. After Dr. Nyboer left, Dr. Keatinge arrived holding a "thermal pill," a $1,000 unit he wanted Cox to swallow.

The thermal pill would allow Keatinge to monitor Cox's internal temperature during the swim. But since the thermal pill was experimental, Keatinge also had Cox insert a rectal probe. It had trailing wires that would be attached to a machine Keatinge would also monitor as Cox swam the Strait.

Eventually everyone in the village turned out to watch Cox go where no human being had gone before. Two problems developed almost immediately. While some of the Inuits inflated the red and blue balloons to signal the start of her swim, and while some carried *umiaks* from their racks and placed them in the water, Cox discovered that many of the Inuits planned to tag along in six additional boats. They wanted to share in the celebration of the border opening. Since the Soviets only expected the pre-approved party, that was a major snafu. None of the Inuits had any clearance to cross the International Dateline, but they had decided to go as far as the Soviets would allow them to go. Just as bad, the weather had deteriorated and none of the Inuits' boats contained lifejackets, all of the boats were old and in disrepair, and none of the Inuits knew how to swim. Cox couldn't figure out which was worse – that, or the fact that one of the Inuit guides, a man named David Soolook, suddenly showed up carrying rifles. He distrusted the Soviets and wanted to take the rifles with him, as though that would be enough to take on the Soviet Red Army. Still, it took a considerable piece of diplomacy by Cox to convince Soolook to leave the rifles behind.

Finally, the moment arrived. Soolook guided a *umiak* full of journalists; Pat Omiak and rest of the crew rode in another. Dr. Nyboer and Dr. Keatinge climbed into an inflated Zodiac they had located at the last minute. The contingent planned to motor up to the southern tip of Little Diomede to the village of Inalik, where, to counteract the current, Cox would start her swim.

Cox wore a black, red, and white-striped Speedo bathing suit, a yellow cap and goggles. Her usual preparation for a cold-water endurance swim involved an acclimation process lasting twenty to thirty minutes. But after her odyssey through Soviet red tape, with the Inuits late and the fog thickening, Cox harbored no mood to dally. So she waded off the coast of Inalik as the Inuits cheered and tossed red and blue balloons into the water. She felt excited, awestruck, and nervous, and most of all was fully aware she was about to swim, her insulating fat and favorable currents permitting, to a strip of land no American had set foot on in forty years. Lynne Cox took one last upright look at the icy, roiling expanse confronting her and, at 10:50 a.m., eased herself into the icy monster. The date: August 7, 1987.

Even the woman who had survived Glacier Bay in Alaska couldn't have been prepared for this kind of cold. The Strait felt like liquid ice, and the sudden shock of it almost knocked the air out of her lungs. Equally onerous, Cox slipped on a rock and ripped her thigh open on sharp clamshells. Cox saw blood trickling down her leg, but was so focused that she ignored the pain, and didn't even think about the sharks. For the first few minutes she sprinted, swimming seventy-two strokes per minute instead of her customary sixty-four.

"I needed to generate heat," Cox said later. "I was also concerned that I needed to have energy throughout the swim, so I didn't want to swim too fast. There was this whole balancing act: the water is icy cold, this is finally the day after eleven years of work, and you've got to make it. By the time the swim started the visibility was down to about fifty feet. I didn't know where I was going."

The *umiaks* positioned on either side of Cox, and just below a large flock of auklets, were supposed to guide her to Big Diomede Island, but almost from the start they fell behind. In no time they fell too far behind and Cox briefly lost sight of them. She remembered the night off Catalina, fear swelling inside her. The Strait remained clogged with fog, closing out the light, and it was drizzling. If Cox got lost she would die before her support crew ever found her, if they found her at all. She grew agitated. Her support crew didn't seem to know where it was going. On the other hand, none of them had ever done anything like this, nor had any of the Inuit guides. Cox couldn't see much of anything and feared that she might miss Big Diomede altogether. Every minute she strayed off course in these 42° waters would severely compromise her chances.

In the Zodiac, Dr. Nyboer and Dr. Keatinge wrestled with the medical equipment, trying to get it to work. Cox swam as fast as her arms would move, but her hands became numb and red splotches appeared on her shoulders. She wondered how the Soviets would see her. They couldn't have seen the Inuits release the balloons. Too foggy. Nyboer and Keating shouted, Nyboer wanting her to roll over so he could take her temperature. Cox had to do it, but didn't want to. The temperature reading would steal precious minutes. Worse, when she rolled over and backstroked, she couldn't produce as much heat as when she swam freestyle.

The first attempt at a reading misfired when a wave rocked the Zodiac, nearly catapulting Nyboer into the Bering Strait. Recovering his balance, he tried again, finding the results alarming. Cox's core temperature, 100.2° at the start of her swim, had dropped to 97°, and she had only been in the water for about a half an hour. She hadn't expected that. Ninety-seven bordered on mild hypothermia. Her cut-off temperature was 94°. All along Cox had planned to stay in the Strait no more than three hours. Anything more and she risked arrhythmia or cardiac arrest. She tried to pick up the pace. An hour into the swim, Cox wondered if she had reached Soviet waters, but saw no sign of Soviets ships. She listened for engines, hearing nothing, not even a vibration. Visibility remained at approximately ten feet. Perhaps she had drifted too far north. Had she really missed Big Diomede? Keatinge and Nyboer, paddling some distance behind her, couldn't help. Soolook, who had caught up to Cox, consulted his compass. According to the reading, the group had drifted alarmingly off course. Soolook quickly made a correction; Cox and the other *umiak* followed. She didn't know what had become of the Little Diomede villagers. Were they still somewhere in the Strait? Or had they turned back?

"I assumed the Eskimo crew would know which way to go," Cox said later, "but it had never been on the other side of the border. The Eskimos didn't know which way the currents went. We couldn't see anything and the current was pushing us to the north. The currents ran one to two knots and I swam at basically two to two and a half knots, but my speed slowed down in that water temperature. I didn't know how fast I was going. I couldn't feel my arms most of the time."

The drizzle turned into sleet and Cox's hands began to splay. Her face felt nothing at all like her face. Her teeth chattered. The doctors wanted another reading. Although Cox didn't want to slow down again, she rolled over. The doctors couldn't get a reading. They tried again. The equipment didn't function. Nobody knew how far north they had drifted, but Soolook and Omiak figured they better turn south.

Close to panic, Cox suddenly felt a vague tremble beneath her body. She listened more closely. It had to be a boat. She couldn't see it, but she could hear it and so could her crew. Someone shot a flare. Her crew shouted. Then, out of the fog, the Soviet boat appeared, about fifteen yards from her. Exhausted, half-frozen, but exhilarated, it dawned on Lynne Cox that she had crossed the International Dateline. From one of the other boats came a shout.

"What time is it?" yelled Coplan.

Lynne Cox knew. She summoned the strength to shout back. "It's tomorrow!"

The border had finally come down. It was now August 8, 1987.

Lynne Cox had visualized this moment for eleven years, but the reality of it was almost unfathomable. Fifty years ago to the day, a peace bridge had opened at Niagara Falls, linking Canada and the

United States. That event was nice; this one was momentous. Cox now swam less than a mile from shore, but her stroke rate had fallen fast and she was suddenly very cold. The water temperature had dropped to 38° and the current had picked up. She felt like she'd been pitched into a washing machine, and her skin burned. But just ahead the fog had cleared and she could make out the rocky cliffs of Big Diomede Island.

With Cox less than fifty feet from shore, the Soviets shouted and pointed south toward the beach. Cox strained to look, finally locating the welcoming committee about a half mile away, milling about on the rock-strewn coastline. When Cox came within ten yards of shore, Keatinge urged her to stop. A rock jutted out of the water. If Cox touched it, she had made it. But everything Cox had ever done had been about extending herself. Would she be satisfied to stop here? She desperately wanted to stop, but couldn't. Because of the cliffs and the rocks, the Soviets had been unable to reach her. So she would reach them.

When Cox made a left turn, paralleling the shore, the Soviets let up a cheer. Cox asked a Soviet soldier in a nearby boat if he would bring the boat closer to her. She wanted them to arrive together, and they did. A man in a green uniform extended a hand toward Cox. So did Vladimir McMillan, a reporter for TASS and the official interpreter for the welcoming committee. Cox pulled off her goggles, stuck them in her mouth, and extended her arms, half smiling. Together the two Soviets pulled Cox out of the Strait. Not far away, a Siberian women held a beautiful bouquet of wildflowers. The day had dawned sunny and lovely on this side of the Strait, Siberia in all its splendor. Time of the crossing: two hours, six minutes, eleven years.

"At first I couldn't get out of the water because the embankment was so steep," recalled Cox. "In the meantime, the journalists' boat and the medical boats were pulling ashore and they were trying to get out as quickly as they could so they could greet me and make sure I was okay. I found out afterwards that the people on the boats never thought I was in distress, or that the swim was difficult. But a big part of the reason for that was that I didn't want to show any distress. Keatinge and Nyboer would have pulled me out of the water. If they knew that

Swimmer Is Bearing Straight for Russia

Los Angeles Times Headline,
August, 1987

168

my teeth were chattering and I was having a hard time keeping my fingers together they would have pulled me out. So I showed no distress."

Cox's legs wobbled so much she could barely stand, and she shivered uncontrollably. The Soviets stood in awe, never unwavering in their belief until now that the water temperature was too cold for human survival. But in the event Cox proved them wrong, they were prepared. They quickly draped Cox in a heavy blanket. One of the Siberian women gave her a pair of beaded sealskin slippers. To Cox's amazement, they fit perfectly. In addition to the rewarming tent, the Soviets had set up two buffet tables manned by a waiter wearing a white smock. He served hot tea, bread, dried fish, and chocolate-covered coconut candy. The Soviets overwhelmed Cox with such applause that she shook even harder.

Unaware that she might be in physical danger, the Soviets held an impromptu press conference that included a man from Radio Moscow, a woman from *Pravda*, and someone from *Vremya*. The Soviets had transported people from all over the Soviet Union to meet them on Big Diomede. Keatinge wanted to get Cox into the rewarming tent, but the Soviet journalists started making speeches. The TV cameras rolled, microphones poking at Cox's face.

"The journalists started asking me four-part questions," remembered Cox. "I was just trying to get my mouth to form sentences and they're asking me things like, 'Do you think your swim will help to generate goodwill between the countries and help increase the chances of a missile treaty between the U.S. and Soviet Union?' And, 'What do you think about the INF treaty?' I was thinking, How do I sound intelligent when my body has gone through everything and I can hardly stand up?"

No one had briefed Cox on what to say; no one in the world but Cox ever thought she would get there. As best she could, she said the reason she swam the Strait was to reach into the future and symbolically bridge the distance between the United States and Soviet Union. And that's about all she could say. Cox's legs trembled and she felt she would collapse. Although coherent, Cox understandably slurred her speech. Dr. Keatinge finally hustled her into a charcoal-heated tent, placing Cox in a sleeping bag. Dr. Keatinge and Dr. Rita Zacharova applied hot water bottles on the back of Cox's neck, under each armpit, and in her groin area. A few minutes later, Keatinge and Nyboer hooked up the rectal probe and measured Cox's temperature. Normally,

Bob Walsh with Lynne Cox at a Tbilisi press conference

it didn't drop significantly during a cold-water swim. This time it had dropped dramatically, registering 94°, just shy of severe hypothermia.

Right after the swim, Cox's heart thumped at 140 beats per minute, way above normal. But within ninety minutes it had decreased to eighty beats a minute. Outside Cox's tent, Joe Coplan, who had brought along a plaque from Alaska Governor Steve Cowper and gifts of black bread, salt, tobacco, and candy, held court.

"Nobody else will ever do this, not in a hundred years," Coplan told the crowd on the Big Diomede beach. "She's the only one."

"I felt a huge sense of accomplishment," Cox admitted later. "Not just not for me, but for the team and for the Soviets who opened their doors to us. I really felt like we had made an opening. But I was also sad that it was over."

The Big Diomede beach party lasted three hours, after which Cox, her crew, and the journalists motored back across the Strait to Little Diomede Island. The villagers had not gone all the way; the Soviets had turned them back at the International Dateline, so they were in a festive mood, made more so later in the day when the villagers spotted a dead baby whale floating in the Strait. They caught it, dragged it ashore, and sliced it up with a chain saw, distributing the meat to each member of the village. They would honor it, freeze it, and eat it. It would sustain them. And then the Inuits made the most respectful gesture it was possible for them to make: To the woman who had accomplished one of the most remarkable things they were ever likely to witness, they offered the heart of the baby whale.

An Onion
A Day

*Bob is like that Waldo character.
You know, 'Where's Waldo?' Bob just
keeps popping up everywhere.*

— Julia Church, Sagamore Associates,
Washington, D.C.

*S*ince cockroaches swarmed over dinner plates, cats prowled the corridors, and bathrooms matched the most malodorous pits on earth, sane Soviet citizens took all precautions to avoid hospitals and medical clinics. A vast majority lacked hot water, and some had no water or sanitation system at all. Many offered little more than beds and used syringes, and almost all had a dearth of operating tables, lamps, gurneys, blood transfusion systems, bandages, cotton, thermometers, diagnostic devices, and sterile surgical gloves. Most women's consultation centers had no fetal heart monitors, ultrasound units, or equipment for monitoring labor and delivery, contributing significantly to the Soviet Union's dismal infant mortality rate. Analgesics, insulin, aspirin, and other painkillers rarely could be found.

Antibiotics were weak, forcing patients to receive injections every few hours.

In most cases, patients took the responsibility of supplying their own food, medicine, bedding, bandages, and plasma. Doctors and nurses were scarce; as ordinary state employees, they earned less money than factory workers, bus drivers, and butchers, and frequently moonlighted in other jobs. When they did show up for work, it often required a bribe to get them to tend to patients or wander off in the woods and cut a splint from a birch tree.

The Soviet Union had some ability to deliver decent medical care, and the best Soviet doctors were excellent. But ordinary citizens rarely received treatment from them. The good doctors selected their patients through a system based on the ability of patients to offer a mutual exchange of favors. Patients who had nothing to offer scrambled for care as best they could. A letter writer to the newspaper *Literaturnaia Gazetta* insinuated that some Soviet doctors didn't know enough to put the gauze on before the tape and then quoted a Soviet surgeon as saying, "What do you want? Our medicine is free, and therefore worth nothing."

Many Soviet citizens didn't do much to promote their own health. They bathed infrequently, poor hygiene causing an unusual condition that not only required medical attention, but qualified for induction into the Yuck Hall of Fame: Many men, even some women, developed painful, golf ball-sized sacks of puss in their armpits.

Until she got sick and wound up in a hospital in Riga, the capital of Latvia, Elana Arustamova had generally received decent medical care. Elana's parents were medical people and Elana had married a doctor. But when she became ill during a vacation, she was placed in what was considered a prestigious sanatorium, catering mainly to high-ranking military people. Elana got a fold-out canvas cot, no medicine, no treatment, no service, and nothing to eat. At least she had a cot; many patients did not and were simply forced to shuffle around the corridors. Elana became so terrified of the place that her husband flew back to his own clinic in Moscow so he could bring her medicine and food.

"If you want to have good medical," Elana explained later, "then you have to have your doctor. That means you take gifts to make sure he's interested, or she's interested, in taking care of you — some French perfume or French cognac, something like that."

172

At least Elana had been admitted to one of the better places. In the lousier ones, patients made liberal use of vodka, mixing it with honey to soothe a sore throat, or rubbing it on stiff joints, or using it to wash out a wound, which was probably preferable to washing wounds out with water. Patients ultimately consumed hospital vodka to the last drop so they could forget the whole excruciating exercise. Since the Soviets put so little money into biomedical science, doctors could not take care of a seriously ill patient. As *Pravda* reported, Soviet doctors fought like "warriors with bows and arrows."

Cardiac infarction killed more Soviet citizens than anything else, but the Soviet medical system rarely offered heart surgery, claiming it to be too risky, and it probably was. The Soviets didn't have adequate blood banking or plasma substitutes and lacked a coherent pharmaceutical industry. They imported — or tried to import — a majority of their drugs from other countries. Most vanished during transit. Most of those that didn't were stored in conditions in which they would not keep.

Even the good hospitals smacked of MASH units. The Soviet government spent an enormous amount of money building a cancer center in Moscow, only to pay for a triumph of shoddy workmanship. The slate tile on the first floor didn't fit together, making walking down a corridor a tricky proposition. In Voronezh, hospital rooms had not been repaired for decades. In fact, in one of those rooms, stucco fell from the ceiling, killing a patient. In the mid-1980s,

Republican Children's Hospital of the Ministry of Public Health of RSFSR.

Department of Hemodialysis

Tarasova Tamara, born on 11.03.1924. She came to the department 15.12.89.
AV-fistula formed 26.12.1989, and programmed hemodialysis began since 24.01.90.
There were blood urea - 19.0; blood creatinine - 697 before hemodialysis began (23.05.90)
The diurnal diuresis is here 1500/1500 ml with acception of 2 tables of furosemid 2 a day.
Blood group is O(I) Rh(+).
There is no contraindication for kidney transplantation.

D-r Nikolay Evreinov.
Moscow
Phone office 438-90-54
home 337-72-57

24.05.90.

173

Soviet officials in the Republic of Tajikistan boasted of pioneering the construction of cheap hospitals. One cost only 5,000 rubles, less than the cost of a new cow shed. The Soviet Union produced talented doctors and scientists, and no end of specialists. But Dr. Roy Farrell of Seattle's Group Health Cooperative, who headed up medical services for the Goodwill Games, observed during his visits to Moscow and Tashkent that most specialists didn't do anything.

"They wrote down a lot of prescriptions," recalled Dr. Farrell, "but nothing ever happened."

When Dr. Farrell made his initial visit to the Soviet Union, he immersed himself in Soviet medical ways, concluding that they amounted to a combination of dedicated, highly educated people who had some creative ideas about how to take care of patients with the limited resources at their disposal, and demented risk takers who used off-the-wall approaches that had no basis in science. The Soviets treated asthma, bronchitis, and other chronic respiratory diseases with invasive, even gruesome approaches, like snaking tubes into the lungs and squirting water or medicine on them. At first, Dr. Farrell couldn't figure out whether the Soviets had made a real leap forward in clinical treatment, or whether their procedures were baseless and simply subjected the patient to unnecessary grief. He finally concluded the latter. For example, he found the Soviets' use of

Posted on March 8, 1997

Need Surgery? Bring Vodka And A Bribe

Letter From Moscow
By Carol Matlack
Edited By Sandra Dallas

Ghostly pale, cancer patient Zinaida Smirnova huddles under a blanket at Moscow's Hematology Research Institute hospital. "It's very hard for us," she says, in the drab green room she shares with four others. The bedside call button doesn't work, and even if it did, nurses are scarce. Her family brings food, medicine, and fresh bedding. Several times a day, Smirnova hobbles down the hall to a toilet shared by 60 patients. Still, she feels lucky because a doctor gives her the chemotherapy she hopes will cure her.

Smirnova is a casualty of the collapse of one of the world's most complex health-care systems. As Boris N. Yeltsin's quintuple-bypass operation last year demonstrated, Russian medicine can still deliver first-class care. But ordinary Russians rarely get it. Most hospitals offer little more than beds. Patients supply everything from plasma to vodka for disinfecting wounds.

Health care in the Soviet Union was never up to Western standards. But the cash-strapped Russian government has slashed spending, leaving hospitals scrambling to survive. Inefficiencies compound the problem. So thousands of Russians die every year from lack of treatment that is routine elsewhere. Only about 2% of people who need heart bypasses, for instance, get them.

The crisis goes back to 1993, when the Kremlin dismantled the centralized Soviet-era health-care system and dumped responsibility for most hospitals onto regional governments. As part of the plan, employers were taxed 3.6% of their workers' wages, with the money going to regional medical cooperatives. Regional governments were expected to kick in enough to pay for health care for the nonworking population. If the program sounds like the Clinton Administration's failed 1993 health reform plan, it should: The Russian system is based on a model developed by Alan Enthoven, a Stanford University health-care economist who advised Clinton.

The Russian plan ran into trouble from the start. The tax is only a third of what's needed, and, at that, payment is spotty because some employers either don't pay workers or pay them in goods. Many Russians moonlight, with no record of their income. Meanwhile, local governments haven't come up with their shares. "In six months, we have gotten hardly a single kopeck," says Andrei Lishansky, deputy chief physician at Moscow's City Hospital No.1, a sprawling 1,600-bed complex.

high-pressure oxygen to treat a variety of infections, even diabetes, utterly draconian.

But Dr. Farrell also witnessed fascinating approaches to treatment. In the absence of high-tech screws and plates and the sterile conditions required to insert them into bones, a Russian-Jewish physician named Illazarov had developed a procedure for immobilizing fractures of the extremities. He created a device like a tinker-toy ring with bicycle spokes. Illazarov put the spokes through the bone and hooked it up to his tinker-toy ring, which he attached to the limb both below and above the fracture. Illazarov could tweak the thing and line it up perfectly by making a quarter turn here and a quarter turn there of the screws. With the fracture held rigidly in place, the patient could walk around in a day or two. An American patient with a similar fracture spent six weeks in traction. Soviet physicians used Illazarov's methods for bone lengthening, applying them in cases where patients had one leg shorter than another, and to elongate the bones of dwarfs. By tweaking these little nuts by a quarter of a turn each day, bones healed and elongated. It showed Dr. Farrell that bone could, over time, be molded almost like plastic.

Dr. Farrell found himself as dazzled by the Illazarov technique as he was disgusted by the filth in the hospitals. It came down to the fact that Soviet medicine was not a high priotiy in a country that sacrificed almost everything to maintain its defense and space programs. That being the case, most Soviet citizens endured the system or learned how to game it. And to the foreigners who encountered him, Vaso Margvelashvili reigned as the ultimate gamer.

A Georgian, Vaso Margvelashvili did not have the ordinary Georgian's dark, striking features. He could have been from anywhere, America, Canada, Russia, Holland, or England, and he spoke several languages fluently. When he translated Russian, it sounded as if he had spent all his life drinking vodka and eating borsht.

Bob with Jim Sheldon of the SOC, and Vaso Margvelashvili

He had all the inflections, mannerisms, and animations. When he spoke English, the slang, rhythm, and flow made him sound straight out of Des Moines, Iowa. Vaso had studied at the Institute of Foreign Languages in Tbilisi, and taken advanced language courses in Moscow, becoming so proficient that he ultimately was named Director of Foreign Relations for Gosteleradio in Georgia. With subsequent experience as a guide and interpreter for Intourist, coupled with an engaging personality, Vaso received many prestigious assignments. Among other Soviet visitors, Vaso helped host U.S. astronaut John Glenn, actor Peter Ustinov, British Prime Minister Margaret Thatcher, U.S. Senator Edward Kennedy, Supreme Court Justice Warren Berger, singer B.B. King, Dr. Armand Hammer of Occidental Petroleum, David Rockefeller, Archbishop Dimitrious The First of Constantinople, the reigning archbishops of Alexandria and Armenia, the Prime Minister of Ceylon, and the Crown Prince of Saudi Arabia. Vaso also worked on CBS's production of *Seven Days in May*, CNN's *Portrait of the USSR*, CBS's *Nature of Things,* and ABC's *Space Bridge Journalists*. He traveled throughout the Soviet Union, all over Europe, the Orient, and Middle East.

Not long after Lynne Cox swam the Bering Strait, Bob Walsh found himself ensconced at the National Hotel in Moscow in a room adjacent to one occupied by American singer Billy Joel. Part of that huge migration of prominent Americans to the Soviet Union in the summer of 1987, Joel had also been assigned to the National. One night, Bob and his traveling partner, SOC board member Mike Scallon, engaged in an evening of spontaneous mirth with Joel and Vaso Margvelashvili, his Soviet host, who later escorted Joel on a trip to Tbilisi for an impromptu jam session.

In addition to his brushes with the rich and famous, Vaso seemed to know practically every sick or dying child in the Soviet Union, and continually provided Bob with their names. A young Russian girl had a congenital heart defect. Bob and Gene Fisher arranged for her to undergo corrective surgery at Providence Hospital in Seattle. A Russian boy, Andrei Verinchek, had a pituitary deficiency, suffered from retarded growth, and required a certain hormone to correct the problem. Bob and Alexander Kozlovsky of the USSR State Sports Committee made it possible for Andrei and his mother, Natasha, to travel to the United States to receive help. Within eighteen months after his treatments began, Andrei had grown a full foot to five-foot-five, well within the normal range for males. Taking into account the follow-up appointments with physicians, the communication between American and Russian physicians, a two-year course of treatments, and the plane flights back and forth, the cost to treat Andrei reached nearly $30,000. U.S. doctors, nurses, and the Seattle Organizing Committee contributed everything gratis.

A year before the Goodwill Games, a terrible accident occurred in Kiev, the capital of the Ukraine, when a hydrofoil ran over a young athlete named Elena Snopova while she practiced canoeing on the Dnieper River. Elena lost both of her legs. When Bob learned of the accident, he had Fisher dispatch a series of telexes to Moscow requesting information about Elena's condition. After Bob showed Elena's records to various American doctors, Fisher sent another telex to Kozlovsky, outlining the plan: Dr. Ernest Burgess, widely known for his work in the development of prostheses, would accept Elena as a patient.

When Elena arrived in Seattle, doctors at the University of Washington Medical Center fitted her with artificial legs, paid for by Marion Williams, a Goodwill Games patron. A few months after Elena and her mother returned home, they visited Kozlovsky.

"Not only could the girl walk," Kozlovsky marveled later, "she could run and jump. None of this had cost anyone in the Soviet Union anything."

Another case involved a sixty-six-year-old Russian, Georgiy Samoilovich, who had been trying to get out of the Soviet Union for a decade to receive treatment for large cell lymphoma. Samoilovich had been denied an exit visa on the spurious grounds that he harbored state secrets from his days in the Soviet army. To complicate matters, the doctors who diagnosed Samoilovich refused to treat him after he applied for a visa. Bob and Gene responded to the case because the request came through Daniel Grossman at the State Department. In part through their efforts, Samoilovich received treatment in the United States.

Not all cases featured positive endings. Tamara Tarasova, a five-year-old Russian girl, required a kidney transplant, but the U.S. doctors Bob and Gene consulted could offer her no hope. Bob tried to arrange a kidney transplant for a Russian boy, Asatiani Alexander Davidovich, but no suitable organ could be located. Rusudan Giorgadze, the daughter of Dr. Nodari Giorgadze, Tbilisi's chief of police, had a deformed arm. Nothing could be done for her condition in Georgia, and it turned out that nothing could be done in the United States, although Dr. Giorgadze presented Bob with a magnificent Georgian horn for his efforts on the girl's behalf.

A Ukranian, Anatoly Grishchenko had flown a helicopter over the radioactive soup released during the nuclear accident at Chernobyl, contracting leukemia. Dr. Robert Day, the chief administrator at the Fred Hutchinson Cancer Research Center, made arrangements for Grishchenko to come to the United States to receive a bone marrow transplant. Although successful, Grishchenko developed a lung lesion, forcing an operation. He never recovered from surgery.

For every ten individuals Bob, Gene, and the Seattle Organizing Committee tried to help — and they received dozens of requests — many more could not be helped.

"The only way to improve that medical system," Dr. Farrell believed, "was to improve the economy. Only when the Soviets produced products their own people could buy and the rest of the world wanted, would the average Soviet citizen be able to receive adequate health care."

In the absence of such health care, the majority of Soviets suffered unfathomably abysmal conditions, relying on their own meager resources and herbal concoctions to remain in good health.

Most Russians enjoyed the *banya*, a place of communal rejuvenation since the eleventh century. The ultimate *banya* was Moscow's Sandunov Baths, whose staircases sported ionic columns, ringed by plaster cherubs and rococo murals. The heart of the *banya* was the steam room, where the most prominent sound was the slap of birch twigs against wet skin. Russians believed that "birching" the body promoted circulation, and that a meal of dried, salted fish and vodka replaced salt lost through perspiration. Russians conducted all business in a *banya* without clothes, rank and status relegated to hooks. Russians considered it a scientific fact that two naked people understood each other better than two clothed people, a line of reasoning many Russians supplemented with a spectrum of unscientific beliefs.

It invited bad luck, for example, to pick the name of a child in advance of its birth, bad luck to buy the baby a present ahead of time, worse to discuss a likely birth date, for fear of jinxing it. In general, Russians did not want to appear to be too happy about something ahead of time: the evil eye would descend upon them. A Russian never said, "I will visit Leningrad next week." That jinxed it. Something could go wrong. Whistling indoors caused a loss of money. If a Russian's left palm itched, the Russian expected to receive money. If his or her left nostril itched, a round of drinking would take place. If a Russian stepped on your foot, it was customary for the Russian to insist that you step on his or her foot to prevent ill feelings the next time you met. If two Russians knocked heads accidentally, they immediately knocked heads again to prevent an argument. If a knife fell, the Russian expected to receive a male visitor. If a fork or spoon fell, the visitor would be female. If a bird flew into a room, someone would die. If a spider crawled up a wall, that was good news; down a wall heralded terrible news. Some Russian brides wore nets over their faces because the knots served as a defense against sorcerers. In parts of Eastern Russia, some people beat their homes with sticks on New Year's Day in order to shoo away demons.

All cultures have repositories of superstitions. But Russians possessed an almost profound preoccupation with devils and omens, fortune telling, religious foolishness, and intense speculation about mysteries and the occult. Perhaps, as many Russians believed, "an onion a day keeps the doctor away." But one Soviet mother became a gamer of a different stripe. She found her own way out of the Dark Ages, purchasing three airplane tickets to the United States.

Saving The Evil Empire

*Bob is my closest man. God sent Bob
to us, really. It was a miracle we met him.*

*– Zizi Bagdavadze, resident,
Tbilisi, Georgia*

She had straight black hair, festive eyes, and a pair of daughters who shared her florid – and typically Georgian — personality. Lili Rtskhiladze's oldest, Nana Bagdavadze, studied oil painting at the Tbilisi Academy of Art and was the more intellectually inclined of the two. Five years younger, Zinaida Bagdavadze attended the same institution as a student of design, approaching life as something of blithe spirit. Everyone called her Zizi.

The horror crept into Zizi's life slowly, almost imperceptibly. At first, she noticed only occasional low-grade fevers and bouts of dizziness, surely nothing serious, she thought. But then an unremitting, draining fatigue gripped her. Zizi had no idea what had gone wrong, nor did Lili and Nana. But when, after some weeks, Zizi's symptoms refused to go away, Lili insisted that Zizi get a medical checkup. When the results came in, none of the women were prepared for the prognosis.

"I will never forget this day when the telephone rang," recalled Nana. "It was the worst of my life."

The blood test contained the breathtakingly scary truth: leukemia, a disease impossible to arrest in the Soviet Union. Without a bone marrow transplant, twenty-one-year-old Zizi would eventually die. Neither Lili nor Nana knew exactly how long Zizi had.

Although her own mother, Margarita Adamia, had died at far too young an age from a bungled thyroid surgery, Lili had difficulty reconciling the awful verdict about Zizi. Except for her symptoms, Zizi had always been so vibrant. And to die young in Georgia seemed to defy national policy, for Georgia had always presented a fascinating phenomenon: In Tbilisi alone, the population of 1.5 million contained nearly 100 people more than 100 years old.

Lili Rtskhiladze

Lili told herself the worst could not happen to Zizi. And more than that, it would not happen. So she took Zizi and Nana to Moscow so that doctors there could run some tests. Those doctors soon discovered that Nana could serve as a suitable bone marrow donor for Zizi, but admitted to Lili they did not have much experience with the transplant procedure. Still, they would do what they could do.

"There were two top doctors who told me they will treat Zizi," Lili recalled. "They were hematologists and had even treated Brezhnev. They told me they had access to some American procedure. They gave Zizi some medication. It cost fifteen cents. It was nothing. They said to go back to Tbilisi and stay in touch. After this, they did some blood work on Zizi, and I was tortured by this procedure. It went on for five years. One of the doctors in Moscow wanted to do a transfusion, but I did not trust this doctor. He wanted to make experiment on Zizi like mice. And I was so scared."

As the vice president of Tbilisi's Chamber of Commerce, a position that enabled her to travel internationally, Lili also had access to certain foreign medical publications that had been declared off-limits to the vast majority of Soviet citizens. Lili scoured them all, trying to find information about bone marrow transplants. Through one of them, she learned about the Fred Hutchinson Cancer Research Center in Seattle, Washington.

"I knew of New York, Los Angeles, and Chicago, but not Seattle," remembered Lili. "But now I begin dreaming of taking my daughter there to the Fred Hutch."

Scientists at the Fred Hutchinson Cancer Research Center had performed pioneering work in bone marrow transplantation. They had been the first to show that patients with acute leukemia who had failed chemotherapy could still be cured. They had performed the first successful transplant for a patient with multiple myeloma, a disease otherwise incurable. The Center's E. Donnall Thomas had done the first bone marrow transplant between individuals who were not twins.

"I had no idea how to have my daughter admitted to this Center," Lili admitted later. "Or even if it was possible. But this doctor in Tbilisi, a friend of mine, she tells me that if I have a chance to get out of Soviet Union to do it as soon as possible."

Lili not only did not know about admittance procedures at the Fred Hutchinson Cancer Research Center, she had nowhere near enough money to pay for a transplant. She didn't even know how much a transplant would cost. But like most Georgians, she possessed a deep faith. She also had one connection in the United States, a Georgian acquaintance who lived in San Diego, and a vital piece of information: San Diego's Scripps Howard Hospital might be able to perform a bone marrow transplant if Fred Hutchinson could not.

While Lili worried over what to do, a friend advised her one day to visit a fortune teller, who performed readings from a stall on a Tbilisi street. Lili normally didn't seek out fortune tellers, but with nothing to lose she decided to give it a try. After Lili explained Zizi's situation, the fortune teller advised Lili not to trust the doctors in Moscow, even describing in unnerving detail the face of one of those doctors.

"After this, I cannot trust this doctor in Moscow anymore," Lili later explained. "And then this fortune teller, she tells me that I have a long way to go to recover my daughter. And that was it. At first, I had no idea to leave my country. But America, for me it was everything. I trust America more than the other countries. And the fortune teller in Tbilisi, somehow I trust her. Can you imagine? Is that something unbelievable? So it was time to go."

Lili purchased three airplane tickets, one for her, another for Zizi, a third for Nana. Because Lili had a position of trust in Tbilisi's Chamber of Commerce, and because her family had always been among the elite ones in Georgia, authorities reluctantly granted her permission to leave the Soviet Union for a period of not less than ten days and no more than ninety.

"Even though our family was really very famous, it was still very complicated to get out of there," Lili recalled. "The big gate, you know? But I waited some for months and some things were done."

"The KGB had a hard time figuring out why I was needed," Nana said later. "So I had to explain to them that the donor must go. For KGB, it was too many people from one family going. They would always come up with some reason not to let you out. So it was some time before we could leave."

About a week before Lili, Zizi, and Nana departed for the United States, Bob Walsh flew to Tbilisi on Goodwill Games business. Lili, alerted to Bob's arrival, had heard ac-

Bob flanked by Nana, left, and Zizi Bagdavadze

counts of Bob's humanitarian work in Georgia. Although she had never met Bob, she asked two of her friends, Armas Saneblidze and Vaso Margvelashvili, if they would tell Bob about Zizi's condition. As Bob listened, his heart went out to Lili and her daughter, but he suspected that arranging a bone marrow transplant might be extraordinarily difficult, if not impossible. In order for the Fred Hutchinson Cancer Research Center to admit Zizi, Bob believed, it might have to reject an application from an American citizen. A transplant would cost a lot of money, perhaps as much as $200,000. Bob didn't even have the $25,000 to $30,000 he later discovered it would take to initiate a bone marrow procedure in the event that Fred Hutchinson admitted Zizi. And certainly the Seattle Organizing Committee couldn't help, floating as it did in red ink. But after his conversation with Saneblidze and

Margvelashvili, Bob didn't hesitant a second, determining it was time to spoil a stranger.

He got hold of Zizi's blood records and, after returning to Seattle, set up an appointment with Dr. Robert Day, the chief administrator at the Fred Hutchinson Cancer Research Center. To Dr. Day, Zizi's case appeared average for the kind of patients Fred Hutch normally admitted. She had a serious disease made worse by the fact that she had never undergone chemotherapy. The pre-conditioning for a transplant would require total body radiation, unfortunate for a woman so young. Money posed a huge problem. Given Washington State insurance laws, no method existed for Fred Hutch to perform a transplant free of charge. However, Dr. Day informed Bob that he would authorize some preliminary tests on Zizi while Bob scrounged for funds.

A few weeks later, Gene Fisher, at work in the Seattle Organizing Committee offices, received a telephone call from a woman at the Scripps Howard Hospital in San Diego who wanted to know where she should forward a bill to Bob Walsh. Fisher did not know anything about a Scripps Howard bill.

"How much is it and what is it for?" Fisher asked the woman, suddenly leary.

"It's $130,000."

"Whoa! What is it and who is it for?"

"Lili Rtskhiladze," stuttered the woman, butchering the Georgian name.

Unbeknownst to Fisher or Bob, Lili, Nana, and Zizi had flown to San Diego and were staying with Lili's Georgian friend and his American wife, Catherine Dorn. Zizi had entered the hospital for tests, but Scripps Howard could not proceed with an actual transplant until it had $130,000. When Bob returned to the office and found out what had happened, he immediately called Lili, then booked a flight to Los Angeles. When Bob, accompanied by Bernie Russi, heard Lili's story and gazed into the hopeful eyes of Zizi and Nana, he promised that Zizi would receive a bone marrow transplant. Bob didn't know how it would happen or where the money would come from. So he asked Lili, Nana, and Zizi to be patient a little while longer.

"Bob loved Zizi instantly," Lili recalled. "I remember this: Bob's eyes were full of tears. He placed his hand on Zizi's knee and said he would do his best."

"Bob was touched personally," Nana reflected. "And you must understand how important that was for us. We didn't know what was going to happen. Our only hope was that Bob would help us."

"It then took Bob one more month to arrange everything," Zizi remembered.

The Fred Hutchinson Cancer Research Center had elaborate rules regarding admissions, most of them insurance-based. Even if Dr. Day had wanted to make an ex-

ception in Zizi's case by providing a bone marrow transplant free of charge, he could not. The Center had no way to absorb the costs. Bob asked for and received the initial seed money for Zizi's preliminary treatment from a source he knew wouldn't turn him down. Ted Turner wrote a check for $25,000 and didn't ask a question. Bob then tapped his own bank account, hit up just about everyone he knew for donations, and somehow wrangled a few dollars out of the Seattle Organizing

Dr. Robert Day

Committee. By the time Lili, Nana, and Zizi arrived in Seattle from San Diego, Bob found himself about $50,000 shy of being able to pay for Zizi's transplant, but he had enough money for the Center to begin the procedure.

"All the time Bob treated us like queens," Nana recalled. "We had very limited pocket money. All you could bring was $300 from Soviet Union, not more. So we were totally dependent on Bob for everything, and everything was paid for. He did some miracles for us."

"The money turned up because the divine was there," Zizi later admitted.

A graduate of the Harvard Medical School, Dr. E. Donnal Thomas had been among the first doctors to believe that marrow transplants could successfully treat leukemia. He conducted many of his early experiments on dogs, since only dogs and humans shared such elaborate genetic diversity. In 1956, Dr. Thomas successfully transplanted two humans with bone marrow from their respective identical twins. While the transplants themselves were successful, both patients died of recurrent disease. Subsequent transplant patients also died, many from infection. Many also suffered from graft-versus-host disease, a problem so vexing that by the early 1960s a majority of researchers believed that marrow grafting would never work. Dr. Thomas didn't share that view. After arriving in Seattle from New York, where he had already conducted two decades' worth of research into bone marrow transplants, he established a laboratory and began recruiting some brilliant, young co-workers.

One turned out to be a native of Essen, Germany. Dr. Rainier F. Storb was tall and angular and presented himself with an academic air. A creature of the laboratory, Dr. Storb did work that was as laborious as it was unglamorous. Like Dr. Thomas, Dr. Storb had spent years probing the mysteries of marrow transplantation technology, asking and answering one bedeviling question after the other. How did new bone marrow cells know where to go after they had been introduced into a host's bloodstream? What made them radar in on the right nesting sites, where they could attach and begin to grow? Why did those cells try to kill the host? Why did this invasion, the graft-versus-host disease, affect the skin, liver, the gastrointestinal tract, and the lungs?

Dr. Storb's research finally began to pay dividends concurrent with several other milestones in transplantation technology. The first successful non-twin transplants between siblings occurred in 1968 and 1969. In 1977, two years after Dr. Storb became an associate at the Fred Hutchinson Cancer Research Center, Laura Graves made medical history, receiving marrow from an unrelated donor and living to tell about it. In the late 1980s, Dr. Storb made one of his most significant breakthroughs, the development of a drug that prevented graft-versus-host disease. His achievement, ironically, resulted in a Nobel Prize for E. Donnal Thomas.

"It bothered me for about a day," Dr. Storb admitted later. "But it really was a collaborative effort. And Donnal protected me from an enormous amount of administrative work which I was not fond of doing."

By a coincidence of scheduling, Dr. Storb happened to be the attending physician when Zizi arrived for her transplant. First, she was taken to an underground room at the Fred Hutchinson Cancer Research Center, where technicians blasted her for thirty minutes every day for a week with opposing sources of radioactive Cobalt 60. Then it was Nana's turn. Two Swedish Hospital physicians inserted harvesting needles into an area near Nana's hips, probed the bone cavities for marrow, suctioned it into a stainless-steel beaker, and placed it in an administration bag.

"And from there they did the transportation from Nana to me," recalled Zizi. "It took five hours."

Lili could only hope that the marrow that flowed intravenously into Zizi would give her daughter a chance to live. Under the best of circumstances, Zizi would have to remain hospitalized at least for a month, probably for six weeks. Then she would have to undergo checkups every day for three months. If alive at that point, Zizi would require annual checkups for five more years. If Zizi survived all that, maybe she would make it. But nobody knew for sure.

"All I could do," Lili conceded later, "was place my hope and faith in God."

Several weeks after the transplant, Zizi was released from the Fred Hutchinson Cancer Research Center. She convalesced for a couple of months in a Seattle apartment that Carmen Matthews of the Seattle Organizing Committee located for her, and made daily trips to the hospital, where doctors maintained close surveillance on her.

"Now Zizi has part of me and we are one," Nana explained later. "Zizi had a wonderful husband. We found out later that Zizi's husband swore he would not sleep in the bed they shared while she was gone. So he slept on the floor all the time Zizi was in Seattle."

"When we went back to Georgia there were lots of articles in the newspapers," recalled Lili. "Bob Walsh became famous because of our story. That's why I was very happy always when Bob came back to Georgia. He became a member of my family."

"Bob was known by everybody before our story," Nana added later. "But after our story he became more famous. And he helped others, too."

"I know of four people who were near to death that Bob helped," Lili recalled.

Lili returned to Seattle several times after Zizi's bone marrow transplant. On each occasion she made a point of going to the Fred Hutchinson Cancer Research Center to meet with doctors and nurses and offer them souvenirs. And each time she visited Fred Hutch, she made it a practice to walk around the building, kissing its entrances.

"I kiss it like it is a church, like a temple," Lili remembered. "Maybe someone would catch me and take me to some mental place. Who is this crazy woman? But I am so grateful, and this is such a beautiful story, what Bob and the doctors at Fred Hutch have done for our family. It is really better than a love story, and all the sheets of paper that tell about how Zizi is saved have tears and melted ink on the pages."

Sweet Science

Bob is the kind of guy who does what he does and doesn't look back. And thank God for that.

> — *Jennifer Potter, Director of Operations, 1990 Goodwill Games, Seattle, Washington*

The Seattle Organizing Committee took a major step toward institutional stability when it hired Kathy Scanlan as its executive vice president. A tall, intense woman in her early forties, Scanlan wallowed in challenges and luxuriated in details. She had been a budget analyst and director of the Seattle Parks and Recreation Department, business manager of Seattle's Woodland Park Zoo, and deputy director of the Seattle Center, an inner-city playground built for the 1962 World's Fair. Scanlan had joined the SOC originally as its Vice President of Operations; in her new role, she would oversee budgets and contracts, coordinate activities with state and local governments, supervise a management team, and implement the broad plans already in place for the sports, arts, cultural, and exchange programs. To do what needed doing, Kathy Scanlan would have to apply all of her administrative wizardry.

Nobody in the SOC had ever successfully organized an event as large, complex, and disparate as the Goodwill Games. Nobody had presented a well-focused economic scenario, or explained precisely how the SOC planned to invite thousands of visitors to Seattle without making a transportation system that was gridlocked daily even worse.

Kathy Scanlan, Executive Vice President

So far, the SOC had largely peddled the idea of an illusory, watered-down Olympics. Before the SOC could expect community-wide skepticism to vanish, before it could begin to generate the nearly $25 million in corporate support it would take to stage the Games, somebody had to articulate why they were going to be a good deal instead of what they appeared to be: a Trojan horse. That somebody was Kathy Scanlan.

She became the third individual to try to harness an organization that had already generated a super tsunami of ill-will and spawned as much chaos as a Balkan election. Most of the intrigues had involved territorial disputes at the top of the SOC food chain. Ted Bowsfield, the SOC's first Chief Operating Officer, had lasted only six months, finally resigning after his attempt to have Bob Walsh removed as the SOC's president failed to draw the support of its board of directors. Next came Shelly Yapp, the director of planning and administration. A policy wonk who craved structure and procedure, Shelly had issued the same complaints about Bob as Bowsfield had: With Bob running things, and continually trying to redefine the scope of the event, the Games would unravel before they were ever assembled. Bob winged through things without providing details, had a dream but no solid plan, and subscribed to a fiscal policy that made Blanche Dubois look like Alan Greenspan, an opinion even Bob's friends shared.

"The bottom line was always Bob's weak spot," recalled Gene Pfeifer, who was one of those friends. "One reason people worried about Bob was because they thought his bottom line was going to become their bottom line."

"Bob could spend money until all the money in the world was spent and gone," remembered Patsy Collins, another of those friends. "He could spend Ted Turner into oblivion."

Not comfortable with Bowsfield gone, never comfortable with Bob's spur-of-the-moment inventiveness, and convinced her professional relationship with Bob wasn't going to work, Shelly Yapp followed Bowsfield out the door, becoming deputy mayor of Seattle. Unfortunately for those they left behind, neither of their departures spared the SOC from internal squabble, external conflict, or rampant controversy. Father Sullivan, the SOC board chairman, nearly quit because the SOC couldn't generate community support or corporate sponsors. James Munn, a prominent Seattle attorney who objected to the Soviet Union's threatened boycott of the 1988 Summer Olympics in Seoul, South Korea, generated $200,000 worth of commitments from the city's downtown business core to topple the Games. Seattle Police Chief Patrick Fitzsimons, chairman of the newly created Law Enforcement Council, a consortium of fifteen agencies that had been empanelled to plan for Games security, threatened to disband the organization unless the SOC provided it with additional funding. John Miller, a Washington State Congressman who served on the House Foreign Affairs subcommittee on human rights, promised to derail Goodwill funding efforts in Washington, D.C., unless the SOC made a concerted attempt to address the issue of Jewish emigration

Ted Bowsfield, Chief Operating Officer

out of Russia. Facing what SOC officials perceived as Miller's political blackmail on the one hand, they couldn't give away a multi-million dollar swimming pool with the other.

The SOC had worked out a deal with one of its board members, David Sabey, to build a world-class pool. The SOC had then approached University of Washington athletic director Mike Lude with a proposal: The SOC would provide the university with a new pool if the university provided the property. The SOC would use the pool during the Games, and the university would reap its benefits in perpetuity. To the SOC's astonishment, and without explanation, Lude's superiors rejected the idea, leaving the SOC to scramble for an alternate site.

While the SOC pondered the mystery of why the University of Washington would turn down a free swimming pool, even when it really needed one, it scrambled to locate a replacement for Bowsfield. Bob found what he believed to be the perfect candidate. But Gene Pfeifer, long one of Bob's greatest supporters, resigned after only six months on the job; he just didn't need the grief.

Kathy Scanlan felt tough enough and capable enough to overcome whatever grief came her way, especially since the SOC, she believed, had an exceptional board of directors and a staff that had already accomplished a lot more than most Seattleites realized. Bob Walsh

Vjacheslav Gavrilin, left, of the USSR State Sports Committee, Bob Wussler of TBS, and Bob Walsh inspect a Goodwill Games venue

had developed extraordinary relationships with the Soviet government. Largely through Jarlath Hume's efforts, Seattle's major artistic groups had joined forces on a plan for a Visual and Performing Arts Festival. Because of David Gogol, a Washington, D.C.-based lobbyist, the SOC's agenda had been advanced expertly inside the Beltway. Gogol had been instrumental in negotiations with the General Services Administration that resulted in the SOC securing inexpensive office space in Seattle's Federal Building, had helped shake loose a $500,000 appropriation to jump-start the Goodwill Arts Festival, and had organized

192

Washington State's congressional delegation in such a way that it would work on the SOC's behalf to acquire additional funds for Goodwill security and exchange projects.

The challenges still confronting Scanlan remained as daunting as the SOC's accomplishments were praiseworthy. Shortly after she joined the SOC, the King County Council voted 9-0 to contribute $8.8 million toward the construction of an $18.8 million aquatic center in Federal Way, ten miles south of Seattle. That solved the SOC's most nagging venue issue, but put the SOC in the burdensome position of having to provide $5.8 million of the remaining balance. The SOC needed $20 million from the U.S. Defense Department to pay for the Goodwill security effort, and more than $8 million from Washington State to supplement that grant. But federal and state politicians squealed at providing charity to Ted Turner's private Olympiad. The SOC needed $100 million in liability insurance, $1.7 million to refurbish the track at the University of Washington, and $300,000 to make improvements at the Marymoor Veledrome, the Goodwill cycling venue, but hadn't received a nickel in corporate support.

Scanlan had to conjure up a plan to build that support. She had to determine how to guarantee that none of the municipalities that would host Goodwill events would lose money when the newspapers fulminated that it was an impossibility. She had to make a spate of management hires and develop marketing, advertising, and volunteer programs. She had to hassle over a $900,000 dispute with the Law Enforcement Council and resolve a host of contractual issues with the City of Seattle, City of Tacoma, City of Spokane, the Port of Seattle, King County, and the University of Washington. University officials quickly proved an exasperating lot, torturing Scanlan and her administrative staff in every aspect of negotiations. Tallman Trask, William Gerberding's chief lieutenant, became such a troublesome character that many SOC staffers winced whenever they had to deal with him.

"The university raped our budget," recollected Jennifer Potter, hired by Scanlan as the SOC's Vice President of Operations. "They had us over a barrel and went right after us."

"Trask was terrible," Scanlan said later. "He hated the Goodwill Games and wanted to make sure every red cent that could be extracted from us would be extracted. We had to deal with a lot of people at the UW who were complete pains in the rear."

As much rancor existed between the SOC and Turner Broadcasting System as it did between the SOC and the University of

Washington. Although the SOC and TBS had a signed contract, the deal always had a multifaceted amendment to it under negotiation. The greatest revenue source available to the SOC would come from the sale of corporate sponsorships, and the SOC needed at least thirty in order to reach its revenue goal. The SOC's agreement with TBS stipulated that TBS would recruit national sponsors, and the SOC local ones. But the contract language was vague as to whether big regional sponsors, such as Fred Meyer and AT&T, also constituted national sponsors.

"After we had done a deal with Alaska Airlines," recalled Scanlan, "TBS told us we couldn't do it. If we hadn't been able to work that out, I was going to recommend that we throw in the towel. If you can't sell to a big regional sponsor like Alaska Airlines, you'll never raise enough money."

The SOC-TBS relationship also abounded with personality conflicts. SOC staffers found themselves on good working terms with several TBS officials, especially Don Ellis and David Raith. A network television veteran who had produced every important sports event in America, including the NFL's infamous "Heidi Game," Ellis had won an Emmy award for his efforts at the 1986 Goodwill Games in Moscow, had an engaging personality, and told fabulous stories. In charge of securing athletes for the Games, Raith performed his duties with extraordinary competence, quickly becoming one of Bob's TBS favorites. Then there was Bob Wussler, who even managed to alienate a few TBS employees.

"He's sure not on my speed dial," Ellis later admitted.

In fact, no sooner had Scanlan become executive vice president of the SOC than she found herself embroiled in a bizarre mess involving Wussler and Bob Walsh. Although an extraordinarily gifted executive, Wussler resented Bob Walsh's relationships with the Soviets, finding it particularly galling when Bob sat on the same side of the table with the Russians during negotiating sessions. It made Wussler look like the adversary, even an enemy. Wussler also bristled over the fact that, whenever he and Bob Walsh found themselves together in Moscow, the Soviets drove Bob around in long, black limos while Wussler got ferried about in slightly less exotic cars. For his part, Bob had no use for Wussler, finding it particularly galling that Wussler badmouthed Ted Turner behind his back. But Bob generally kept his feelings to himself.

One night, Bob Walsh joined a dozen TBS people at a restaurant in Chicago. Wussler had complained in general terms about the SOC and issued specific gripes over the fact that TBS had not received an expected line of credit from a Seattle bank. When it came time for dinner, Bob made the mistake of depositing himself between TBS's Vivian Lewand, who orchestrated Goodwill merchandizing efforts, and Ellen Stone, who ran the network's marketing pro-

David Raith, Turner Broadcasting System

grams. Unfortunately, this happened to be near the center of the table where Wussler preferred to sit. When Wussler made his grand entrance, late as usual, the only available chair was at the end of the table. Wussler spent the entire dinner in a froth, glaring at Bob. By the time dinner ended, Wussler's mood rivaled that of a Doberman with a migraine. He commanded that Bob join him in the adjacent bar, where he launched into a rant about the Seattle Organizing Committee and the Seattle bank. Bob listened quietly for a few moments, then turned to face Wussler.

"Wussler, why are you such an asshole?"

Bob might as well have used Wussler's shoe as a chamber pot. Wussler's eyes narrowed into reptilian slits and peered at Bob in the manner of a lizard spying a fly before flicking it with its tongue. The next thing Bob remembered was waking up in a hotel bed feeling like Jackie Chan had just gotten through with him. Wussler had nailed him with a sucker punch, pancaking Bob's face into something reminiscent of a 1912 first baseman's mitt. When flabbergasted TBS employees raced into the bar and saw Bob fully engaged in the middle of the next week, they stared at Wussler as though he had loudly broken wind during High Mass at the Vatican. Wussler quickly ordered them to forget the incident; it had never happened.

The next day, with Bob feeling like the morning after Mardi Gras and his face a constellation of blue, green, and purple bruises, Wussler telephoned.

"Hey," Bob heard Wussler say, "I understand we had a little fight last night."

"The Goodwill Games are cancelled," replied Bob, slamming down the phone.

That set off a panic among Ted Turner's minions in Atlanta, who frantically tried to figure out what to do next. Turner tried to reach Bob by telephone in Washington D.C., where Bob had flown later that morning for meetings with lobbyist David Gogol and Andrew Card, President Ronald Reagan's deputy chief of staff. But Bob refused to accept calls from Turner or anyone else at TBS.

"Wussler was always pretending he was John Wayne," recalled Jarlath Hume.

"I wish I had been there so I could have dropped that sonofabitch in his tracks," the SOC's Bill Sears subsequently admitted. "You hit a guy like Walsh the wrong way and you could kill him."

"I sat in a meeting with Wussler once and he was mean to this guy on his own staff," remembered Kimberly Brown, president of Bob Walsh & Associates. "He made some comment about this guy's manhood that was really inappropriate, and then he laughed about it."

Goodwill argument comes to blows

Tacoma News Tribune Headline

When word got out that a top TBS official had KO'd a top SOC official, Wussler denied the incident, telling The Associated Press, "I have no problem with Walsh. In fact, I get along just fine with the Seattle people. Of course, in any relationship, you're not going to agree on everything."

Bob eventually took a call from Turner, who told Bob he had heard reports of Wussler's pugilistic prowess. Turner agreed to talk to Father Sullivan, the SOC's Chairman of the Board, and Scanlan about the episode. Barely transitioning into her new role, Scanlan and Father Sullivan flew to Montana, where Turner had a ranch, to meet with Turner and TBS's Paul Beckham. Although Scanlan later told John Clendenon of Tacoma's *News Tribune*, "We have a good working relationship with TBS" and "Whatever personal differences exist are not worth public comment," they were certainly worth private comment. Father Sullivan and Scanlan presented Turner with a letter, drafted by Scanlan, that condemned Wussler's actions and demanded his removal. Turner listened patiently and promised to make a change. A few weeks later, he did, casting Wussler aside. Wussler still had a job, but Turner barred him from further contact with the SOC.

In addition, a financial settlement called for TBS to issue an apology plus pay Bob Walsh a sum of money, about $50,000. Several SOC board members wanted to sue Wussler personally, but neither Bob nor Father Sullivan thought that an appropriate solution, especially since suing Wussler really meant suing Turner. Scanlan agreed; a lawsuit would become a major distraction. She needed to keep the SOC and Bob Walsh on a tight track, a difficult enough assignment considering the SOC's tenuous finances, and especially considering that Bob and Kathy rarely found themselves on the same page.

Kathy saw the SOC's responsibility as organizing a huge festival of sports, arts, and culture. She couldn't fathom why Bob continually sought out extracurricular projects to add to the Goodwill matrix, including his bid to host a quarterfinal match of the World Chess Championship. Scanlan simply assumed the chess tournament would lose money, driving the SOC even farther away from its financial goals.

Considering the vast scope of the challenges confronting her, Kathy Scanlan probably didn't need to know that Bob Walsh had also been plotting to smuggle a Russian vixen into the United States.

The Heartbeat Of Georgia

Bob was the first American I ever met, and I thank God for it. Bob is like a second father to me because he gave me life for a second time.

*— Kakha Merabishvili, resident,
Tbilisi, Georgia*

*T*he other Georgia is sealed almost hermetically in its customs, traditions, and beliefs. One of those beliefs is that a guest comes from God. All Georgians believe it, and it is a belief that rules the Georgian heart. Georgians are also predisposed to the belief that each and every life is cause for major celebration, and Margo Diakonidze-Merabishvili of Tbilisi was already twice blessed: two sons, both healthy, both happy, both gifts. Margo prayed for them each day in her Georgian Orthodox Church, and said many more prayers the day she delivered her third son, whom she named Kakha.

Three months after his birth, Kakha suddenly began to cry and turn dark blue. Margo had Kakha examined by a physician in Tbilisi, who explained that Kakha's heart was all wrong, and that he probably would die. Refusing to accept the diagnosis, Margo immediately took Kakha to Moscow to see Dr. Vladimir Burtakovsky, the head of the prestigious Medical Research Institute. When Dr. Burtakovsky looked at Kakha, he was shocked. And when several of his colleagues confirmed his diagnosis, Dr. Burtakovsky told Margo that Kakha would probably die within a year. But in case Kakha didn't die, Margo should return to Moscow when Kakha was two-and-one-half for a special test.

"So after this," Margo recalled, "every day we faced death."

Kakha survived to two and a half. When Margo again took him to Dr. Burtakovsky, the physician expressed surprise that Kakha was still alive and informed Margo that Kakha required an operation.

"But the operation cannot be performed until Kakha is six years old," Dr. Burtakovsky told Margo. "Until then, there is nothing to be done."

"We did everything after that to help the child when he had his heart attacks," remembered Margo. "We had a special liquid that we gave him to widen the vessels in his heart, and we kept hot water in a tub so we could put Kakha in it to open his vessels even more and spare him one more day. So when Kakha becomes six, we go back to Moscow and he has this operation. The doctors put this thing in him, this device to keep him alive. The doctors say that before Kakha is eleven, another operation should take place."

Margo brought Kakha back to Moscow two years later, but Dr. Burtakovsky refused to perform the second operation, insisting it was too risky. She brought Kakha back again the next year, Dr. Burtakovsky once more insisting surgery was too dangerous. When Margo returned to Moscow the following year with Kakha, Dr. Burtakovsky said he would never perform such a chancy operation. Margo believed in God and in miracles and refused to accept her son's apparent death sentence. She scoured the Soviet Union searching for help, and Margo knew how to search. A writer, Margo had been awarded title "Honorable Journalist of the Country." Margo's younger sister, Zina Diakonidze, also a journalist, exhausted her contacts to find an answer for Kakha as well. Always Margo and Zina ran into two immutable truths: Kakha would die without surgery; no Soviet doctor, even doctors who had won Stalin and Lenin prizes, had the expertise to perform the kind of operation Kakha required.

"It was like if the famous Dr. Burtakovsky cannot take risk, nobody can," Margo reflected. "Still, this doctor kindly allows me to be only mother who can be with her son when he goes in hospital. And not to put Dr. Burtakovsky in awkward situation, I began to work there as a cleaning woman. I am journalist, but now I clean hospital to be with my son."

After nearly two decades of relentless panic that her son's body would suddenly shut down, Margo came to realize that her only option was to take Kakha out of the Soviet Union. Through something she had heard on the Voice of America, Margo knew there were outstanding surgeons in Europe and the United States who might be able to help. She also knew that her chances of receiving permission to leave the Soviet Union with Kakha were practically nonexistent. Every time she presented her case to the Central Committee in Moscow, which she did repeatedly, the committee denied her request. She begged at other departments, including the Council of Ministers. She implored government officials in Tbilisi for help, but they told her that she needed at least eight different signatures from people who would have to vouch that, if permitted to leave the Soviet Union, Margo would return. She could not get them.

"Everybody supported me," Margo explained later. "But they did not dare help. They did not want to admit that this operation could not take place in Soviet Union. They would have my Kakha die before they admit to this."

By the time Kakha Merabishvili staggered into his nineteenth year, his breathing impaired, his liver enlarged, his skin color a dangerous shade of blue, Margo's hope was hanging by a thread, ready to break.

"And then," Margo recalled, "we received the miracle."

Bob Walsh, made aware of Kakha's plight by his friend, Vaso Margvelashvili, asked for a copy of Kakha's medical records. When Kakha's Moscow doctors wouldn't release them, Margo arranged through friends to have the documents stolen from the Medical Research Institute and sent to Bob.

"The doctors would not give us the history of Kakha's disease," recollected Margo, "because they did not dare. This has to do with prestige of Soviet Union."

The records that Margo's friends swiped from the Medical Research Institute amounted to a two-page statement and an x-ray. While Gene Fisher attempted to locate heart specialists who might consent to perform surgery free of charge, Bob mentioned Kakha's plight to Cynthia Day. Cynthia worked at Seattle's Providence Hospital and was married to Dr. Robert Day, the lead administrator at the Fred Hutchinson

Cancer Research Center. Cynthia recommended one of Providence's top heart specialists, Dr. Lester Sauvage, the founder and director of Seattle's Hope Heart Institute. Dr. Sauvage had invented the coronary artery bypass procedure and pioneered a line of artificial arteries, known as the Sauvage Graft. He had written 240 scientific papers on heart and blood vessel surgery research, and three books, including *The Open Heart: Stories of Hope, Healing and Happiness.* Mother Teresa not only gave the book a glowing review, she wrote one of its two forewords.

Dr. Lester Sauvage, Hope Heart Institute

Dr. Sauvage's examination of Kakha's records disclosed that the young Georgian was massively messed up with two major problems. One was "Tetralogy of Fallot." Kakha had a hole between the major pumping chambers of his heart. Blood did not flow freely from his right ventricle to his lungs, and he had a displaced aorta and an enlargement of the right ventricle. Kakha couldn't produce enough oxygen to supply his body's major organs, so he tired easily and had developed a bluish color.

Kakha's second problem was "Dextrocardia," which is Latin for a diabolical condition: He had been born with his heart upside down and backwards on the right side of his chest.

The job of repairing Kakha would require the talent of several world-class experts and numerous strategy sessions to determine how the operation should be performed. But Dr. Sauvage didn't hesitate a moment, telling Bob that if he and Gene Fisher could get Kakha to America, surgery would be performed at Providence at no charge.

"Bob worked on the political and logistical aspects," recalled Margo. "And again I go to Central Committee, and I fight for this. This was a call of a mother's heart. And maybe everybody who has

201

heart, he feels a mother's heart. At last, they agreed to give us permission to leave the country."

The night before Kakha left for America, a young girl showed up at Margo's house holding candles and a gold cross. The Orthodox Patriarch had heard about Kakha and was sending his prayers.

"And then Bob took all cares so the life of my son could be presented to me for the second time," Margo said later. "And this was unbelievable. To take the child from USSR then, you could not even imagine. But Bob, he take Kakha. And my sister, Zina, she go. I could not go. I had black hair before all this. But the blackness of my hair I leave at the Ministry of Health in Moscow."

When Kakha arrived in Seattle, accompanied by his aunt, Zina Diakonidze, he could hardly walk. "We took him right to a hotel and he practically collapsed," Fisher explained later. "He was blue and staggering. I thought he was going to die at any minute. I thought it was a miracle Kakha's story ever reached Bob Walsh."

Dr. John Doces, a member of the Providence staff, had joined Dr. Sauvage to determine precisely what had to be done to repair Kakha and how the operating team should proceed during surgery. Dr. Peter Mansfield, Dr. Sauvage's partner, came aboard to execute the plan in the operating room. The surgery would be formidable and tricky. In a patient population of, say, one million, tetraology occurred fifteen to twenty times a year. The operation was performed frequently on new-

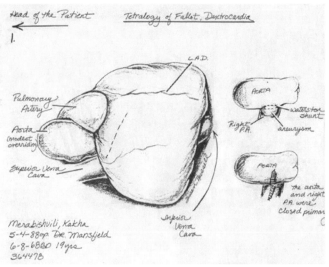

Dr. Peter Mansfield's notes on Kakha's heart condition

borns and infants in their first year of life. But Kakha had reached nineteen and his heart had undergone significant changes. In addition, tetraology combined with dextrocardia gave Kakha's doctors an unprecedented challenge. Dr. Mansfield, who had encountered both conditions in other surgeries, had never encountered both simultaneously in a career involving thousands of operations. Dr. Sauvage had never personally encountered it, nor had Dr. Doces. Given the rarity of Kakha's condition, and given that the Soviets probably could ably could

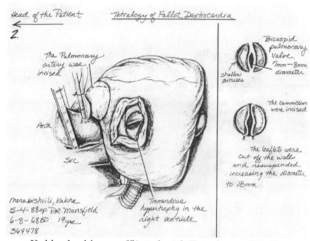

Kakha had been afflicted with Tetralogy of Fallot and Dextrocardia

not have provided adequate post-operative care, Dr. Mansfield found it little wonder Kakha's Soviet doctors had been so reluctant to do anything. Even if Kakha had survived a Soviet surgical knife, he probably would not have survived post-op complications. The potential for something going wrong bordered on staggering.

Dr. Sauvage, Dr. Doces, and Dr. Mansfield first had to figure out how to approach Kakha's perversely positioned heart. Then they had to determine how much traction they could place on it and when to place Kakha on the heart-lung machine. They would have to rotate Kakha's heart so far that it wouldn't be able to perform its normal pumping duties unless they put Kakha on bypass. So they had to design the procedure in such a way that they would go to bypass before they made the final rotation of the heart.

"We had to plan in three dimensions," Dr. Mansfield revealed later. "If I approached the surgery from one direction, what was on the other side of where I was working? I could damage Kakha just by taking a stitch that ran a little too deep. I would have to rotate Kakha's heart without compromising it and work underneath it. It would be sort of like working backwards in a mirror. It was a question of being able to see the situation well enough once we got inside Kakha."

Fortunately, Kakha had had a shunt put in his heart when the

Soviet doctors operated on him thirteen years earlier. Without it, he would have died, for the shunt made it possible to receive enough oxygen from his blood to keep him alive. But where a child grows, a shunt does not. The larger Kakha grew, the more inadequate the shunt. As less and less blood traveled to his lungs, he developed a bluish tint and his body started to shut down.

Dr. Mansfield believed that Soviet doctors could have operated successfully if they had regularly been doing the kind of surgery Kakha required. Since they hadn't, Dr. Mansfield felt they had been wise not to try. Not even an average American cardiac physician had the ability to perform this type of surgery. Dr. Mansfield also knew

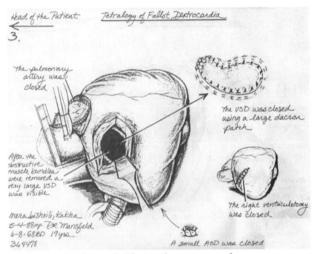

It took Dr. Mansfield nine hours to perform surgery

that, once Kakha got on the operating table, the young Georgian would be there for a very long time.

When Kakha's moment arrived, the operation took nine uninterrupted hours. After Dr. Mansfield's team placed Kakha on the operating table, Gene Fisher and Kakha's aunt, Zina Diakonidze, went outside to wait. They smoked cigarettes furiously, Fisher assuming he was on a death watch.

"It was a pretty intense surgery. It required a great deal of reconstruction inside the chest cavity," recalled Dr. Mansfield. "There was a lot of scarring from the previous surgery. The key is when you take the patient off pump and give the heart back the responsibility of doing the pumping. But Kakha came off the pump just fine. We measured the pressures in his chambers and they were all essentially normal. His oxygen level was high. His color was good. We knew he was going to be fine."

"What happened with Kakha," Zina said later, "was like gold falling from the sky."

Margo Merabishvili attended her Georgian Orthodox Church every day before Kakha's surgery, saying silent prayers before the icons. She didn't think much about her nineteen-year ordeal, but carried Kakha's smile with her everywhere while he was away. Finally, the telephone call came, then the telex from America. Margo wept when told of its contents. Her son would live.

"A different child came home to me," remembered Margo. "Kakha had a swollen face and was different. But before long, he was healthy. I will always pray and thank God for Dr. Peter Mansfield and Dr. Lester Sauvage, who, with their hands, solved the heart of my son. I will always send love from the heart of the mother to such wonderful people as Gene Fisher and the believers of a church in Seattle who donated money to help cover some of Kakha's costs. This should be said because people of our country should know what happened. And for me today, the United States is a country where I feel friends, though I have never been there. After this, how can I look at Bob without tears in my eyes? God send me Bob. And when I say that, I have many pictures in front of me. I have been blessed with renewed life for my son as a result of the humble help of Mr. Walsh and Gene Fisher and their American friends. Who is Bob for me? It's hard to explain with words what I feel. But I pray to God every day that He will forgive not only my sins, but those of Bob as well for the life he has given my son. I look forward to seeing Mr. Walsh in heaven on Judgment Day."

Voices Of Doom

It was kind of amazing that, with all of this covert, suppressed dissension going on, things actually worked.

> – Gene Fisher, Director of Special Projects,
> 1990 Goodwill Games,
> Seattle, Washington

Seattle's newspapers splurged ink constantly over the real and imagined drawbacks of the Goodwill Games, Rebecca Boren of *The Weekly* and Joni Balter of *The Seattle Times* issuing the most frequent denunciations. Most members of the Seattle Organizing Committee believed that neither understood the SOC's mission or vision. In fact, the majority of SOC staffers thought that both were moralizers bent not on covering an unfolding story but on portraying SOC personnel as hapless bunglers. Boren spent considerable time sniffing at the SOC's perimeter for whiffs of disorganization while Balter worried in hundreds of column inches that the Games amounted to a financial fiasco in the making.

Based on their articles, neither Boren nor Balter seemed to share the view of their counterpart, Art Gorlick of the *Seattle Post-Intelligencer*, that the Games presented an opportunity to cover a spectrum of issues no Seattle journalist had ever experienced. Neither seemed to subscribe to the opinion of Emory Bundy, a Soviet scholar involved in the Goodwill Exchange Program, that Seattle had a chance to become a frontline actor at an epic moment in U.S.-Soviet history. Both apparently ignored, or were unaware of, the keen U.S. State Department interest in the Games. Both, in the view of SOC functionaries, felt compelled to fulfill the prediction of Peter Ueberroth, who organized the 1984 Summer Olympics in Los Angeles. In a *Post-Intelligencer* article, Ueberroth predicted that "doomsayers and pseudo experts" would prattle endlessly that the Goodwill Games would become a civic disaster. Both reporters made Ueberroth a prophet.

Six months after Kathy Scanlan became Executive Vice President of the SOC, Boren launched a scud missile that described the organization in terms of Laurel and Hardy carting a grand piano up a flight of stairs. By Boren's reckoning, the SOC lagged two years behind in planning, had failed to locate sponsors, and that its tepid efforts "didn't fit into a rational set of civic priorities." Boren lamented that the SOC's budget had become "a moving target," and she condemned the SOC for failing to provide local law enforcement agencies with sufficient resources to plan for security.

"At the heart of what's wrong with the Goodwill Games," wrote Boren, "is that it remains the enterprise of a few individuals rather than a concerted community effort. The likelihood that we would find ourselves in this pickle should have been obvious from the first mixing of the brine."

The SOC had commissioned an economic impact study, in small part as ammunition to use against naysayers like Boren, in large part to use as a tool for funding requests from the Washington State legislature. The study showed the Games, at least to the SOC's satisfaction, would impact Washington's economy to the tune of $311.6 million and provide $16 million in additional tax revenue. Boren doubted the study's validity. The SOC had arranged with TBS for the network to spend $5 million to promote Washington State as a tourist destination. Boren doubted the Games would attract many visitors. Boren remained steadfastly unswayed by any survey that cast the Games in a positive light, arguing against every estimate, motive, projection, and statement issued by the SOC.

"And then you had Joni Balter," recalled Bernie Russi, who had taught journalism at Marietta College. "In a Sunday edition of the *Times*, she wrote one article saying that nobody was going to come to the Games. In another part of the paper, she wrote an article talking about the horrible traffic crisis we were facing. Joni always tried to turn everything we did upside down to find the worms on the bottom of it."

It was true, as Boren insinuated, that the SOC had become riddled by internal dissent. Scanlan didn't care for media maven Bill Sears, who disliked Scanlan and had no use for one of Scanlan's hires, Gretchen Sorensen, whom Sears considered incompetent. Scanlan also thought marketing whiz Mike McDermott as useless as bleached driftwood. Most everyone in the SOC, except Scanlan, believed sales guru

Doug Hauff, SOC

Doug Hauff to be a blowhard. Although Scanlan claimed to respect Jim Sheldon, the Vice President of Sports, Bob Walsh remained convinced that Scanlan wanted to fire Sheldon. Jarlath Hume, the Vice President for Community Affairs, and Carmen Matthews, the Program Manager for Community Involvement, came to loggerheads. BWA President Kimberly Brown didn't care much for either Hume or former City Prosecutor Doug Jewett. Gene Fisher believed that Peter Kassander, the SOC's liaison with the State Department, behaved like some kind of secret agent and especially resented SOC staffer Don Dow's attempts at upside-down reading of memos and telexes on Fisher's desk. And then, of course, both Ted Bowsfield and Shelly Yapp had tried to topple Bob Walsh, which didn't sit well with Hume, who thought Yapp didn't know what she was talking about half the time. One board member had become ensnared in a divorce, while another made wild accusations that a third board member had bedded his bride. In other words, the SOC appeared to be a perfectly normal organization.

A reporter who enjoyed universal respect among her peers, for her ability to flesh out facts and compose them with style, Balter had a reputation as a phenomenally dogged inquisitor. Her stories suggested that she believed Seattle business leaders had been pressured by the SOC into thinking that if they didn't support the Goodwill effort, Seattle would wind up with a black eye. She quoted critics who said the Aquatic Center in Federal Way would be too small and that the Seattle Police Department would be overwhelmed. And, as Ueberroth predicted, she hammered on the inevitably of Goodwill gridlock. "For many," wrote Balter, "the Goodwill Games will be nothing more than a series of world-class traffic jams."

"I couldn't abide Joni," Scanlan admitted later. "No matter how many times we told Joni we intended to break even, no matter how many times we told her our projections showed we would break even, it didn't matter. She needed to take a course in municipal finance, or maybe a course on how to add up a column of numbers. She didn't understand anything."

While Scanlan agreed with Boren that the SOC had initially been a "mess," it was also true Boren failed to understand the process. The SOC's organizational chart had not been drawn well in advance nor implemented by committee and consensus. The Games had bubbled to life through a rapid fusion of disparate organizations — the SOC, the Goodwill Arts Committee, One Reel, International Event Management, Turner Broadcasting System, the USSR State Sports Committee, federal, state, and local governments — spread from Seattle to Atlanta to Washington, D.C. to Moscow, each entity trying to negotiate with the other, with private contractors, and special interest groups.

The Soviets especially required great care and feeding. They wanted to talk long and often, usually in Moscow. The USSR State Sports Committee wanted the SOC to pay for a Soviet TV producer to travel to the U.S. to consult with TBS and SOC about the Opening Ceremony. The Ministry of Culture wanted the SOC to help pay for the prize winners at the Riga Film Festival to travel to Seattle. The Soviets wanted their own logo on Goodwill souvenirs, another in a succession of demands. Given the high maintenance the Soviets required, the peevishness of TBS, the molasses pace of government, and especially their own limited resources, SOC officials inevitably encountered chaos, responding to each tempest and issue somewhat in the manner of Indiana Jones: They made it up as they went along.

Boren especially didn't understand, or care, that creating the Games from scratch was more difficult than staging the Olympics. The Olympics were four times the size of the Goodwill Games, but the Olympics had history, TV, advertisers, sponsors, and no need to justify its existence, much less demonstrate its credibility.

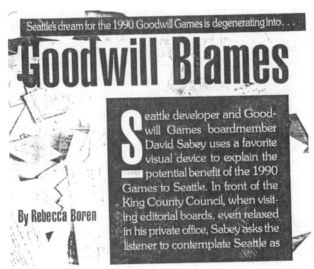

Seattle's dream for the 1990 Goodwill Games is degenerating into. . .

Goodwill Blames

Seattle developer and Goodwill Games boardmember David Sabey uses a favorite visual device to explain the ▬ potential benefit of the 1990 Games to Seattle. In front of the King County Council, when visiting editorial boards, even relaxed in his private office, Sabey asks the listener to contemplate Seattle as

By Rebecca Boren ▼

Rebecca Boren's article in The Weekly skewered the SOC

Each Olympic venue had an eight-year lead time to get ready; Seattle had half that. So there had to be instant analysis, wizardry on the fly, and a relentless belief it would all work out in the end. How the SOC assembled the Goodwill engine, and what outcomes loomed, failed to interest Boren, who didn't so much care about process as she cared about controversial stories that drew attention and comment. Two years before her diatribe at the SOC, she journalistically pepper-sprayed Bob with an article that questioned

A high hurdle: paying Games bills

5/6/90

The public cost is rising; gap could hit $2.6 million

Seattle Times Headline

his ability to deal effectively with the Soviets, even though she never spoke to Bob about his career or credentials. Two years later, she did not bother to explore the significance of the largest U.S.-Soviet exchange in the history of the Cold War, even though it was being assembled right under her nose. She fulfilled her journalistic obligation to question, but flunked her obligation to understand. So she staked out the pit stops, reporting on the occasional blown gasket and flat tire, missing the strategy of the race entirely.

"After we got U.S. Bancorp as a sponsor, I had this conversation with Boren," Scanlan explained later. She said, 'Well, you know, you only have one bank. What about Seafirst and all these other banks?' I said, 'Well, Rebecca, the whole idea is that there's only one bank, the official bank.' She didn't get it. You have to think of an organizing committee as having the full life cycle of a business. It's a startup, and then it operates, and then it folds. It has all the classic attributes of a business only all sped up. When it starts out it's undercapitalized, it doesn't have a structure or staff, and then pretty soon you've got a structure and a staff. Then it's over, and the last ones out are the attorneys and accountants."

Kathy Scanlan had been hired to develop a strategy that would enable the SOC to overcome its single biggest obstacle when talking to potential sponsors: whether the Games were really going to happen. As she structured her staff, and as the SOC expanded its marketing efforts, the Goodwill Arts Committee developed its own publicity programs. One of the more intriguing evolved into a competition to identify a project that would come to represent the Games in the way the Space Needle represented the 1962 World's Fair. An anonymous donor provided $5,000 as the prize for the winning project, and the winning idea proposed launching a piece of sculpture into space through a joint U.S.-Soviet effort. The sculpture, designed to be visible in the Northern Hemisphere for the six months prior to the Games, would symbolize a new era between the countries. Americans would build the sculpture at a cost of $3.5 million; the Soviets would launch it. A normal launch would cost $6 to $8 million; through Bob Walsh's efforts, the Soviets agreed to launch the sculpture for just $150,000. Jarlath Hume proposed a July launch to coincide with the fifteenth anniversary of the Apollo-Soyuz flight. For working purposes, the SOC titled the project "The Goodwill Constellation."

Some of the $71.1 million the SOC required to stage the Games began to trickle in soon after Scanlan, her staff, and Herb Bridge, president of Ben Bridge Jewelers, convinced a few major companies that the Games represented a marketing opportunity rather than competition for civic donations. In fact, shortly after Boren's article hit the streets, the SOC locked up a series of major financial commitments: $1.5 million from Group Health Cooperative, $1.5 million from

KING-TV, $1.4 million from TCI/Viacom, $1 million from the Alpac Corp., $1 million from U.S. West, $850,000 from McCaw Cellular, five other packages ranging from $15,000 to $125,000, and the whopper, $2 million from The Boeing Company.

By the time Boeing came aboard, the SOC had also received a commitment from the USSR Ministry of Culture to send the Bolshoi Ballet to Seattle in the summer of 1990 — Bob had always believed the Soviets would cave in — and had made a significant decision about the direction of the Goodwill Games Exchange.

"We wanted to do the largest exchange in the history of American-Soviet relations," remembered Doug Jewett. "An exchange conference had just been held in upstate New York. Some 150 Soviet citizens participated, the largest exchange ever at that time. And I said, 'Let's multiply that by a factor of ten.' That's pretty much how we decided we were going to do an Exchange Program for 1,500 people."

It was precisely the kind of math that Bob Walsh could appreciate.

Sex, Spies, & Lies

It went without saying that you were going to sleep with your boss. We grew up in a culture where it was okay that you were a woman and okay to be reminded of it. If you are not propositioned, you are not attractive. Something is wrong with you.

> – Elana Arustamova,
> Russian-American Foundation,
> Seattle, Washington

*W*henever Bob Walsh ventured to Moscow, he dropped by the United States Embassy, a complex that included one of the more intriguing monuments to Cold War espionage. The chancery, located in an eight-story building in the center of the Embassy grounds, had stood barren for more than a decade. Years of construction had slammed to a stop in 1985 after shame-faced U.S. officials discovered thousands of listening devices embedded in its red brick walls. Precisely how the Soviets implanted them remained a mystery that had received a thorough but inconclusive review. Specu-lation had it that attractive Russian female workers, packing the bugs, had simply waltzed past vodka-challenged U.S. secu-rity guards, whose supervision of the site smacked, in retrospect, of the work of

Inspector Clouseau. After it was revealed the building had been compromised, Congress launched hearings.

Before those hearings commenced, Bob had engaged Sergeant Clayton Lonetree in several benign conversations while the young Marine was stationed at the U.S. Embassy's gate. But soon after Congress initiated the chancery probe, Bob took particular note that Lonetree's photograph began appearing in newspapers, along with accounts of his court martial in Quantico, Virginia, for providing secret information to the KGB. Lonetree had gotten in trouble apparently because of Violetta Seina, a stunning Russian woman who had worked as a translator at the Embassy.

Lonetree had often taken long rides on the Moscow Metro, admiring the murals and other artwork. On one trip he had a "chance" encounter with Seina, immediately falling prey to her seductions. Lonetree's infatuation grew into a love affair and, ultimately, an introduction to Seina's "Uncle Sasha." At the urging of "Uncle Sasha," later identified as Aleksei Yefimov, one of the "best, sharpest, and toughest Soviets" in service to the KGB, Lonetree provided information about the physical layout of the Embassy and names of officials whom Lonetree believed to be CIA agents. Three months after meeting Seina, U.S. military officials transferred Lonetree to the American Embassy in Austria where, presumably wracked by guilt, he confessed his involvement with Seina and "Uncle Sasha." Although Lonetree insisted the information he provided was of little value to the KGB, patriots denounced him as a traitor. His trial received front-page attention and was the gossip of the Moscow ministries Bob frequented, particularly the Ministry of Foreign Affairs, and especially when the verdict came in: Lonetree had been sent to do a long stretch in Leavenworth.

Bob could identify with the Marine's predicament to the extent that it related to infatuations with Soviet translators. Most of the ones Bob encountered were invariably drop-dead beautiful, fluent in several languages, and experts in the art of flirtation. Bob scribbled mental post-it notes to remind himself that any dalliance with a Soviet translator courted unimagined grief as well as the attention of the KGB, which Bob came to discover was not so much a network of administrators and agents operating in service to the Soviet Union as it *was* the Soviet Union.

The KGB's principal work involved war against spies and agents, the investigation and exposure of political and economic crimes by Soviet citizens, the protection of Soviet borders and secrets, and an array of missions designed to prevent unorthodox political and social attitudes from taking root. The KGB monitored education in schools, infiltrated sciences, controlled the military and police, muzzled dissent, and acted as the official state censor. In every metropolis, city, town, village, hamlet, hut, and hovel, the KGB established informant networks to investigate the behavior and attitudes of nearly 300 million people. The Soviet government's definition of sanity ran along these lines: Since no sane person would engage in dissident activity, anyone who did so was insane by default and needed treatment.

At its numerical peak, the KGB employed more than 1.5 million agents and informants, operating within a Byzantine architecture of chief directorates, directorates, sub-directorates, departments, and service sections. The First Chief Directorate included the spawning ground for spies. Special Services I, its intelligence division, provided the Politburo with the unfiltered results of all clandestine activities undertaken by the KGB. Special Services II penetrated the intelligence agencies of other countries. Department V, part of Special Services II, concerned itself with the kind of intrigues normally seen in a James Bond movie. Rudolf Abel, a Russian who infiltrated the United States on a forged passport in 1948, became one of the great success stories of the First Chief Directorate. Abel lived in New York, posing as an artist, and operated a spy network that stretched from North America to Central America. Abel had been so effective that after his cover was blown, Allen Dulles, then CIA chief, said, "I wish we had a couple like him in Moscow." The U.S. exchanged Abel to the Russians in 1962 for Francis Gary Powers, the U-2 spy-plane pilot whom Bob Walsh later hired to do fill-in work on KABC in Los Angeles.

The Second Chief Directorate focused most of its efforts on the internal political control of Soviet citizens and foreigners who resided in or visited the Soviet Union. Foreign tourists became such a priority that the Second Chief Directorate devoted its largest department to their monitoring, sometimes employing "journalists" and "translators."

One "journalist" assigned to Bob Walsh and the Seattle Organizing Committee was Vladimir Geskin, a correspondent for one of Moscow's leading sports newspapers and a "sports journalist" quite unlike any Bob had ever encountered. Geskin once made a telephone call to the Soviet consulate in San Francisco and added Bruce McCaw, a Seattle-based wireless technology entrepreneur, to a visa list with just a casual suggestion. Another time, when Bob wanted to meet with an official in the Soviet Ministry of Foreign Affairs, Geskin handled all arrangements. Geskin introduced Bob and other SOC members to Soviet cosmonauts and involved himself in negotiations in one of Bob's other projects: an attempt to convince the Soviet government to permit Soviet fighter planes to make an appearance at the Opening Ceremony of the Goodwill Games.

The Soviet translators assigned to SOC personnel offered other intrigues, starting with the fact that the vast majority of them could have been centerfold material. In addition, they always did their homework. The SOC's Bernie Russi found himself in Moscow once, waiting to catch a plane. His translator asked if he would like anything to eat. Bernie said no, just coffee. The translator left and returned with a slice of angel food cake.

"Are you sure," she said, "that you don't want some cake?"

"No thank you," Bernie said.

"Oh, that's right!" she replied. "You like chocolate cake."

"How do you know I like chocolate cake?" Bernie asked. "We haven't talked about chocolate cake."

Helen Shiskana quickly became one of Bob's favorite translators. Helen stood about five-foot-three, sported an inferno of red hair, a quick wit, and occasionally played the tease. Unlike millions of Soviets who existed on the cusp of poverty, Helen resided in a luxurious apartment near the Moscow River and wore designer clothes. Her father, Cyril, had been one of the top men in the KGB, and a couple of Helen's former husbands had apparently been aligned with it. Helen had lived briefly in the United States and then for six years in South Africa, where her father served as an "ambassador." She later studied international law at Moscow State University.

"After that I went to work for the Ministry of Foreign Affairs," Helen explained later. "I also trained to become a simultaneous interpreter. I had a chance to leave my work — it was possible if you had the right KGB connections — and work for different ministries. Ultimately, I was sent to the Ministry of Sport. One day, Alexander Kozlovsky told me Bob Walsh was coming to Moscow, and I asked him, 'Who the hell is Bob?'"

Bob's introduction to Helen occurred on a trip he took there with Bernie Russi and Lynne Cox, then planning a series of swims across the Soviet Union as an encore to her successful navigation of the Bering Strait. Helen drew the assignment of translating for Bob's group and received raves for her humor and spunk, particularly after

*Helen Shiskana, far left, translates a speech by the
deputy mayor of Leningrad*

the manner in which she interpreted a speech by the deputy mayor of Leningrad. While the deputy mayor droned on about the siege of Leningrad during World War II, Helen stood next to her, translating: "Now the deputy mayor is saying blah-blah-blah. The deputy mayor is saying that the Communist Party will live forever, blah-blah-blah. And now the deputy major is saying more bullshit."

Helen had no compunction about telling Bob anything he wanted to know about the Soviet Union, including everything he wanted to know about sex, Soviet style. The official view on that subject held that any variety deviating from straight forward bedroom boinkings between married couples was depraved, making homosexuality taboo and punishable. The Soviets also outlawed most forms of erotic art. They did not believe that love should necessarily be a prerequisite for marriage; marriage was, in many cases, a prerequisite for gaining access to privilege, more often a prerequisite to finding an apartment in Moscow. Although Soviet officialdom frowned on divorce, legal termination of marriage was relatively easy to obtain. Russians ended their marriages at a considerably higher rate — approximately one out of every three — than in Western Europe and North America, a lot of breakups stemming from alcoholism and plenty due to socially acceptable philandering. Many Party officials, along with other resourceful Russian men, "sponsored" mistresses. To the Russian men who could afford them, mistresses served as status symbols, like telephones.

Abortion was a non-issue. About 1,000 Soviet women died each year as a result of abortions versus about fourteen per year in the United States. The main reasons: Abortions were often performed without anesthetic and took place in unhygienic conditions. That Russia led the world in per-capita abortions could be traced to the fact that the contraceptive revolution in the West, marked by the development of the Pill, barely cracked Soviet borders, and condoms, euphemistically called "Article Number 2," were always in short supply. Abortion had never been a matter of choice for Soviet women; it had been a necessity stemming from the lack of any alternative.

"If you did it legally there was publicity involved: you had to stand in line," recalled Elana Arustamova, a Russian woman who worked briefly as an interpreter in Moscow. "They had lines for abortion. If you knew a doctor and could pay, you could get the abortion under the table right there and then. Some doctors concentrated their practice on illegal abortions and had a good source of income. But it was not safe. Nobody ever talked about these things in public. They didn't teach us these things in school, either."

Although prostitution officially did not exist, it flourished to the degree of making minor heroines out of the more entrepreneurial harlots. Since the Soviet system provided the majority of people with so few opportunities for social advancement, and almost nothing in the way of glamour, prostitution became a predictable response. One tier of prostitute — the kind Bob had once seen frequenting the restaurant/bar in the Belgrad Hotel — included women who didn't possess many skills beyond their ability to spread them and bed them. Practically every hotel where foreigners stayed had prostitutes working in them, and about half were employed by the KGB. Another level of prostitute, also affiliated with the KGB, ensnared foreign ambassadors, diplomats, couriers, businessmen, and journalists. Cheka, the early Soviet secret police, sometimes used female agents to help separate couriers from their diplomatic pouches. OGPU, a Cheka successor and KGB forerunner, compromised the ambassador from Afghanistan by catching him making love to an opera singer who was working for the OGPU. In 1953, the CIA station chief in Moscow, Edward Ellis Smith, was seduced by a "state worker" posing as a maid and sent home in disgrace. During the eight-year term of Maurice Dejean as French ambassador to Moscow, both he and an aide, Colonel Louis Guibaud, fell victim to sexual seduction. Dejean even sustained a beating by a KGB officer posing as the enraged husband of the woman who seduced him. Some females were pressed into service if the KGB discovered they had dated foreigners. Some signed on out of patriotism, others joined to support impoverished relatives, still others spotted an opportunity for a better lifestyle.

"I was offered job as sexual entrapper," Arustamova remembered. "This KGB guy told me it wasn't much to do, just meet once in a while with some men and talk to them. Well, I wasn't stupid. So I did not become sexual entrapper. The KGB was not something you wanted to deal with. I went to a foreign language school. We had special department, the Fourth Department. It was KGB. I wanted to work for Intourist. They said, 'Okay, you need a license,' and they sent me to this Fourth Department. This guy there says, 'We can give recommendation, but you need a paper saying you'll be reporting to us on everything you see and hear and what these tourists are doing.' I said no. He also wanted me to spy on my roommate. I told him no. So I never got a license."

"The sexual part is a great lining to the cake," Helen Shiskana reflected. "But no one ever insisted on it or said do it, you know what I mean? It was not the incorrect thing to do. It was sort of up to the person."

The Soviets attached Helen to Bob on several of his junkets to Moscow. She liked him, and Bob thrilled over her. Bernie Russi believed Bob would have married Helen if she had wanted to marry him. But Helen knew she was way too much for Bob to handle.

"Besides," recalled Helen, "I knew there was another Russian woman waiting just around the corner for him."

Fire & Ice

Most of Bob's ideas are amazingly creative. I think it's even more amazing that he follows through and pulls them off.

> – Nicole Preveaux,
>   Seattle, Washington

Bob Walsh and Kathy Scanlan approached the Goodwill Games from fundamentally different points of view. Handed a project, a budget, and a team, Scanlan became the quintessential manager, always ramming all of her assignments through to completion. Considering the scope of her current one, Scanlan faced an unenviable mandate: organize and operate the Goodwill Games against a backdrop of relentless harangues with the University of Washington, the Turner Broadcasting System, and Seattle's government and law enforcement agencies — and do it on a shoestring budget. Since Scanlan had no mind to fail, she demanded devotion to the bottom line.

While Bob Walsh served as the SOC's president, his role was not as clearly defined as Scanlan's. Bob played liaison, point man, negotiator, and diplomat, generating torrents of belief in the value of the Games. Where Kathy defined the Games as a series of athletic competitions, arts and cultural events, business and trade conferences, and people exchanges, each to be organized, budgeted, staffed, and executed, Bob preferred fluidity in their definition, his version of the Games always ripe for updating and editing. Kathy's problem with Bob was that he continually rewrote the playbook, often calling audibles that made her game plan more difficult and expensive to implement.

Kathy especially believed in the sanctity of the budget, the Magna Carta of her universe, and it drove her to fingernails-on-blackboard distraction that Bob made paper airplanes out of it. Many of Bob's projects involved great expense and were usually without, in Kathy's estimation, material purpose or merit. Scanlan's budgetary rigidity made little sense to Bob, who believed that the Games presented the SOC with a once-in-a-lifetime opportunity to orchestrate real, first-of-a-kind, cross-cultural exchanges with an adversary once responsible for an American boom in bomb shelters. So while Scanlan immersed herself in operating systems and strict timelines, Bob plunged into the experience of the moment.

Lynne Cox's swim of the Bering Strait, and her less-publicized crossing of Lake Baikal in Siberia, had nothing to do with the Games until Bob enlarged his vision to include them. And both, in Bob's view, had worked out magnificently. Cox had been toasted by Mikhail Gorbachev, who hailed her "courage" and "daring," and by Ronald Reagan, who called her "the essence of the American spirit." She had even gone to Italy to meet the Pope, where she discovered that he had once been a swimmer. In Bob's mind, every opportunity that presented itself could be incorporated into his Goodwill dream. Bob incorporated as many as time and money would allow, and many for which no money existed.

Bob and Gene Fisher, for example, planned a Seattle visit for several chefs from Tbilisi, Georgia, to participate in a cooking exchange, much of the cost subsidized by the SOC. Bob and Gene also arranged for a handful of Soviet state employees, representatives of Gosteleradio and Goskomsport, to move to Seattle to work for the SOC, the first time any Soviets would toil for a nonprofit U.S. organization. Bob and Gene also orchestrated dozens of projects that resulted in minor diplomatic coups. For the first time in history, Gosteleradio aired TV commercials promoting tourism in Washington State. For the first time, Soviets and Americans worked on a program to promote better understanding of the culture and history of the Native Americans in both countries whom Cox's swim had brought together. For the first time, Soviet officials negotiated with U.S. State Department officials about an exchange with the U.S. Job Corps. For the first time, the U.S. and Soviet governments discussed the opening of an air link between Seattle and Leningrad.

When Bob got up every morning, he instinctively desired to invite the world to do something. Kathy appreciated, although she did not fully comprehend, how Bob pulled viable projects out of the ozone. Bob respected Kathy's administrative acumen, although he didn't always understand why his ideas often had her barking at the moon. Because many of Bob's projects knocked gaping holes in her budget, Kathy occasionally came down hard on Bob. Bob always listened to her laments, except when he didn't want to, which was often. So their relationship evolved into a territorial skirmish between the consummate manager and the intuitive entrepreneur, an ideological struggle between structure and improvisation, a knockdown, drag-out between a woman who found Ozymandian lyricism in fine print and a man given to doing his own legal work on bar napkins. Had Bob been both president and executive vice president of the Games, they would have had as much chance of making a coordinated landing as a dust bunny in an Oklahoma twister. Had Kathy held these offices alone, the Games would have had no distinguishing flavor. To produce something extraordinary, Bob and Kathy needed each other. And now they had each other.

Kathy had arrived at the SOC already wary that living with Bob was like living on an earthquake fault line. Bob only thought big and bigger, and his thinking was fragmented and ephemeral. If that made him creative, it also made him dangerous. Bob romped across high wires, blindfolded, made constant excursions into melodrama, and was utterly unrepentant about it. Bob not only stood logic on its head, he beat it with a stick.

There had been that bizarre incident at the Seattle Opera House, Bob's elaborate celebration of the Seattle Seahawks' Tenth Anniversary. Kathy had not forgotten her encounter with Bob on that occasion, when he had maintained that an elevator breakdown had caused the entire show to go south on him. So immediately after becoming executive vice president of the SOC, Kathy had let him know that he wasn't going to be happy with the way she ran the organization.

"You're not going to like this," she told him. "I am a far stronger person than you are. Frankly, I'm far more decisive, and I'm a lot tougher than you are. You are not going to be happy with this."

Kathy did not want to wind up with a failed project, and Bob had, she felt, the capacity to punch her ticket to impoverishment. But she could no more control Bob than she could the media or the weather.

Kathy embraced Bob's projects that had direct relevance to the Games, such as a North American tour of *Bolshoi On Ice*, which dovetailed into the Goodwill Arts Festival. But the Association of International Sportswriters convention that Bob hosted in Seattle symbolized precisely the kind of wild line item that made Kathy chafe. During an impromptu trip to Istanbul, Bob extended an invitation to a bunch of sportswriters to hold one of their semi-annual drinking sprees in Seattle — at the SOC's expense. Sixty scribes descended upon Seattle from Brazil, China, the Congo, Kuwait, Tunisia, Hungary, and Bulgaria. Bob reasoned that if the SOC liquored, pampered, and lavished booty on the writers, they would ultimately crank out volumes of positive copy about the Games, thereby lifting the Goodwill credibility bar internationally. While they did exactly that, Bob's exercise in unbudgeted hospitality cost the SOC a bundle in air fare, hotels, gifts, and miscellaneous expenses. Bob viewed the convention as a huge success. Kathy couldn't figure out how a press clipping in a Congo newspaper, however glowing, enhanced the SOC's bottom line.

While Bob often became the difference between a mainstream Goodwill project occurring or not occurring, a lot of his other stuff, in Kathy's view, bordered on the peripheral. For example, in the middle of Bob's involvement with a Soviet-American Kids-to-Kids radio bridge, Bob romped around the Soviet Union on the SOC's ruble in the company of Lynne Cox after her successful trip across Lake Baikal in Siberia. Bob thought the publicity was great as it provided the SOC reflected glory. Kathy couldn't justify the expense. And she particularly considered Bob's idea for the Opening Ceremony bogus almost beyond comment.

Bob wanted several Soviet cosmonauts and U.S. Air Force flyers to perform together and invited representatives of the Soviet Flying Research Institute to Seattle to discuss the matter — at the SOC's expense. When Bob informed Soviet sportswriter Vladimir Geskin, who pretty much validated Kathy's thinking on the subject, he got an earful.

"To send Soviet combat jets to the United States — even the idea is crazy," Geskin explained to Bob. "It would be the same to have the American jets in the USSR. The bureaucrats are wild when they hear of this."

Of all the projects that blasted craters in her budget, none infuriated Kathy more than the quarterfinal match of the World Chess Championship between former champion Anatoly Karpov and Johann Hjartarson of Iceland. Or-

Bob Walsh and Bruce Marr talk chess with champion Anatoly Karpov, right

ganized by the meticulous hand of Fisher, the tournament had nothing to do with the Goodwill Games per se, but was promoted as an adjunct to them. The entire affair polarized the SOC staff and made Kathy go postal.

"I was ready to kill Bob," Kathy admitted later. "There wasn't any redeeming value to that damn chess tournament. It was crazy and so bloody boring. It was like watching paint dry."

"I loved the things Bob did," recalled Carmen Matthews, involved in bilateral exchanges. "They were why I worked for the Goodwill Games."

"The chess tournament was one more goddamned thing," remembered Jennifer Potter, the SOC's Vice President of Operations. "We didn't need the agony of that."

"I can understand people who are organizationally driven," Jarlath Hume conceded later. "There's no room in that kind of organization to do a bone marrow transplant. But that was what Bob did. It was an accumulation of things that made the Goodwill Games special. Bob was the perfect person for it. But most people don't think that way. Most people think in much more linear terms."

"Kathy's job was to put on the Games," Bernie Russi later insisted. "The rest of these things, or a lot of these things, was fluff

224

coming out of Bob's head. Kathy would go along with them because Bob often got them so far along that they couldn't be cancelled without a problem."

"Kathy didn't grasp the importance of these kind of things," SOC media director Bill Sears subsequently added.

The three people who took the most objective view of the internal goings-on at the SOC were probably Gene Fisher, Jarlath Hume, and Bernie Russi. All appreciated Bob and Kathy for their respective talents and recognized the value that each brought to the party. Of course, precisely because they were objective, many on both sides of the Walsh-Scanlan tug-of-war often accused each other of a lack of loyalty to one camp or the other, some even speculating ridiculously that others were double agents out to serve their own interests. But the friction was real.

"I got along with Kathy up to a certain point," recalled Sears, "and that point was when she brought in some people from Los Angeles to set up the press center. That was my jurisdiction. I told her how I felt, she got huffy about it, and I was pretty much in the outhouse from that point on. She tried to get me fired. She tried to get Jim Sheldon fired as well."

Bill Sears, SOC

"I never wanted to get rid of Sheldon," Kathy explained later. "Bill Sears I might have wanted to get rid of. He just didn't work very hard."

"Kathy got rid of Mike McDermott because he was my guy," recollected Bob. "She wanted to get rid of Sheldon, too. She should have fired Doug Hauff. He was a used car salesman. Kathy had a strange way of picking some people she thought were good, like Hauff and Gretchen Sorensen."

"Gretchen was regarded by some people as being savvy politically," Fisher said later. "I thought she was a little girl trying to do a woman's job."

"Kathy was in favor of putting on the sports events," recalled Bob. "Anything outside that was not good. I believe she wanted to eliminate the arts and cultural exchanges and just do sports."

"I was always in favor of the Arts Festival, the cultural exchanges, and our core projects," Kathy later insisted. "I never had any difficulty with the arts because Jarlath was in charge."

"Kathy would have taken Bob out if she could have," reflected Sears. "She had plans. She needed to change us three — me, Sheldon, and McDermott — in order to get control."

Sears employed several passive-aggressive countermeasures against Kathy, particularly after she hired Gretchen Sorensen, whom Sears called "a government hack," to serve as director of "non-sports media." When the Goodwill Games finally began receiving favorable press notices, Sears clipped the "tear sheets" and tacked them to his office walls to irritate Kathy. When Sears filled his office walls, he tacked more tear sheets in the hall.

Another time, Sears drew an assignment to publish an updated SOC media guide. He deliberately left Sorensen out of it. Without mentioning the omission, Sears showed the proofs to Bernie Russi.

"Looks fine to me," Bernie told Sears. "Let's go with it. But maybe you should show it to Jarlath Hume."

"So Jarlath looks at it," Sears explained later, "and he says, 'Well, where's Gretchen in here?' I says, 'Well, is Gretchen supposed to be in the book? Nobody told me she was supposed to be in the book.' Jarlath says, 'Well, she has to be in the thing. She's our press person with non-sports media.' Well, the book had actually been printed when I showed it to him. And you know, the sons of bitches made me do it over."

When Sears required the services of a secretary, he selected Larkin Wyatt, who had once worked at the Convention and Visitors Bureau. No sooner had Wyatt come on board than moves were made to dispose of her. Sears argued that Wyatt worked for him and no one else at the SOC. The major complaint from Kathy's side of the aisle had it that Larkin Wyatt disrupted the office by singing in the hallways.

"So, I said, 'Jesus. Well you could probably use a little music in this dump,'" remembered Sears. "Their real beef was that I didn't kiss Kathy's ring, or any other part of her extremities."

"Thank God for Bernie Russi," Jennifer Potter said later. "He was the lion at Bob's door. He protected Bob, but he had the ability to inspire trust and confidence on the part of everybody. If Bernie had been a different person, the problems between Bob and Kathy would have been larger."

"For a couple of years it was a war zone and we got along about like fire and ice," recalled Kathy. "We were really different personalities. But we managed to emerge good friends."

But when Kathy discovered that the SOC had lost $200,000 on the quarterfinal match of the World Chess Championship, her disgust spanned every color in the rainbow. Bob spared Kathy a grand mal seizure by failing to inform her that he had also put together a cruise for the chess officials to Devil's Island — at the SOC's expense.

The Lonely Side Of Love

Bob is a true believer. That's why he got in-volved in his second marriage. He wanted the Soviets and Americans to get together so badly that he got together with a Soviet woman, much to his regret.

— Don Horowitz, Board of Directors, 1990 Goodwill Games, Seattle, Washington

When Bob Walsh's gaze first fell on Nina Aksyonova, he all but melted on the floor of the Moscow airport, Nina over-whelming him with her practiced charm and trophy good looks. Nina had long, luxuri-ant hair, the high, arching cheekbones of a model, centerfold legs that reduced Bob to a quiver, and eyes — Nina means "pretty eyes" — that seduced him without Nina even trying. Nina also proved to possess every other quality Bob sought in a woman — intelligence, a sweet disposition, and a sense of humor — and was, as was he, avail-able. She had eagerly agreed to travel with Bob, Gene Pfeifer, and Bernie Russi to Tbilisi for the signing of Bob's wine deal, and by the end of the trip Bob was so hope-lessly moonstruck that he conjured a plot to get her to the United States.

A Soviet translator, Nina had been married once before, to the son of a famous dissident writer, and seemed as inclined toward a new romance as Bob. He courted her in Moscow with mounting enthusiasm over the span of several months while attending to Goodwill Games exchange activity, and kept in constant contact with her from the United States by telephone. Bob soon began to contemplate marriage and knew Nina had thought about it as well.

Emotionally, Bob felt ready. Eight years had lapsed since his divorce from Ruth, and Bob had never been serenely single. He'd dated a woman briefly that he'd met during one of the Emerald City marathons and enjoyed romantic larks of fluctuating degrees of intensity with a couple of other women who left him less than spellbound. He'd had an ongoing relationship with a sexy French woman, Nicole Preveaux, but marriage to Nicole didn't seem quite right, a feeling she apparently shared since Nicole had entered into a fling with a handsome French chef. The other consideration, oddly enough, turned out to be Ruth Walsh. Ruth had remarried, becoming Ruth McIntyre, and it pleased Bob that Ruth was happy. Bob and Ruth had even become friends again, and Bob felt free to move toward a new commitment.

Politically, marriage to Nina presented problems. Since she was a Soviet citizen, marriage would almost require a defection. Bob and Nina had discussed it, and Nina was excited to make the move to the United States. Important to Bob was that he had Bernie Russi's blessing. Bernie considered Nina a wonderful woman, trusting and loving in every way, and Bob valued Bernie's judgment more than anyone else's. As a bonus, marriage to Nina, and their new life in America, would symbolize the ultimate Goodwill Games exchange: The president of the Seattle Organizing Committee hitched to a beautiful Russian translator.

So Bob proposed, Nina accepted, and they made their move while Bob was in Moscow, ostensibly for another round of Goodwill Games meetings and the opening of a Leroy Nieman art exhibition. Only Russi and Gene Fisher, the SOC's director of special projects, became privy to Bob's plan to whisk his bride-to-be out of the Soviet Union.

It required a bit of subterfuge. Bob never let on to any of his Moscow friends that he planned to spirit Nina out of the Soviet Union. Nina then obtained a visa that enabled her to enter North America in Vancouver, British Columbia. To Bob's surprise, Soviet authorities granted the visa. Nina did not really have a valid reason to travel to Vancouver, and without one her visa request should have been denied. Nina also traveled alone, or so Soviet authorities thought, not the normal procedure, either. But it happened this time. Bob didn't know why, nor did he ask. To make certain Soviet security officials did not see them together, Bob and Nina boarded the Vancouver-bound airplane separately.

"When Bob took Nina to America," recalled Alexander Kozlovsky, a deputy at the USSR State Sports Committee, "I received a call to my office and one of the gentlemen from the KGB who was in charge of security informed me that Walsh had tricked everyone. The KGB was unaware Bob was taking Nina away."

Nina remained in Vancouver for close to a month while U.S. Customs and Immigration processed her application to enter the United States.

"It wasn't easy getting her in," remembered Dick Smith, who presided over U.S. Customs and Immigration in Seattle. "There were some concerns about Nina's background, some concerns about security issues."

During that month, Bob made frequent trips to Vancouver and dispatched several of his closest friends to visit Nina. Don and Linda Horowitz spent a weekend with her, as did Bernie and Julie Russi.

"She was very attractive and we certainly did our best to make her feel comfortable," recalled Horowitz, a member of the Seattle Organizing Committee's board of directors. "Bob was so happy. Bob kept saying how wonderful she was to him and for him."

On the day Nina finally arrived in the United States, Bob's friends roasted him at the Westin Hotel in downtown Seattle. During the proceedings, Bob introduced to a long table of roasters that included TBS chairman Ted Turner, basketball legends Bill Russell and Lenny Wilkens, former client and NBA star Jack Sikma, and Rick Welts, now president of NBA Properties in New York, the woman who would play the role of wife number two in the pantheon of Walsh weddings. To most of Bob's friends, Bob and Nina seemed like the perfect couple.

"I liked her right from the start," Bernie Russi admitted later. "I was all for it."

"Nina looked like she came from royalty," reflected Valerie Yurina, one of Bob's closest friends. "She was polished and elegant."

"Nina was very pretty," recalled Amy Boisjolie, who worked as Bob's assistant at the Seattle Organizing Committee. "I tried to do everything I could to make things easy for her when she came."

"The first time Bob brought Nina into the office he paraded her around," remembered Kimberly Brown, president of Bob Walsh & Associates. "After she left, Bob came back and said, 'Isn't she just the most beautiful person?' He thought Nina was the most beautiful woman in the world."

Lenny Wilkens, a friend of Bob's for nearly fifteen years, agreed to host the wedding in the backyard of his Bellevue, Washington, house and stand up for Bob as his best man. With Lenny coaching the Cleveland Cavaliers, Bob rarely saw much of his former client during the professional basketball season, but they spoke frequently on the telephone and occasionally got together during the summer months, which Lenny spent in Seattle.

The day dawned postcard perfect. Under radiant sunshine, with the bride stunning and groom gaga with anticipation, the ceremony took place beneath a thick stand of Douglas fir and Western red cedar, the Rev. William F. Sullivan presiding. Ruth McIntyre smiled happily from the gallery.

"Bob and I had finally pulled together a relationship that was becoming unique and wonderful out of the devastation caused by the wreck of our marriage," Ruth explained later. "I wanted happiness for Bob. My concerns were the cultural differences. I wondered what it would have been like for me if I had been taken from America and plopped in the Soviet Union. But Bob had been spending so much time there that he was aware of those cultural impacts. Bob felt very certain that this was right, and I knew he would do whatever he could to ease the way for Nina."

"Bob was very, very happy; he looked great," recalled Kimberly Brown. "He was really honored that this had happened at Lenny Wilkens' house."

And equally pleased that Bill Russell showed up.

"Nina looked beautiful and Bob seemed very happy," Ruth remembered. "The only thing I sensed was that Nina looked nervous. She didn't seem to be very happy."

The rest of the assembled guests sensed the same thing soon after Bernie Russi escorted the bride to the altar when Bob uttered the two most catastrophic words in the English language — I do.

*Lenny Wilkens, left, served as best man when Bob Walsh
married Nina Aksyonova*

"At the end of the ceremony Bob turned to kiss Nina," recalled Valerie Yurina, "and she just turned her head away, kind of like she was sickened by it. It was a really odd moment."

To most of the invited guests, Nina suddenly seemed almost too pretty, her figure too perfect, her previous charm not quite real.

"Nina just wasn't with it at the wedding," Horowitz said later. "It seemed like she didn't want to get married at all, and that made the wedding really uncomfortable."

"The sense I had was that there were problems already," recalled Carmen Matthews, who worked on Goodwill Games exchanges. "Nina was furious that Bob paid too much attention to the two little Ostrom girls."

"Bob just danced with them," Bernie Russi remembered. "They were twelve or thirteen years old. And Nina went ballistic. It was pretty clear things weren't right. Nina could be perfectly natural one moment, and then in a flash she would become very mad. My wife, Julie, had been suspicious of Nina almost from the day we went to Vancouver to spend a few days with her. When we left, Julie said, 'Did you know that not once did she ask anything about Bob or about Bob's family? There was never any expression of admiration or love of Bob. Don't you think if somebody was about to marry, or at least consider marrying somebody, that they'd want to know something about his family or his background?'"

"I didn't want to believe what I thought was the truth because Bob was so happy," Horowitz later advised. "But I felt like she was using Bob. She went through the motions, and not too many motions."

"After the wedding we went to the Olympic Hotel downtown

and Nina was still furious with Bob there," Matthews said later. "Three hours after the wedding and she was in a fit over something, and they got in a fight. It did not bode well."

"The problem with Bob," Horowitz reflected, "was that he was alone and lonely. He was in love with love and you can make mistakes that way."

"Bob is a poor judge of women," Karl Moynes, one of Bob's long-time friends, remarked later. "I think he got married because of the novelty of it all."

"I don't pretend to psychoanalyze people," Father Sullivan later admitted. "But I did not at all anticipate that the thing would run into trouble so quickly."

Like Ruth, most of Bob's friends worried that Nina would have difficulty adjusting to America, and that it would play havoc with their marriage. Like Kimberly Brown, several of Bob's friends suspected that Nina was not interested in Bob at all, only in pursuing a life of luxury.

"I kept seeing self-interest on her part and Bob deluding himself," Horowitz confessed later. "I start out with the presumption that somebody is for real. Nina overcame that presumption and kept overcoming it. I could never understand why Nina acted the way she did."

"I felt badly for Bob that he was with someone who just wasn't nice," recalled Kimberly Brown. "And she was jealous. Nina thought that Bob and I had some- thing go- ing on. But she w a s pretty much that way with a n y w o m a n Bob was involved

Bill Russell, left, banters with wedding guest Don Horowitz

with or knew. After you got to know Nina it made you wonder what it was that made Bob fall so hard."

"I wondered whether she just hadn't used Bob as a ticket to the United States," Russi later reflected.

"Nina was smart and sophisticated, but she is one of the most unhappiest people," believed Nana Bagdavadze, another of Bob's friends. "She will have golden houses and diamonds, but she will never be happy — I guarantee."

Not long after the wedding, Bob Walsh & Associates received a marketing award. All the BWA staffers attended a dinner honoring the company. Most were women. Bob brought Nina to the banquet.

"Nina just froze up and wouldn't talk to anybody," Russi recalled. "She thought Bob was making out with all the women in his company."

"At Christmas time, I brought a gift to Bob's house," remembered Bob's assistant, Amy Boisjolie. "When Nina came home she was sure we were having an affair. She was very insecure. Nina had to be the center of attention. If she wasn't, you paid a heavy price for it."

"After Bob and Nina got married, she wanted a house," recalled Valerie Yurina. "So Bob sold his condominium downtown and bought them a house. And then a few months later, Nina wanted a fur coat. Bob had just bought the house. He told me he couldn't afford to buy her this coat, that he was going to tell her no. When he did, Nina got hysterical. She had to have the coat. So Bob ran down and bought her a coat. No matter what Bob did, it was never enough for Nina."

"Responding to a desperate phone call from Bob, Julie and I spent Christmas night with Bob and Nina one time trying to keep them, although not literally, from killing each other," Russi later admitted. "She had thrown Bob out of the house. She was angry that Bob had gone to a Bob Walsh & Associates Christmas party and had stayed a half-hour longer than he had promised. There was some Russian thing she had wanted to go to. I said, 'Nina, when was that party?' She said, 'It was the 6th of December.' I said, 'Well, this is the 25th of December. Don't you forgive and forget?' Her response was, 'No. He must be punished.'"

"I did not know how Bob came to be president of the Goodwill Games, but the choice was perfect," Kozlovsky said later. "As I understood the idea of the Games, it captured Bob totally. As the president, Bob went far beyond the Games as they were. He was permanently generating new projects. Bob was so totally captured by the idea of the Games that he seemed to try and turn almost

234

everything into a project of the Games. So it was with Nina. And thus he trapped himself."

Bob and Nina's marriage soon combined the tension of *Aliens* with the plot of *I Married A Monster*. Rarely a day went by that Bob didn't feel like he'd been strung up with piano wire, Nina strumming it fiendishly.

Intervention In Armenia

Bob won't let people say no. He's going to make the thing work. He's an extremely rare personality.

> *– Rev. William J. Sullivan, former president,*
> *Seattle University,*
> *Seattle, Washington*

The earthquake that shook the northern region of Armenia at 11:47 a.m. on December 7, 1988, produced devastation almost beyond comprehension. Three distinct tremblers, each lasting between ten and fifteen seconds, spiked in a Richter reading of 6.9, instantly transforming half of the republic's territory into a tapestry of death, misery, ruin, and ash. By the time the shaking and settling had stopped, 25,000 people were dead and 500,000 homeless. Seventy-nine cities, regions, and villages had been laid to waste, including Spitak, which was utterly flattened. Two hundred and thirty manufacturing enterprises, thousands of schools, and countless social and cultural institutions had been destroyed. The quake even cracked the foundation of the Hotel Tbilisi in Georgia's capital city, 250 miles from its epicenter.

Several hours after news of the disaster swept the globe, Gary Furlong, a personal-injury attorney, took a red-eye out of Seattle, his destination the U.S. State Department's Office of Foreign Disaster Assistance in Washington, D.C. Furlong, who had just been named the new chairman of the King County Disaster Relief Team, had a keen interest in Russia and the Soviet Union and wanted to volunteer his organization's services. But when Furlong arrived at OFDA, officials told him that while the Soviet government

The 6.9 quake that struck Armenia killed more than 25,000

welcomed donations of supplies and medicine, it would not allow American doctors, paramedics, or nurses to enter Armenia.

Furlong figured as much. While he realized Armenia was woefully ill-prepared to deal with still-unfolding carnage, he also recognized that the Soviets harbored profound paranoia that anyone in the West would discover the truth. Refusing to let it go at that, Furlong tracked down Bob Walsh's telephone number from U.S. Senator Brock Adams' office and called for advice. Gary Furlong and Bob Walsh had never met, but Furlong knew that Bob was president of the Seattle Organizing Committee, that the SOC had experienced difficulty generating support for its efforts in Seattle, and that Bob had connections to Soviet government officials. Furlong suspected that an earthquake response might put Seattle in the news and generate interest in the Games.

Bob immediately agreed to help Furlong, dispatching telexes to Gennadi Gerasimov at the Soviet Foreign Ministry and to Soviet ambassador Yuri Dubinin. The telexes vouched for Furlong, made it clear that Furlong only intended to conduct a private relief effort, and proposed a quick solution to Soviet customs and immigration concerns. Meanwhile, Furlong met with Third Secretary Georgy Markosov at the Soviet Embassy.

"We have access to doctors and experienced paramedics who are prepared to fly to Armenia to render assistance," Furlong told him.

"You already know our position," replied Markosov. "No Americans in Armenia."

"Are you aware that Bob Walsh has offered to help?"

The Russian's attitude changed perceptibly.

"I'll get back to you this afternoon after I consult with Moscow," said Markosov.

The Soviets normally took weeks to make any kind of decision, even relatively insignificant ones. But a few hours after Gerasimov, Markosov, and Dubinin had discussed the contents of Bob's telexes, Gary Furlong, who had never traveled outside the United States, found himself making frantic plans to fly to Soviet Armenia. The Soviets had agreed to Bob's proposal that Furlong and his team be allowed to fly directly to Yerevan.

Gary Furlong

That solved several problems. Under ordinary circumstances, American relief team personnel would first have to obtain visas to enter the Soviet Union. Normally, that paper trail would snake through the Soviet Embassy in Washington, D.C., and then on to Moscow; the process would have taken weeks — even without delays, miscommunication, or misplaced paperwork. Once the disaster team received visas, it would have had to fly to Moscow, where the airplane's cargo would be unloaded and inspected. Only then would it be permitted to fly into Yerevan.

Since Furlong's relief team had no time for that, Bob suggested the Soviets waive standard procedures and permit Furlong's team to fly directly to Yerevan without visas so it could get to work immediately. Bob promised to screen and certify all individuals making the trip to assure that they weren't agents of the federal government or media representatives. Bob also vowed to provide the Soviet Embassy, via telex, with registration information on the U.S. aircraft that would enter Soviet airspace. When the U.S. transport arrived, the Soviets could send up their fighter planes; their pilots would be able to check the registration identification on the tail of the U.S. transport jet against those Bob provided. If they matched, the American transport would be given a Soviet escort into Armenia. If they didn't, the Soviets would shoot the American plane down.

This venture not only marked the first public-private American relief effort conducted anywhere in the Soviet Union since 1923 (U.S. soldiers had done relief work in the Soviet Union during World War II), it became the start of what the International Red Cross would ultimately describe as "worldwide, public-private relief symbiosis." And it only happened because of a major, here-to-fore unheard of concession by the Soviets: They would allow Americans without visas to enter Armenia solely on Bob's word.

Furlong had never orchestrated a relief effort anywhere in the world. He had, however, made frequent visits to the Office of Foreign Disaster Assistance, studying how the organization set up disaster responses, and the technical components of planning a relief mission. Now he had three primary tasks: Get his team into Armenia, get it going, and get it out. After exploring several options to transport his team, equipment, and supplies into Soviet territory, Furlong contacted Flying Tigers, a cargo service that operated all over the world. He began with a weekend night clerk at Los Angeles International Airport; a couple of hours and supervisors later, Furlong had the company's vice president of operations on the phone. Furlong explained the situation and asked if Flying Tigers could help. Within a relatively short period of time, Furlong had a plane, a crew, the necessary fuel, and one-way transport to Armenia. Flying Tigers could get Furlong and his team into Armenia; because the airplane would depart shortly after arrival, Furlong would have to make other arrangements to get his team home. The plan fell short of perfect, but a frenetic Gary Furlong had few other options.

When the Flying Tigers 747 arrived in Seattle from LAX, Dr. Roy Farrell coordinated the packing of the plane with blood plasma, medicines, blankets, tents, and other gear. An emergency physician at Group Health's Central Hospital in Seattle, Farrell held the responsibility of orchestrating medical services for the Goodwill Games. He had already made a few trips to the Soviet Union and had a decent understanding of conversational Russian, much of his language expertise owing to his participation in a one-month exchange with Soviet doctors in Tashkent, Uzbekistan.

"Within a week of the earthquake we were on the scene," recalled Dr. Farrell. "During that week, we put together a 747 full of medical supplies and equipment. We had a mobile field hospital and

Dr. Roy Farrell

three search and rescue dogs from Alaska. Once word got out that we had permission to enter the Soviet Union, everybody wanted to get on that plane. Donations came from everywhere. We even had Armenian physicians from California and the Midwest."

When the Flying Tigers 747 stopped at JFK in New York en route to Yerevan, Furlong and a small group of doctors joined the flight. As the plane departed, Bob telexed Victor Gribanov at the Soviet Embassy in Washington, D.C., providing him with the tail identification letters: L V M L O.

"The landing in Armenia was hairy and the pilots were real nervous about it," remembered Furlong. "You had to come through the mountains. In the two days preceding our arrival there had been two mid-air collisions there. I heard that the air traffic system was just overloaded. Then the Soviets gave altitude in meters where we calculated in feet. Their tower people did not speak English very well. Our interpreter did not speak traffic-control Russian. There were real tensions in that plane as to what the hell was going on. When we were getting ready to land in Yerevan, I was sort of doing a last-minute briefing and I asked whether there were any questions."

"Yeah," someone shouted from the cockpit. "How are we getting home?"

"I don't know," Furlong replied.

Nearly everyone on the plane burst into laughter.

"They thought I was kidding," Furlong recalled later.

"No, really, how are we getting home?" asked another voice.

"I told them again I didn't know," Furlong remembered. "Then there was a quieter laugh, and then there was dead silence."

"Fuck, you're serious!" came another voice.

"I told them I was," Furlong explained later. "The only thing I knew was that Aeroflot would bring six people out a day through Moscow back to the United States. Aeroflot had told us it would do that. Or Aeroflot had told Bob Walsh. I wasn't sure."

"I knew that this was the first 747 Armenia had ever seen," recalled Dr. Farrell. "The airport was thronged with people gaping at this double-decker airplane. It took fifty-two trucks to unload it."

"We arrived at night," Furlong advised later. "As we taxied in, the pilots commented about one of the planes on the ground."

"Look who's here," one of the pilots said.

The other pilot peered out the side window. "Shit. What's he doing here?"

"God only knows."

Overhearing the two pilots, Furlong glanced at the plane sitting on the tarmac.

"Who's plane is that?" he asked.

"You don't wanna know."

"No, really, I wanna know. Who is this guy? What's the name of this guy's company?"

"Pan Aviation. Out of Miami."

The name meant nothing to Gary Furlong and he couldn't get any more information out of the pilots, so he turned to the task at hand, becoming aware soon after disembarking the 747 that the Soviets had not prepared for Furlong or his team. They didn't know what to do with them and couldn't answer any of Furlong's questions. After standing in a heavy rain for what seemed to be hours, Furlong snapped.

"Look," Furlong said to a man who seemed to be in charge, "if I don't have a meeting with someone of a certain level within an hour, and if my guys aren't taken out of the rain, we're going to put all this shit back on the plane and we're leaving. And I'm going to tell Moscow it's your goddamn fault."

"Do you want me to interpret 'goddamn?'" asked the Soviet translator.

"You bet I do!" barked Furlong.

Fifteen minutes later, a man identifying himself as a "deputy minister" introduced himself to Furlong.

"He could have been the janitor for all I knew," Furlong admitted later. "But he was sitting in a nice office. He said the arrangements for getting our team into the field would have to be made the next day. There would be someone at the hospital for me to talk to. So the next day I went to talk to this guy at the hospital. The first thing he wants to know is what our team will give him to let us go into the field."

It stunned Furlong that the man wanted a bribe. Dead bodies had been stacked everywhere. Thousands of people suffered from exposure. Countless others remained trapped beneath flattened buildings. Each member of Furlong's team had gladly given up the Christmas holidays to fly to Armenia to assist earthquake victims, only to encounter an asshole who wanted a kickback in exchange for allowing Furlong's team to save lives and treat the injured.

"I was surprised the guy could be so goddamn calloused," recalled Furlong. "The deal we finally cut was that, in return for a bus for our team and a person with the authority to get my team anywhere it wanted to go, I would get him ten doctors over the next six months to perform surgeries. Obviously, I had no intention of doing that. But the long and the short of it was that I found out the value of ten surgeons was a bus and KGB guy."

Furlong had gotten his team in, arranged transportation, and gotten it going. Now he had to get back to the United States to see what he could do about getting his people out of there. As Furlong departed on Aeroflot for Moscow, Dr. Farrell and his medical colleagues began performing operations and search-and-rescue services.

"We went out to a little town near the epicenter and set up camp in a park," remembered Dr. Farrell. "One night we went to a collapsed building with the dogs. We took them into a department store that had collapsed like a house of pancakes. The Armenians are Christian; to go through this department store with Santa Clauses and Christmas trees, well, it was gut wrenching when you thought about all the people who were crushed and killed in the building."

Furlong flew from Moscow to New York, where he was promptly targeted by a news media eager to have him criticize the Soviet government's apparent inability to manage the crisis in Armenia. Taken aback by his instant celebrity status, Furlong grew more astonished when the news media failed to understand that no country, not even the United States, could be prepared for a quake of the length and magnitude that jolted Armenia. And it irritated him, especially as

*Bob Walsh welcomes
Houston basketball
coach Guy Lewis to
the 1984 Final Four*

*Bob Walsh, left, and Gene Fisher, right, of SOC with
Georgian chess champion Eddie Gufeld*

*Bob Walsh and
Nicole Preveaux,
with ex-President
Richard Nixon,
the 1986
Goodwill Games,
Moscow, Russia*

Bob Walsh welcomes ex-President Ronald Reagan to the 1990 Goodwill Games, Seattle, Washington

Bob Walsh greets the Rev. Jesse Jackson at the Pepsi Friendship Center during the 1990 Goodwill Games

L to R: Kristin Hayden, BWE shareholder Sharon Lovejoy, and Bob Walsh in Tbilisi

*L to R:
Rev. William
Sullivan,
Marat Gramov,
and Bob Walsh
at the 1986
Goodwill Games*

*Bob Walsh welcomes First Lady Barbara Bush
to the 1990 Goodwill Games*

Dave Syferd, left, and Bob Walsh discuss procedural issues with Juan Antonio Samaranch, president of the International Olympic Committee

Bob Walsh with Arnold Schwarzenegger and former Olympic gymnast Olga Korbut

Bob Walsh, left, with Tatiana and Alexander Kozlovsky in San Francisco

*Bill Russell
and Bob's sister,
Toni Walsh*

*Georgia President
Eduard Shevardnadze
greets Bob Walsh
in Tbilisi, Georgia*

*During a junket to Vilnius, Lithuania, to check out "Circus on Ice,"
Bob played hockey against a rather unusual goalkeeper*

Tbilisi Toast:
Bob Walsh
with "tamada"
Vaho Tskhadaze

President and Hillary Clinton welcome Georgian ambassador
Tedo Japaridze and his wife, Tamara, to the White House

Bob and
Nina Walsh
with Larry King
at the 1990
Goodwill Games

L to R: General John Shalikashvili, Georgian ambassador Tedo Japaridze, Eduard Shevardnadze, and former U.S. ambassador William Harrison Courtney, outside Shevardnadze's residence in Tbilisi, Georgia

Bob became acquainted with industrialist Armand Hammer during the Opening Ceremony of the 1990 Goodwill Games

L to R: Jack Lemmon, Peter Jacobson, Toni Walsh, Elizabeth (Mom) Walsh, Nicole Preveaux, Bob Walsh, Tom Watson and Monty Hall at a celebrity golf tournament in 1985

Bob Walsh with Vice-President Hurbert Humphrey at KABC Radio, 1967

Bob Walsh with boxing champion Sugar Ray Robinson at KABC Radio, 1967

fatigued as he was, that the media peppered him with inane questions; either the news media hadn't listened to his answers or it wanted to trip him up.

Furlong could have been critical about a lot of things he'd seen and heard in Armenia, especially the bribery, corruption, and siphoning off of money and goods intended for the relief effort. People in the Armenian community had told Furlong not to route medicine, equipment, or money through Moscow because Armenia would receive only a small percentage of it. Moscow would snatch the majority, much of it winding up on the black market throughout Russia. But Furlong certainly wasn't going to tell any secrets — not while he still had a team on the ground in Armenia, and not while Bob Walsh still had the Goodwill Games in Seattle to produce. So Furlong danced the media dance, then hopped a shuttle to Washington, D.C., where he used U.S. Senator Brock Adams' office to search for a way to get his team out of Armenia and back home by Christmas.

Furlong weighed the pros and cons of routing options on several carriers. Aeroflot had offered to take out six people at a time from Moscow to either New York City or Washington, D.C., but that would be a slow, tedious process. He checked with Donald Trump's people. Trump had a stake in TWA, but Trump had no interest in assisting Furlong, who explored additional commercial avenues, including Yerevan-Moscow-London, Yerevan-Istanbul-London, and Yerevan-Frankfurt-London. Pan Am had a flight out of London for New York on the evening of December 21, which would get many of Furlong's people home by Christmas thanks to a deal Furlong cut with Continental Airlines to fly his people home for free, wherever they lived, if they made it to the U.S. by December 22.

Furlong wanted his team to make that Pan Am flight, but just in case, he scratched around for other flights. Then he remembered Pan Aviation. He didn't know anything about the company or the mysterious individual who owned it, but he located Pan Aviation's telephone number and called it. A receptionist grilled Furlong about the nature of his call, then transferred it.

"What do you want?" said the gruff voice on the other end. "Where are you calling me from?

"Senator Brock Adams' office."

"Do you work for the senator?"

"No."

"What are you doing there? How do you know the senator?"

Furlong explained that he once ran one of Adams' political campaigns in Washington State, but had no official connection to the senator and was not on Adams' payroll. Adams had permitted Furlong to use one of his offices, and there was nothing more to it than that.

"Look," said Furlong, "all I want to know is if you can get my team out of Armenia and into Europe."

"Okay. I'll talk to you about it. Come down and see me."

Furlong asked several people in Adams' office what they knew about Pan Aviation. All of them advised Furlong to stay away from it.

"He has airplanes in Armenia and seems willing to help," said Furlong. "So I'm going to Miami."

"Just watch your ass," advised one of Adams' staffers.

So Furlong jumped on a plane to keep his appointment with Pan Aviation's major-domo, Sarkis Soghanalian. On the flight down, a pair of reporters, one from *The New York Post* and the other from *The Miami Herald*, both of whom recognized Furlong, struck up a conversation. By coincidence, they knew all about Soghanalian and were en route to interview him.

Furlong quizzed the reporters, eager to learn more about the man the Flying Tigers pilots told him he didn't want to know anything about. According to both, Soghanalian occupied a shadowy netherworld teeming with the kind of implausible figures ordinarily found in a John Le Carre novel. The bottom line on Soghanalian: March out 50,000 naked soldiers and Soghanalian could equip them out of stock with uniforms, boots, weaponry, bullets, explosives, vehicles, and helicopters. And what he didn't have in stock he could get: grenade and rocket launchers, Uzi's, precision sniper and antisniper rifles, ammunition, whatever the client ordered.

Sarkis Soghanalian ranked among the largest private arms dealers in the world and was known in the trade as "The Merchant of Death." As the glamour guy of the industry, Soghanalian sold weapons everywhere on the planet that insurrections and armed conflicts could be found. Soghanalian had a murky and ill-defined relationship with United States government agencies and law enforcement officials. He apparently worked on and off for them but was currently under indictment for selling attack helicopters to Iraq.

A Lebanese citizen of Armenian decent, Soghanalian had been born and reared in a Beirut suburb and grew up to become a freelance gunrunner; he had nearly been murdered once for selling arms to Lebanese Christian groups. When he arrived in the United States, he had

$46 in his pocket. He struggled for years, working in a small garage in upstate New York while selling arms to Lebanese Christians whenever he could arrange financing. Then he reportedly picked up the CIA as a client and his fortunes turned around. Over the next two decades, Soghanalian's buyers came to include a roster of bloody headline makers: the Lebanese Christian Forces in their war against the Palestine Liberation Organization; the Argentine military junta in its war in the Falkland Islands; Nicaragua's radical Somoza. Soghanalian apparently had branches of his illusory and high-profit operations in Miami, Beirut, Madrid, Athens, Geneva, and Baghdad.

Soghanalian had boasted that he was not only an arms dealer, but a military consultant who frequented battlefields to visit customers and provide morale for the troops. He maintained that his sales exceeded $1 billion per year and his annual income topped $12 million. He had held legal residency in the United States for more than two decades and, according to the grapevines that whispered in Soghanalian's sphere, had reportedly received jars of severed human ears from his clients.

Furlong would find out much later that Soghanalian had gone to jail for bank fraud and money-laundering, and that he had conspired to sell high-tech weaponry, including rocket launchers, to Saddam Hussein for his country's use against Iran, and then against the United States during the Persian Gulf War. According to U.S. assistant attorney Susan Tarbe, Soghanalian was "a con man who had perverted the American dream."

Yet following his release from prison, Soghanalian helped U.S. agents uncover a Middle East-based counterfeiting scheme. The Sarkis Soghanalian that Gary Furlong met was about sixty years old and weighed more than 300 pounds. He owned a stable of Arabian horses, a fleet of jets and helicopters that whisked him and his weaponry anywhere at a moment's notice, a palatial home on Biscayne Bay, and additional homes in Athens, Madrid, Paris, and Los Angeles. His main office occupied part of a private hangar at Miami International Airport.

The office actually amounted to a compound surrounded with a barbed-wire fence, guarded by several frowning men with guns. Two of them escorted Furlong to Soghanalian's quarters.

"Are you CIA or are you State Department?" Soghanalian asked, bypassing pleasantries.

"Neither," said Furlong.

"Are you working with Senator Adams?"

"No, I'm nothing, you know? I'm telling you the truth. If I lie to you, you are not going to believe me. If I tell you the truth, you are not going to believe me. At least this way, I'm honest."

"Fuck you," said Soghanalian, walking away.

For the next three days, Soghanalian interrogated Furlong about his relationship with Senator Adams, pushing to find out who Furlong really was and what Furlong could do for him, although Soghanalian seemed to have nothing specific in mind. Soghanalian talked about the Soviets, about several regional conflicts, and even told Furlong where weapons were manufactured and how they were bought and sold. Soghanalian generally displayed a friendly attitude, but Furlong detected an undercurrent of menace in his personality. During the course of their conversations, they discussed a range of options for getting Furlong's team out of Armenia.

"Maybe the best thing," Soghanalian finally told Furlong, "is to just send my private jet to collect the doctors."

Soghanalian eventually returned to prison for an array of scurrilous deeds. But had he not provided that plane, a number of the weary American doctors, paramedics, and nurses would have been at Heathrow Airport in London on December 21st, ready to board a Pan Am 747 bound for Kennedy International Airport in New York where they could catch the free Continental flights home. The London flight pushed off Heathrow runway 27R at 18:04 hours and leveled off at cruise altitude at 18:56 hours. Seven minutes later, the 747 disappeared from Heathrow's radar screens. Most of the wreckage from Pan Am 103 was found in Lockerbie, Scotland.

Barbarians At The Gate

The personal and professional abuse that Bob has taken is outrageous. He's a very passionate and emotional person. I'm not sure Bob has a tough enough shell.

— Kathy Scanlan, Executive Vice President, 1990 Goodwill Games, Seattle, Washington

*N*ot every project worked out the way Bob Walsh envisioned. Several couldn't find wings, a few became abortively messy affairs, and a couple degenerated into darkly comic soap operas, including one involving Vjacheslav Gavrilin of the USSR State Sports Committee. Bob had lobbied Soviet authorities for more than a year to assign two operatives to the Seattle Organizing Committee. After much fuming on the Soviet side over the unprecedented nature of Bob's request, Gosteleradio agreed that Valentin Yegorov would become its liaison in Seattle. The USSR State Sports Committee dispatched Gavrilin to the SOC six months later in what amounted to a minor diplomatic triumph for Bob: Yegorov and Gavrilin became the first two Soviet officials permitted to join a nonprofit United

States organization, both receiving monthly salaries of $3,000. But while Yegorov made valuable contributions to the SOC, Gavrilin proved to be a slacker with Magoo-like incompetence, impossible to please, particularly with respect to his housing arrangements.

Accompanied by his wife and granddaughter, Gavrilin scoffed at the original apartment the SOC secured for him since it did not include a suitable play area for the young girl. That forced a beleaguered Gene Fisher to scour Seattle for alternate lodgings that Gavrilin requested be furnished with a plethora of frivolous knickknacks. Once settled, Gavrilin did little to earn his keep, spending the vast majority of his work time on the telephone trying to broker deals for himself.

"For some reason," Fisher recalled, "Gavrilin was always calling Korea."

Annoyed at squandering $3,000 a month for nothing, Kathy Scanlan and Bernie Russi insisted that Bob fire Gavrilin, who departed without much fuss but with a colorful flourish. When Bob and Bernie inspected Gavrilin's vacated apartment, they discovered he had emptied much of its rented contents and shipped them back to Moscow. In frustration, Bob dispatched the following note to Alexander Kozlovsky at the USSR State Sports Committee:

Mr. Alexander Kozlovsky
Deputy Chairman
USSR State Sports Committee

Dear Sasha:

We are sorry to notify you that several items from the Soviet Representative's apartment in Seattle are missing. From the number of boxes shipped to the Soviet Union, it is possible they somehow found their way to Moscow. We have had to pay for the missing items. They include:

1 Norelco Coffeemaker
1 8-inch sauté and 1 pan
1 blender
1 6-pack towel set
2 hand towel assortments
2 bath towel assortments
1 Regal 9-piece cookware set
1 13-piece cutlery set

5 pieces of a Corelle 6-piece range top cookware set
1 Eureka vacuum cleaner

Best Regards,
Bob Walsh
President
Seattle Organizing Committee

Kozlovsky's reply both irritated and delighted Bob. As Kozlovsky explained it, Marat Gramov, the head of the Sports Committee, disliked Gavrilin intensely, as did most of Gavrilin's former co-workers. When the opportunity arose, Gramov had simply palmed his troublesome underling off on Bob, then held a champagne and vodka celebration to mark Gavrilin's departure to America. To make amends, Kozlovsky published a story about the theft in Moscow newspapers that included a photo of Gavrilin and a complete inventory of the missing items.

For a long while, Bob bumped into bad news in clusters, and in the case of Diane Ballasiotes, the news turned tragic. A project manager who had previously worked on numerous NCAA events and the Goodwill Games for both Bob Walsh & Associates and the Seattle Organizing Committee, Diane had just taken a new job when, one morning, she failed to report to work. After a couple of days elapsed with no word from Diane, Bob received a frantic call from her mother, Ida. Bob telephoned Seattle police, who refused to believe Diane's absence was anything serious: She was, they insisted, a young, attractive woman probably out having a good time. Bob refused to believe it and contacted Vern Thomas, a former King County sheriff and the SOC's veteran Director of Security. Bob advised Thomas that Diane's disappearance was uncharacteristic, asking him to use whatever influence he had to intervene. It did no good. Diane's body later was discovered on Seattle's Beacon Hill: She had been abducted and murdered.

A subsequent scam perpetrated by one of Bob's employees did nothing to lift his spirits. Just before the 1989 Final Four, whose championship game Bob and the NCAA's Tom Jernstedt arranged to become the first live telecast of an American sports event in the Soviet Union, Bob discovered that one of his staffers had sold, for $15,000, a nonexistent luxury box at the Kingdome. The staffer, a Goodwill Games employee, had slipped into the offices of Bob Walsh & Associates, made off with BWA stationery, and concocted gibberish to the effect that BWA had a luxury box and Final Four tickets available. The employee then located a couple of rubes and "sold" the box and tickets to them for fifteen grand, which they handed over to Bob's man at a 7-Eleven store. Bob didn't discover the swindle until two men, both in a dither, showed up one day at the Seattle Organizing Committee offices.

Bob didn't recognize either man, but listened intently, and with mounting shock, as the men angrily detailed how they had paid $15,000 for Final Four tickets and a luxury box at the Kingdome. The whole thing had been a charade and Bob Walsh & Associates, which organized the Final Four, was responsible.

"This is all your fault!" one of the men stammered.

"I don't know anything about it," Bob protested. "This is the first I've heard about it. Look, our company had nothing to do with any Final Four tickets or luxury boxes."

"But we paid $15,000 to a man who said he worked for you," the other man barked.

"Do you always hand over $15,000 to strangers at 7-Eleven stores?" Bob asked.

When neither man could furnish an adequate reply, Bob requested a description of the culprit, recognizing him immediately. He quickly hauled him into the office, where, at Bob's recommendation, Kathy Scanlan fired him. The $15,000 never turned up, and the two individuals who had been separated from their cash never came back.

As Bob attempted to keep a public lid on the in-house scam, he learned that two of his Goodwill-related projects had fallen apart. In cahoots with Kozlovsky, Bob had plotted the unconventional idea of arranging a National Football League exhibition game at Lenin Stadium in Moscow. But the NFL nixed it, fearing that political upheaval in Eastern Europe presented too grave a risk. Then the National Hockey League foiled Bob's attempt to have an all-Soviet expansion franchise awarded to Seattle.

Finally, Bob discovered to his disgust that Seattle had lost its Super Bowl bid, a project on which he, John Nordstrom, Gene Pfeifer, Bill Sears, and Ted Bowsfield had labored for six years. The Seattle Bid Committee had practically been assured of winning the bid for the 1992 event by NFL Commissioner Pete Rozelle after a formal presentation to the Super Bowl Site Selection Committee that included actor John Houseman, the taciturn law professor of *The Paper Chase* TV series, extolling Seattle's case on video. But two problems wrecked the effort. The Nordstrom family first sold the Seattle Seahawks to California real estate developer Ken Behring, whom most league officials loathed, and then King County Executive Tim Hill and Chamber of Commerce President George Duff formed a second Seattle bid committee, designed to blatantly usurp the work of the original one Bob chaired. The NFL did not look favorably on the contrived consortium. But rather than sort out which bid committee was the "official one," the NFL simply awarded the 1992 Super Bowl to Minneapolis.

Bob got undercut by Hill and Duff in a much more significant way than the loss of a Super Bowl. Following one of Bob's junkets to Moscow and Tbilisi, he found out that the Chamber of Commerce had created a new entity called "The King County Sports Council." The Council included sixty-two can-do guys from Seattle's business glitterati, purported to offer support to local sports franchises, and promised to pursue sports events and coordinate event proposals with local business leaders. Bob recognized the implications immediately. Henceforth, the Sports Council would make all "official" bids for NCAA football, basketball, and soccer tournaments, not Bob Walsh. The Sports Council would serve as the city's "official" broker with the United States Olympic Committee and U.S. sports federations, not Bob Walsh. Hill and Duff had created the Sports Council with the clear intent of running Bob Walsh out of business.

In announcing the Sports Council's formation, Duff declared that its mandate was to act as an "honest broker" in planning professional and amateur sports events, a brazen insinuation that Bob was somehow dishonest. Duff also said, "The Sports Council is poised to aggressively market Seattle as a prime sports events city,"

Bob Walsh and Kimberly Brown greet Final Four teams

251

something Bob had successfully accomplished for almost a decade. What Duff thought he could accomplish with the Sports Council presented a riddle neither Bob nor any of his close associates could solve.

"None of those guys on the Sports Council had any experience bidding on sports events," recollected Bill Sears, who ran the SOC's media department. "Nobody on the Council had relationships in the NCAA, the USOC, or anywhere else."

In the seven years prior to the Sports Council's formation, eleven national events had been held in Seattle, generating $245 million in direct spending to the state of Washington. Bob had played a major role in every one. Even *The Seattle Times*, never reluctant to tattoo Bob in public print, conceded that the economic impact of Bob's events exceeded $300 million. In just the two previous years, and despite Bob's incessant globe-hopping on behalf of the Goodwill Games, Bob Walsh & Associates had played the coordinating role in hosting consecutive editions of the NCAA Men's West Regionals, NBA All-Star Weekend, back-to-back NCAA Women's Final Fours, and an NCAA Men's Final Four.

Sears wondered if the Sports Council had the connections to pull off something like that. Or if the Sports Council could create, develop, and produce something like the Emerald City Marathon. Bob Walsh & Associates had its tentacles all over the sports world, bringing so many events to Seattle that one national magazine rated the city as one of the "hottest sports markets" in the United States. But Duff had positioned the Sports Council to take over everything to ensure that Seattle would never again get blindsided by something like the Goodwill Games.

For a long time, Bob Walsh received only one piece of good news, a copy of a Turner Broadcasting System press release. It said:

> It is with regret that I have accepted the resignation of TBS Senior Executive Vice President Robert Wussler. We wish him success in his new challenge as President and CEO of COMSAT Video Enterprises.
>
> R.E. "Ted" Turner
> TBS President and Board Chairman

The way Bob figured it, Wussler had at least been responsible for one positive development: The $50,000 settlement Bob received from TBS after Wussler punched him out had gone to pay off the remainder of Zizi Bagdavadze's medical bills at the Fred Hutchinson Cancer Research Center.

A Flight
Of Fancy

*Bob always had the personality of a
Soviet cosmonaut and made time to
have fun with us. All of us consider
him part of our family.*

*– Remas Stanskievicius, former Soviet
cosmonaut, Moscow, Russia*

*B*ruce McCaw possessed a passion
for speed, airplanes and race cars especially
mesmerizing him. One of the principal
shareholders in McCaw Communications,
a company that would one day be reincar-
nated as AT&T Wireless, McCaw's fascination with flying began in the 1960s. By
the late 1980s, McCaw had cofounded,
nurtured, and sold Horizon Air Industries,
negotiated the purchase and sale of several
hundred million dollars' worth of aircraft
and airplane parts, and was well into building a fleet of private planes that he maintained in a small hangar at Boeing Field near
Seattle. Because he had the resources, time,
and a commercial pilot's license, McCaw
flew his airplanes all over the world,
whenever he pleased.

Of all the flights McCaw had taken, or would ever take, none turned quite as bizarre as the one he took six months before the Opening Ceremony of the Goodwill Games. At first, there did not seem to be the remotest chance McCaw would be permitted to take the trip. But because of McCaw's relationship with Bob Walsh — McCaw Communications had been one of the first financial supporters of the Goodwill Games — and because he encountered a sportswriter who had unfathomably good connections inside the Soviet government, McCaw soon found himself jetting to a place that no American president, senator, congressman, or ambassador had seen since 1942. It happened like this:

During a Goodwill Games-related conversation with King County Councilman Ron Sims, Bob Walsh learned that Sims' sons played Little League baseball. That got Bob to musing: When the Aeroflot flights carrying Soviet athletes, officials, and tourists arrived in Seattle for the Games, why not send those Little Leaguers back to Moscow to teach Soviet youngsters about the sport? Even better, why not back load every Aeroflot flight to Moscow with American tourists? The Soviets would save on expenses; the SOC might make some money. Bob and Gene Fisher pursued this project with special energy, handing off much of the technical work to Washington, D.C., lobbyist David Gogol, who quickly ran into a bog of regulatory and diplomatic issues: No precedent existed for charter flights between the United States and Soviet Union; no flight path existed; Soviet planes couldn't go very far without refueling; for security reasons, the U.S. government didn't want those planes making frequent stops or flying over strategic areas. By the time Gogol untangled those messes to the satisfaction of the U.S. and Soviet governments, the Russians had agreed to send a special delegation of Soviet cosmonauts to Seattle, replete with an American observer in the cockpit.

The Soviet contingent that blazed the new air route from Moscow to the Emerald City became the largest to land in Seattle since the end of World War II. It included space veteran Igor Volk, who had once mowed down a cotton field with the wing of a jet fighter, and Bob Walsh's sportswriter buddy, Vladimir Geskin.

"When the Soviet plane touched the runway," recalled Ed Parks, manager of international relations at the Port of Seattle, "it caught a side wind, one of the wings dropping within three feet of the ground. We found out later that the Russians had flown in literally using old *National Geographic* maps."

During their visit, the cosmonauts attended a reception at the Boeing Company's Museum of Flight, where McCaw, a member of the museum's board of directors, was introduced to Volk. Volk didn't speak much English, but McCaw found he could communicate well enough with the Russian to know he enjoyed Volk's company. Feeling

likewise, Volk spontaneously invited McCaw to return to the Soviet Union with him. The cosmonauts would leave in three days and fly to Moscow after a short layover at Magadan in the Soviet Far East. Although intrigued with the invitation, McCaw thought there was no chance at all that he could obtain a visa on such short notice. The process usually took weeks.

Then Geskin jumped into the conversation, insisting that he could procure a visa. Dubious that any sportswriter, even one from a country where almost nothing was as it seemed, had that much clout, McCaw dismissed the idea. But the next morning Geskin called and instructed McCaw to send his passport to San Francisco by Federal Express. McCaw did. The day after that, Geskin called again, telling McCaw to pack his bags and report to Seattle-Tacoma International Airport the following morning. When McCaw arrived at Sea-Tac, a policeman emerged from the throngs and handed McCaw his passport, complete with a visa that entitled him to enter the Soviet Union. First amazed, McCaw grew skeptical, then became more than a little concerned. McCaw had heard a lot of crazy stories about Russian airplane flights, and even crazier stories about Russian pilots. But once McCaw spotted Volk, his concerns dissipated. Igor Volk had probably logged millions of flight miles. His country had proclaimed him a hero. So Bruce McCaw got on the plane.

Bob Walsh, who followed him aboard, had business in Moscow with Alexander Zasokhin, chief of Foreign Affairs in the Supreme

Igor Volk signs an autograph

Soviet's Chamber of Nationalities, with whom he would discuss a proposal to open a Russian consulate in Seattle. Bob had also taken it upon himself to invite several other Americans to Russia for what essentially was a sightseeing junket. Only Bernie Russi declined to make the trip.

"Screw it," Bernie told Bob. "I'm not getting on *that* airplane."

When Ed Parks got on it, he wondered who would pay for the fuel. The Russian pilots had glittering reputations but no money. Parks also noticed that the plane, which had once carted around Nikita Khrushchev, smelled like a combination of sweat, garlic, and urine.

And the seats rocked all the way back to the floor. To add to the ambience, Parks saw that the Russians had loaded up the plane, which had no refrigeration or ice, with fish. Parks understood why the Russians seemed unconcerned as he next observed them haul aboard enough beer and vodka to replenish the Ogallala Aquifer, with Wild Turkey for chasers.

From the beginning, this oddball flight seemed ill-fated.

Parks made an educated guess that air traffic control had cleared out all planes in the area so the Soviet Ilyushin jet

Soviet officials at the Port of Petropavlovsk

could safely take off. Bob Walsh figured he knew why: Some of the Russian pilots had already gotten so drunk that the tower didn't want to take any chances. Volk then got into an argument with the American observer, a United States Air Force lieutenant colonel who had accompanied the Russians on their flight to Seattle and was scheduled to return to the Soviet Union with them. It ended with Volk throwing the squawking lieutenant colonel off the airplane.

McCaw selected a seat near Emory Bundy, the director of the Goodwill Games Exchange, who had no idea what the itinerary included. When the plane suddenly lost power, both Bundy and McCaw wondered if they were going anywhere at all. An hour later, after power had been restored, the airplane shot down the runway, picking up speed, but taking forever, it seemed, to achieve sufficient acceleration for takeoff. Bundy sat apprehensively as the runway diminished, feeling like the plane was glued to the ground.

"I never thought we'd get in the air," Bundy remarked to McCaw once the plane was aloft.

"Forty-six seconds exactly," replied McCaw, checking his watch. "It took us forty-six seconds to get in the air."

The plane, which barely crested the top of a hill, had needed the entire runway to get airborne.

"Scary," Bundy mumbled.

Any façade of professionalism rapidly disintegrated after that. Igor Volk seemed nominally in charge of the plane, but Volk was swilling vodka and getting swacked, leaving control of the aircraft to a couple of other pilots who didn't exactly have their minds focused on aviation. For example, when Parks wandered toward the cockpit for a look-see, he noticed the navigator passed out over his maps and charts, a bottle of beer still in his hands. Later, when Jarlath Hume, the SOC's Vice President of Community Relations, ambled into the cockpit, he not only observed the slumbering navigator, he saw Bob Walsh flying the airplane. In a vodka haze, Volk had invited Bob and several other Americans to have a go at steering the jet. When Hume looked back toward the cabin, he saw the regular Soviet pilots singing and doing vodka toasts, one right after the other.

The plane had been scheduled to fly to Magadan, but Volk, on a whim, decided he didn't want to go there. He wanted to go to Petropavlovsk instead, where some of the Soviet pilots had dachas. That triggered alarm bells in Hume and Bundy. Of all the cities in the Soviet Far East, none inspired more intrigue than Petropavlovsk. Located in the northeastern part of the country on the Kamchatka Peninsula, Petropavlovsk separated the Bering Sea to the east from the Sea of Okhotsk to the west, its geographical highlights including twenty-two active volcanoes. Petropavlovsk officially sustained itself with a fishing industry. Unofficially, it had always been one of the Soviet Union's most strategic areas, serving as the sanctuary for the Soviet Navy's ballistic-missile submarine fleet, and the base from which the

Soviets shot down Korean Air Lines 007 on September 15, 1983, with a loss of 269 lives.

While Bundy watched as the Soviet pilots engaged in more vodka toasts and unlicensed Americans manned the controls of this airborne saloon, the best he could figure out was that some of the Soviet pilots had been trying, apparently without success, to get permission to land in Petropavlovsk. Bundy wondered what might happen if Volk attempted to make an unauthorized landing. Bob Walsh speculated that the Soviet pilots had been told they couldn't go to Petropavlovsk, but wasn't sure if it was the Americans who had said they couldn't or the Russians.

When McCaw entered the cockpit, he noticed the Russian radio operator frantically leafing through an English and Russian dictionary and immediately understood the dilemma. The airplane did not have a bilingual navigator on board because Volk had thrown him off the plane at Seattle-Tacoma International Airport.

McCaw sat down and surveyed the instruments. He asked Bob's wife, Nina, if she understood any of the technical words in Russian; she did not, nor did she seem to care, occupied as she was verbally brawling with Bob. McCaw studied all the levers, trying to figure out what controlled what. After a

Ed Parks, left, and Art Gorlick of The Seattle Post-Intelligencer tour Petropavlovsk

while, as the plane soared over Alaska, he heard voices from air traffic control — a thick-as-molasses Southern drawl the Soviet radio operator couldn't understand. After a few minutes, McCaw cut in.

"Hello?"

"Who are you?" said air traffic control.

"Well," said McCaw, "I'm just one of the passengers. I thought I'd help out."

"What?" came the startled reply. "What's going on?"

Volk grabbed the radio, saying he wanted to change the flight plan from Magadan to Petropavlovsk.

"Negative," the radio crackled. "We cannot authorize that destination."

As the plane headed over the Bering Strait, just a couple of hours from Petropavlovsk, Volk called the base commander there and told him the plane was coming in. Again, air traffic control radioed back, saying the plane did not have permission to land in Petropavlovsk. So McCaw and the Russian co-pilot started fudging their track a little bit, telling air traffic control they were turning because of weather. Within thirty minutes, they would be in Soviet airspace and the Americans wouldn't be able to do anything about it anyway.

When the plane landed in Petropavlovsk, night had fallen and the temperature hovered at -35°, appropriate since it was the closest major city to the Arctic Circle and only about a shot and beer chaser from Oymyakon, in the Yakutsk Autonomous Republic, a place where the overpowering cold could split railroad tracks.

The group had been led to believe they were going to be housed on a cruise ship. But Petropavlovsk had no cruise ships. In fact, the base commander had no idea what to do with the Americans, so he merely asked to see all passports, although he wouldn't stamp them as he wanted no record that any of these people had ever been in Petropavlovsk. He finally made the decision that the Americans should count their money and write down on a piece of paper how many dollars they had. Although utterly useless information, the base commander at least had something on paper he could put in a file that nobody would ever look at anyway.

The "cruise ship" turned out to be the rustiest ship afloat in the frozen harbor. The mayor of Petropavlovsk had managed to organize a banquet on two hours notice. To celebrate the first group of Americans in his city in more than forty years, he got drunk. Following the feast, Volk, McCaw, and Gene Fisher repaired to the local *banya*, where they lolled until the sun came up.

The next day, the group received a tour of Petropavlovsk. After Hume became the first American to ski Petropavlovsk's slopes, the contingent left for Moscow where Bob, Hume, Geskin, and other Soviet officials participated in negotiations relating to a joint exhibition of Soviet cosmonauts and U.S. Air Force personnel during the Opening Ceremony of the Goodwill Games. As usual, the Soviets trotted Bob off to a large press conference and gave the Seattleites tours of several ministries. McCaw tagged along, observing Bob commingle with his hosts.

"What impressed me," recalled McCaw, "was how much the Russians respected Bob at this pivotal point in the Cold War. His ability to do things with them was clearly based on trust. To see what Bob had accomplished through his diplomatic skills was amazing. After that, I saw the Goodwill Games in a whole new way."

So did Ed Parks. While shopping on Arbat Street, Parks encountered a Russian who offered to exchange some of Parks' currency. While Parks listened to the Russian's terms, Moscow police swooped in and arrested him for participating in an illegal currency exchange.

"It took two hours to spring poor Ed from jail," Fisher explained later.

Summit At The Summit

Going to the edge, pushing into new territory, makes you make the most of every moment. It's where you learn and grow the most. You learn to appreciate life, to be alive to other people, and to the animals . . . all of the magic of this planet that we are on.

> – Jim Whittaker, American mountain
>   climber and adventurist,
>   Port Townsend, Washington

*J*im Whittaker started to climb mountains as a Boy Scout in 1943, and for the next four and a half decades nature served as his church. He conquered summits and sailed seas, achieving his most enduring fame on May 1, 1963, when he ascended what the Nepalese identify as Sagarmatha ("Goddess of the Sky"), the Chinese refer to as Qomolangma ("Mother Goddess of the Universe"), and Americans know as Mount Everest. Whittaker's status as the first American to reach the top of the world's most famous mountain brought him international celebrity. He soon became friends with several members of the Kennedy family who were outdoor adventurists, and those friendships thrust him into the family's political inner circle. Whittaker ran both Bobby and Teddy

Kennedy's Washington State Presidential campaigns, and in 1968 served as one of Robert F. Kennedy's pallbearers.

Because of Whittaker's high public profile, Bud Krogh and Warren Thompson, both lawyers and mountain climbers, approached Whittaker in mid-1987 with an idea that only someone of his stature could entertain. Krogh, who had paid his penance for his role in the Watergate affair, and Thompson, vice president of Seattle's Seafirst Bank, entertained the notion of organizing an international peace climb of Mount Everest involving Americans, Soviets, and Chinese.

Whittaker considered the idea simultaneously brilliant and unrealistic. Such an expedition would involve the politics, cultures, languages, and diets of the United States, USSR, China, and Tibet. But more than that, Whittaker couldn't fathom how he would be able to convince Soviet and American

Warren Thompson, 1990 Peace Climb

climbers to join together with the Chinese in a sanctioned expedition in the forbidden province of Tibet. The Soviets and Americans still didn't trust each other much, although some of that mistrust had dissipated since Mikhail Gorbachev had become Soviet premier. On the other hand, the Soviets and Chinese remained at such odds that some observers had predicted war between them. And if somehow Whittaker could convince the Soviet and Chinese governments to momentarily shelve their hostilities, he knew that the history of international expeditions, even those involving climbers from friendly nations, was littered with mishap and miscalculation.

So for a long while, a peace climb of Mount Everest seemed to Whittaker too impractical to take seriously. But the more he mulled over the potential of such a unique ascent, the more intrigued he became, especially after recalling the words of Johann Goethe:

263

"Whatever you can do, or dream you can do, begin it. Boldness has genius, power, and magic in it." The world, Whittaker had always believed, was a magical place, and a peace climb would be a magical way to explore it. A peace climb presented the chance, even if it seemed far-fetched, to lead mountaineers from the three powers primarily responsible for environmentally degrading the planet to the top of the world. If they made it, they would demonstrate that the highest goals on earth could be achieved.

When it dawned on Whittaker that April 22, 1990, marked the twentieth anniversary of Earth Day, he knew precisely when he wanted members of his unassembled expedition to hold hands, plant

flags, and remove decades of debris from the world's most rarefied junkyard. From a practical standpoint, Whittaker would have to obtain a permit to climb Mount Everest, find a way to fund this almost inconceivable voyage to the clouds, and, most daunting of all,

Dr. Michael Weidman

figure out a way to convince the Soviets and Chinese to participate.

Even Everest veterans of Whittaker's stature do not prance up that mountain on a whim. Permits are difficult to obtain, paperwork often begun years in advance of a climb. Everest permits are, in fact, prized commodities, sold and resold in the mountaineering marketplace for thousands of dollars. But Whittaker soon caught a break. Dr. Michael Weidman, a member of the American Alpine Club, had a permit to climb the Tibetan side of Everest in the spring of 1990. Weidman offered to sell it to Whittaker for $5,000 — Weidman had bought it for $2,000 — on the condition that he be allowed to join the expedition. Weidman didn't rate as much of a climber, but Whittaker had little choice: Weidman's permit became the only one available to Whittaker. With it, Whittaker would be able to spend the next two years focusing

264

on how to make the climb happen rather than on wondering whether it could.

Whittaker's next step involved getting the Chinese on board. Meeting in Beijing with members of the Chinese Mountaineering Association, an organization responsible for approving all climbs in China, Whittaker outlined his dream. The Chinese reacted with instant suspicion, dismissing Whittaker's plan as politically impossible. The Chinese told Whittaker they had no idea what the Russians thought of his idea, but they had a very good idea about the implications of inviting the Russians into China. And Jim Whittaker could not respond to Chinese inquiries about the Russians since he didn't know a soul in the Soviet Union.

But Whittaker knew who did. Although not acquainted personally with Bob Walsh, Whittaker had heard about some of Bob's involvements with the Soviets and read about his activities as president of the Goodwill Games organizing committee. When Whittaker approached Bob about the peace climb and asked whether Bob could be of any assistance, Bob didn't need prodding. Bob was not a political animal, but he knew the Soviets hated the Chinese, that the Chinese loathed the Soviets, and that both mistrusted the Americans. He also recognized that no Americans had climbed any mountain in the company of Soviet and Chinese Communists, and that the Chinese hadn't permitted Soviets in their territory in more than thirty years. As a political matter, and particularly with China in the equation, a peace climb made little sense. As a practical matter, it seemed implausible. But Bob never engaged himself in pithy conversations, much less confound himself with great ponderables. Whittaker wanted to climb a

Bob Walsh, left, and Jim Whittaker (rear) with
USSR State Sports Committee officials

mountain; Bob would find a way to facilitate it. Besides, a peace climb of Everest, at least in Bob's mind, seemed no more impossible than Lynne Cox's swim of the Bering Strait. So Bob wired telexes to several officials at the USSR State Sports Committee, outlining the project and emphasizing its value as he perceived it. He expected nothing but grief. Instead, the USSR State Sports Committee expressed no objection, even inviting Whittaker to Moscow to discuss it.

When, several weeks later, Whittaker and Walsh faced twenty members from the committee, Bob launched into the particulars of the project. Whittaker then talked about the symbolism of a group of climbers trusting their lives to comrades whose governments had long been at odds with each other. Whittaker concluded by saying, "On the top of the highest summit in the world, Soviet, Chinese, and American climbers will celebrate their common achievement. We will demonstrate to the world what can be accomplished, what odds can be overcome, through cooperation and friendship. Our three flags will fly on the summit together."

After Whittaker finished his presentation, he met a Russian, Alexandr "The Tractor" Ivanitesky, who had won the freestyle gold medal in wrestling at the 1964 Tokyo Olympics. Ivanitesky seized Whittaker's hand and said, "This will be the most important thing you will ever do in your life."

L to R: Gerry Kingen, David Sabey, and Jim Whittaker in Tbilisi

The Soviets invited Whittaker to appear before a larger contingent of officials the next day to make a second presentation. To Whittaker's astonishment, the Soviets quickly agreed to join the peace climb on the condition the Chinese government issue a formal invitation to Moscow.

"It was easier than I thought it would be," Whittaker admitted later. "Maybe it was because Mikhail Gorbachev was running the Soviet Union. Maybe I just gave one hell of a speech. Anyway, afterward we went to the homes of some of these Russians, drank straight shots of vodka, and everybody got smashed. Later, when I got home, I was asked how I was able to go in there and convince them to join the expedition. I said one reason was because Bob Walsh paved the way. The Russians trusted Bob completely. It was amazing. While we were in there, Bob seemed to me to be almost worshipped by the Soviets."

Several weeks later, Whittaker and Warren Thompson traveled to Beijing to meet a second time with the Chinese Mountaineering Association. Once again, Whittaker delivered his pitch, this time reporting that the Soviets had been receptive and would participate if the Chinese issued an invitation. But the Chinese remained leery, finally telling Whittaker they would not do it unless they were sure the Soviets would accept.

"I suddenly felt extremly sorry for professional diplomats," remembered Whittaker.

The Chinese then announced they could not yet make a commitment and sent Whittaker and Thompson on sightseeing junkets for three consecutive days. When the Chinese finally summoned them to a meeting, they disclosed that they would permit a peace climb involving Soviets and Americans, but wouldn't participate themselves. Whittaker understood instantly what was wrong.

"The Chinese were afraid of failing," Whittaker explained later. "They weren't very good climbers; the Tibetans were exceptional climbers. What if the Soviets and Americans got to the top and the Chinese did not? It would be a terrible loss of face."

Whittaker determined the only way to achieve full participation in the climb was to offer his personal guarantee to the Chinese that they wouldn't fail. So he told them he would train them on Mount Rainier in Washington State to prepare them for the assault on Mount Everest.

"I even promised that no country would go to the summit unless all three countries were represented," Whittaker revealed later.

Whittaker didn't tell the Chinese that he would have a diabolical time fulfilling that promise. The lust for Everest was such that if the American and Soviet climbers got within reach of the summit and the Chinese did not, the Americans and Soviets would simply leave the Chinese behind.

It took the Chinese about five months to respond favorably to Whittaker's proposal and promise, which prompted Whittaker to the next stage of his plan: a search for funding. The expedition would cost hundreds of thousands of dollars, perhaps in excess of a million, taking into account equipment and supplies, airfare, lodging, and training expenses. But Whittaker caught another break. While attending a trade show in Las Vegas, he struck up a conversation with Leon Gorman, president of L.L. Bean, about the peace climb. When Whittaker mentioned he had been attempting to fund the climb through Olympic-style sponsorships, Gorman reached into his sport coat, pulled out his checkbook, and autographed a check for $100,000. With that precedent, Whittaker went on to land Boeing, Seafirst Bank, and 166 smaller companies as sponsors. Whittaker's expedition raised additional funds through the sale of t-shirts featuring the International Peace Climb logo. It had a dove on a summit, the word "peace" in three languages, and Chinese, Soviet, and American flags at the base.

Whittaker decided the expedition would include five climbers from each country. Each team would also include a leader, deputy leader, doctor, base camp organizer, and interpreter. The total finally grew to thirty individuals, the largest expedition Whittaker had ever organized. Whittaker added two more wrinkles. No climber from any of the countries could have previously reached the crest of Everest, which meant that Whittaker, now sixty years old, would not be going to the top. And each team had to include a female.

Applications swamped Whittaker when he announced that he sought the best high-altitude climbers in America who met those qualifications. Whittaker found two close to home, Ed Viesturs, a veterinarian, and Robert Link, a carpenter. Both had been guides for Rainier Mountaineering. Whittaker also selected Steve Gall, a guide and ski instructor from Aspen, Colorado, and La Verne Woods, a tax attorney and marathon runner from Seattle, who had explored the Cascade, Olympic, and Sierra ranges, climbed in Africa, New Zealand, and the Himalayas, and reached 23,000 feet on the Soviet peak, Mount Lenin.

"It started out as a wild dream," recalled Whittaker. "It got further along with help from Bob Walsh. Now all we had to do was make it happen. And so we began."

Whittaker trained the climbers on Mount Rainier, which they summited by five different routes, and then took them to Mount Elbrus in the Caucasus for additional work. After a break of several months, and a few weeks before the Opening Ceremony of the Goodwill Games, Whittaker and his American team arrived in Lhasa, the Buddhist holy city, to join the Soviet and Chinese teams for the ascending trek through Tibet.

Almost immediately after the expedition established base camp at 17,500 feet on the Rongbuk Glacier, it ran into a crisis that threatened the entire enterprise. The Soviet climbers had forgotten — conveniently, Whittaker thought later — to bring along the special titanium oxygen tanks, masks, and regulators Whittaker specifically had requested — and paid for.

"Must have left them back in Moscow," one of the Soviets told Whittaker, who managed to get news of the setback to his wife, Dianne Roberts, in Port Townsend, Washington.

It took Dianne a week's worth of negotiations with Senator Ted Kennedy's office in Washington, D.C., the U.S. Embassy in Moscow — many Russian telephones were jammed because of a political upheaval in Lithuania — and the U.S. Embassy in Beijing to arrange for the equipment to reach base camp. Then the expedition suffered another crisis when Whittaker's leg started to swell. Terrified he had a blood clot, Whittaker departed the team and endured a 300-mile jeep ride over washboard dirt to a hospital in Kathmandu, Nepal, fearing that was the end of his Everest journey. When he arrived he found a city in the midst of riots.

"The hospital was full of dead bodies and wounded rioters," recalled Whittaker. "So I got on an airplane and flew to a hospital in Bangkok, Thailand."

After doctors there assured Whittaker he had a torn calf muscle and cleared him to return to the expedition, it took him six days by plane, jeep, and foot to reach base camp, where he promptly ran into another snafu. The American climbers believed the proper approach to Everest demanded a climb as high as possible during the day, then a return to a lower base camp at night to reduce the risks of extreme altitude. The Chinese agreed with the Americans; the Soviets did not. They believed the way to approach Everest was to climb as high as possible, and stay there. Whittaker knew such a philosophical difference would create practical problems, not the least of which was that the Soviet climbers would rapidly deteriorate physically, placing the fate of the expedition in jeopardy. But the Soviets wouldn't listen.

Then another crisis erupted. La Verne Woods, the American woman who had been selected to assault the summit, became so ill that doctors suspected she suffered from pulmonary edema. The medicos had little choice, ordering Woods down to base camp, where drivers took her to Kathmandu. From there she flew to Bangkok, where doctors diagnosed a massive blood clot in her thigh.

"It probably would have killed her within twenty-four hours if it had gone untreated," Whittaker later admitted.

The next big issue to plague Whittaker involved oxygen. The Soviet climbers did not want to use it, but Whittaker finally got them to agree to at least carry it and use it if they fell behind the other climbers.

"But they violated the rules we'd set down," Whittaker later explained. "And it's a scary thing. People die more quickly without oxygen. As it turned out, the Soviets had no intention of keeping their promise. They left the high camp without their oxygen tanks."

What happened next figured. The Americans and Chinese reached the summit together, but were forced to wait an additional forty-five minutes, risking frostbite and hypothermia, for the wheezing Soviets to arrive.

"They were really dragging," Whittaker recalled. "But they did stand on the summit, their arms around each other, demonstrating what could be done through friendship and cooperation. But our climbers were really pissed at them for having to wait up there at the top, which they might not have been able to do if the weather had been bad. The Soviets could have blown the whole climb. I was in Camp 3 when this happened. When I heard that the Soviets were not using bottled oxygen, it made me angry and the Soviet in charge turned pale as a ghost. He said he would take care of them when they got back. Well, they got back down. And then these two Soviets who had lagged behind, they came down, kissed everybody, and told us they knew what they were doing. And then they got absolutely drunk."

Over the next several days, fourteen other climbers ascended to the top of Mount Everest while Whittaker supervised the burning and burying of two tons of trash from previous expeditions.

"When we left," Whittaker remembered, "our camp was so clean there was no sign that anyone had ever been there."

The Chinese lifted martial law in honor of the expedition and invited the climbers to the Great Hall. The Soviets invited them to the Kremlin, and Bob Walsh invited them to the Opening Ceremony of the Goodwill Games.

"A couple of neat and interesting things came out of that climb," reflected Whittaker. "After I got home, Dianne and I received a letter from a schoolteacher in Georgia who taught disadvantaged children. The teacher had a boy in her class who had not spoken in two years. Somehow, the boy had picked up on the climb, and one day he suddenly blurted out, 'Have they made the summit yet?'"

Peace climbers reach the summit of Mount Everest, spring 1990

"One of the Soviet climbers was Slava Gorbenko from Odessa," Dianne explained later. "When he came over to climb Mount Rainier, he took Jim aside and told him he had two-year-old twins. One had been born with a congenital heart problem that required surgeries a couple of years apart. The first surgery had taken place in Russia, but the second one would be extremely risky. Slava asked Jim if there was anything he could do. While the climbers were still on Mount Everest, we called around to find out if there was any way we could bring the boy over for surgery. Ultimately, we were contacted by this organization called Healing The Children in Spokane, Washington. One thing led to another and they found a doctor and hospital that were willing to donate their services. The boy went into the operating room blue and six hours later he came out pink. It was as dramatic as that."

"When Slava went home," Whittaker recalled, "he told us that any American, anybody, any friend of mine who wanted to come to Russia, he would do anything he could for them. And that was exactly what our expedition had been all about."

271

Ringside At History

Bringing tourists from the USSR to Seattle and putting them into families? This frightened me. Taking into account the language barrier, the differences in traditions and tastes, you can understand why I was afraid.

> – Alexander Kozlovsky,
>   Russian Olympic Committee,
>   Moscow, Russia

*A*fter more than three years of laborious sledding, Bob Walsh, Kathy Scanlan, and the Seattle Organizing Committee's eight vice presidents stood poised to roll out $133.9 million worth of creativity and sweat. While they had operated with an abiding conviction that the most enduring value of their grand experiment in citizen diplomacy would emerge from the unencumbered interaction of Soviet and American citizens, the Goodwill Games Exchange posed as much risk as it offered potential reward. The 1,500-member Soviet contingent would be ten times larger than any that had previously visited the United States, but neither the SOC nor the U.S. government had any control over which Soviets would attend. The United States Information Agency had pushed for a cross-section of Soviet society to help assure diverse participation, but remained convinced the Soviets would sabotage the spirit of the exchange by infiltrating the Games with Communist Party officials and KGB agents in the guise of tourists.

The SOC had a more practical worry. When 1,500 Soviet citizens, Communist Party officials or KGB agents notwithstanding, swarmed into Seattle, the vast majority would be traveling outside the Soviet Union for the first time. Few would speak English, some might become ill, many could get lost or disoriented, and several might attempt to defect. The SOC and Rotary International, which mobilized 5,000 American host families to receive the Soviets, prepared for every contingency, but had no way to guarantee a problem-free exchange.

The Goodwill Exchange Conferences presented another level of risk. Seven times larger than any previous conferences involving participants from the U.S. and USSR, it had taken $5 million to assemble them, the cost covered by more than 100 foundations, corporations, and government agencies. Coordinated by former Seattle city prosecutor Doug Jewett and chaired by Prof. Herb Ellison of the Jackson School of International Studies at the University of Washington, each of the sessions would include ten to thirty participants from the Soviet Union and a comparable number from the United States.

The sessions had been segmented into components spanning a swath of issues: eleven Citizen Initiatives Conferences on topics ranging from U.S.-

Bob Walsh on the diving board at the King County Aquatics Center

Soviet economic partnerships to mutual environmental issues; three Leadership Conferences; and a Human Rights Conference, co-sponsored by the Helsinki Commission and American Bar Association. The latter particularly worried the Soviets, who believed that an open examination of their human rights record would degenerate into a diplomatic embarrassment and detract from Soviet athletic achievements during the Games.

"The fresh air of freedom had just touched Moscow and Leningrad," recalled Alexander Kozlovsky. "But people who were at power before *perestroika* were still at their chairs. So when we received the list of the invitees to these discussions from Bob Walsh, we almost lost our consciousness. It was a full list of the extreme radical wing of Soviet society, whom we regarded as enemies of the state. Two of my closest associates went to Seattle to try to persuade Bob not to organize those discussions. But step by step we were forced to surrender. As we say it in Russia, 'horror has big eyes.'"

The Goodwill Games Exchange represented only a fraction of what the SOC planned to offer. Fifteen months in the making, the International Trade Exhibition matched 200 foreign buyers from forty countries with 300 U.S. exporters. The $16.7 million Goodwill Arts Festival, developed so customers could feast slowly, featured a breathtaking menu that would light up stages, concert halls, and galleries at twenty-seven locations for the summer of the Games. The Festival's main components, *Moscow: Treasures and Traditions*, the Bolshoi Ballet, and an epic production of *War and Peace,* would be supplemented with hundreds of dance, theater, and circus performances, film and folk festivals, music concerts, and historical and contemporary art and photography exhibits.

Moscow: Treasures and Traditions offered a crash course in Russian art history, the majority of the icons, paintings, engravings, porcelains, and costumes dating back five centuries. Sergei Prokofiev's $2 million *War and Peace* would become the largest show in the history of the Seattle Opera, and the first new American production of Tolstoy's masterpiece in twenty years. The entire company of the Bolshoi Ballet, the crown jewel of Soviet arts, would perform the U.S. premier of *Ivan The Terrible*, marking the ballet's first American appearance since 1975.

The SOC and TBS had spent months wrangling over the theme, look, and feel of the Opening Ceremony. Under the direction of New York producer Barnett Lipton, the two-hour show would include four acts consisting of 2,000 people and feature special appearances by Ronald Reagan, Arnold Schwarzenegger, Armand Hammer, Reba

McIntire, Kenny Rogers, The Moody Blues, saxophonist Kenny G, New Age keyboardist David Lanz, and the Vladimir Chamber Choir. The Opening Ceremony would also present, as Bob Walsh had always known it would, an aerial spectacular starring Soviet cosmonauts and U.S. Air Force flyers.

As the Opening Ceremony approached, Bob's most palpable worry concerned events in Eastern Europe. Cracked by pickaxes, the Berlin Wall had tumbled in a mist of champagne spray, leaving a sixth of the earth's landmass bubbling with political upheaval and social rearrangement. Estonia, Latvia, and Lithuania marched in protest over their forced absorption into the Soviet Union. Anti-Soviet riots had erupted in Georgia and Azerbaijan, where bloody banditry had become a routine feature of everyday existence. Soviet troops had fired on demonstrators in Central Asia even as anti-Communist picketers waltzed through Red Square exhorting Mikhail Gorbachev to admit his failures. A dissident playwright ran Czechoslovakia. As East and West Germany negotiated terms of a merger under the watchful eye of Soviet Foreign Minister Eduard Shevardnadze, border guards sold hundreds of miles of wire fencing that had once been used to keep anyone from entering or escaping. Communist Party bosses had been booted from their limos, to the delight of customers who clamored for burgers at McDonald's on Gorky Street.

Gorbachev had opened a door to history by attempting to implement the rule of law, curbing the power of the KGB, and shattering the monopoly of the state media. But his nation had spun wildly out of control, worrying Bob and everyone in the SOC that if the Soviet Union imploded, the Games would become an unintended victim. The Soviets might back out; for security reasons, the U.S. government might refuse to issue visas to foreign diplomats, athletes, coaches, journalists, and tourists.

Lithuania threatened to topple no end of apple carts. Angered that its independence movement jeopardized *perestroika*, Russia had cut off Lithuania's oil and natural gas supplies and seized its television and radio stations. Lithuania responded by withdrawing its athletes from Soviet sports competitions, demanding to compete in the Goodwill Games as an independent country. When the Soviets balked, Bob got dragged into a quagmire of undiplomatic muck. He conducted several meetings in an attempt to mediate a solution, ultimately recommending that athletes from Lithuania and other Soviet republics be permitted to carry their national flags at the Opening Ceremony. But that olive branch pacified practically nobody.

The Lithuanian snag became one of several Bob and the SOC endured on the eve of the Games. In addition to a ticket problem and a

financial tug-of-war with the Seattle Fire Department, the SOC found itself embroiled in a wrangle with the City of Seattle over, of all things, liability insurance. The city now wanted increased coverage for participant suicides, lightning strikes, and tornadoes in a geography where no tornadoes existed. Then, a month before the Opening Ceremony, Bob learned that Gorbachev would not be able to attend the Games;

Bob Walsh made the cover of several magazines prior to the Games

neither would President George Bush nor Vice President Dan Quayle.

"The Games are still seeking stature," observed *Seattle Post-Intelligencer* columnist Art Thiel. "Don't be surprised if the Opening Ceremonies headliner is Bart Simpson."

Less than a month before the Opening Ceremony, Bob received a confidential telex from Anatoly Kolesov, Deputy Chairman of the Ministry of Sports and Physical Culture, suggesting that a Middle East terrorist organization planned to seize Soviet and American citizens and athletes and hold them hostage.

"In view of great public and political significance of the Goodwill Games in Seattle," Kolesov further advised, "extremists may attempt to carry out actions during the Games to attract the attention of the world public. Certain extremist groupings have not given up the idea of laying their hands on mass destruction weapons."

Bob forwarded Kolesov's concerns to the FBI and Turner Broadcasting System, but TBS paid little heed, almost having arrived at the conclusion that a terrorist attack might actually improve Goodwill television ratings.

The network had scheduled eighty-six hours of sports and related features and assembled a small army to execute the telecasts. Executive producer Tony Verna, who had invented instant replay in 1963, recognized the Games wouldn't duplicate the grandeur or tension of the Olympics, but believed that Goodwill athletes would be competitive and their stories compelling. Trouble was, TBS bean counters had done enough math to know that what Ted Turner had called "the biggest event in the history of cable television," also stood a decent chance of becoming one of the biggest financial calamities in the history of cable television.

TBS had overspent on publicity and undersold advertising spots, conservative estimates placing TBS's looming losses at anywhere from $10 to $25 million. Turner, who hoped the Games might one day become a valuable commercial property, brushed it off.

"The 1990 Goodwill Games," Turner predicted, "will be much bigger and better than the 1986 Goodwill Games."

"Growing from nothing to a speck," a New York advertising executive zinged in reply, "isn't much."

Turner had grown far larger than that. In the four years since the first Goodwill Games, he had evolved from maverick entrepreneur into certified visionary, his much-criticized purchase of the MGM film library now seen as one of the shrewdest acquisitions in media history. CNN stood on the verge of becoming the most powerful news source in the world, with Turner at the forefront of an information revolution that would one day be looked upon as having had as much to do with the collapse of the Berlin Wall as the hammers that brought about its physical demise.

But most TBS senior management people focused on the short-term — whacking budgets, curtailing advertising campaigns, releasing hotel rooms, canceling publicity tours, and placing the SOC in the position of hoping that a run on tickets during the Games would salvage its budget. The SOC had little other recourse. Banners, streamers, and flags had been strewn along Seattle streets, Soviet cruise ships had arrived on the waterfront, and more than 370 SOC staff and 11,000 volunteers stood poised to execute the show. The time had arrived to light the Goodwill torch, trade pins and opinions, welcome the largest and most diverse group ever to fly out of Moscow, and then settle back and deal with a lawsuit, a defection, and a Russian who would become the quintessential party pooper.

277

The Glasnost Games

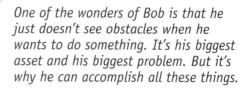

One of the wonders of Bob is that he just doesn't see obstacles when he wants to do something. It's his biggest asset and his biggest problem. But it's why he can accomplish all these things.

> – Carmen Matthews,
> 1990 Goodwill Games Exchange,
> Seattle, Washington

*B*ob spent a substantial part of the Goodwill Games hosing down a deluge of diplomatic conflagrations. His mea culpas actually started before the Opening Ceremony when he was forced to apologize first to an apoplectic commander stationed at Elmendorf Air Force Base in Anchorage, Alaska, and then to a staffer in the Bush White House over an episode that nearly erupted, through no fault of Bob's, into an international incident.

Igor Volk and seventy other pilots from the Flying Research Institute departed the Soviet Union for the Goodwill Games as planned on what was July 13. However, when they crossed the International Dateline, they found themselves back into July 12, creating a hellacious mess since they weren't scheduled to arrive until Seattle's

July 13. Predictably, when the Soviet Ilyushin 62, accompanied by two SU-27 military fighters, reached Canadian airspace, alarm bells started to clang. And by the time the Soviet jets arrived in U.S. airspace, all good God was breaking loose. The United States Air Force dispatched fighter planes to intercept the Soviet entourage and escort it to Elmendorf.

"We intercepted them 100 miles northwest of Nome," recalled Capt. Monica Aloisio, an Air Force spokesperson. "We picked them up on long-range radar."

Since no Soviet planes had penetrated American airspace without authorization since World War II, it wasn't long before the Elmendorf commander, in a mighty froth, blistered the telephone lines, demanding explanations. Unfortu-

L to R: Bob, Mari Watanabe, and Bernie Russi of the SOC

nately, his call found its way to Bob.

"Who is this?" shouted the commander.

"Bob Walsh."

"Who the hell is Bob Walsh? And who in the hell are these pilots? And what am I supposed to do with them?"

Bob explained they were an elite group of cosmonauts en route to the Goodwill Games to participate in an air spectacular over the University of Washington's Husky Stadium.

"Nobody told me anything about this!" screamed the commander, who informed Bob in no uncertain terms that he wasn't buying Volk's lame excuse that the Russians had arrived early because they had gotten screwed up by the International Dateline.

Bob apologized for the miscommunication, promising that he would contact the State Department and White House and have either or both confirm to the commander's satisfaction that the cosmonauts were a legitimate part of the Games.

Bob hung up and called the White House. By a stroke of luck — it was after working hours in Washington, D.C. — he reached

279

Andrew Card, by now a special assistant to President George Bush. Card had not only advised Bob on several Goodwill Games-related issues, he had assembled a White House task force to coordinate the federal government's involvement in the Games. Bob apologized to Card for calling so late and explained the situation at Elmendorf. Card said he would handle the commander and contact State and Defense. Thirty minutes later, Bob received a telephone call.

"I'll let them go," said the still-stewing Elmendorf commander, "but not without an escort."

A couple of hours later, an entire international fleet approached Seattle: The Soviet Ilyushin 62 and a couple of Soviet SU-27 military fighters, a pair of U.S. F-15 fighters, and two Canadian jets that practically nose-dived toward the airport before racing up and away into Seattle's wild gray yonder.

Once the cosmonauts settled in, Bob learned to his horror that some of them had plotted to take an airborne joy ride with the Blue Angels. Bob advised both the cosmonauts and Blue Angels that such a stunt would create a security problem that would reverberate all the way to the Defense Department. But the cosmonauts and Blue Angels went joy riding anyway, forcing Bob to apologize on behalf of the Seattle Organizing Committee to several U.S. military types in Washington, D.C.

That furor had barely dissipated when the first wave of Soviet officials, athletes, coaches, and tourists arrived at Seattle

Uniting The World's Best

International Airport. Two hours later, the Aeroflot plane that brought them returned to Moscow with ninety Americans. Although Bob's idea had worked spectacularly, it could have ended disastrously. The Soviet plane had not stopped to refuel; when it arrived in Seattle, its tanks were on empty.

One of the Soviet visitors, Nikolai Rusak, the new head of the USSR State Sports Committee, had been in Seattle only a matter of hours when Soviet hockey star Sergei Federov sought asylum with the Detroit Red Wings. The defection, which generated headlines world wide, deeply offended Rusak and his deputy, Alexander Kozlovsky. Bob and Dick Smith, the regional director of U.S. Customs and Immigration, spent days trying to persuade Federov to rejoin the Soviet national team. When their efforts failed, Bob apologized profusely to Rusak and Kozlovsky, and then found himself apologizing repeatedly in the aftermath of the Opening Ceremony, a colorful, two-hour production that concluded with the "Fly Over" of Husky Stadium by U.S. Air Force personnel and Soviet cosmonauts. Bob apologized first to the staff at University Hospital: noise from the Soviet and American jets disturbed the patients. Bob

L to R: Ted Turner, Tracie Ruiz, Mike Conforto and Bob Walsh

apologized next to Native American dancers after TBS cut their performance out of its television broadcast. Then Bob apologized to the Chinese Consulate General, who took umbrage at a remark former President Ronald Reagan made during the Opening Ceremony. In fact, Bob apologized to the Chinese Consulate General twice, issuing the second apology because a Goodwill t-shirt that depicted the flag of Taiwan omitted the flag of the People's Republic of China. That taught Bob a significant lesson: The Chinese valued apologies above all.

Even though Bob had nothing to do with it, he apologized to Seattle Mayor Norm Rice after Rice's exclusion from the Opening Ceremony. He apologized to Rev. Sam McKinney, a preacher at Mount

Zion Baptist Church, who thundered to a congregation that included actress Valerie Harper that Games organizers amounted to a bunch of incompetent fools for failing to include Seattle's African-American mayor in welcoming festivities. Following South Korea's victory in the judo tournament, Bob apologized to that nation's officials: the North Korean national anthem had inexplicably been played instead of South Korea's.

One night during the Games, SOC staffers took a boat cruise. Bob could not attend, having too many apologies to make. In fact, Bob had such a lengthy list of them that Mari Watanabe, an SOC employee, had to schedule apology appointments for him.

Bob could have apologized to Weyerhaeuser's Howie Meadowcroft, who got steamed that his company had been roped into paying $18,000 to fly Ronald Reagan to Seattle. Meadowcroft blamed Bob, who did not apologize because he had nothing to do with Reagan's transportation. Bob could have apologized to University of Washington administrator Tallman Trask, but instead took great delight over the fact that Trask got booted out of Husky Stadium during one of the track and field events for failing to comply with security procedures.

Bob did not have to apologize for, and was even spared from comment about, the ring of Colombia, South America, pickpockets that preyed briefly upon Goodwill fans and tourists. The public never found out about it. Nor did Bob have to address the International Event Management fiasco, a psychodrama that played out three days after the Opening Ceremony when IEM, an SOC partner, walked off the job in a dispute over payments for some cellular telephones. But Bob could not be spared the Anatoly Firsov affair. A two-time Olympic hockey player and a member of the Supreme Soviet, Firsov arrived in Seattle drunk, got drunker by the day, finally becoming so horrendously bombed that he lost all control of his bodily functions. As President of the SOC, Bob got figuratively plopped into the man's mess.

"He had literally poisoned himself with alcohol," remembered Jennifer Potter, the SOC's Vice President of Operations. "He was staying in a private home and was defecating and throwing up all over the place. He wouldn't sleep in his room. He slept on the living room sofa and soiled everything he was so drunk."

Bob had to recruit Ralph Munro, Washington's Secretary of State, to handle the situation, involving as it did diplomatic considerations. Munro had no other option but to send Firsov back to the Soviet Union.

The Soviets didn't object to Firsov's ejection, but they bleated bitterly when thugs attacked a Russian tourist, sending him to a hospital. The SOC lamented to Seattle police that several Americans posed as Soviet tourists for the purpose of duping bar patrons into buying them free drinks in local watering holes. Seattle-area fishermen fumed about missing several days of the prime salmon season while Goodwill yacht races were held. A horde of born-again Christians fussed when the SOC prevented them from giving Bibles to Soviet visitors. Seattle hoteliers and merchants griped that they didn't reap the financial bonanzas they had expected. Airline carriers who figured on ticketing thousands of Goodwill visitors barked loudly when anticipated business failed to materialize. And this probably figured: Media critics who had argued that the timing of the 1986 Goodwill Games wasn't the best because they occurred when the world was threatened by tension, complained that the timing of the 1990 Games wasn't the best because the world was threatened by peace.

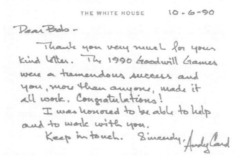

Andy Card later became George W. Bush's White House Chief of Staff

TBS, of course, anguished over its ratings. They came in 50 percent higher than in 1986, but only half of what the network projected, partly because the Games failed to attract several notable performers in track, swimming, and gymnastics, and partly because the Games were either ignored by several major news organizations or roundly criticized. For example, to highlight its coverage, *Sports Illustrated* selected a photograph from a deserted Marymoor Velodrome, site of the cycling races, with the following caption: "Where was everybody? Certain venues didn't pack 'em in." *Sports Illustrated* neglected to mention that the photograph had been taken twenty-five minutes after the final race. The magazine never printed an explanation or correction.

"Nobody really knew about the Games outside of Seattle," recollected the SOC's Bernie Russi. "Some people probably thought they were sponsored by Goodwill Industries of America."

Because TBS elected not to market the Games as a festival of sports, arts, culture, and exchanges, it missed the opportunity to tell compelling stories that may — or may not — have lifted the perception of the Games beyond the level of a sawed-off version of the Olympics. For non-Seattle residents, it required an arts junkie to understand that one of the most remarkable visual and performing art festivals ever staged in the western United States ran concurrently with the Games, or State Department-level expertise to appreciate the Goodwill Games Exchange. But TBS's Games had never been the SOC's Games.

A few snafus aside, the SOC's Games played out almost perfectly. Nearly 2,500 athletes from fifty nations participated without incident. No major security issues surfaced. Rebecca Boren's fear that the SOC's planning efforts would be inadequate proved groundless. Joni Balter's "world-class traffic jam" failed to materialize. The weather was spectacular, ticket sales brisk, and the SOC almost hit a bulls eye with its budget. In almost every way that mattered — security, venue operations, traffic flow, event scheduling — the Games could not have gone more smoothly. More than 800,000 people attended sports events and thousands more enjoyed plays, ballets, and art exhibits. The Goodwill Arts Festival that Jarlath Hume conceived and nurtured became a critical and financial smash. More than 2,000 people a day streamed through the Washington State Convention Center to gander at the wonderworks of *Moscow: Treasures and Traditions.* The Bolshoi Ballet sold out all of its performances, including an extra show in just thirty-nine minutes. In all, the Goodwill Arts Festival attracted more than 500,000 spectators, generating $6 million in ticket revenues. During the festival's summer-long run, 500 newspapers and magazines published more than 1,500 articles about it, including glowing reviews in *The Wall Street Journal, The New Yorker,* and *The New York Times.*

The International Trade Exhibition resulted in $10 million of immediate deals, and in the three months following the Games more than 225 trade relationships had been formed, fueling $37 million in direct U.S. export sales. The Pepsi Friendship Center, where Soviet and American citizens shared perspectives and life experiences, drew thousands of people daily. The Goodwill Conferences, even the controversial symposium on human rights, drew acclaim, and the home stay program, always fraught with risk, turned into a triumph — despite the drunken Politburo member, and even though the Soviets sabotaged the spirit of it by sending over hundreds of Party leaders as a reward for their service.

"It was really cool," recalled Molly Raymond of the United States Information Agency. "For the first time in history, 1,500 Soviets ran around in the United States. I can't imagine what the Kremlin thought. Everybody had Russians in their houses and driving their cars. It was extraordinary and unprecedented."

Following the Games, Kathy Scanlan found herself in demand by organizations all over the United States, and the demand for other SOC staffers ran high. However, the local demand for Bob turned decidedly cool. Still, in the immediate afterglow, Bob did not let rejection bother him much. For Bob, the value of the Games had been in watching Soviet and American citizens experience each other on an unprecedented scale. The value had been the opportunity to create climates for Lynne Cox to swim the Bering Strait and Jim Whittaker to orchestrate his "Summit on the Summit" of Mount Everest. To Bob, the Games meant that Elena Snopova would walk, that Kakha Merabishvili would never again turn blue, that Zizi Bagdavadze would have a chance to remain a daughter, a sister, and a wife. They meant that perhaps somewhere in Armenia, someone had been snatched from the rubble of an earthquake.

It did not fail to strum Bob's heartstrings when the *Post-Intelligencer*, on the eve of the new millennium, published a major Seattle retrospective of the decade of the 1990s. The Goodwill Games received all of one sentence.

The Great Depression

Bob was criticized from the moment he stuck his head above the crowd. But things don't happen without people who have vision and are willing to put their ass on the line. Bob is one of those people. And to me that makes him a hero.

– Steve Morris, Seattle-King County Convention & Visitors Bureau, Seattle, Washington

*J*In the months following the Goodwill Games, Bob Walsh's life deteriorated into a series of tribulations and lonely nights. Nina Walsh moved out and filed for divorce, leaving Bob so morose and bewildered that he accepted an invitation to Ted Turner's Montana ranch, where he spent a couple of days commiserating with Jane Fonda about the tortures associated with wedlock to an ex-Soviet translator. The pastoral interlude in Montana high country also helped Bob clear his mind so that he could confront a calamity only slightly more palatable than his marriage to Nina had been. In part because of his preoccupation with the Games, in part because of the formation of the Seattle Sports Council, Bob had no new projects in the works and exceedingly few prospects of fanning any into flames. Bob

Walsh & Associates had dwindled to four employees, coming perilously close to folding shop.

Three personnel losses hit Bob particularly hard. Amy Boisjolie, his special assistant during the Games, and BWA President Kimberly Brown, had both found new jobs, and Gene Fisher had vanished without a trace. Bob called all over town trying to locate Gene, always coming up empty. If the divorce, defections, and Fisher's disappearance left Bob feeling like a poster child for abandonment, the Sports Council had rendered him desperate and disillusioned.

After wresting away Bob's events business, the Sports Council had been all talk and no walk, its impotence even drawing a rebuke from *Special Events Report*, a Chicago-based newsletter. "Thanks to the Sports Council," the newsletter reported, "1992 will mark the first year since 1983 that Seattle will be without a major sports event. The Sports Council's main agenda appears to be shackling Bob Walsh."

According to the Seattle Convention and Visitors Bureau and the consulting firm of Hansen & Associates, the

Certificate of Appreciation
is presented to
BOB WALSH
In recognition of your excellent contribution to the
Defense support effort to the 1990 Goodwill Games
20 July - 5 August 1990

Secretary of Defense

Goodwill Games had resulted in a $155 million economic boon to the Puget Sound region. Adding that to the other events Bob and BWA had produced, the combined economic impact stood at nearly $400 million. Since 1984, direct spending in the State of Washington as the result of Bob's projects had averaged $35.1 million per year. Even Joni Balter of *The Seattle Times*, usually eager to march Bob out behind the journalistic woodshed, had been moved to comment, "No major national sports events have found their way to Seattle since Walsh was effectively sent to his room to sulk after the Games ended. . . . One driven individual, however flawed, can accomplish far greater things than a clunky committee."

As an arm of the Chamber of Commerce, the Sports Council did not have sufficient resources to bid for professional or collegiate sports events. Even if it had been funded adequately, it had one problem Chamber of Commerce president George Duff could never solve: None of the sixty-two members of the Sports Council had a clue about how to bid for or promote a sports event.

When the National Hockey League announced an ambitious round of expansion, the Sports Council failed to line up a potential ownership group. Because of Seattle's successful staging of the Goodwill Games, the city practically had its pick of qualifying competitions in advance of the 1992 Barcelona Summer Olympics. Yet the Council failed to land the U.S. Synchronized Swimming Trials for lack of follow-through, and then botched a bid for the U.S. Track and Field Trials.

"Losing the track trials, especially on the heels of the Goodwill Games, made us look idiotic," recalled Bill Sears, the former media maven of the Seattle Organizing Committee. "Bob Walsh wouldn't have lost those trials."

Nor, Sears believed, would Bob have bungled an opportunity for Seattle to host some of the 1994 World Cup soccer matches, as the Sports Council did.

Bob pitched Ted Turner about making Seattle the permanent American site of the Goodwill Games, but TBS and the SOC had squabbled so often Bob knew TBS would never again yield control of the Games to a local organizing committee. Bob also explored the possibility of pursuing a bid for the Winter Olympics and briefly entertained a fanciful notion about the Summer Olympics. In Bob's mind, Seattle had clearly demonstrated it could handle an international sports competition, and the SOC had proved it could pay its bills. Kathy Scanlan had closed shop on the Goodwill Games having satisfied every local vendor, and only TBS was still due money from the SOC, about $1 million. The deficit sufficiently irked Bob that he wrote a letter to Turner promising to repay the $1 million if it was the last thing he ever did. But he knew he would not be able to overcome what he was convinced would be stiff local opposition to the Summer Olympics. A bid would be shouted down for the same reasons the Goodwill Games had originally been scorned, and Bob believed to a certainty *The Seattle Times* would describe any pursuit of the Olympics in terms of a pie-eyed Bob once again straddling the line between cockamamie and hocus pocus.

Bob tinkered briefly with reviving the Rainier Bank Golf Classic and Emerald City Marathon. But with the Goodwill Games still a vivid experience, small-scale events no longer interested him. For a while, he dabbled with a promoter who wanted to stage a marathon in Vietnam's Ho Chi Minh City, but that interested him even less. Without much enthusiasm, he tried to locate commercial sponsorships for the 1992 Soviet Olympic team. He even flew to Lithuania to check out a production called "Circus On Ice," which featured bears on ice skates. But it didn't have much profit potential, so Bob departed Lithuania only with the experience of having played hockey with a circus bear to show for the trip.

Of all the things that misfired, went wrong, or never were in the aftermath of the Goodwill Games, none caused Bob more grief than his sorry association with former gymnastics heroine Olga Korbut. A ballerina of the balance beam, Korbut had burst upon the world scene at the 1972 Munich Olympics with a performance so riveting that she had instantly become an athletic icon. But the Olga Korbut that Bob encountered bore no resemblance to the smiling, pigtailed teenager forever immortalized in ABC-TV Wide World of Sports videos. Olga had morphed, in Bob's view, into a chain-smoking She-demon.

When her athletic career ended, Korbut moved to Minsk, becoming administrative director of the Byelorussian gymnastics team. Bob and Olga met at a gymnastics competition prior to the Goodwill Games, reuniting when Bob agreed to help Olga establish the "Olga Korbut Foundation" in association with the Fred Hutchinson Cancer Research Center. To help Olga launch her foundation, Bob sought out NBC's Maria Shriver, who had accompanied her husband, Arnold Schwarzenegger, to the Goodwill Games. Bob presented Shriver with

*L to R: Bob Walsh, aquatics coach Dr. Sammy Lee, Olga Korbut,
Kristi Yamaguchi, Dr. Robert Day*

the idea of doing a major TV profile of Olga. Shriver not only did the piece, she proposed a made-for-TV movie, to be produced in conjunction with her husband. The project had just started to take off when it fell apart, largely because of Korbut, who insisted on an exorbitant salary and then blew off a series of personal appearances Bob

arranged for her to promote her foundation. Olga's unreasonable demands and dictatorial behavior dissuaded Bob from further involvement with her. Then, following several nasty donnybrooks, Bob finally terminated his relationship with Olga. "Olga was a piece of work," remembered Dr. Robert Day, chief

Bob Walsh with Maria Shriver and her brother, Bobby

administrator at the Fred Hutchinson Cancer Research Center. "She was pretty much just out for herself."

The Moscow Circus proved a bigger fiasco than Olga Korbut. The first two North American tours of the circus in 1988 and 1989 generated substantial profits, and Bob had no reason to suspect another tour wouldn't attract sellout crowds. But just as the third edition of the Moscow Circus opened, Seattle got smacked by a preposterous blizzard, silencing the city under a foot of snow and ice, and ruining ticket sales. Bob Walsh & Associates, which had taken out loans from Security Pacific Bank to cover up-front costs of the event, had no revenues to pay back the loans. That not only left BWA in trouble, and it left Bob personally on the hook: He had guaranteed the loans.

From the distance of several months, Bob sometimes wondered whether the Goodwill Games had been worth the effort. His marriage had fallen apart, his business had dwindled to nothing, and his moods had become increasingly dark. Still, he missed the Games and the permanent energy it required to produce them. He also remained proud of what they had left in their wake.

Before the Games, Russian airplanes never flew to Seattle. Aeroflot now offered direct flights from Moscow every other day.

290

Before the Games, no Russian vessels docked at the Port of Seattle. Now, Russians fishing boats cruised in and out of the port two or three times a week. Russian-American trade had reached an all-time high, and dozens of Seattle-based companies participated in joint ventures with new Russian partners. An American consulate had opened in Vladivostok in the Russian Far East, and a Russian consulate would soon open in Seattle. Bob believed, and he knew Ted Turner did as well, that the Games had played a small role in ending the Cold War.

"A lot of things ended the Cold War," Turner later told Bob. "A lot of straws went on that camel's back. Who is to say which one finally broke it? What I do know is that the Games occurred at a very significant point in U.S.-Soviet history and opened a dialogue with the Soviets that would not have occurred without the Games. If nothing else, the Games showed the kind of cooperation that could exist between our two countries in the absence of the Cold War."

Bob saw all kinds of tangible symbols of what the Games had meant to his career. The Soviet Union's chief parliamentary body, the Supreme Soviet, citing his relief efforts following the Armenian earthquake, had presented Bob with its highest award, the Memorial Medal. Bob had been honored as Washington's Man of the Year, awarded the "Friend of Man" trophy by the Association of Washington Generals, and named "Washington's Travel Person of the Year" and the "American Diabetes Man of the Year." He received the "World Citizen Award" from the World Affairs Council and even flew to Marietta College in Ohio to receive its Distinguished Alumnus award. Bob had also been appointed to eight community boards and tapped as a consultant to seven corporations, including Southland and Pacific Northwest Bell.

But Bob could not live without projects, and no amount of awards, prizes, and board nominations put money in his pocket. For a long while, Bob had no idea how to resurrect his business or what to do with his life. He vowed he would never marry

Bob with actress Glenn Close

291

again. After his All-American marriage to Ruth and the nightmare with Nina, enough was enough.

The only glimmer in Bob's eye for the first eighteen months after the Games came when he learned that the Russian government had approved a new law that permitted foreigners to own business enterprises in the former Soviet Union for the first time since 1917.

Bob had plotted out a dozen possible ventures when he received an emergency telephone call: His presence was required quickly in St. Petersburg, Russia.

St. Petersburg Partners

I have always found Bob to be a rare commodity in the world. His intent for all the things we dealt with was developed for all the best of reasons.

> – Don Ellis, former executive producer at NBC and TBS, Cape Cod, Massachusetts

*A*natoly Sobchak's cheery mood curdled shortly after Bob Walsh entered his ornate office. Although pleased to welcome Bob after the lapse of many months, the mayor of St. Petersburg, Russia, had urgent business to discuss and he motioned Bob to take a seat at his conference table, littered with the usual bottles of soda, mineral water, vodka, and brandy.

"The United States government is not responding quickly enough to this situation," Sobchak began. "Something must be done very quickly. Do you know what is occurring here?"

Bob did not, at least not specifically.

"Catastrophe," said Sobchak. "This is now the hungriest city in all of Russia."

Sobchak, who had met Bob during the 1986 World Chess Championship when

St. Petersburg was known as Leningrad, explained that while other Russian cities, including Moscow, could trade products for farm produce, more than 70 percent of St. Petersburg's industrial output during the Cold War had been devoted to military hardware. In the debris of the former Soviet Union, Peter the Great's crowning achievement no longer had markets for its tanks. Now, on one of the city's most fashionable streets, Nevsky Prospekt, shoppers largely had a choice between cans of Finnish sardines and American M&M candies.

"Many people have no food at all," Sobchak added bitterly. "The U.S. does not recognize what's at stake here. The economic conditions could lead to demonstrations and riots against democracy. If the government uses force to suppress them, it will almost certainly end Russia's brief experiment with democracy."

"What can I do?" asked Bob.

"We need humanitarian assistance," said Sobchak. "Victor Lopatnikov of the Ministry of Foreign Affairs agrees on this. And we need it as urgently as possible. We know of your efforts here in Russia, and in Armenia, and with the Georgians. I would like you to meet with Eduard Shevardnadze."

Mikhail Gorbachev's former Foreign Minister now headed up the Foreign Policy Association, a Moscow think tank.

"The situation in St. Petersburg will get even worse," Shevardnadze said through his interpreter after greeting Bob. "The city needs everything: food, clothes, medicine. Do you have any ideas?"

"Perhaps," Bob replied after giving it some thought, "we could look at forming an international team of inspectors to monitor the distribution of aid, like the way inspectors supervise the disarmament of nuclear weapons."

"What must we do for St. Petersburg to fully recover?" asked Shevardnadze. "To establish a vibrant economy?"

"Once we have addressed the hunger crisis," Bob said, "St. Petersburg must develop its communications, technology services, and financial services."

"You have my support," Shevardnadze said.

Bob left Shevardnadze a little overwhelmed. Although he had several ideas he thought might benefit St. Petersburg, he had few resources to execute them beyond an active imagination. But as was so often the case, Bob encountered a financial archangel at precisely the moment he needed one. Shortly after his meetings with Sobchak and

Shevardnadze, Bob received a telephone call from Bill Becker, a senior vice president at Westin Hotels and Resorts in Seattle.

"I have a new project I'd like you to consider," Bob heard Becker say. "We want to establish a presence in St. Petersburg and would like you to help."

Like dozens of United States companies, Westin itched for the potential riches in the former Soviet Union. Becker wanted to establish a Westin presence in St. Petersburg, one of Russia's most attractive cities, and assemble a consortium of businesses to rebuild the city's infrastructure. As Becker explained it, the consortium would own and operate hotels and restaurants, deliver communications and computer services, establish business centers, offer management training and security services, assist St. Petersburg in upgrading its transportation system, develop hospitality and entertainment sectors, and provide financial

L to R: Isa Garcia, Alexander Kozlovsky, Sergei Sviridov in St. Petersburg

and insurance expertise. Since Bob enjoyed unparalleled political relationships in Russia, Becker thought he was exactly the man to lead the consortium's efforts.

"Let's get together," said Becker, adding that if the St. Petersburg project proved successful, he planned to expand the concept to Tbilisi, Minsk, and Kiev.

Bob couldn't wait. Since the conclusion of the Goodwill Games his professional life had, with one or two exceptions, amounted to a rash of misses. Bob Walsh & Associates had no exciting or profitable projects looming, and the company struggled financially. The chance to do something in St. Petersburg would fulfill Bob's desire to work again with the Russians and, even better, St. Petersburg would host the 1994 Goodwill Games. The board of directors at the Turner Broadcasting System still hadn't killed them.

"I think what we need to do," Bob advised Becker after they had met for the fifth time, "is first address the humanitarian needs of St. Petersburg. That's the main priority right now. And I think I've got a way to do that."

Bob explained that he had worked on several projects with the CARE Foundation, the international relief agency.

"They might be willing to become a partner," Bob suggested.

"Good," replied Becker. "We want to get involved in St. Petersburg as soon as possible. I'd like you to think big and not worry about expenses."

After Becker and Bob agreed on a compensation package, Bob went to work on behalf of "St. Petersburg Partners," first arranging for a contingent from the consortium to meet with Sobchak, the Russian Ministry of Foreign Affairs, and organizers of the 1994 Goodwill Games. Bob next escorted Westin officials to meetings at the United States Information Agency in Washington, D.C., and to the Consulate General in San Francisco, where they met a young Russian, Sergey Volkov, to whom Bob had been introduced during the Goodwill Games. Bob had always been impressed with Volkov's business sense and command of English. With Becker's blessing, Bob offered Volkov the opportunity to move to Seattle and supervise the St. Petersburg project.

But shortly after Volkov accepted the position, Bob began to hear rumors that Westin was having second thoughts about investing in St. Petersburg. They caught Bob by complete surprise: Becker had seemed so committed to a Westin involvement in St. Petersburg. Bob confronted Becker about it.

"Is Westin committed or not?" Bob asked.

"The project is merely going through a hiccup," Becker insisted. "Look, I'm committed to it. Just think big, and don't worry about finances."

Bob worried. While Becker had become a major player at the Seattle Westin, the hotel chain's owner, Hiroyoshi Aoki, who lived in Japan, called all the shots and apparently had a deeper aversion to investing in Russia than Becker realized. Bob also stewed because, in his haste to turn St. Petersburg Partners into a success, he had not yet received a signed contract from Becker.

"I'll handle it," Becker told Bob. "Remember, you just keep thinking big."

So Bob proceeded with plans for a second swing through St. Petersburg. But four days prior to departure, the Westin executives who had been ticketed to make the trip suddenly cancelled. Worried anew, Bob went anyway with several executives from the CARE Foundation.

Bob had hooked up with CARE in the aftermath of the Goodwill Games when Peter Bloomquist, the director of its Pacific Northwest office, told him that CARE had been seeking ways to more effectively market itself to a younger audience largely unfamiliar with the foundation's signature item, "The CARE Package," a staple of international relief since World War II. Bob agreed to work on CARE's behalf, first launching a marketing campaign to raise CARE's profile, then recruiting actor Lou Gossett Jr. to tape public service announcements.

"I have another idea," Bloomquist told Bob. "As you know, our primary selling point is that CARE is an international charity. And I'm sure you're aware that the National Basketball Association is expanding globally. I was thinking that maybe you could use some of your contacts to get us involved with the NBA."

Bob called Rick Welts, his former employee, at NBA headquarters in New York. One thing led to another, and CARE ultimately signed a three-year contract to serve as the NBA's official international charity.

In turn, CARE hired Bob Walsh & Associates to attract publicity and financial support for its relief efforts in the Soviet Union, and then Bob introduced CARE to St. Petersburg Partners, the Russian Ministry of Foreign Affairs, Aeroflot officials, and finally to David Chikvaidge, a spokesman for former Soviet Premier Mikhail Gorbachev. Bob also arranged, with the help of Lili Rtskhiladze and her daughter, Nana Bagdavadze, who had friends in Moscow, for part of the CARE group to attend a reception hosted by Gorbachev and Shevardnadze, which, unfortunately, was cancelled by a devastating snow storm.

CARE's first project in the former Soviet Union, "St. Petersburg Outreach," started as a fund-raising program — Bob's former Goodwill Games volunteers anted up $25,000 — aimed at reducing the famine and misery that plagued the city. While CARE officials had not initially been convinced that any former Soviet republics required emergency intervention, they changed their outlook after Bob took them to St. Petersburg and Moscow, signing an agreement with the U.S. government to monitor the delivery of 165 million tons of food and supplies to the Commonwealth of Independent States. Each CARE package contained flour, beans, milk, lentils, and vegetable oil, enough to sustain an individual for fourteen days. The NBA also made a contribution: Each CARE package featured one item of sportswear. CARE later learned that some of the old women in St. Petersburg had lit candles to Michael Jordan because his picture adorned many of the t-shirts.

While Westin eventually became one of CARE's primary sponsors, St. Petersburg Partners didn't fare nearly as well. Westin pulled the plug on the project and did so for a reason beyond even Bob's wild imagination. Hiroyoshi Aoki, Westin's owner, became angry with the Russian government when it would not return to Japan four tiny islands in the Kuril Archipelago, located between the northern tip of Japan and the southern end of Russia's Kamchatka Peninsula. Since Russia wouldn't give up the islands, Aoki would not do anything to help the Russians.

Bob didn't know whether he'd been screwed or skewered. He didn't blame Becker for the project's collapse, but Bob had changed the focus of his company to accommodate St. Petersburg Partners, hired Volkov, and now had no business to show for it. Presented with that set of circumstances, Bob reasoned that his only option was to fly into a war zone.

The Black
Sea Scrolls

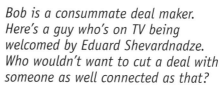

*Bob is a consummate deal maker.
Here's a guy who's on TV being
welcomed by Eduard Shevardnadze.
Who wouldn't want to cut a deal with
someone as well connected as that?*

> *– Dave Ross, CBS Radio correspondent,
> Seattle, Washington*

*G*eorgia turned so dangerous following the dissolution of the Soviet Union that it more closely resembled a Third World robber's paradise than an emerging independent republic. Ethnic conflicts plagued its borders, terrorists played havoc with its rail and communications systems, and testosterone-inspired hooligans roamed its streets, brandishing assault weapons, sometimes shooting at anything that moved. At the top of what passed for a government reposed a despot masquerading as a democratically elected president.

Zviad Gamsakhurdia, a former Shakespearean scholar, had long been one of the country's leading anti-Communists. He had led protest movements against Soviet repression that landed him in jail and rose to prominence just before the Berlin

Wall crumbled. When Georgia made its break from Moscow months before the Soviet Union came to an unlamented end, it turned to Gamsakhurdia, making him the nation's first freely elected president, largely because no other figure could so charismatically galvanize the anti-Soviet feelings of the Georgian electorate. But after claiming he would restore Georgia's state sovereignty, Gamsakhurdia surrounded himself with bodyguards, vicious dogs, and Mafiosi muscle. Egged on by a shrew of a wife who had clear political designs of her own, Gamsakhurdia soon materialized into a dictator who jailed his opponents and shot the demonstrators who opposed his policies.

Gamsakhurdia conducted his most significant pageant of warfare against restless minority populations in two Georgian territories, South Ossetia, situated to the northeast of Tbilisi, and Abkhazia, a stunning strip of Hawaii-like coastline on the Black Sea that had once served as the playground of the Soviet elite. The South Ossetians desired to align themselves with North Ossetia, part of the Russian yolk, which prompted Gamsakhurdia to send in his troops. When the Abkhazians declared their own independence, an act that flushed 300,000 ethnic Georgians out of the territory, Gamsakhurdia embarked on a campaign of ethnic cleansing that failed when Moscow sent in troops to support the Abkhazian cause. Russia still sought a tethered Georgia, Soviet Union or no Soviet Union, and got its way, leaving Abkhazian leaders the rulers of a nearly depopulated Eden.

Gamsakhurdia had been in office less than a year when almost every democratic force in Georgia clamored for his removal. The opposition reached critical mass when anti-Gamsakhurdia forces, including a rebel faction of the Georgian National Guard and the "Mkhedrioni," a paramilitary group of "Georgian Knights," conducted a siege of the Georgian Parliament that ran uninterrupted for three weeks over the Christmas holidays in 1991-92. The tempest that played out on Tbilisi's streets, as much a battle between rival Mafias seeking to control gangland territory as it was a skirmish for political advantage, resulted in Gamsakhurdia's ouster, more than 100 deaths, and the destruction of one of Tbilisi's most elegant landmarks, the Hotel Tbilisi.

Although Gamsakhurdia left Georgia in shambles, his successors, Tengiz Sigua, Tengiz Kitovani, and Jaba Ioseliani, the latter a dapper ex-thief and leader of the Mkhedrioni, had unwittingly placed themselves behind an international eight-ball. By ousting a democratically elected president, however bogus he might have been, they instantly transformed Georgia into an international pariah. Georgia did not belong to the Commonwealth of Independent States, went unrecognized in the West, and quickly deteriorated into a rogue nation paralyzed by murder, muggings, and starvation. Bandits loyal to Gamsakhurdia looted supply trains that traveled the main routes to Russia and Armenia. Abkhazian separatists blew up bridges, isolating Georgia from oil and power. Gasoline stations closed, marooning the population. Inflation shot so high that no statistics could track it. Recognizing that Georgia would hemorrhage to extinction under such conditions, Sigua, Kitovani, and Ioseliani formed a Military Council, promising to hold democratic elections. Soon after, they invited Eduard Shevardnadze to return to his homeland to become the "face" of the country.

The son of a schoolteacher, Shevardnadze had precisely the kind of international profile needed to lift Georgia out of its bloody quagmire. Shevardnadze had been Georgia's Minister of Internal Affairs, Secretary of the Tbilisi City Committee of the Communist Party, First Secretary of the Central Committee of Georgia's Communist Party, and Soviet Foreign Minister under Mikhail Gorbachev. As Foreign Minister, he dined with kings and presidents, deployed Soviet troops from Afghanistan, and helped broker the reunification of Germany and the end of the Cold War.

Although Shevardnadze possessed a résumé that glittered in the West, Georgians greeted him more with trepidation than joy. To Georgians who believed that he had not always been a defender of human rights, and to Georgians who loathed his close ties to Moscow, Shevardnadze seemed no candidate for canonization. In spite of their misgivings, Georgians had little other option than to entrust the fate of their country to their most decorated prodigal son. On October 11, 1992, Georgians elected the sixty-four-year-old

L to R: Bob Walsh, Eduard Shevardnadze, and Dave Ross in Tbilisi

Shevardnadze by 90 percent of the vote to the post of Speaker of Parliament. Less than a month later, Parliament elevated Shevardnadze to head of state, essentially making him the country's de facto president.

Bob Walsh waltzed into Shevardnadze's tempestuous domain one June evening, intent on fueling a slew of projects. Bob had ideas for Georgia, even as Georgia reeled and bled. He had no money or investors, but nurtured a dream. Bob traveled with Dave Ross, a Seattle radio talk show host, who had a curiosity about the consequences of the Soviet collapse. Bob arranged for Ross to interview a rash of Georgian officials, including Shevardnadze and Ioseliani.

Among other things, Ross came to discover that Georgia needed medical equipment, humanitarian assistance, and Western investment, and in the worst way. He also noted with some fascination that the Georgians counted on Bob to help them. And since Bob had already demonstrated an uncommon loyalty to Georgia through a series of medical interventions, the Georgians also wanted Bob's participation in an array of joint business ventures, including the redevelopment of several resort areas on the Black Sea coastline not controlled by the Abkhazians.

To further those projects, Bob and Dave had breakfast with Ioseliani one morning in his Tbilisi apartment. Once a playwright, novelist, and drama teacher, Ioseliani remained a Mafia leader and

politician, positions not mutually exclusive in Georgia, of considerable, controversial, and fearful stature. A convicted bank robber who radiated insouciant thuggery, Ioseliani had publicly promised to blow the brains out of anyone who opposed him. Anyone doubting his word had only to look at how he had commandeered

L to R: Jaba Ioseliani, Bob Walsh, and Dave Ross

the Metechi Palace, a huge luxury hotel built by an Austrian chain in 1989, by peppering the lobby with bullets.

"When Bob and I got there," recalled Ross, "Ioseliani had just been the intended victim of an assassination attempt. I was feeling kind of nervous about this."

In fact, the car bomb attempt on Ioseliani resulted in six deaths, injuries to 200 people, and the near devastation of two Tbilisi city blocks.

"Ioseliani's apartment was ringed by about 100 armed guards," Ross said later. "There were four other guards inside his apartment, and two more on the balcony."

After breakfast, Ioseliani served cognac. Ross got his interview, Bob and Ioseliani discussed Georgia's problems, and Ioseliani informed Bob that he would lend his support to whatever Georgian projects Bob decided to pursue.

"Later that afternoon," Ross remembered, "one of Ioseliani's closest advisors was assassinated."

Although there did not appear to be many investment opportunities in Georgia outside of kidnappings, Ross observed that Bob refused to go home empty-handed. Bob introduced Ross to a fabulous group of young Georgian singers and dancers who gave the Americans a one-hour command performance. Afterward, Bob signed the group to an exclusive contract to tour the United States. Later, at the newly established Georgian Stock Exchange, Bob wandered the floor trying to cut a deal — for the second time in his career — to import Georgian wine to the U.S. market. At a Georgian sports club, Bob signed some of its athletes to exclusive contracts. He sealed yet another agreement with the Georgian government that made Bob Walsh & Associates the official U.S. In-

Bob Walsh signed Georgian singers and dancers to an exclusive contract

formation Center for Georgia. Although he knew Bob had traveled to Georgia many times, Ross hadn't a clue that Bob had become such a celebrity. Bob seemed to know everybody in every official and unofficial capacity.

"One night," Ross recalled, "we went to a party at the home of one of Georgia's assistant ministers of defense. The streets outside were filled with young men wielding machine guns. We were drinking the local liquor, toast after toast. I'm not really used to this, and so I'm just keeping my lips shut. I'd been getting away with it for a long time until our host notices I'm not drinking my fair share. When he realized how many toasts I'd missed, he made me make them up in front of the others. I was completely snockered by the time we finished. I just finally passed out on the couch. All this time, Bob was still signing deals. By the time we left, I think Bob bought half the city."

Snockered or not, Ross perceived that Tbilisi had no suitors other than Bob. Astute investors, even dumb ones, would not pursue opportunity in a country where the façades of prominent buildings stood riddled with bullet holes. But Ross could see what Bob saw. Georgia made unique products, kept labor costs low, and had an educated population. Once the country settled down, once the shooting stopped, an investor with imagination and courage could really develop something. Ross did not know if Georgia would ever become serene enough to attract significant Western investment, but he flew out of the sniper's nest convinced that, at the very least, Bob had positioned himself to reap a financial bonanza.

Celestial Ambitions

I know that this upset a lot of people, and I know that people thought Bob was crazy. But from our perspective, we looked at this and thought it was really exciting. I mean, shoot a rocket ship around the world?

— Ed Parks, former director, international relations, Port of Seattle, Seattle, Washington

Gennady Alferenko looked like a balding rock star, had the mind of a scientist, the curiosity of a detective, the ambition of an entrepreneur, the soul of a philanthropist, and the politics of a dissident. For twenty years, the former geophysics engineer from Siberia had chafed at the way the Soviet government stifled the initiative and creativity of its citizens, always wanting to do something about it. But what to do and how to do it escaped him until 1986 when he came across an article in a London newspaper about an organization called The Institute for Social Inventions. It had been formed, Alferenko noted, with the aim of encouraging the "innate inventiveness of the British public, and collecting, researching, publicizing, and carrying out its ideas."

After Alferenko read the article, he decided to create a philanthropic foundation that would warehouse and fund the most socially responsible ideas Russians had to offer. Philanthropy, Alferenko believed, could be a powerful force for social change, which may have been the principal reason the Soviet government opposed it.

Before Alferenko launched his brainstorm, no philanthropic organizations existed in the Soviet Union, Communist Party dogma insisting on the contrived fiction that the state met all needs of the Soviet people. Alferenko understood the Soviet government would hardly condone an organization with such a potential to rouse the rabble, but figured a way around that. By assembling a voluntary association of individuals who had no official status, and keeping them below the Soviet radar screen, he could get his foundation registered, open a bank account, and start operating. It took him a year, and he did it this way: In a published notice in *Komsomolskaya Pravda*, he announced the formation of the "Foundation for Social Innovations," explaining that its purpose was to create a "National Bank of Ideas." Alferenko encouraged readers to submit creative methods for improving living standards, the economy, anything they deemed worthwhile. Once in receipt of the ideas, *Komsomolskaya Pravda* would publish the author's photograph, his or her biography, and a short description of the project, along with a bank account number. If other readers thought the project beneficial, they could send money to that account number.

Alferenko's first article about The Foundation for Social Innovations generated 15,000 responses in what also amounted to a stroke of perfect timing. *Glasnost* and *perestroika* had achieved full flower, turning Soviet citizens flush with optimism about the coming changes in their society. Simultaneously, hundreds of American citizen diplomats poured into Moscow proposing one idea and project after the other.

Alferenko soon started to receive an average of 100 letters a week and rubles along with them. Before long, The Foundation for Social Innovations had eight million rubles in the bank, enough for Alferenko to make grants to applicants whose projects seemed to have the greatest potential. One of the first projects, given impetus by Lynne Cox's swim of the Bering Strait, became "Siberia-Alaska," which helped underwrite the reunification of Yupik Eskimos from Russia and America near the region of the Bering Strait. Another idea came from a Soviet factory worker who proposed that the foundation start a campaign to assist in the rehabilitation of Afghan War veterans. Called the

"Duty Program," it generated ten million rubles and ultimately evolved into a company that manufactured artificial limbs for disabled and crippled soldiers. "Closed Cities" became a popular project. Dozens of former Soviet cities had been declared off limits for military or strategic reasons, and Alferenko's foundation desired to open some of them. The foundation arranged for a young American pilot, Tony Aliengena, to cross the former Soviet Union from the northwest to east, landing in twelve of the country's most secret cities en route.

Another of Alferenko's successful grants went to the "Samantha Project," named in memory of famed child diplomat Samantha Smith. In 1982, the eleven-year-old American had written to Soviet leader Yuri Andropov asking why he "wanted to conquer the whole world." To assure her he had no such intentions, Andropov invited Samantha to the Soviet Union where she received a welcome usually reserved for a space hero. When, some years after meeting Andropov, Samantha died in an airplane crash, Alferenko wrote in *Komsomolskaya Pravda*, "Death did not stop Samantha's heart. It beats in the breasts of millions of her contemporaries. For them, Samantha is still alive — they have not acknowledged her death. They carry on Samatha's cause, the struggle for the continued existence of the planet."

The Foundation for Social Innovations implemented a constellation of public movements before the breakup of the Soviet Union. After the breakup, copycat foundations blossomed all over Russia as the country, enduring a maelstrom of economic turmoil, moved to privatize many of its inefficient Soviet-era industries in the hope that a viable market economy would follow.

If the passing of the Soviet Union left no economies of consequence in any of its fifteen former republics, it also left behind one first-rate sector of Soviet enterprise — weapons and space technology. An article in *Aviation Week & Space Technology* described one privatization effort related to those industries, although not many took it seriously. Under a headline that said, "He Can't Mean It," the author wrote, "About those bizarre schemes the Russians have for commercializing everything under the sun, here we go again. It seems that Mikhail Maley, a defense advisor to Russian President Boris Yeltsin, wants to go commercial with the giant SS-18 Intercontinental Ballistic Missile. Maley proposes — arms controllers take note — to fill the missile's nose with tons of food, blankets, tents, and other rescue supplies. When an emergency occurs in an isolated part of the world, the

Russians will lob an SS-18 ICBM over the stranded parties and 'bomb' them with sustenance."

At the time Maley proposed dispatching CARE packages via intercontinental ballistic missile, Alexander Bazlov served as General Director of Photon, a Russian aerospace company located in Samara, where the Soviets had built rocket ships. A forty-one-year-old rocket designer, Bazlov believed that Samara would be transformed into a city of unemployed technical scientists unless projects could be found to keep the workers working. Bazlov preferred a project that would attract world-wide attention to the Russian space industry to demonstrate that private entrepreneurs in the New Russia could do anything anybody else could do, and do it more efficiently.

To give life to his vision, Bazlov recruited Dmitry Kozlov, the chief designer at the former Central Specialized Design Bureau, Ilia Baskin, a new Russian millionaire, and Yuri Lvov, president of a St. Petersburg bank. Then he brought aboard Gennady Alferenko, who created an umbrella organization, the Europe-America 500 Consortium. The consortium determined that its first project should look very much like a Cold War doomsday scenario.

The Europe-America 500 Consortium wanted to shoot a rocket directly at the United States, timing the launch to coincide with two anniversaries: It had been 500 years since one of history's most fortuitous achievements, or accidents — the discovery of America; and thirty-five years since the Russians had launched Sputnik. The consortium had one other hook: 1992 had been designated the International Year of Space. The consortium's space shot would not only showcase conversion opportunities of Russian rocket technology, it would mark the first time a satellite had been sent from one country to another, serve as the official celebration of the end of the Cold War, put thousands of Soviet scientists back to work, and become a one-of-a-kind publicity stunt.

The first time Irina I. Kibina heard about the space shot, she thought that the people running the Europe-America 500 Consortium had been consuming too much vodka. Irina hailed from Novgorod the Great, Russia's first capital. A graduate of Novgorod State University with degrees in English and German, Irina worked as an executive vice president at the Marco Polo Beresta Palace Hotel, managing its accounting, advertising, and finance departments. Irina sat enjoying an after-work drink in the restaurant at the Hotel Mir in Moscow one evening when a colleague began talking about a plot to shoot a rocket at the U.S.

"After this evening at the Hotel Mir, I went away and forgot all about it because this could not happen," recalled Irina. "These guys were crazy. Definitely crazy. Shoot a rocket around the world? I was just sitting there holding my tongue thinking that, of course, this will fail, and my God, this will never happen. But then some months went by. And then one person from Novgorod was invited to work with this Consortium of Europe-America 500. His name was Oleg Otchin, the mayor of Novgorod. He was technically instituting all activities, like a director."

One night, Irina received a telephone call from Oleg.

"Do you have a multiple American visa?" he asked.

"Yes, of course," she replied.

"Pack your bags now and come to Moscow. We're going to America."

"What for?"

"The space launch."

"I didn't know what to do or what to say," remembered Irinia. "But I packed my things and left for America."

For the longest time, Gennady Alferenko didn't know where his space capsule would land, could land, or should land. And while the Europe-America 500 Consortium's idea of shooting a rocket at the United States was a novel one conceptually, it required major financing. In addition to raising money, Alferenko also had to locate an individual on the U.S. side who could coordinate activities there. Alferenko needed someone who wasn't afraid of unusual projects, someone who could convince the United States government that the space shot wasn't completely crazy. So who in all of America could Alferenko recruit to help him pull off such an incredible stunt? Did a man like this even exist?

The Entrepreneurs

Bob is one of the few private American citizens who could develop a position of trust with some of the top leaders of the Soviet government. I'm glad he is here to carry on.

– Dr. Armand Hammer, industrialist, Los Angeles, California, 1990

Richard Nelson had never met anyone who could conceivably have Bill Russell on line 1, Ted Turner on line 2, and Eduard Shevardnadze on line 3, and he likely would have missed the opportunity if not for his daughter, Gretchen, the Vice President of Events at Bob Walsh & Associates. Gretchen had regaled her father for months with Bob Walsh anecdotes, insisting he owed it to himself to meet such a unique individual. When the rendezvous finally occurred, Nelson quickly came to the conclusion that Gretchen hadn't exaggerated a bit.

"The more that I listened to Bob," Nelson remembered, "the more I seriously began to believe that Bob, while not exactly a mainstream entrepreneur, was at least a conceptual genius."

They discussed Bob's involvement in the 1990 Goodwill Games and his recent escapades in Moscow, St. Petersburg, and Tbilisi. Nelson found himself particularly impressed with the manner in which Bob conjured up and carried out projects, and the resiliency he demonstrated when they didn't work. St. Petersburg Partners had been a case in point. Bob spent several months working for a consortium that aimed to rebuild the infrastructure of St. Petersburg, Russia, only to watch the project crumble when the consortium's lead partner, Westin Hotels and Resorts, bailed on him. Bob's response not only caught Nelson off guard, it was not the kind of reaction Nelson saw in many people.

Instead of giving up on St. Petersburg Partners, Bob had spun it into the East-West Goodwill Foundation, an out-of-the-box, non-profit Washington corporation designed to aid countries in the Commonwealth of Independent States with emergency relief and professional business training. Bob had opened offices in St. Petersburg and Moscow, worked up a budget, and given Sergey Volkov, who had been slated to supervise St. Petersburg Partners, the responsibility of managing East-West Goodwill.

"Have you ever thought," Nelson queried Bob, "about using some of your contacts from the Goodwill Games to do some business over there in Russia?"

"Absolutely," replied Bob. "In fact, I've got several leads."

Bob explained that Alexander Kozlovsky, the former deputy minister of the USSR State Sports Committee, had told him about an outfit called Russian Capital Ltd. The Moscow-based company apparently had excellent political connections with the new Russian government and the funding to become a major commercial player in the New Russia, which was in dire need of every product and service imaginable. While Russia had incomparable natural resources and mineral wealth, few Russians had the money to exploit them or expertise in writing and following a business plan. From his conversations with Kozlovsky, Bob could sense the opportunity in Russia in an unlimited spectrum of ventures. But Bob didn't know which ones to go after, or how to proceed even if he identified what he wanted to do.

"I'd like to get some people together," Nelson told Bob. "I'd like them to hear you out and maybe offer some suggestions."

So one afternoon in late July of 1992, five individuals convened in Nelson's office, where Donald Nielsen, Donald Horowitz, and Ronald Studham listened as Bob and Dick outlined several opportunities awaiting the right touch. Out of that brainstorming session came the idea to form a Russian trading company. The new entity, Bob Walsh Enterprises, would be capitalized by selling shares of stock at $2 each to a special group of investors with the goal of initially raising $700,000. Once banked, the money would be used to purchase a 60 percent interest in Bob Walsh & Associates and to fund the opening of a full-service pharmacy in Tbilisi, Georgia, which Georgian President Eduard Shevardnadze had urged Bob to do. Bob suggested that he travel to Tbilisi to locate at least 10,000 feet of retail space to house the pharmacy, tentatively known as "Walsh Mart." If the venture proved too risky because of the murder and mayhem still afflicting Georgia, BWE would postpone investment in Tbilisi and establish a "Walsh Mart" in Moscow.

Each new BWE board member brought relevant expertise to the fledgling company. A licensed pharmacist, Nelson operated Objective Medical Assessments Corporation, a company that employed physicians and medical professionals to provide expert opinion in personal injury and disability cases. He had also once served as the Medicaid Director for the State of Washington. Nielsen had built the Virginia-based Hazelton Corporation into the world's largest biological and chemical research company before retiring, relocating, and immersing himself in Seattle's public education efforts. Studham had a banking background, and Horowitz, a former board member of the Seattle Organizing Committee, a law practice.

Several investors signed on within a matter of weeks, the initial sales of BWE stock generating $450,000. Although the new board of directors agreed that no other business would be pursued in the former Soviet Union until $700,000 had been raised, BWE added two employees to help out with BWE and BWA projects. Bernie Russi, Bob's former mentor at Marietta College, would become a company administrator, and Suzanne Lavendar, a perky twenty-five-year-old, would act as a staff assistant.

Bob Walsh heaved a sigh of relief at the formation of Bob Walsh Enterprises. Bob Walsh & Associates faced substantial debt owing to two unavoidable calamities, the 1990 Moscow Circus and the formation of the Sports Council. By Bob's calculations, the Sports Council had sucked $300,000 worth of business away from BWA, and more losses loomed. Seattle had been awarded the 1995 Final Four in large part because of Bob's efforts during the 1984 and 1989 tournaments. But with the Sports Council orchestrating Seattle's event business, and not doing a very good job of it, Bob had no role in the 1995 Final Four, leaving him to commiserate over the loss of $200,000 such a role probably would have generated. BWE not only represented a remedy for the ailing personal and financial health of Bob and BWA, it presented an opportunity to start over with a clean financial slate, new investors, and what appeared to be boundless opportunities, especially now that Russia had declared itself open for Western investment.

Dozens of U.S. companies had already launched operations in the former Soviet Union. The Vermont-based ice cream chain, Ben & Jerry's, had reaped windfall profits in a remote outpost called Petrozavodsk, 600 miles north of Moscow. Tim's Potato Chips, owned by Seattle-area resident Tim Kennedy, had established a thriving business in Moscow. While it might take considerable research for BWE to successfully separate viable businesses from duds, making money

Stories about Bob Walsh appeared frequently in Georgian newspapers

seemed less an issue than how much money could be made, especially since Bob had practically greased BWE's way into the Russian marketplace. Bob had so many contacts in the former Soviet Union that BWE enjoyed natural advantages even as a startup. BWE would be able to save on expenses by using the name "Walsh" in its marketing efforts. Bob's photograph had appeared in dozens of Soviet newspapers during the Goodwill Games, and his face had been seen on millions of TV screens. The publicity he had received during the U.S.-Soviet exchanges and humanitarian efforts would now

WHO THE HELL IS BOB?

produce an immediate level of market awareness in whatever businesses BWE involved itself.

BWE's board wanted to minimize risk to reassure current investors and attract new ones. But Russia factored into that. While Russia offered fabulous potential, it could not govern, feed, or protect itself. Things had turned so sour that some Russians had even been quoted in Moscow newspapers to the effect they wished they had never been cursed by democracy. It brought too much misery. But democracy could not be blamed entirely. An Englishman named Maurice Baring had written a book titled *The Mainspring of Russia*. In it, he said in part:

> Russia is a country where the cost of living is high and the expense of life is out of proportion to the quality of goods supplied, where labor is bad and slow, where medical aid and appliances are inadequate, where the poor people are backward and ignorant, and the middle class slack and slovenly, where progress is deliberately checked and impeded in every possible way. It is a country governed by chance where all forms of administration are arbitrary, uncertain, and dilatory, where all forms of business are cumbersome and burdened with red tape, where bribery is an indispensable factor in business and administrative life, a country burdened by a vast official population which is on the whole lazy, venal, and incompetent.

It stood as a vivid and accurate picture of the New Russia — except that Baring had written his gloomy passage in 1914, three years before the Russian Revolution. Thus, seventy years of Communism had gone for naught, new Russians now bearing the burden of dead generations.

The U.S. government warned American entrepreneurs not to enter the Russian marketplace without professional guidance, or without trusted relationships with Russian nationals who could make things happen, not just make promises. BWE had that much going for it, plus one Russian eager to become its partner.

Sergei Kugushev operated Russian Capital. A former Soviet deputy minister of construction, Kugushev had assembled a dynamic management team bursting with ideas. Russian Capital employed thirty-five people and had offices in Moscow and Bangkok. After Kozlovsky, through Bob, made BWE aware of Russian Capital, BWE's board decided on two courses of action. Bob and new BWE board member Jack McMillan would travel to Tbilisi to check out what potential a

"Walsh Mart" might have in the Georgian capital, and a contingent of BWE investors would venture to Russia to explore opportunities there.

McMillan sashayed through life as a tall, handsome, silver-haired snapshot of the American dream. Married to one of the Nordstrom daughters, Jack had, along with Bruce, John, and Jim Nordstrom, transformed what once had been a local shoe store into a series of successful national retail outlets praised industry-wide for their attention to customer service. McMillan served on a variety of boards, supported the arts, and was an unabashed sports fan.

Although McMillan had traveled the world, he was wholly unprepared for the scene that confronted him when he and Bob arrived in Tbilisi. Dozens of people greeted the flight — so many, in fact, that McMillan wondered if maybe a rock star hadn't shown up. When McMillan finally figured out the crowds had amassed to greet Bob, he had a suspicion that perhaps Georgia represented an even greater land of opportunity than Bob had led him to believe.

The endless toasting didn't sway McMillan from that point of view; to the contrary, he enjoyed that as much as he did the Georgian people, clearly as charming as Bob had advertised. The notion that Georgia might not be ready

Bob Walsh articles also appeared in Russian-language newspapers

for American investment crystallized in McMillan's mind when, following a series of meetings with Georgian government officials, Bob and Jack arrived at the Tbilisi airport to catch an airplane home. While they sat on the tarmac, waiting to take off, the cockpit caught on fire, forcing them to evacuate the plane. Shortly thereafter, bombs exploded not far from where the plane burned up. Then several soldiers detonated grenades, barked things in Georgian, and shot up the place.

"I'll give anybody $5,000 right now if they can get me out of this country!" McMillan yelled.

"Maybe," said Bob, seizing the moment, "we could make some additional money supplying Shevardnadze's government with more military equipment."

Vexed by his short-term predicament, a battle-fatigued Jack McMillan understandably failed to appreciate the long-term economic consequences of investing in Georgia. When he returned to Seattle, McMillan couldn't inform BWE's board fast enough that he wouldn't invest a cent in Georgia, certainly not now, perhaps not ever.

Moscow Cowboys

Bob is one of the more remarkable people I've ever met. You'll go a long way before you ever find anyone else exactly like him.

– Wally Walker, president & CEO,
Seattle SuperSonics,
Seattle, Washington

*A*n iron gate largely obscured by thick, dark woods signals the entrance to *Blizhny*, a compound of dachas about twelve minutes by car from Red Square. *Blizhny* was where, from 1932 until his death in 1953, Joseph Stalin conceived his gulags and plotted his purges, and also where a contingent of investors from Bob Walsh Enterprises roosted when they arrived in Moscow to explore opportunities for their new Russian trading company. BWE's main mission: To determine whether Russian Capital Ltd. qualified as a suitable business partner.

A holding company, Russian Capital desired to form partnerships with American investors who wanted to take advantage of the free-market frontier opening up in the New Russia. Its president, Sergei

V. Kugushev, a gregarious sort about one Happy Meal shy of 400 pounds, explained to BWE speculators that he had a menu of investments available almost certain to generate substantial wads of cash. Russian Capital planned to delve into all sorts of areas, banking ranking as its top priority.

Russian Capital would first purchase several provincial banks. The banking sector had expanded rapidly, and Russian Capital did not want to miss out on the opportunities still ripe for plucking. Since the breakup of the Soviet Union, the number of Russian banks had increased from four to more than 1,500. Russia had become the easiest country in the world in which to form a bank, but the most difficult country in which to withdraw money. If a Russian wanted to withdraw 500 rubles from his or her account, he or she had to notify the bank in writing three days ahead of time and specify what he or she wanted to do with the money. The bank officer had the right to decide whether the request was worthy, this done to assure that funds would not be filtered through the black market. Even when a bank officer granted a withdrawal, Russian banks were so inefficient that it often took two weeks to complete a single transaction, only one reason why most Russians, who had squirreled between $5 billion and $12 billion under mattresses, elected not to put their money in banks. In Moscow alone, 300,000 people had dollars to spend, and plenty of new places to spend them, but no place to invest those dollars.

Russian Capital wanted some of that action. It required only 100 million rubles, about $250,000, to set up a bank. If Russian Capital and BWE formed a joint venture, they could create a financial repository for Russian citizens who had dollars and other Western currencies. In fact, why just stop at a bank? Russian Capital and BWE could collaborate on a Russian financial store and offer an array of services.

Moscow Cowboys L to R: Mike Garvey, Dick Nelson, Don Nielsen,
Tom Lovejoy, and Bob Walsh with their Russian interpreter

The partnership could sell mutual funds, offer investments in stocks, bonds, and real estate. And then, of course, the financial store could make money on the back end through commissions on investment income, consulting, and asset management fees. No one had ever done anything like this in Moscow, and it wouldn't be difficult for Russian Capital to obtain the necessary licenses. Sergei stressed that the bank would feature a Western-style look and feel to inspire confidence in customers, adding that he believed the bank could generate $25 to $50 million in its first year alone. After that, the Russian Capital-BWE banking partnership could expand into Latvia, perhaps even to a region near Mongolia, north of the Chinese border, which teemed in raw materials, minerals, and lumber.

Russian Capital had ambitions beyond banking. It planned to export "finished goods and products" to Third World countries that had tradable currencies, and to develop a business that sold trucks, cars, helicopters, and electromechanical equipment. As Sergei explained, significant profits could be made by selling new or used Jeep Cherokees through the Russian Far East, or by selling American luxury automobiles, especially Cadillacs and Lincoln Town Cars. If Russian Capital and BWE entered this business, they could price each vehicle $5,000 above cost and enjoy a 25 percent profit margin.

Profits also loomed in book and newspaper publishing. Russian Capital had a relationship with Simon and Schuster in New York and might launch a periodical aimed at financial investors, such as *The Wall Street Journal*, in addition to distributing Simon and Schuster titles in Russia.

Sergei further believed that Russian Capital and BWE could open a department store that featured upscale Western apparel and accessories, citing the Nordstrom chain as an example. Moscow had only one department store that sold fashionable clothing, and it was Italian.

Pharmaceuticals presented a lucrative opportunity, especially if Russian Capital and BWE cooperated on a mail-order drug store. Huge profits appeared probable, especially since both Sergei and Bob Walsh had contacts in Russia's Ministry of Health. After obtaining the necessary licenses, Russian Capital and BWE would simply place advertisements in major Russian newspapers. The orders would cascade in floods.

Russian Capital had its eye on three pieces of property, one near the Moscow airport suitable for a warehouse, and another near downtown that seemed perfect for a hotel, perhaps a Holiday Inn or

L to R: Don Nielsen, Lynn Garvey, Melissa Nielsen, Mike Garvey

Embassy Suites. The third property, which encompassed 250 acres in a prestigious Moscow location, could be developed into exclusive country-club-style homes for Russia's emerging rich. Because no other housing development like this existed anywhere in Moscow, Sergei believed it would sell out immediately. As a bonus, purchasers could be converted into Russian Capital-BWE banking customers.

Russian Capital had also explored investments in farm equipment, oil, minerals, and food processing, still one of the most inefficient businesses in the former Soviet Union. The Russian government lost 40 percent of all crops produced in the fields prior to getting them to market. Russian Capital had already prepared a business plan to take advantage of this situation.

The KGB's security systems had been put up for sale, Russian Capital securing exclusive rights to them. State-of-the-art, these systems could be adapted for use in houses and buildings. In fact, Russian Capital had access to all sorts of "strategic goods" that had once been part of the Soviet defense system. Russia, for example, had a glut of unused rocket ships that could be sold for well below world market prices. Sergei had worked with several rocket scientists who had plans to privatize old Soviet military hardware. The Russian government would permit only a few companies to engage in this type of business, but Sergei believed Russian Capital would have little difficulty receiving licenses.

BWE investors later discovered that the Russian government maintained a huge warehouse crammed with old Soviet missiles. Enthused with this opportunity, and inspired by a little vodka, BWE board chairman Don Nielsen proposed to investors that they purchase thirty or forty missiles. The way Nielsen figured it, Russia had satellite launch vehicles stacked up like wood that could be peddled in the United States.

Sergei had dozens of other investments to tout. But first BWE investors called upon Kirill N. Ivanov, the vice minister of the Ministry of Foreign Economic Relations of the Russian Federation. Ivanov presented yet another opportunity: garment manufacturing. Moscow had twenty-five factories that made clothes, and for a relatively small investment BWE could obtain exclusive rights to any of the plants. And, for probably $100 per month in wages, surely no more, BWE could hire as many people as it wanted to work in them.

Viktor V. Rakov, Deputy Managing Director of the International Monetary Department of the Central Bank of the Russian Federation, told BWE investors that Moscow had no parking lots, at least none that were secure. BWE could lease land and operate the lots, making windfall money. One BWE board member, Sharon Lovejoy, queried Rakov about opening a dry cleaning business. Rakov replied that Moscow had only one dry cleaning business.

"My wife took a dress there once and it took two months to get it cleaned," Rakov told her.

"Where do you get your suits cleaned?" Sharon asked.

"Russians do not get their suits dry cleaned," Rakov explained.

"Why not?"

"Well, Russian suits don't get dirty."

BWE investors next moved to Petrozavodsk, a city of half a million people 600 miles north of Moscow and just to the east of Finland. Petrozavodsk lacked most modern conveniences, including indoor plumbing, but a Ben & Jerry's ice cream store had opened there, becoming the most successful outlet in the entire Ben & Jerry's chain. Petrozavodsk and the surrounding Karelia region also abounded in mineral resources and forest land, and had an extensive fishing industry. BWE investors took an overnight train to the area, a thirteen-hour trip, largely to talk timber.

Seven lumber mills in the area exported product to Great Britain, Germany, and Italy. Three had Western equipment, but the other four barely functioned. With an investment in new equipment, mill operators would produce finished wood products for residential and commercial use. This idea especially intrigued BWE investors. Russia possessed a third of the world's lumber; the U.S. faced a deficit due to excess logging and environmental squawks.

Karelia's fishing industry could generate decent profits, but a large percentage of the fish catch spoiled before anyone could eat it. The problem could be rectified with new processing equipment, storage facilities, and freezing capacity. Karelia also contained deposits of high-quality marble and granite, some of it currently purchased by Israel and Great Britain. With an investment in new mining equipment, investors stood to claim a significant return.

BWE investors ran their shopping list past Paul Griffith, the president of a company called Sibir, which employed seventy people in the former Soviet Union. Griffith confirmed that lucrative investment opportunities existed all over the New Russia, but warned BWE that it must select a reliable partner.

"It's important," he told the partners, "to know what you are doing, whom you are doing it with, and what governmental requirements will be placed on each business and enterprise."

Jeffery Kadet, who worked for the accounting firm of Arthur Andersen, explained to BWE investors that it was critical for any new business in Russia to maintain two bank accounts, one for hard currency and the other for rubles, as well as two sets of books, one for Western accounting, the other for Russian accounting. Kadet also advised that BWE carefully choose its accountant. This individual personally signed tax returns and accepted liability if anything went wrong, giving the accountant enormous power in any business.

BWE investors found their junket to Russia eminently worthwhile. The size and scope of their investments would be restricted only by the amount of money they were willing to spend and the degree to which they wanted to exercise their imaginations. But they had to act quickly, as Russia was being privatized in rapid fashion.

The Moscow and Petrozavodsk trips suggested to BWE investors that their best opportunities for success existed in timber and pharmaceuticals, and in the kind of activities at which Bob excelled, such as Russian exchange visits, sports teams traveling back and forth, and humanitarian activities. Bob's skills in these areas could become important components in enhancing BWE's reputation, and thus its ability to do business in the former Soviet Union.

Sergei Kugushev bubbled over the possibilities, informing BWE investors he would travel to Seattle in several weeks for further discussions. In the meantime, BWE needed to complete its $700,000 stock offering and determine how much to invest initially, how a partnership would be structured, and what investments had the best chance for quick success. While BWE had to sort through a lot of issues, there was no denying the fact that Bob Walsh Enterprises had an opportunity to pull the trigger on several deals of a lifetime. Sergei V. Kugushev, soon to be their new partner, had practically guaranteed it.

Stalin Slept Here

Everything was complicated if you weren't paying somebody off. You could get better service if you dealt under the table. But we did things above board. We wanted to do something that would help the Russian people. That was Bob's intent. We didn't get into it just for an investment to put money in our pocket.

– Sharon Lovejoy, former board member, Bob Walsh Enterprises, Seattle, Washington

*A*lthough Bob Walsh Enterprises ranked as neither the largest nor smallest United States-based company attempting to take advantage of the boundless opportunities in the New Russia, it may have been the most adventuresome. Before BWE investors could seriously consider opening a financial establishment in Moscow, before they could import timber to the Pacific Northwest — an absurd idea on the face of it — and before they could invest in a marble quarry, an oil field, or in Jeep Cherokees, they needed to locate one or two simple projects with quick-profit potential that wouldn't require substantial investment. Right away, BWE found three that blended perfectly with Bob Walsh's cocktail of oddball ventures: televangelism, nesting dolls, and Stalin's dacha. But in order to make these or any other opportunities pay off, BWE investors had to indoctrinate themselves in the "rules" of the New Russia as they applied to American-run businesses.

In the New Russia, no clear legal structure existed for business and investment. Personal relationships superceded business relationships. Politics ruled all. It had to be assumed that everything would take three times longer to accomplish than in the United States. In the New Russia, contracts had no validity. They simply provided a nice place to start a conversation. Even so, the terms had to be structured in such a way that both parties constantly had leverage on one another so that the next step in the project could be completed. In the New Russia, business was transacted in cash, sometimes briefcases full of it. It had to be understood who owned what, but taken into account that it was not always possible to verify. When a Russian said that he and his coworkers owned the company where they worked, there was no way to prove it; neither was there any way to prove they didn't. The Russian government frequently created laws on the spot to meet an immediate need, but then changed those laws if they were found to be in conflict with existing regulations. New taxes and duties could be introduced with little or no warning.

The New Russia welcomed almost any idea or enterprise — with the possible exception of American televangelism, which Bob Walsh had the dubious honor of foisting on an unsuspecting Russian public.

Bob Walsh never really forgave himself for doing that. Not particularly religious anyway, Bob considered televangelism to be "religion" at its worst, and televangelists as little more than pitchmen who dealt in scripture rather than in Ginzu knives and — but wait, there's more! — miracle mops. But when Bob introduced televangelism to the former Soviet Union, he had little choice. BWE still had shaky financial legs — so far, it was all money out and no money in — and needed cash flow. The company only had a few projects in the works, none of which were going to make anyone wealthy, and a couple that might have made it fizzled on their launching pads.

One dud involved the Chevron Corporation, which wanted BWE to broker an association with Major League Baseball. Chevron asked for ideas, then a proposal, but after BWE fulfilled its request, the oil company giant approached Major League Baseball on its own, cutting BWE out of the deal. BWE had also been approached by Follett, the largest bookstore operator and textbook wholesaler in the United

States. A company with a reputation for supporting education, Follett wanted to develop a relationship with the National Collegiate Athletic Association by creating "The Spirit of America Games," an event designed to bring together male and female student-athletes from different universities for a series of athletic-academic competitions with cash prizes awarded by Follett. The first Spirit of America Games, developed by Follett executive Jim Baumann, had been conceived with the idea of sending a positive message to America's youth that scholastic excellence was as noble a pursuit as athletic eminence. The NCAA thought so as well, but corporate America never saw fit to support the project financially, and it withered away.

So with little cash coming in the door, BWE needed to find something, and that something turned out to be introducing the newly independent republics of the former Soviet Union, now newly plagued by Western drugs, pornography, and American motion picture violence, with the supposed antidote of American televangelism. In subsequent years, when he watched TV evangelists whimper and thunder in the name of God while trying to get into viewers' pockets, Bob would come to look upon his role in the project as insidious as if he had knowingly contaminated the region with the Ebola virus. But the "Channel 4 Moscow" opportunity had the potential to generate cash faster than any other investment BWE had on the table.

In Touch Ministries was headquartered in Atlanta, Georgia, and operated by Dr. Charles Stanley, pastor of the 12,000-member First Baptist Church, who preached, numbingly, about the merits of leading a Christian lifestyle. A few phone calls were made, a few meetings set up, and within a matter of weeks entire populations stretching from the seascapes of the Baltics to the sands of the Kara Kum desert in Central Asia had their souls saved from damnation by a TV preacher.

According to BWE's contract, In Touch Ministries produced a videotape once a week that featured Stanley ranting piously. Bob Walsh Enterprises received the tape, which contained an audio track in Russian, three weeks prior to air time. Bernie Russi then sent the tape to Moscow, where it was retrieved by one of Bob's Goodwill Games friends, Sergei Sviridov, who took it to the studios of Channel 4 for air play in Russia and retransmission to parts of the Commonwealth of Independent States. In Touch paid Channel 4 $12,000 to broadcast each week's program; BWE snatched a 15 percent commission, which amounted to $7,200 per month for a period of the contract length, twenty-six weeks.

In Touch sought out BWE because, when it had originally broached Russian authorities on its own, it got ushered out the Kremlin door. With the help of Alexander Kozlovsky, Bob changed Russian thinking about accepting the Christian programming, regretting the move, despite the cash it provided. For one thing, almost as soon as In Touch's videotapes started to air, a tsunami of born-again Christians clamored to place their infomercials before the children of Communism. This set off a yelp by the Russian Orthodox Church, which believed, owing to 1,000 years of existence and seventy recent and vivid years of persecution by the Soviet government, that if anyone owned the religious franchise rights in that part of the world, it certainly did. With the collapse of the Soviet Union, the Russian Orthodox Church had just begun to make a comeback, only to run up against formidable competition in the guise of rich, quasi-religious operators from America. The Russian Orthodox Church's howl grew so deafening that Boris Yeltsin and the Russian government finally had to place a limit on the number of televangelism programs they would allow on the air.

Every time Bob traveled to Moscow after that he became consumed by guilt. Murderers stalked the city. The AIDS virus ran rampant. Hundreds of Hare Krishna yo-yos defaced street corners. Prostitution flourished. The Russian Mafia had seized control of the country's critical assets and historic treasures. And to this sorry state of affairs, Bob had contributed a TV evangelist who pontificated to hundreds of thousands of souls in the former Soviet Union, many of whom didn't believe in God but had a profound fear of the devil. To ease Bob's guilt, Bernie Russi stumbled on a possible rationale, becoming, in the process, a master of spin doctoring. Bernie's notion was that, for the first time in a century, the Russian government supported the Russian Orthodox Church. So by introducing televangelism into Russia, BWE had, if only unwittingly, helped the Russian Orthodox Church reestablish itself. The mere fact that BWE had buttressed the foundation of a 1,000-year-old religion certainly warranted $7,200 a month — perhaps more.

BWE expected to make more than $7,200 a month selling nesting dolls. In fact, after completing a financial analysis of the project, BWE determined that it could make as much as $25,000 a month. And BWE would do it by coupling the former Soviet Union's passion for basketball with its love of nesting, or *matroyska* dolls. Popular everywhere in Russia, the dolls were made by turning blocks of wood on a lathe and carefully hollowing out the interiors to produce a succession of progressively smaller pieces that "nested" inside one another. A single nesting doll could contain three, five, seven, ten, or even more successively smaller and identical dolls. Just before the Soviet break up, the hottest-selling nesting dolls in Moscow featured Lenin inside of Stalin inside of Khrushchev inside of Brezhnev inside of Gorbachev.

When BWE launched itself optimistically into the nesting doll business, the traditional varieties drew their inspiration from folk tales, fairytales, history, art, and culture. Some Russian schoolchildren used the brightly painted, lacquered dolls to learn how to count.

BWE acquired blank nesting dolls and hired artisans to depict professional basketball players on them. The big money, BWE figured, would come from the sale of Michael Jordan dolls. So the company commissioned the manufacture of a test doll, then a series of test dolls featuring members of the Seattle SuperSonics. The National Basketball Association loved the idea of nesting dolls crafted in the image of its players and gave Bob the green light to proceed. The red light came on for a reason nobody had even thought of: Russian artisans — at least the ones BWE uncovered — could not produce artistically accurate representations of African Americans. For that reason

and others, BWE abandoned the nesting doll idea, and Bob would rue the day. Four years later, in 1996, the hottest-selling nesting doll outside Red Square featured a series of Chicago Bulls players — Dennis Rodman inside Scottie

BWE investors tried to promote stays in Stalin's Dacha

Pippen inside Toni Kukoc inside Luc Longley inside Steve Kerr inside Michael Jordan. The Russians who produced the Chicago Bulls nesting dolls reportedly made millions.

With the nesting doll idea both premature and dead, BWE started to market Stalin's dacha. Several BWE investors had stayed there during an exploratory trip to Moscow and Petrozavodsk, coming away convinced that other American travelers would embrace the dacha the way they had. Since marketing the residence of a murderous maniac as "home away from home" was hardly tantamount to marketing a stay in Lincoln's bedroom, BWE spent gobs of money on advertising materials, including an elaborate brochure, which it mailed to more than 400 travel agencies throughout the United States.

On Your Next Trip To Moscow You Can Get A Room.
Or You Can Get Stalin's Dacha

blared the brochure's headline, followed by colorful copy describing the various amenities of a butcher's paradise. Despite a bargain price of $1,500 per night, and catchy ads — "Sleep Where Stalin Slept!" — in *Business Week* magazine and *The Wall Street Journal*, more people played golf on the moon than spent a relaxing evening enjoying the heated towel racks in Stalin's dacha.

So BWE made no money on that venture, decent money brokering televangelism to the Commonwealth of Independent States, and zip on nesting dolls. Undaunted, Bob Walsh moved forward with his usual aplomb. The logical progression from dachas, televangelism, and nesting dolls became, in Bob's practiced view, rocket ships.

Rocket Man

I sat down with Bob and these guys who were planning this thing. I just knew it was going to cost a fortune. I was thinking that somebody would lose his shirt. I never could understand how we were going to make money on it.

– Jack McMillan, Board of Directors, Bob Walsh Enterprises, Seattle, Washington

As Bob Walsh loitered in the lobby of the Radisson Hotel in Moscow one evening, he was approached by two Russians who appeared to be in their early forties. Bob did not recognize either man, but they recognized him, having frequently spotted his photograph in newspapers. After introducing themselves as Gennady Alferenko and Peter Gladkov, they ordered vodka and got right to the point. Alferenko and Gladkov represented the Foundation for Social Innovations, and Alferenko, in excellent English, highlighted several of its more ambitious projects. The foundation currently represented a consortium of scientists and wealthy individuals who planned to revive the Russian space industry. And while the project they had in mind was admittedly unusual, Alferenko and Gladkov hoped Bob would soon recognize its merits.

To demonstrate their seriousness of purpose, Alferenko and Gladkov wanted Bob to accompany them the next day on a two-hour airplane flight to the city of Samara, 600 miles southeast of Moscow. Even if Bob couldn't or wouldn't support the project, the trip would at least be a novelty: Bob would become the first private American citizen to get a peek at Samara's secrets. Alferenko and Gladkov had already taken the liberty of arranging for an Aeroflot charter. If Bob was agreeable, they would send a limousine for him the next morning.

A city of 1.3 million situated at the confluence of the Volga and Samara rivers, Samara had housed a branch of the Central Design Bureau that perfected Soviet rocket technology. During the Communist era, the nature of the work in Samara had been so secret that the individuals who toiled in its factories were routinely refused permission to travel outside the city limits. But things had changed. With the Cold War over, the Russians hadn't been building many rocket ships or space capsules, and the lack of demand meant that thousands of scientists and technicians were about to lose their jobs. Unless something was done, Samara's rocket factories would have to be shut down. To prevent that, the consortium planned a demonstration that would draw attention to Russia's expertise. To engage Bob's support, Alferenko and Gladkov wanted him to tour Samara's rocket plants, seeing for himself that Russians could provide rocket launches at a far cheaper price than anyone in the West.

Bob's interest quickly turned into pie-eyed fascination. Arriving in Samara, again in the company of Seattle talk show host Dave Ross, Bob saw that its rocket plants extended for what seemed to be blocks and contained row after row of rockets, many several stories high, and hundreds, perhaps thousands, of half-built space capsules. Bob and Dave strolled through the maze of machinery, Bob flummoxed about what to do. Alferenko and Gladkov proposed shooting one of these things at the United States and wanted Bob in league with them.

Bob wondered what Alferenko and Gladkov really knew about launching rockets, and briefly winced over what he suspected the U.S. government would think about such a proposal. And he knew for certain the reaction he could expect from the board members at Bob Walsh Enterprises: massive eye-rolling and forehead slapping, piteous yelps and bleats, followed by a swift dismissal of the project as an addle-brained scheme.

331

Bob Walsh tours the rocket factory in Samara, Russia

Alferenko and Gladkov explained that the rocket would contain a payload of Russian artifacts, commercial items, and a message of peace from President Boris Yeltsin. The capsule would orbit the earth for a week, generating international publicity, and land somewhere in or near North America at a predetermined area. If Bob picked the spot, the Russians would hit it. The Russians would also put up most of the money. They needed Bob's help in obtaining the necessary approvals from the U.S. government and working through other logistics on the American side.

"The thing to keep in mind," Alferenko pointed out, "is the unprecedented nature of this project."

"Nothing like this has ever been done — ever," added Gladkov. "Imagine the headlines."

Bob imagined, the fundamental implausibility of Alferenko's proposal arousing his passions. Of all the projects in which he had been involved, none seemed more unusual than this. And despite looming objections, the project presented a unique challenge, precisely the kind that got Bob's juices flowing in a white-water current.

While Bob and Dave toured the rocket factory, it did not occur to Bob to consider any of several possible consequences or calamities that could result from such an impromptu launch. What if the Russians didn't know what they were doing? What if they fired the rocket and the descending capsule missed the designated target? What if it crashed into the Space Needle or punched out a crater the size of the Coliseum on Figueroa Street in Los Angeles? Even if the rocket went where it was supposed to go, to what degree would it interrupt air and

332

ship traffic from Tokyo to the West Coast of the United States? How much would it cost to insure the project? Did Lloyds of London handle this kind of thing? None of these weighty matters made the slightest difference to Bob, who didn't ponder long over whether his profit would be a king's treasure or a beggar's alms. He simply wanted to do it.

Following a tour of the factory, Alferenko and Gladkov escorted Bob and Ross to the office of Dmitry Kozlov. Short, squat, and minus an arm, Kozlov nevertheless had a pair of attractive Russian women flitting about, attending to his every whim. After lunch, Kozlov's assistant prepared a contract. At Bob's suggestion, the Russians agreed to aim their rocket at a point 200 miles off the coast of Washington State, although most Russian space capsule landings were on land, not water. Once the capsule struck the Pacific Ocean, the Russians would retrieve it with a research vessel and transport it to one of the piers at the Port of Seattle. Then everybody would have a big party.

The contract took all of two pages, the gist of it being that the Russians would underwrite most of the costs and Bob Walsh Enterprises would line up American spon-

Bob Walsh, Dave Ross check out a rocket ship

sors. The Foundation for Social Innovations would transfer $50,000 to Bob Walsh to be used as start-up costs. Bob would have to come up with an additional $50,000 to cover labor and expenses on his side, but since the Russians planned to spend more than $200 million, Bob felt he was getting a bargain. Besides, if he finessed this the right way, he had a chance to wind up with 40 percent of any profits, tons of publicity, and no downside.

If Bob had really penciled it out, he would have conceded he had no idea how much money the space shot would cost, or where he would scrounge up his portion of the money. But he'd always wanted to do a space project with the Russians. He had nearly pulled one off two years before the Goodwill Games when he worked on "The Goodwill Constellation," a project that died for a lack of sponsors. The Russians had wanted to launch a piece of sculpture into space to serve as the celestial symbol of the Games, but there had been no money and not enough time to get it done.

Although Gretchen Nelson and Suzanne Lavendar both had become well acquainted with the odd whims of their boss, Bob Walsh, this rocket idea seemed so far off the wall that it wasn't even in the building.

"It was easily the most ridiculous thing I'd ever heard of," recalled Gretchen.

"It was the most illogical project I'd encountered," Suzanne said later. "I had no idea how we would get it done, or what was going to happen."

The launch would take place at the Plesetsk Cosmodrome in northwestern Russia on November 16. Once disengaged, the capsule would circle the earth 111 times and land, just before Thanksgiving, 200 miles off the Washington State coast — practically a bullet burn from the Trident Nuclear Submarine Base.

Not long after Bob returned to Seattle from Samara, the telephone rang at the U.S. Department of State in Washington, D.C. Whoever answered it soon became privy to a scoop: A bunch of Russians planned to shoot a rocket directly at the United States. The caller seemed fairly certain there would be no accidents, such as the capsule straying off course and taking out half of Eugene, Oregon. The State Department functionary also heard details about a humongous Russian spy ship lurching toward the West Coast of the United States, and some vague plans for the largest Thanksgiving Day dinner in the history of the world. Since Bob Walsh was not sufficiently convinced that the State Department person he had spoken to took him seriously, he telephoned his Beltway allies at Sagamore Associates. A federal affairs consulting firm, Sagamore had undertaken its share of weird projects, but had never had a rocket as a client.

Julia Church, a Sagamore assistant vice president, specialized in federal grant programs. When she learned that Bob had gotten mixed up in a plot to shoot a Russian rocket at the United States, she laughed.

Ted Bristol, a Sagamore vice president, coordinated a variety of federal appropriation efforts. When he heard that Bob had gotten mixed up in a plot to shoot a Russian rocket at the United States, he laughed. But Bristol knew enough about Bob to know that Bob always had things going on that stretched the imagination to the outer limits. And the more Bristol thought about it, the more he realized he would have to talk about the space shot in such a way as to make government bureaucrats believe it was something more than what he suspected they would believe: an idea straight from the ninth ring of Saturn.

David Gogol, the founder and president of Sagamore Associates, had more than twenty years of experience at unraveling the complexities of federal, state, and local government. When Gogol heard that Bob had gotten mixed up in a plot to shoot a Russian rocket at the United States, he didn't laugh.

David Gogol and Bob Walsh went back several years, Gogol more than once keeping Bob's projects from perishing in the Bermuda Triangles that constitute the U.S. government. In fact, Bob saw Gogol as one of the unsung heroes of the Goodwill Games, playing key roles in a number of projects and dicey endeavors. A first-rate problem solver, Gogol had developed a reputation for taking on projects just far enough outside the governmental box as to strain credulity. In a way, offbeat projects had become one of Gogol's signatures. But even

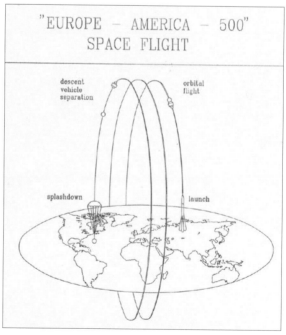

The plan called for the rocket to blast off from northwestern Russia, loop around the world 111 times, and parachute into the Pacific Ocean off the Washington State coast

335

Gogol recognized that this one was so far outside normal channels as to attract the attention of men brandishing butterfly nets.

Gogol did not see Bob as crazy; to the extent anyone understood Bob and his projects, Gogol did. But Gogol recognized that Bob didn't always think of his projects as businesses. Gogol kept trying to figure out how a space shot would make any money, and the only way he could think of was for the Russians to do more than one launch, maybe as many as ten, to really demonstrate the cost effectiveness of Russian launches — about $3 million in Russia versus $60 million in the United States. Typically, Bob had been vague about the business side of the space shot, simply saying that Gogol should take care of any government requirements.

Gogol first had to figure out where to start. Washington worked on paper, so Gogol had to generate paper. But what paper? The U.S. government offered no neat little applications to fill out that requested a Russian rocket launch with an American splashdown. Gogol had done Senate Banking Committee work, gotten in the middle of the New York Loan Guarantee Act, the Chrysler Recovery Act, and the FHA Revitalization Act, but had never been the point man on a project involving a rocket that had been towed to its launching pad following several rounds of vodka in a Moscow bar. As Gogol puzzled over the situation, it occurred to him that the rocket project was not only possible, but eminently doable, only the United States government presenting an obstacle. So Gogol started by doing some research, making a few phone calls, and crafting a compelling argument on the project's behalf. He soon understood the scope of his task.

The Pentagon would have to be assured that, under international agreements governing the peaceful use of space, the Russian government would take sole responsibility for the safety of the mission. NORAD would want to know the coordinates of the spacecraft's orbit and splashdown, how relevant agencies would be notified if a change in orbit occurred, and how communications would be monitored during the space flight. The Nuclear Risk Reduction Center would require an inventory of the capsule's payload, including verification that it didn't contain nuclear, toxic, or radioactive materials. The Federal Aviation Administration's Licensing Division would need an application for a Foreign Aircraft Permit and a Certificate of Insurance. The International Civil Aviation Organization, headquartered in Montreal, would have to be alerted since it established rules governing flights over oceans. The U.S. State Department would have to be briefed on protocol, insurance, and liability issues. The U.S. Coast Guard would have to be notified since it would be the Coast Guard's responsibility to coordinate marine traffic in the splashdown area. The Department of Transportation, U.S. Navy, and Port of Seattle would be interested in that Russian retrieval boat — mainly the kind of equipment on it — while the FBI and U.S. Customs and Immigration would be interested in the Russian crew. Gogol would have to locate a customs broker, perhaps even a shipping clerk, and acquaint himself with U.S. import rules.

After Gogol and Bristol examined the myriad technical aspects of their assignment, they started knocking on the doors of an alphabet soup of federal agencies. Everywhere they went, they were either brushed off or told in excruciating detail that they were complete idiots.

Gogol and Bristol continued to receive rejection notices until one day when they explained the project to a Naval attaché, who revealed that Gogol and Bristol needed an exchange of diplomatic notes between the Russian Admiralty and its counterpart in the United States. That elated Gogol. If those notes could be secured, he would have generated paper. So he telephoned Bob and told him he needed a letter from the Russian Admiralty to the U.S. Navy requesting permission for a large Russian boat to enter U.S. waters and the Port of Seattle.

"I was amazed at how quickly Bob secured the letter," recalled Gogol, who was also not surprised that all hell broke loose when the Navy received it.

Bob quickly received a summons to Room 7835 at the U.S. Department of State. When Bob, BWE's Bernie Russi, Sagamore's Ted Bristol and Julia Church, and Peter Gladkov of the Europe-America 500 Consortium arrived, they anticipated a pleasant conversation with no more than five government representatives. Instead, fifty of them jammed the room, many military types, their uniforms awash in medals, their faces adorned with scowls.

When Bob wrote his name on the sign-in sheet, he noted the assembly included hot shots from the Pentagon, FBI, Joint Chiefs of Staff, National Security Council, U.S. Department of State, United States Information Agency, Federal Aviation Administration, U.S. Department of Transportation, Nuclear Risk Reduction Center, National Space and Aeronautics Administration, U.S. Coast Guard, U.S. Customs and Immigration, the Immigration and Naturalization Service, and one, beet-red guy from the Canadian government who seemed poised to go off like Krakatoa.

As a class, government bureaucrats did not like surprises, especially loathing projects without precedent. The bureaucrats in Room 7835 roundly viewed the space shot as surprising and unprecedented. On top of that, many of them had already told Gogol and Bristol they were idiots for attempting the project in the first place.

They began their inquisition by directing several hardball questions at Bob. Who the hell are you? Why are you doing this? How the hell did this happen? They demanded specifics about coordinates, launch telemetry, and all sorts of technical stuff. Neither Gladkov nor Bob had come prepared to talk about technicalities or specifics; they didn't know anything anyway. All Bob could say was what he had already said: The Russians planned to launch a rocket to celebrate the end of the Cold War. The capsule would land within a thirty-mile radius of where the Russians said it would. The space shot would be an unbelievable event. And more than 50,000 Russians had worked on the project.

Sign-in sheet from Bob Walsh's meeting at the U.S. State Department

It particularly frustrated the bureaucrats gathered in Room 7835 that they had no authority to end this space shot then and there. But they had neither the authority to order the Russians not to launch the rocket, nor any jurisdiction over the splashdown since it would occur in international waters. The bureaucrats had been reduced to denying the Russian retrieval vessel permission to enter the Port of Seattle.

"Who's going to pay for the space shot?" a man from the State Department quizzed Bob.

"It's my understanding," Bob replied, "that Gennady Alferenko, the president of the Foundation for Social Innovations, has several wealthy investors. He's raising additional money through the sale of lottery tickets."

"Lottery tickets?"

"Alferenko wrote an article in *Pravda* asking readers to guess where in the Pacific Ocean the space capsule would land. I think he's sold several hundred thousand dollars' worth of tickets."

"Where exactly do the Russians think this thing's going to land?" queried a representative from the FAA.

"I really don't know exactly," Bob said. "I'm not an expert on that. But the Russians say it will be somewhere in a twelve-by-twelve map grid."

"With that kind of parameter," the FAA man pointed out, "all airline operations would have to be suspended along the West Coast for probably twenty-four hours."

"There's always a possibility the capsule could splash down early or late," Bob said, scoring no points.

"How will the government be alerted when the capsule enters American air space?" asked a man from the Defense Department.

"Oh, when stuff enters U.S. air space, we don't know that?" asked Bristol.

"What's being done to decontaminate the capsule?" another bureaucrat asked.

"As far as I know, nothing," said Bob. "Is that an issue?"

The representative from the Canadian government fumed more than anybody in the room, pointing out that if the launch lagged just ten or fifteen minutes off schedule, a reasonable assumption given historic Russian tardiness, it could have a major impact on Canadian air space and disrupt shipping traffic going in and out of Canadian ports.

"What if it lands on Vancouver or Victoria?" he asked. "What safety precautions have been taken to protect those cities?"

"Uh, well, nothing so far," Bob replied.

As Bob got up to leave the meeting, a man from the National Aeronautics and Space Administration (NASA) approached him, puffed out his chest, and with a clamor of indignation began jabbing Bob with his index finger.

"*You,*" the NASA man seethed, "don't shoot rocket ships! *We* shoot rocket ships!"

Miracles To Go

I am teacher in Tbilisi. So that everybody knew that there was a Bob, I took it as my responsibility to teach my students about Bob.

    – Nelly Saroyan, resident, Tbilisi, Georgia

*T*hirty-five minutes from downtown Tbilisi, Georgia, a road that appears to have been struck by an asteroid shower snakes through a series of twenty-story concrete towers that sprawl in depressing uniformity along the city's eastern perimeter. Made of cinder block, splattered with mortar, and featuring wobbly iron balconies aflutter with laundry, the buildings became a blight on the city as soon as the Soviet government slapped them together in the 1950s. They have no heat, electricity, or running water. They have not been painted or repaired in years. Most foreigners who gaze at this place shudder. *What has gone wrong here?* For the 300,000 people who call this peeling, pocked, and rusted semi-suburb home, the answer is obvious. The Soviet government stuck them there and forgot about them. The impoverished Georgian government can only wince and look away.

Nelly Saroyan has never complained. Three times a week she stoically descends seven flights of stairs, collects her allotment of water, and totes it in buckets back to her apartment to fill the kitchen sink, the bathtub, and the toilet. A woman with large, almond eyes that twinkle despite her circumstances, Nelly long ago learned to expect nothing.

Her father, Saroyan Varazdat, walked more than 200 miles from his home in Spitak, Armenia, to Tbilisi, Georgia, in 1931. Eight years later, he entered obligatory military service. Wounded twice during the Great Patriotic War, he survived a stretch in a concentration camp and then returned to Tbilisi, where he met Kaloyan Arusyak, whose parents found their way to Tbilisi after escaping the genocide of Armenians

Soviet-style apartment complex in Tbilisi, Georgia

in Turkey. Born to Saroyan Varazdat and Kaloyan Arusyak on Mtatsminda Street in Tbilisi on July 2, 1950, Nelly grew up to become a schoolteacher of such extraordinary skill that the Soviet government pressed her into divulging her classroom methods to other Tbilisi teachers.

She spoke Georgian, Russian, and Armenian with precision, English with a flair, and sang songs in French and Italian. After mastering foreign languages, Nelly turned her attention to business, learning banking and securities. Then she immersed herself in the study of health care, even passing examinations administered to Georgian nursing students. After a period of time at Georgia's Institute of Therapy, Nelly became drawn to healing and alternative medicine, devouring books about Shiatsu — treatment by finger pressure — and psychology. She read more books about general psychoanalysis and parapsychology. Slender, frail, dark-haired, and olive-skinned, Nelly also became a deeply religious woman. She prayed nearly every day at her

Armenian Church and had a literal and profound belief in miracles and reincarnation. Nelly told everyone that miracles occurred all the time. She had witnessed many miracles herself and counted on a regular occurrence of them to successfully negotiate the planet.

Two months after insurrectionists chased Zviad Gamsakhurdia out of Tbilisi, Nelly joined "Caucasus Concern," a relief agency that provided aid to the hundreds of thousands of refugees displaced by Georgia's civil conflicts in Abkhazia and South Ossetia. Children had always been her first love, and she had a special attraction to orphans. Nelly became a whirlwind whenever she encountered a child left homeless or injured, or one who required medical treatment, and no miracle conveniently announced itself.

Nelly had been made aware of a ten-year-old Tbilisi girl, Ia Mirotadze, who was afflicted with such a severe case of glaucoma in

Ia Mirotadze

her right eye that she faced losing her sight. Ia's mother, Manana Papinaghvili, an unemployed music teacher, had stood in the farmer's market in the middle of Tbilisi every day holding a sign she had written herself. It said, "PLEASE HELP LITTLE GIRL WHO NEEDS AN OPERATION ABROAD, OTHERWISE SHE WILL GO BLIND." Manana had taken Ia to Moscow for an eye operation three years earlier; it had failed. Ia's condition had deteriorated to such an extent that the doctors at Moscow's most widely acclaimed eye center refused to perform a second surgery, deeming it too risky. Even if the Russian doctors had been confident enough to perform surgery, Manana did not have the $60 to pay for her daughter's operation. As a last resort, she had drawn a sign on a piece of cardboard and gone to Tbilisi's public market to beg for help.

Nelly learned of Ia's plight from a friend of Manana's, and she made it her business to seek out the woman and offer her assistance. In the absence of a miracle, Nelly had no idea how she would help Manana and Ia until she recalled how Bob Walsh, a man she had personally never met, had once intervened on behalf of two young Georgians.

Nelly remembered that Kakha Merabishvili had received a heart operation in the United States. Zizi Bagdavadze had obtained a life-saving bone marrow transplant. Bob had helped arrange for both surgeries. Bob's acts of generosity had been widely reported in Georgian newspapers, making a huge impression on Nelly.

"I am for ten years a teacher at Experimental School No. 1," Nelly explained later. "One day I received a call from some people who wanted me to translate papers. The person signing from the American side was Bob Walsh. I knew that at that time, he was President of Goodwill Games, and his arrival was an event in Tbilisi. When I hear that there is such an American man as Bob, you don't forget because at that time you don't meet Americans every day in my country. Soon after I make translation I read an article in our newspaper saying that a Georgian boy had his heart operated on and that Bob was the person who arranged everything. When I heard Bob was not in my country for international business, but heart-to-heart relationship, I highly appreciate this act. I decided to find out who was that boy, and he turned out to be a pupil of my school, Kakha Merabishvili. I decided that it would be good if all the teachers and pupils read this article. Then they will tell this story to their friends. It was pleasant to hear children speak about Bob. They expressed so much admiration that I decided to write letter of gratitude."

Nelly's next letter to Bob, four years after the Kakha and Zizi surgeries, detailed Ia Mirotadze's predicament. But Nelly didn't receive an answer, mail service being nonexistent in Tbilisi. Some weeks later, Nelly discovered by watching television that Bob had returned to her city. According to the news account, he had just arrived from Russia, where a medical contingent from the Fred Hutchinson Cancer Research Center, the Methodist Hospital in Houston, and the National Marrow Donor Program had put on symposia for the Ministry of Health. Bob had directed travel logistics for the group, chaired by Elmo R. Zumwalt, the former commander of U.S. Naval forces in Vietnam. Zumwalt, the news account mentioned, had an active interest in the marrow donor program. After he had ordered the spraying of Vietnam's jungles with the defoliant Agent Orange, his own son, also a soldier, had contracted cancer and died. Bob had been with Zumwalt for a week, then had flown to Tbilisi for a meeting with Eduard Shevardnadze about a series of East-West Goodwill humanitarian projects.

Bob had long thought that Shevardnadze had one of the most difficult jobs imaginable. More than half of the Georgian population had no visible means of support. Carefully brokered cease fires in Abkhazia lasted about as long as a bottle of wine. Random shootings and robberies occurred with breathtaking frequency on Georgia's highways. There had been an epidemic of assassinations. With no power base he could trust, Shevardnadze faced a major juggling act. In order to institute democratic reforms, he needed to sweep out the old Communists and replace them with men from a younger generation. But that remained impossible politically. All Shevardnadze could do was turn to the West for monetary support and humanitarian aid, which was why he had written a letter to Bob Walsh.

The Honorable Robert Walsh
East-West Goodwill Initiative
Seattle, Wash.

Dear Mr. Walsh:

The Republic faces national emergency in the area of pharmaceuticals and basic medical equipment. We are grateful to you for the offer of help. Your kind and generous gesture will be highly appreciated. We will be pleased to receive any kind of assistance which may ease our present crisis. And certainly we would welcome small-scale technical projects aimed at organizing local production of pharmaceuticals. The Government of the Republic will give most favorable treatment to all investments in the medical field. Thank you and please accept my best wishes.

Sincerely,

Eduard Shevardnadze

After arriving in Tbilisi to discuss the contents of that letter, Bob settled in at Krtsanisi, a gated compound that included Shevardnadze's personal residence and a half dozen other buildings the government used for state functions. Krtsanisi reposes on a hillside, the second-floor veranda offering a panoramic view of four bends of the Kura River, a stretch of Rustaveli Avenue as it winds past Freedom Square, and the outlines of Gorgasali Square and The Old Town. To the northeast loom the Khrushchev-era apartment buildings where Nelly Saroyan began her journey. After arriving at Krtsanisi, where she finally met Bob face-to-face, she briefed him about the little girl who was losing her eyesight, asking if there was anything he could do to help.

"It seemed that I had known Bob for centuries," recalled Nelly. "I was sure that he shall do something with Ia."

Bob agreed to help, subsequently handing the project off to BWE staffer Suzanne Lavendar with instructions to locate a doctor who would perform the operation free of charge. After Dr. Howard Barnebey, one of the nation's leading eye specialists, agreed to become the medical miracle of Nelly's prayers, Bob arranged for both Ia and her mother to fly to Seattle for the surgery.

In addition to the glaucoma in Ia's left eye, the pupil and iris in her right eye were badly distorted. So, Dr.

Krtsanisi Government Residence, Tbilisi, Georgia

Barnebey, who diagnosed that Ia had about six months of sight left, placed an implant and tube in her left eye to reduce the high pressure and restore her sight.

"The one eye of Ia's was saved and the second eye, so to say, whatever could be done was done," Nelly said later. "Everything was done free. I believe in miracles and from time to time I even watch them. I can add that people who believe in miracles always come across miracles. And this was one of them."

In the first year after they met at Krtsanisi, Bob and Nelly collaborated to save, repair, and assist several other ailing Georgians. It proved to be a good warm-up. Soon they had thousands of cases on their hands.

The Voyage Home

*I went down to the harbor to look
and there was this incredible boat.
There were all these Russian sailors
in town and people were whooping
it up with vodka and caviar. I
figured that only Bob Walsh could
be doing something like this.*

> – Sara Benveniste, former project
> coordinator, Bob Walsh Enterprises,
> Seattle, Washington

On November 16, 1992, at precisely
12:45 A.M. local time, a three-stage Souyez
rocket lurched off its launching pad at the
Plesetsk Cosmodrome in northwestern
Russia. Vanishing from view in a matter of
seconds high above the Barents Sea, the
rocket carried a 3,300-pound Resurs satellite, descent module, and a payload of cu-
rios, including a cut-glass replica of the
Statue of Liberty, icons from the Russian
Orthodox Church, the wedding rings of a
Russian couple who planned to marry in
Seattle, peace messages from Boris Yeltsin
and the Dalai Lama, and twenty containers
of Russian cultural gifts and commercial
products. It had taken fifty-five technical
scientists in Samara and 50,000 construction workers, strung from one end of the
former Soviet landscape to the other, nine

months to transform the Europe-America 500 Space Flight project from high fancy into a celestial reality.

If all went according to plan, the space capsule would loop around the earth 111 times over a span of six days before parachuting into the Pacific Ocean 120 miles southwest of Gray's Harbor, Washington, two hours after sunrise on November 22 — 18.27 Greenwich time, 10.27 Seattle time. From there, it would be retrieved by the *Marshal Krylov*, an oceanographic research vessel, and transported to Pier 42 at the Port of Seattle.

Most of the deeper pockets at Bob Walsh Enterprises viewed the space shot as an epic boondoggle. It did not figure into the company's business strategy, and BWE board chairman Don Nielsen, an archly efficient businessman, hadn't been favorably swayed by Bob's observation that the project had the blessing of Boris Yeltsin and Patriarch Alexei II of the Russian Orthodox Church. In Nielsen's mind, the space shot simply underscored the fact that BWE engaged in business not to make money but to satisfy Bob's whimsical compulsion to roam in a world of Mad Hatters and Cheshire Cats. Nielsen would have, if he could have, ordered Bob to wear a cowbell any time he came within 100 yards of a checkbook.

"If Bob has $10, he'll give you $15," Nielsen conceded later. "Bob is generous to a fault and trusting to a fault. He's been screwed blue and tattooed. Bob has left millions on the table over the years, millions."

If Nielsen believed that Bob constantly grabbed at bubbles, the more liberally inclined BWE board members recognized this wasn't entirely the case. Bob had also brought millions to the table. He had negotiated 246 professional sports contracts before he reached his fortieth birthday, delivered dozens of endorsement deals, and ridden herd over every detail of every one of his projects, sometimes to the profound frustration of a string of BWE project directors. Bob just didn't do business in an orthodox way. Where his critics embraced predictability, Bob wallowed in the unpredictable. Where they sought fixed targets, Bob aimed his crosshairs on moving ones. When Bob took on a project, he never sorted out its obstacles upfront. He riveted first on his goal and then swept away problems as he encountered them, the exact opposite of most people, who initially listed so many hurdles that they became too intimidated to take action. The bottom-liners in Bob's universe enjoyed the thrill of watching Bob will his fairytales into existence, but they blanched at his methods. They counted, audited, and projected numbers, but never tested the boundaries of their own imaginations. For Bob, the space shot constituted one of those adventures too rich to ignore, and epitomized his belief that one need not dunk a basketball, swat a game-winning home run, win the Nobel Prize, reach the summit of Mount Everest, hit the lottery, or appear in movies to ride the wild dream.

Bob, Bernie Russi, Gretchen Nelson, and Suzanne Lavendar spent months plotting a series of ceremonies, art exhibitions, business seminars, entertainments, aerospace symposia, and parties to surround

Russian "research" vessel, The Marshal Krylov

the capsule's arrival, an event that had already been described by one newspaper as "the most unusual publicity stunt of the twentieth century." They had invited 350 Russians to the United States to celebrate the moment, organizing a "Washington Welcome" replete with marching bands, a flag corps, cheerleaders, and a VIP reception. And they had planned a Thanksgiving dinner for 7,000 people aboard the *Marshal Krylov.*

None of those efforts entirely alleviated U.S. government squeamishness once the rocket blasted off. Bob received frequent, late-night telephone calls from a directory of federal agencies demanding answers to a myriad of questions. Had the capsule achieved orbit? Where was it now? Was it on track? Although no expert, Bob reported to every federal official who called that, as far as he knew, everything appeared to be on target. The only piece of technical information he could relay was that the Russians had scheduled corrections of the orbital parameters during the second and fifth twenty-four-hour periods of the flight to ensure that the capsule's trajectory went through the specified splashdown area, and that the Russians were monitoring the trajectory of the descent capsule with short-wave range transmitters. Still not convinced, Washington rerouted air and ship traffic in the splashdown area.

But government anxiety proved pointless. Six days after the rocket disappeared over the Barents Sea, the capsule struck the Pacific Ocean 150 miles off the Washington State coast. It took the *Marshal Krylov* eleven hours to locate it, scoop it out of a rainy sea, and transport it to the Port of Seattle. The launch, orbit, landing, and retrieval had all gone exactly as the Russians planned, and just as Bob believed it would.

The *Marshal Krylov* weighed 23,000 tons, spanned ninety feet in width and 696 feet in length, making it just large enough to accommodate the 605-foot Space Needle laid end-to-end. Thousands of Seattleites jammed Pier 42 when the humongous vessel entered Elliott Bay, agog at its arrival, agape at the size of it.

The Europe-America 500 Space Flight capsule

"It was probably the biggest ship ever to steam into Seattle," recalled Ed Parks, director of international relations at the Port of Seattle.

"An incredible vessel," remembered Dick Smith, the regional director of U.S. Customs and Immigration. "No one here had ever seen anything like it."

But Smith didn't quite view the *Marshal Krylov* with the same effervescent enthusiasm as Bob Walsh. Smith regarded the *Marshal Krylov* — named after Nikolay Ivanovich Krylov (1903-72), once a Soviet rocket force commander — much in the same way that he would have looked upon Medusa on a bad hair day. The *Marshal Krylov* had the ability to electronically snoop on everything in the Puget Sound region, containing as it did an ungainly but effective bouquet of electronics that made life awkward for people in the customs business. Antennas sprouted everywhere — antennas for tracking automated and manned space crafts, antennas for receiving telemetric and trajectory information — and it literally featured tons of complex gear. It even had a hangar for two K-27 helicopters and a twelve-ton amphibious all-terrain vehicle to transport the capsule to the Boeing Museum of Flight. Perhaps its most dangerous feature, however, crowded the entire front of the boat, collectively waving and smiling. None of the 450 young Russian sailors who stood there had seen a female in six months.

After the *Marshal Krylov* docked, Bob hosted a reception for

Bob Walsh with a Russian Naval Officer

Admiral Verich and the crewmen of the Russian Navy. That launched a week of merrymaking interrupted only by two pieces of serious business. Three days after the *Marshal Krylov* arrived, Bob received a telephone call from a field agent working for the Federal Bureau of Investigation who informed him that the agency had received a tip that someone, probably an American, had slipped aboard the ship on one of the guided tours with the intent of passing classified documents to the Russian Navy.

"I'm not in a position to give you specifics," the FBI man told Bob, "but we'd like to get somebody on that ship so we can check things out without arousing suspicions."

"How about if I take one of your agents to one of the admiral's parties?" Bob asked.

Bob attended parties every night on the *Marshal Krylov*, inviting Seattle dignitaries, BWA staffers, his friends, and his sister, Toni. His FBI "guest" turned out to be an attractive young female, whom Bob passed off to the admiral as an "accountant" at Bob Walsh Enterprises. Although she received a front-row seat at one of the admiral's soirees, she failed to crack the espionage case, discovering only that a spigot in the admiral's quarters delivered copious amounts of vodka, which explained why he spent most of the week sloshed.

Bob spent most of the week popping in and out of receptions, renewing friendships he'd made during the Goodwill Games, and hoping the space shot would generate enough revenue to cover expenses. Bob had blown through Gennady Alferenko's $50,000, spent an additional $64,000 of company funds to make certain the event became a success, and knew BWE's board of directors had to be antsy.

"This rocket thing was one of the seminal events in the career of Bob Walsh," recalled Parks. "He brings in this huge Russian spy ship, he pissed a lot of people off, and then there was a party every night and it was great."

"We got telephone calls from all over the world," Suzanne Lavendar said later.

"This was a fairytale come true," remembered Irina Kibina, the Russian interpreter who had first learned of the space shot at the Hotel Mir in Moscow. "Never in my imagination did I think this was possible. But when I finally saw the capsule in Seattle it showed me that anything is possible."

The week's other glitch occurred one night after the admiral hosted a rousing bash. Bob and his sister, Toni, remained behind after the other guests departed, at which point the admiral's mood turned suddenly sour. He informed Bob that he and his crew had not been paid for retrieving the space capsule, that he was angry, and would not permit the capsule to be unloaded the following morning.

"He told Bob he was going to take the ship out of Seattle," remembered Toni. "I was nervous. Bob started negotiating. I wondered how Bob was going to deal with this man who was standing up for his crew. Bob and the admiral went back and forth, and I don't know how Bob did it, but he convinced the admiral not to take the ship away. Somehow, Bob was able to tell the admiral exactly what he wanted to hear."

The admiral appeased, his crew unloaded the twelve-ton all-terrain vehicle, placed the capsule on it, and transported it to the Boeing Museum of Flight, where it became part of a permanent exhibition. Unfortunately for Bob, who spent the next three days dealing with the defection of three Russian sailors, the space shot did nothing to aid the bottom line of Bob Walsh Enterprises, which sustained a $42,000 setback on the project.

Although the loss miffed BWE board members, they soon had to concede that, where Bob was concerned, ironies seemed to string out in seamless succession. If it hadn't been for the aborted Goodwill Constellation project four years earlier, Bob would not have been as susceptible to working on the space shot. If it hadn't been for the space shot, Bob would have had no chance to recoup the $42,000 on an amazing little scheme involving the Russian Space Agency, a Malaysian billionaire, and the Kingdom of Tonga.

The Wild, Wild East

Bob is an intuitive genius, and I don't use that term lightly. He has an incredible instinct for what can work.

— Jarlath Hume, president, Hume Enterprises, Seattle, Washington

Sergei Kugushev came off as smart and engaging, there was no denying that. And although he rhapsodized over the sparkling financial prospects of Russian Capital Ltd. and Bob Walsh Enterprises, it became difficult to tell whether Sergei had a viable business vision or whether he simply spun fiction. He had claimed, for example, that a Russian Capital-BWE banking venture would attract $25 to $50 million in deposits its first year of operation. But based on the business plan he submitted, that figure had plunged to $15 to $20 million. Sergei offered a quick explanation for the discrepancy — the new figure did not reflect deposits made by institutional investors — and the main point remained simple: Russian Capital and BWE couldn't go wrong investing in a financial institution.

Russian Capital just required $100,000 immediately from BWE to launch the venture.

Several BWE investors found Sergei's request on behalf of Russian Capital unorthodox, if not bizarre. The Russians wanted $100,000 before a BWE-Russian Capital partnership had been formalized and registered, before any licenses had been issued, before any mutually agreeable business plan had been drafted, much less adopted, and before Russian Capital put in any money of its own.

"It's a simple matter of trust," Sergei told Bob Walsh after he arrived in Seattle. "This might not be regular business procedure in America, but we do things differently in Russia. Besides, obtaining licenses will be no problem."

Sergei had not lost a molecule of enthusiasm for any of the proposals he had showered on BWE investors in Moscow, and he came prepared to discuss an avalanche of new ones. A few of Sergei's government friends had been haggling with the Japanese over four small islands in the Kuril Archipelago — the same islands that had prompted Westin owner Hiroyoshi Aoki to thwart the St. Petersburg Partners project. Although punished by volcanic eruptions and swarms of blood-sucking mosquitoes, the islands had superb fishing grounds. An investment in the Kuril Islands would pay quick dividends, Sergei enthused.

"My friends believe that investment in fish processing technology will convince the Japanese to give up their quest of the islands," Sergei told Bob, who wondered how in hell the Kuril Islands had managed to cross his radar screen twice.

Sergei also agreed that money could be made by selling used computers. Only six or seven computer companies had penetrated the Russian marketplace, but all sold new computers. Priced inexpensively, used computers represented an entirely new market. Money could be made even faster selling cellular telephones. And a huge market existed for used reading glasses. Russians bought used reading glasses even though the prescriptions were all wrong.

BWE's board liked the idea of importing lumber from Russia. At first glance, it sounded kind of crazy — the Northwest had zillions of trees — except for the fact that almost all of the region's old-growth was gone, and what wasn't gone soon would be. Given that any number of lunatics would take chain saws to the last old-growth tree left standing in the Northwest, and given the swelling controversy over endangered spotted owls, a lumber import business could become highly profitable. Russia contained 2.7 billion untouched acres of birch, spruce, pine, and aspen, all of it cheap. BWE only had to purchase some of it and sell it to processing plants in Oregon and Washington. The way it penciled out, BWE could earn nearly half a million dollars for every shipload it imported and sold — assuming, of course, that a high percentage of harvested trees resulted in high quality lumber, and assuming that timber prices remained stable. If they plunged, BWE would be stuck.

Pharmaceuticals represented a faster opportunity for cash. By opening the Russian equivalent of a Drug Emporium, Russian Capital and BWE could sell proprietary aspirin and vitamins and eventually add new product lines, including anti-stress drugs and personal hygiene, health, and beauty products. The pharmaceuticals could also be produced in Washington or Oregon manufacturing plants, and BWE would not have to warehouse a lot of inventory in Russia. In fact, limited inventory meant less opportunity for theft, less of a chance that BWE would have to pay bribes to get its products to the marketplace, and less exposure to the Russian Mafia, whose tentacles had started to touch every aspect of Russian society.

The *"mafiya,"* a word first applied to corrupt Soviet bureaucrats in the early days of *perestroika*, included a cocktail shaker of disenfranchised members of the Communist Party elite and KGB, professional criminals, former operatives in the Soviet underground economy, and miscellaneous thugs who sprouted from the rubble of the Soviet Union, encountering an environment that allowed them to take root and flourish.

In the Soviet era, the state owned and controlled all goods and services, chronically in short supply. Illegal private enterprise filled the void. It began with the theft of state property — *anyone who does not steal from the state steals from his family* — and escalated as the main Soviet economy deteriorated, finally making thievery such a national sport that entirely illegal private industries sprang into existence, even creating underground millionaires. Since the acquisition of wealth rested on the control of goods and services diverted from the state, a vast and complex pattern of bribery and corruption formed, violence becoming part of the cost of doing business.

Once Communism had been swept aside, Western advisors proposed that the Russian government privatize business and industry to give — theoretically — each individual a stake in the new economy.

That effectively placed the entire former Soviet Union up for sale. But since only organized crime had sufficient operating capital to benefit from privatization, the *mafiya* took control of the Soviet Union's critical assets and natural resources. It seized shops, stores, depots, hotels, real estate, and factories. It gobbled up Russian coal by the tons, Azeri oil by the lakeful, salmon by the shiploads, vast treasures in precious metals, and forests of Siberian timber. It sold its ill-gotten gains at absurdly low prices, and *mafiya* suppliers grew rich, even developing stakes in Western economies by distributing some of their assets into foreign banks.

The Russian government could do little to thwart such an incomprehensible scale of rape. The old Soviet government had operated with the skewed belief that as it perfected socialism, the social basis for crime would disappear. So it invested little in modernizing its police, training prosecutors, or improving its court system, leaving the new Russian government absent a legal culture. Coupled with the fact that Russia had no laws against organized crime, no protection of government witnesses, no mechanisms for controlling private banks, no sanctions for money laundering, no inspectors to verify the source of foreign capital, no tax audits, and a citizenry conditioned to a climate of theft, the country not only became vulnerable to criminals, it permitted organized crime to interact with the economy.

The *mafiya* coalesced into a pyramid. At the base, small-time speculators, smugglers, and lackeys operated Russia's kiosks, selling fruit, cigarettes, chocolate, and vodka at exorbitant prices in order to turn a profit and, in turn, pay off racketeers. The men in the middle — the men who generated all the headlines — protected and extorted businesses, involved themselves in prostitution, robbery, and drugs, and either eliminated competitors or made troublemakers disappear. The *mafiya's* chiefs, who emerged from the Soviet bureaucracy and KGB, made their fortunes smuggling resources out of the country, controlling licenses, and siphoning off funds from profitable government contracts. Organized crime spent a considerable portion of its wealth bribing representatives of state agencies and the judicial system, and even began a direct participation in the flimsy legal process. When either of those two things didn't work, the *mafiya* used violence to influence political decisions. It also controlled the press through investment, intimidation, and assassination.

According to the Russian government, 352,000 persons were killed or maimed by criminals between the time of the Soviet breakup in late 1991 and the end of 1993, a year in which more Russians died of *mafiya*-related violence than were killed during nine years of war in Afghanistan.

None of this had yet become obvious when Bob Walsh Enterprises blissfully launched its business in the former Soviet Union. The press had started to publish scare stories — bodies dredged from the Moscow River, a head discovered in a plastic bag in a St. Petersburg stairwell — but BWE had been sufficiently ignorant of the growing *mafiya* phenomenon that it plunged ahead, clearly cognizant of lurking dangers but certain they could be avoided or circumvented.

In addition to the new opportunities presented by Kugushev, Bob Walsh had been apprised of several possible investments. Through Caucasus Exchange in Tbilisi, he had been offered a chance to sell answering machines and cigarettes in the Georgian capital. Bob and Dr. Robert Day of the Fred Hutchinson Cancer Research Center had discussed establishing an adoption agency in Moscow. Although the Russians had laws prohibiting "out-of-country" adoptions, they were haphazardly enforced. Bob had also received a feeler through one of Alexander Kozlovsky's contacts that, while unusual, showed promise. The GUM department store, Moscow's largest, had come up for sale. BWE could purchase it for $200,000, and GUM was probably worth millions.

BWE board member Jack McMillan had also learned about a real estate opportunity. The City Council of Moscow wanted to sell a nineteen-story shell of a building on approximately 7.9 acres for $800,000-$1 million. Although in shambles — it even had a tree growing from a crack on the second floor — the building could be renovated and leased as prime office space.

BWE board member Mike Garvey recommended that the board select two or three investments and focus on them — it really didn't matter which ones. Obviously, some investments would exceed BWE's financial resources while others would fall outside the board's expertise.

The more BWE board members deliberated, the more convinced they became that lumber imports, pharmaceuticals, and banking made the most sense. So the board authorized BWE management to spend $10,000 to hire a consultant to determine if BWE could successfully acquire Russian lumber and sell it in the United States, requested that Sergey Volkov develop a plan for the pharmaceutical business, and formalized its relationship with Russian Capital so the financial store could proceed.

BWE registered the new joint venture, Bob Walsh & Partners Company, LTD., with the Russian government, electing to headquarter its operation in one of the Free Enterprise Zones in Moscow where taxes were waived. The Russian side of the venture included Kugushev, president of Russian Capital; Sergei Stepenkov, vice president of Russian Capital; and Bob's friend, Alexander Kozlovsky, the key to the deal. BWE did not have much beyond its collective professional instincts to judge Kugushev and Stepenkov, but Kozlovsky had vouched for them and Bob Walsh vouched for Kozlovsky.

With that, BWE's board agreed to make a $100,000 investment in the new financial store, subject to a signed partnership agreement, the successful transfer of partnership monies into a new joint bank account, and receipt of legal papers from the Russian government. Several days after BWE board chairman Don Nielsen informed Russian Capital of its decision, BWE received a phone call from Russian Capital demanding to know why the $100,000 had not been wired to the joint bank account. Although Nielsen explained that he could not wire the money without all documentation, Russian Capital phoned a few days later, again demanding the $100,000. Against the better judgment of many on its board, BWE wired the money.

BWE heard nothing from Russian Capital for a week, then two weeks, then a month. Six weeks after the fact, BWE board members learned that one of the principals in Russian Capital had been blown up in a Moscow elevator.

North By Northwest

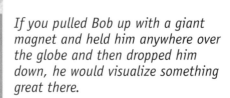

*If you pulled Bob up with a giant
magnet and held him anywhere over
the globe and then dropped him
down, he would visualize something
great there.*

> – Ruth McIntyre, businesswoman/educator,
> Seattle, Washington

*W*hile Bob Walsh never spent much time savoring his triumphs, he brooded over setbacks for years. One that always gnawed on him involved an attempt to place a National Basketball Association franchise in Vancouver, British Columbia. Even after thirteen years, Bob chafed at the thought that he and his then-assistant, Rick Welts, had sold the NBA on a prospective Canadian owner, the erstwhile Nelson Skalbania, only to watch Skalbania back out of the deal and insult NBA owners in the bargain. While Skalbania's undiplomatic exit merely humiliated Bob and Rick, it had shredded Simon Gourdine's NBA career. Viewed as the primary candidate to ascend to commissioner upon the retirement of Larry O'Brien, Gourdine's political stumping on behalf of Skalbania had cost him credibility within the ownership ranks and, ultimately, his own job as the league's deputy commissioner.

But the NBA bore scant resemblance in mid-1993 to the NBA Skalbania had so cavalierly snubbed in 1981. A spate of expansion had not only brought the Minnesota Timberwolves, Charlotte Hornets, Miami Heat, and Orlando Magic into the league, increasing its membership from twenty-three to twenty-seven teams, the NBA had been revolutionized economically by the profound popularity of three players, Larry Bird, Magic Johnson, and Michael Jordan. Franchises that had been worth no more than $20 million in 1981 now sold for $100 million or more. The NBA generated massive revenues, not only nationally, but internationally through global marketing efforts made possible by satellite television that carried games all over the globe.

And yet here was Vancouver, British Columbia, one of the most attractive cities in North America, a city that had once been approved for an NBA franchise, still without one. Vancouver not only had a new, $140 million, 20,000-seat arena on the drawing board, the Vancouver economy had turned bullish, the city had a substantial pool of wealthy investors, and the Vancouver Canucks of the National Hockey League had long played to enthusiastic crowds.

Bob Walsh and Bernie Russi had spent countless hours trying to generate project ideas that might fill the coffers at Bob Walsh & Associates when they lit upon the notion of brokering a franchise for the Vancouver market. Upon contacting Rick Welts, they discovered the league had pondered expansion into Canada, and that Toronto, an attractive bridesmaid in previous rounds of expansion, had emerged as the frontrunner. Neither Bob nor Bernie felt Toronto had much of anything on Vancouver, and that if the two of them could add an NBA team to Vancouver's sporting mix, a commission, normally called a "success fee," would go a long way toward funding Bob Walsh Enterprise's fledgling operations in the former Soviet Union. It would also, in Bob's view, serve as redemption for everything that had gone wrong thirteen years earlier.

BWE's board of directors overwhelmingly endorsed the Bob-Bernie plan for Vancouver. While the company's stock offering had been fully subscribed at $700,000, cash flow at BWE's subsidiary, Bob Walsh & Associates, had dwindled to a trickle. BWE's board had already instructed Bob to locate a few domestic projects with quick profit potential, and he'd located several, although none paid very much. BWA had a minor contract to promote a fundraiser that included the cast from the TV show *Northern Exposure*, and another marketing deal with an outfit called "Name Droppers," which provided tours of Seattle-area highlights, largely focusing on the former homes — and grave sites — of movie and rock stars such as Jimi Hendrix and Bruce Lee. BWA also had a contract with the National Collegiate Athletic Association to promote the sale of sponsorships for the 1995 Final Four, and Bob had become personally involved in an attempt to help Bill Russell acquire an NBA merchandizing license, which carried a substantial commission. But nothing had come of that yet.

Another of Bob's projects had cleared away a three-year-old debt. When the Goodwill Games ended, the Seattle Organizing Committee owed Turner Broadcasting System $1 million. At the time, Father William Sullivan and Kathy Scanlan told TBS it couldn't pay; the SOC was tapped out. The debt sufficiently rankled Bob that he wrote a letter to Turner, telling him he would pay the $1 million if it was the last thing he ever did. Bob had no idea how he would come up with $1 million until he met an executive from AAA, a company that provided emergency road services. Bob set up a meeting between AAA and TBS, and Bernie took it from there, ultimately crafting a proposal that called for AAA to pay TBS $5 million in cash in exchange for what TBS defined as $12 million of advertising time. In a roundabout way, Bob and Bernie had more than paid off the SOC's $1 million debt to TBS, and Turner had been as surprised as he was elated over the arrangement. Bernie's efforts had also resulted in a $350,000 commission for BWE.

Bob and Bernie both believed that if they could spark a flame between Vancouver and the NBA, the payoff could be twice as large. BWE board chairman Don Nielsen figured a Vancouver contract might earn the company as much as $250,000 in billable hours, and a final success fee — Nielsen thought $500,000 to $600,000 reasonable — could be invested in Russian trading opportunities and additional domestic projects.

Bob and Bernie flew to New York to formally run the Vancouver franchise idea past Welts, much in the way Bob and Rick had run the Skalbania idea past Simon Gourdine in 1981.

Welts had come a long way since leaving BWA. Two years after joining the NBA, he had watched the "Crackerjack Old Timers Baseball Game" on TV. When one of the old duffers hit a home run, it had made every sports news show in the country and given Welts the idea of creating an entire day of special events to surround the annual

NBA All-Star Game. Welts' brainchild eventually became "All-Star Saturday," a series of special exhibitions that included a Slam Dunk Contest, a Long Distance Shootout, and a Legends Game. The day-long promotion became such a smash that Welts was promoted to NBA's Director of Events, a new position that required him to supervise a staff of one — himself. He had gone on to become president of NBA Properties, practically a global conglomerate in itself, and an annual member of *The Sporting News'* "100 Most Powerful People In Sports."

"Bob and I loved the Vancouver market, and it killed both of us that we would have had a team in there but for a couple of million dollars," remembered Welts. "We both felt there was great merit the second time around. So Bob got on the phone, talked to people at the NBA and with potential owners, trying to make a match. It was classic Bob."

Bob and Bernie stopped next in Vancouver to meet with the Griffiths family, which owned broadcast properties and the Vancouver Canucks under the corporate name Northwest Sports Enterprises, Ltd. The Griffiths also had a stake in Northwest Arena Corporation, whose principal asset was the $140 million arena planned for downtown Vancouver. Arthur Griffiths Jr. operated the sports side of the company, while Michael Horsey, once president of the B.C. Pavilion Corporation, ran Northwest Arena Corporation.

Neither Griffiths nor Horsey had given much thought to Vancouver becoming an NBA city, both believing that Vancouver didn't have much of a chance of acquiring a franchise. What Bob and Bernie failed to tell Griffiths was that they had inside information to the contrary. What Griffiths failed to tell Bob and Bernie was that, like Skalbania before him, he didn't have nearly enough money to purchase a team. However, Griffiths had no compunction about hiring Bob Walsh & Associates as a consultant. If Bob and Bernie wanted to run around and find out what there was to find out, so be it. What neither Bob nor Bernie knew was that they soon would be chasing their tails.

Next they called Russ Granik and Jerry Colangelo. Granik, the NBA's Deputy Commissioner and Chief Financial Officer, represented the league on the Expansion Committee, while Colangelo, the owner of the Phoenix Suns, served as chairman. Granik neither encouraged nor discouraged Bob and Bernie from proceeding with a Vancouver bid. However, Colangelo advised them to make a courtesy call to Barry Ackerley, the owner of the Seattle SuperSonics, geographically the closest franchise to Vancouver.

Most NBA owners disliked Ackerley intensely. So did Seattle media. Ackerley's main company, Ackerley Communications, sold billboard advertising and occasionally created headlines for illegally cutting down city-owned trees that stood between passing drivers and his outdoor advertising. Bob had never done business with Ackerley, nor did have much desire to, since Ackerley had practically forced Bob's good friend, Lenny Wilkens, to leave the Sonics franchise. To Bob's surprise, Ackerley said he wouldn't oppose Vancouver's entry into the league. In fact, he said he would instruct Bob Whitsitt, president of the SuperSonics, to help Bob put together an application. Ackerley even offered Bob the opportunity to review the team's books.

Bob and Bernie then visited the Orlando Magic and Miami Heat, the most recent expansion franchises, inquiring about their applications to the Expansion Committee. They contacted every NBA owner, president, and general manager, paying special attention to the owners on the Expansion Committee — Colangelo, Jerry Buss of the Los Angeles Lakers, Larry Miller of the Utah Jazz, Harold Katz of the Philadelphia 76ers, and Bert Kolde of the Portland Trail Blazers, who stood in for reclusive billionaire Paul Allen. They devised a plan for Griffiths and Horsey to meet with key people from all the franchises for the purpose of introducing Griffiths, selling Vancouver, and extolling the virtues of his city and new arena. They mailed coffee-table picture books of Vancouver and a personal letter from Griffiths to individuals at each team, secured letters of support from Vancouver business leaders, developed a promotional program for the Vancouver media, churned out a press kit, and sought the support of Vancouver newspapers. They even invited NBA executives to visit Vancouver and conduct press conferences. Bob and especially Bernie did so much work on Vancouver's behalf that the Griffiths agreed to enter into a full contract with BWA, and the success fee was better than Nielsen originally hoped: $750,000.

As Bob had a habit of doing, he expanded the parameters of his project. Running in NBA circles for the first time in more than a decade, he signed Westin Hotels and Resorts to a contract calling for Westin to compensate Bob Walsh & Associates for securing the business of NBA teams. After Bob signed the Atlanta Hawks to use Westin exclusively, he went after Westin for a sponsorship for Dream

Team II, the United States basketball entry in the 1996 Summer Olympic Games.

The first substantive piece of news Bob and Bernie received about the Vancouver project came when the NBA eliminated all U.S. cities as candidates for the next round of expansion. The better news came when the NBA Expansion Committee announced that it would visit Vancouver and Toronto to inspect the cities, check out their facilities, and talk to the potential owners. The Expansion Committee requested that Bob orchestrate the group's Vancouver tour.

Leaving nothing to chance, Bob and Bernie arranged for the Expansion Committee to be greeted at the Vancouver airport by Royal Canadian Mounted Police in full dress uniforms and a cast of sexy cheerleaders festooned with the new logo of the "Vancouver Mounties," their proposed name for the team. The presentation went so well that Katz, the 76ers' owner, blurted out that he wanted to relocate his own franchise to Vancouver. Bob left Vancouver convinced that only a major screwup would deny Vancouver a franchise. And it began to take shape just a week later when Arthur Griffiths Jr. pulled a vanishing act.

A Sister In Need

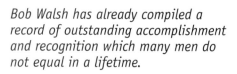

Bob Walsh has already compiled a record of outstanding accomplishment and recognition which many men do not equal in a lifetime.

— Ronald Reagan, governor, State of California, 1972

*A*s Bob Walsh puzzled over the whereabouts of Arthur Griffiths Jr., wondering why Griffiths had suddenly become such a flake, he started to receive a series of telexes from Tbilisi, Georgia. Most came from the Ministry of Health, each describing horrors taking place in the tiny Caucasus republic, and all containing urgent requests for aid. President Eduard Shevardnadze wrote one of the most poignant appeals. It detailed how his troops had been routed by the Abkhazian army and subsequently attacked by ex-president Zviad Gamsakhurdia's rebel forces during a retreat across the Enguri River into Samegrelo, a region into which Jason and the Argonauts once sailed in search of the Golden Fleece. Not only was the loss of Abkhazia humiliating — Abkhazians comprised just 1.8

percent of Georgia's 5.8 million population — it had triggered the evacuation of thousands of refugees. The clash with Gamsakhurdia's soldiers became onerous in a different way.

Ousted from power two years earlier, still intent on reclaiming his rule in Georgia, Gamsakhurdia had nearly captured the strategic Port of Poti on the Black Sea, forcing Shevardnadze to cut a deal with the Russians. In exchange for arms to fight Gamsakhurdia, Georgia had been strong-armed into joining the Commonwealth of Independent States, a move that effectively permitted the Russians to operate military bases on Georgian soil. Although some Georgians reacted with outrage to Shevardnadze's bargain with the Russians, it had given Shevardnadze just enough ammunition to effectively fight Gamsakhurdia. Now, with everyone in the West preoccupied with Bosnia, Shevardnadze prevailed on Bob again.

Telex ID#187654

To: Bob Walsh
East-West Goodwill Foundation

From: Eduard Shevardnadze
Through: Amiran Kadagishvili

The Gudauta (Abkhazian) side once again violated the cease-fire agreement and began a large-scale assault upon the city of Sokhumi. Disarmed defenders of Sokhumi, after selflessly fighting a fierce battle, left the city with tens of thousands of civilians. However, the separatists were not content and continued hostilities. The only safe area where the refugees could hide from the barbaric atrocities perpetuated by the mercenaries was in the mountainous region of Svaneti. Therefore, over 100,000 refugees, among whom the overwhelming majority are women, children and old people, are currently seeking shelter in the mountains.

It has been snowing for some time now. Dozens of people have died of hunger and cold, and what is particularly tragic is that there are infants among the dead. Food and warm clothes as well as various conveyances to bring the refugees out of Svaneti are being sent there. This, however, is not enough. The acute economic crisis raging in Georgia makes it impossible to use every means to save those in trouble. Unless immediate, decisive measures are taken, the current disastrous situation will turn tragic.

The situation is being seriously aggravated by the supporters of the ex-president, who have cut off the major communications arteries. Svaneti shall be declared the zone of distress. I request that you and all neighboring countries, the people of goodwill, to empathize with the Georgians in trouble. Do not let tens of thousands of children, women and old men die of hunger and cold. We are in dire need of warm clothes, foodstuffs and medications. I want you to know that Georgia expects and believes that you will help promptly. The delay is tantamount to death.

May God Bless You,

Eduard Shevardnadze

Despite Bob's heavy load of domestic projects, he plunged into the Georgian relief effort full throttle. First, he reorganized the East-West Goodwill Foundation, changing its name to the Walsh International Relief Fund. Its long-term goal: assist developing countries with disrupted or shattered infrastructures. Its short-term goal: disaster relief. To accomplish the latter on Georgia's behalf, Bob telephoned, faxed, and wrote letters to Rotary International, Seattle's Group Health Cooperative, CARE, the Boeing Company, and Northwest Medical Teams of Portland, Oregon,

Tbilisi's refugee haven, The Iveria Hotel

which had contributed medical supplies to the 1988 earthquake relief effort in Armenia. He then turned the bulk of the project over to a new BWE employee, Kristin Hayden, who quickly proved to have a flair for organizing a relief project. Within five weeks, Bob and Kristin had built a network of organizations and volunteers to gather and move medical supplies to the Republic of Georgia.

Northwest Medical Teams organized the medical shipments. The U.S. government, through the Fund for Democracy, contributed money. CARE provided 200,000 food packages and assorted clothing. Rotary facilitated their transfer to Seattle's Boeing Field via Oak Harbor Freight Lines, which loaded the supplies on 747s donated by the Boeing Company. Matrix International of West Virginia handled international freight and customs issues. When the WIRF mercy flights reached Istanbul, trucks moved the supplies to Tbilisi, where they were turned over to CARE and Georgia's Humanitarian Aid Commission. Nelly Saroyan, who had once introduced Bob to a young Tbilisi girl who had required an eye operation, became one of the primary distribution controllers.

The first delivery included 8,800 pounds of IV solutions, calcium medicines, vitamins, mineral supplements, and medical supplies, a total of 14,900 pounds. Five subsequent deliveries totaled more than 40,000 pounds of medicine and equipment.

"It was at this time that I attended a meeting in the House of Parliament and made a speech about Bob Walsh," recalled Nelly. "Everybody was surprised by what Bob did and wanted to know more about him. I mentioned that by nature Bob is a man who is always ready to assist. And this was very difficult period. People were shot. There was so much pain. We were in a blockade and could not get petrol. There were problems with electricity. Almost everybody had guns. It was cold, and people were stuck in the mountains. When President Shevardnadze put out the SOS that we are in danger, Bob said he shall do his best, and he was the man who did it. Bob shared our pain and sent Boeings with relief to Georgia.

"He sent medicine when we had no medicine. There were so many happy faces of people who got this blessing that who can count them all? And how these happy faces wished that people like Bob were more in the world. When the relief was in the Central Storage, a man came to the warehouse. He told us that if he could not find what he needed, his young son would die. Luckily, what he needed was in the list of Bob's relief. Tears appeared in the eyes of people who saw this. The man's son was saved. After that Bob's visits to Tbilisi were very different. Crowds of people appeared at the airport to express their respect for Bob.

"I can't speak about Bob as a businessman but I can speak about him as a human being and foreigner. When he saw that such a country exists as Georgia he came to Georgia. And after that he kept on coming, when there was severe coldness, when we were frozen without light, without food, and even though they were shooting. Sometimes I think Bob knows Georgia better than Georgians. He likes Georgian feasts. Georgians have some special way of psychotherapy of the table because they expose so much warmth there. Do you think anything that happens doesn't happen from the will of God? Do you think there are not miracles? I shall tell you now that Bob is a Georgian. And if not now, then Bob was Georgian in another life. It can be a mistake. Nowadays there are many mistakes."

Walsh Pharma

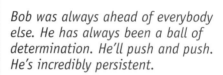

*Bob was always ahead of everybody
else. He has always been a ball of
determination. He'll push and push.
He's incredibly persistent.*

*– Toni Walsh, sister of Bob Walsh,
Seattle, Washington*

*B*ob Walsh occasionally ran afoul
of the men minding the purse strings at Bob
Walsh Enterprises, but never more so than
in the aftermath of the looming Russian
Capital fiasco. True, Bob had not made Russian Capital vanish off the planet, but vanish it had. Bob had vouched for his former
Goodwill Games comrade, Alexander
Kozlovsky, and Kozlovsky had vouched for
Russian Capital. The successive vouchers
had cost BWE $100,000, compelling evidence in the opinion of some board members that yet another of Bob's ventures had
gone missing down a rabbit hole.

BWE had wired the money to a
German bank as its half of an investment in
a new Moscow financial supermarket. But
weeks had passed and Russian Capital had
secured no licenses to operate the bank, or

sent along partnership paperwork. The deadline for receiving the documents had come and gone, then come and gone again. Bob had called, faxed, and telexed Russian Capital repeatedly, never hearing a word in return. He also called Kozlovsky several times, but the former deputy minister of the USSR State Sports Committee found himself at a loss to explain Russian Capital's inexplicable behavior. Kozlovsky could only speculate that it had smacked into a bog of government legalisms, and that it would ultimately prove to be as good as its word.

Bob knew the truth ran deeper. Russian Capital, Bob had come to believe, hadn't been as interested in forming a series of joint ventures with Bob Walsh Enterprises as it had been looking for a source of cheap money that it could turn around for a quick profit. Some Russians, Bob learned, had made as much as 100 percent on their money by loaning it out on a short-term basis, leaving Bob to conclude Russian Capital had never wanted any involvement with BWE other than that. Now, given its silence, trying to collect the missing $100,000 seemed as hopeless as nailing the perpetrator of the elevator blast that had taken out the Russian Capital operative. Bob didn't ponder long over the dead man. He had never met him.

BWE investors mulled over retaining an attorney, or possibly registering a claim against Russian Capital with the Russian government. But Bob recognized that BWE had no chance to recoup the $100,000 that way. Russia had few laws, no way to enforce the ones it had, and a relatively minor white-collar crime would interest no one in a country which, according to *Izvestia*, had degenerated into rampant mayhem. Since the formation of Bob Walsh Enterprises, Russian authorities had reported 30,000 murders and gangland-style assassinations in Moscow and St. Petersburg. In Moscow alone, more than 8,000 people had been reported missing from their apartments, which had become attractive commodities in the city's real estate market. Russia had fallen under the rule of the gun, leaving Bob the problem of finding a creative solution to retrieve BWE's $100,000. In the interim, he hoped the company would hit a financial motherlode in lumber, vitamins, and aspirin.

While the lumber opportunity remained promising, pharmaceuticals represented a more attractive option in its potential for payback. For Bob, the launch of "Walsh Pharma" had as much emotional appeal as it did economic potential, for it was really a fancy extension of something he had been doing for years anyway. From his earliest days as president of the Goodwill Games, Bob had taken vitamins to the Soviet Union to fulfill requests made by Soviet officials at the ministries of Sports, Culture, and Foreign Affairs.

Walsh Pharma hadn't been designed in the manner BWE investors originally envisioned. The initial idea, suggested to Bob by Georgian President Eduard Shevardnadze, had been to open a pharmacy in Tbilisi — an impractical idea, to say nothing of dangerous, with a civil war raging. BWE investors explored selling pharmaceuticals in Russia via mail order, or opening a Moscow pharmacy, an upscale "Walsh Mart," to cater to Russia's emerging rich. The lack of suitable retail and warehouse space and the specter of

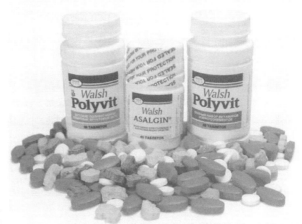

Walsh Pharma's first products included Walsh Polyvit and Walsh Asalgin

the Russian Mafia had sabotaged that plan. But Walsh Pharma circumvented such potential troubles. BWE contracted to have Walsh Pharma products manufactured in the United States and delivered by air to Moscow, where they were collected by a courier driving a nondescript car and distributed directly to the customer. Since Walsh Pharma didn't have to inventory much product in Russia, it wouldn't present a profile that would interest many gangsters. And by using air freight to get product to Russia, Walsh Pharma avoided Russian seaports, all of which were notoriously corrupt.

"The government controlled every aspect of distribution," recalled Sergey Volkov, who built Walsh Pharma's distributor base. "Because of the nature of the product, there was no cash involved, just wire transfers and bank transactions. It was a less exciting opportunity for the criminal people, as opposed to liquor or tobacco, both sold anywhere for cash. We totally controlled the project and didn't have to rely on anybody outside the company."

BWE planned to start small, expand as Walsh Pharma's budget would allow, and deliver a product equal in quality but less expensive than products distributed in Russia by French and German competitors. After BWE developed business, supply, distribution, and marketing plans, it took Russia's Ministry of Health three months to license Walsh-brand vitamins and aspirin. BWE then spent $10,000 to cover the manufacturing costs of 3,000 bottles of test products. Volkov took a couple of cases to Moscow and made the rounds of the city's pharmacies, trying to sell them.

Two months later, a Scandanavian Airlines Boeing 767, with 300 cases of "Walsh Polyvit" and "Walsh Asalgin" (aspirin) in its cargo hold, roared down the runway at Seattle-Tacoma International Airport bound for Moscow. Four months after Walsh Pharma products began appearing on Moscow store shelves, the company received an order from the Ukraine, which sought to purchase $100,000 worth of aspirin, and several vitamin inquiries from Georgia and Latvia. Flush with that success, BWE investors decided to open an office in Moscow to handle Walsh Pharma product exclusively, and to hire an American manager to promote the label.

BWE did not lack for willing buyers, nor did it experience much difficulty locating vitamin manufacturers and distributors. But it faced considerable trouble funding a buildup of product inventory in the United States and creating brand awareness for the product in Russia. BWE investors believed that, if properly marketed — that meant tens of thousands of dollars of advertising per month — Walsh Pharma had the potential to become a $10 million-a-year business in three years and a $50 million business in five years when additional products were brought on line. But until BWE had more capital to invest, Walsh Pharma could not begin to generate substantial revenue, making the $100,000 investment in Russian Capital such a sore point. With that hundred grand, BWE investors could have conducted a television advertising campaign and done a direct mailing to at least 400 of Moscow's 600 pharmacies.

Bob made it a priority to get the $100,000 back. Although Kozlovsky argued on behalf of BWE continuing to cultivate a relationship with Russian Capital, BWE's board had no further interest in the company. BWE management sent a letter to Russian Capital requesting immediate repayment, then a second letter. Several weeks went by before BWE got word that Russian Capital had wired $100,000 to BWE's bank account. But the money never showed up, Russian Capital attributing the snafu to a "bank error." When several other attempts to retrieve its money failed, BWE's board came to the same conclusion Bob had — that Russian Capital had taken the $100,000 and placed it offshore somewhere to collect interest.

Bob figured he had only one chance to get the money back, and that was to pull a fast one. He sent a telex to Russian Capital explaining that he had told Paul Beckham of Turner Broadcasting about the missing $100,000, and that he had an appointment scheduled with Ted Turner. Beckham and Turner would find it newsworthy, Bob advised, that a prominent Russian company had ripped off a small American company. If Russian Capital didn't return the $100,000 within seven days, Bob would go on Cable News Network and expose Russian Capital as charlatans. Bob included in his telex a reminder that his appearance on CNN would be televised all over the former Soviet Union. Before seven days elapsed, Russian Capital not only returned BWE's $100,000, it sent an additional $25,000.

Bob had never called Beckham, had no impending meeting with Turner, and had about as much of a chance of going on CNN and accusing Russian Capital of international skullduggery as he had of getting drafted by the Boston Celtics. Bob celebrated his hoodwinking of Russian Capital by taking a short vacation in Hawaii, where, to his everlasting chagrin, he hoodwinked himself.

Trouble In Paradise

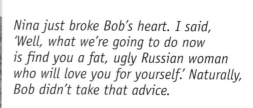

*Nina just broke Bob's heart. I said,
'Well, what we're going to do now
is find you a fat, ugly Russian woman
who will love you for yourself.' Naturally,
Bob didn't take that advice.*

– Valerie Yurina, Seattle, Washington

*O*f all the places Bob Walsh ventured, none enchanted him more than the Hawaiian island of Maui, and especially its quaint whaling village of Lahaina. Bob made his first junket there in the late 1960s when he honeymooned with Ruth Walsh, and over the years he became so entranced with the sun, palms, and tropical charms that he purchased a condominium at the Lahaina Shores Beach Resort, two blocks from the main tourist action. The condo provided Bob all the excuse he needed to make three or four pilgrimages a year to Maui, the locale of two seminal events, the first in 1984.

Following the death of Dr. Marty Kushner, a friend who had served as team physician for the Seattle SuperSonics during Bob's tenure with the club, Bob determined that Lahaina was the perfect environment in which to pen his Last Will and Testament, a beach scribbling that called for the proceeds from Bob's life insurance policy to be used to fly fifty of his best friends to Hawaii to celebrate his life and mourn his death.

He executed the document during an interlude in which he was "of sound mind and body," subsequently agreeing with the notion he had been absent the "sound mind" part when he made his second key decision while frolicking under Lahaina's swaying palms. In fact, for years afterward Bob couldn't explain why he did what he did, offering only a glazed-eyes look reminiscent of a frying-pan trout.

Bob could tick off the names of a litany of women he might have married. He possibly could have married Karen Benea, an early flame from Boston, or Barbara Deems, whom he'd romanced at Marietta College, or maybe Karla Barton, a Seattle runner he'd encountered during the Emerald City Marathon. Perhaps he should have even married Nicole Preveaux, the French dish he'd deep-sixed in favor of Nina Askyonova. Bob might have married one or two other women whose names

The palm under which Bob Walsh penned his Last Will and Testament

had fled his memory banks. Marriage to any of the aforementioned, or even to a pert, U.S. Defense Department cutie with whom he had briefly swooned, might have been recorded on the plus side of the matrimonial ledger. But for some reason, Bob never found nor married the right woman, although the first candidate, Ruth, had been right far longer than she had been wrong.

The lamentable and expensive truth: Bob had a knack for locating the wrong female with jackal-like precision and marrying her with boggling speed. Bob had wanted to marry Ruth from the moment he spied her in the studios of WNAC-TV in Boston. He had the will, and therefore found a way, to spirit Nina out of the former Soviet Union and marry her to the bewilderment of throngs in Lenny Wilkens' backyard. After his marriage to Nina ended, Bob vowed never to marry again. But then he took another of his innumerable junkets to Moscow, where a thunderbolt greeted him.

As BWE board member Jack McMillan recalled it, he and Bob stood in the lobby of the Metropol Hotel when an attractive young woman approached, introducing herself as their interpreter. She worked, she said, in the employ of Russian Capital. As soon as Bob searched Milana Koulagin's eyes, surveyed her shoulder-length, India ink hair, and spied her superb profile, he was a goner, envisioning a panoply of illicit thrills. Later that day, as Bob, Milana, and Jack consulted with investors from Russian Capital, Milana talked about her mother, who was ill. Exhibiting his usual sympathy, Bob invited Milana and her mother to Seattle.

BWE board member Dick Nelson may have foreseen Bob's fate before anyone else. Nelson and several BWE investors had been

in Moscow, holed up at Stalin's dacha when, one evening, everyone except Bob trouped off to a performance by the Moscow Circus. When

Sergei and Marina Sviridov with Bob and Toni in Hawaii

the group returned to the dacha, Bob and Milana stood alone, talking.

"She was sort of leaning against the door," Nelson remembered. "You've never seen anybody look so beautiful in your life. She looked like one of those sirens from Greek and Roman mythology who lured sailors to their deaths on rocky coasts with seductive singing. We looked at her and looked at Bob. Right then we knew Bob was in big trouble. But at that moment in the dacha, Milana would have been irresistible to anybody."

Two months later, following a rash of Bob's telephone calls, Milana and her mother took him up on his invitation and flew to Seattle. Milana never went home, at least not permanently, striking dread in the hearts of all who had ever known Bob.

Ruth McIntyre, Bob's first wife, fretted over the same issues that had worried her about Nina, while Bob's sister, Toni, harbored a sinking feeling from the moment Milana arrived in America.

Initially attracted to Milana's stunning looks, Bob might have also contemplated marriage as a way of making amends for the Nina debacle. But when Bob asked Milana to marry him, she professed reluctance; they had been acquainted only a couple of months. On the other hand, Bob had been so kind to her mother. So Milana finally said yes. Only after Milana accepted Bob's proposal did the thought flit across his field of consciousness that marriage to a woman half his age might not be so ideal after all. But Bob quickly shook off the feeling. He felt that this marriage was the right thing to do, and that Milana would make a wonderful wife and companion. So he plotted a trip to Hawaii.

Just before Bob, Milana, and Milana's mother jetted off to Maui, ostensibly for a short getaway, Bob telephoned Tom Jernstedt, the NCAA official with whom he had staged a couple of Final Fours.

"I've got good news," said Bob.

"What news?"

"I'm getting married again."

"Well, I'm thrilled. I couldn't be more pleased, Bob."

"Yeah, but maybe you won't be pleased. I'm marrying another Russian."

"What? You stupid shit! I can't believe that!"

"Not only that, she was a Russian translator."

"I just unloaded on Bob," Jernstedt remembered. "I told him it was definitely one of his dumber moves."

Jernstedt's concern focused on the age difference, reminding Bob that he had a male friend who had also married a much younger woman. And the poor guy had just endured a huge domestic calamity. The guy's wife had left him and, with the divorce pending, had acquired a new squeeze. The new boyfriend liked everything about her except her average-sized breasts, apparently favoring balloons. So the estranged wife had breast implants, and her estranged husband received the bill — a $5,000 hit so the new boyfriend could fiddle with his soon-to-be ex-wife's new and improved knockers.

When Bob and Milana arrived in Hawaii, Bob tried to summon the courage to tell Bernie Russi, who had accompanied him and Milana, what he was going to do. But Bob couldn't bring himself to do it, knowing full well that Bernie would have tossed him headfirst into

Maui's Haleakala Crater. So while Bernie relaxed at the Lahaina Shores Beach Resort, Bob got on the telephone and worked out arrangements for a blood test, marriage license, and a preacher, knowing full well Bernie was in the adjacent room, oblivious.

After Bernie flew back to Seattle, Bob quickly called Bernie's son in Denver, confessed his impending deed, and solicited advice.

"Don't do it," Bernie's son advised.

"I think I'm going to do it," said Bob.

"Then get a prenuptial agreement."

"It wouldn't matter anyway."

About the time Bernie arrived back in Seattle, Bob motored up the coast toward Kaanapali, found a gorgeous spot near the ocean and, for a second time, married a Russian translator. Bob brooded for a long time over what he had done, and why he had done it, never arriving at a satisfactory answer other than right time, right place, right body, right face. For the most part, Bob could not have been more baffled over his behavior than if a cluster of coconuts had dropped from a palm and conked him upside the head.

When word of the marriage spread through Bob's professional and social ranks, it was greeted not with congratulatory nods of approval, but with condemnation worthy of a moral inquiry. Bob's personal life had frequently been engulfed by turbulence, but the wedding to Milana went way over the top.

Bob's hairdresser, Valerie Yurina, had sought to head off what she was certain would become another conjugal disaster.

"I talked to him," Valerie admitted later, "I told Bob, 'You can't get married again until you go through our little committee.' The next thing you know he's married again."

"When I found out about it," recalled Kimberly Brown, the former president of Bob Walsh & Associates, "I couldn't believe it. What was he thinking?"

Bob was thinking that Milana was just what he needed. He thought that his friends didn't understand the situation, and that they didn't know Milana in the way that he did. Still, it didn't keep Bob's friends from shaking their heads.

"It defied all logic" recalled Ed Parks, who worked in international relations at the Port of Seattle.

"You don't marry a twenty-year-old when you're in your fifties," Virginia Swanson, the director of the Seattle Parks Department, said later. "You'd think Bob would have seen that."

Kristin Hayden, a Bob Walsh Enterprises employee stationed in Moscow, worried about Milana's expectations. Kristin had studied as an exchange student in the Soviet Union during the Cold War era, spoke Russian fluently, and knew the mental workings of the Russian female as well as any American woman on the planet. Most of them, Kristin knew, would have impossibly high material demands if placed in Milana's situation.

"Bob's friends thought he was insane to marry Milana, and they told him so," Kristin remembered. "But the whole way he went about this, the secret wedding, just showed that he knew he wasn't going to have a lot of support. She was a young Russian woman who spoke very good English. She was bright. So Milana comes over to live a life of luxury, and in a twenty-two-year-old Russian mind, who knows what that might be? It's sort of a built-in problem right from the beginning."

As Bob deliberated over what to do about his new domestic situation, he got some news from Milana: Bob had, so to speak, slipped one by the goalie. Barring his own leap into the Haleakala Crater, Bob stood to become a first-time father at the age of fifty-four.

O' Canada

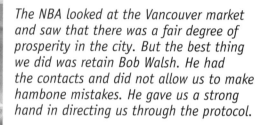

The NBA looked at the Vancouver market
and saw that there was a fair degree of
prosperity in the city. But the best thing
we did was retain Bob Walsh. He had
the contacts and did not allow us to make
hambone mistakes. He gave us a strong
hand in directing us through the protocol.

> – Mike Horsey, President,
>   Northwest Arena Corporation,
>   Vancouver, British Columbia

*A*ccording to Bob Walsh's calculations, only two possible explanations existed for Arthur Griffiths Jr. weaseling out of an opportunity to purchase a National Basketball Association franchise for Vancouver, British Columbia. Either he didn't have the money and had made himself scarce while he chased after new investors, or financing problems had surfaced with the $140 million basketball arena, General Motors Place. But if Griffiths didn't come around soon, Vancouver wouldn't get a team. The NBA had established three different deadlines for a prospective Vancouver ownership group to submit its operating plan and financial statements. All three had been missed, and Bob had no reasonable explanation to offer the NBA, at least none he was prepared to divulge. He certainly couldn't mention that he considered Griffiths Jr. a lightweight, nor could he report that Griffiths' mother had expressed virulent opposition to the family's purchase of an NBA team. So Bob found himself in the awkward spot of having to create an ever-expanding portfolio of excuses on Griffiths' behalf for Joel Litvan, the NBA's legal counsel, and Jerry Colangelo, head of the Expansion Committee.

The excuses finally piled so high they forced Bob Walsh Enterprises to act. With a potential $750,000 commission at stake, Don Nielsen, chairman of BWE's board of directors, agreed to try to put together a group of individuals who had the capacity to invest $5 million each. Nielsen determined that if he could raise enough funds, BWE might be able to claim a small ownership position in the franchise.

Bob and Bernie Russi, who had done the bulk of the legwork on the Vancouver project, sought investors on their own, finally chancing upon Bruce McCaw, who had been a friend of Bob's since well before the Goodwill Games. A McCaw-Griffiths match, Bob reasoned, had intriguing possibilities. Both families had interests in media, communications, and sports, although McCaw's passions ran to flying and race cars, not basketball. Hoping to create a match, Bob met Bruce in Vancouver, where McCaw's PacWest Racing Team had been preparing to participate in the Molson Indy of Vancouver.

McCaw already knew about the potential for investment in both a Vancouver NBA franchise and the $140 million arena going up downtown. While McCaw made no commitment to invest, he told Bob he might be amenable to contributing $5 million and would allow Bob to use his name with the NBA in connection with the Vancouver ownership group. But just as Bob was about to deliver that news to NBA owners, he received a disturbing telephone call from Bert Kolde, chairman of the Portland Trail Blazers.

Kolde didn't know that Bob had already packed his bags for the McDonald's Basketball Championships in Munich, Germany, where he hoped to determine from the NBA officials he would encounter there if any hidden objections existed to Vancouver's application for a franchise. But Kolde spared him the trouble. There was an objection, and a big one. Barry Ackerley, the owner of the Seattle SuperSonics, had inexplicably turned sour on Vancouver. He had called NBA owners and Commissioner David Stern, insisting that Vancouver's application would hurt his franchise. Kolde's disclosure stunned Bob. Ackerley had told him he supported Vancouver's application. Ackerley had even instructed Bob Whitsitt, the Sonics president, to help Bob facilitate the application process.

Bob quickly got on the phone with Whitsitt, who confirmed that Ackerley had executed one of his legendary reversals. Ackerley not only stood firmly opposed to Vancouver, he was prepared to put up a major fight to keep Vancouver out of the league. When Bob told Whisitt that he planned to call Ackerley personally, Whitsitt predicted that Ackerley would wait three days before he returned the telephone call. When Ackerley wanted to make people squirm, Whitsitt advised, he routinely waited three days to call back. Sure enough, Ackerley returned Bob's call three days later, explaining that he not only opposed the Vancouver franchise, but that he had never been in favor of it in the first place. He went on to say that he had not been asked his opinion about Vancouver, and only knew about Vancouver's application by reading about it in the newspapers. Bob nearly called Ackerley a liar, but caught himself, reminding Ackerley instead of their previous discussions about Vancouver. Ackerley denied they had occurred.

Hanging up, Bob suspected why Ackerley went south on him. Ackerley had been angling for a series of improvements at the Seattle Center Coliseum, where the SuperSonics played, and had been unable to convince the City of Seattle to do anything about his complaints. If Vancouver entered the NBA, Ackerley would be unable to threaten to move his team north of the border, destroying his only leverage with the City of Seattle. Bob phoned Colangelo, who suggested that everyone who supported a Vancouver franchise would probably be better off without Ackerley's endorsement. If Ackerley favored something, the other owners would be inclined not to support it.

Three weeks later, Bob, Bernie Russi, Mike Horsey, Harley Hotchkiss, and Arthur Griffiths Jr., who had made himself scarce while he sought new investors, presented Vancouver's application to Stern, Deputy Commissioner Russ Granik, and members of the Expansion Committee. Griffiths did little to impress NBA officials, who nevertheless became enamored with Hotchkiss, a partner in the Calgary Flames of the National Hockey League, and smitten with the idea of McCaw investing in the league. McCaw symbolized precisely the kind of globalization-era owner the NBA sought.

Bob said nothing one way or the other about McCaw, simply allowing Expansion Committee members to assume that McCaw stood prepared to make a major investment in the league when, in fact, he had only thought about committing $5 million. By the end of the presentation, and with McCaw's name lingering in the air, Bob had a pretty good idea Vancouver would be awarded a franchise if a viable ownership group could be put in place. And he considered himself fortunate to escape the meeting without having to answer specific questions about McCaw or his money. In fact, every time the subject started to come up, Bob launched into a Vancouver travelogue, or talked about international marketing, or extolled the natural rivalry that would develop among the Northwest corridor teams in Seattle, Vancouver, and Portland. Once, when Harold Katz, the owner of the Philadelphia 76ers, broached the subject of McCaw and his money, Bob quickly played a colorful video about Vancouver that made Katz forget his question.

The Vancouver ownership group finally came together in way Bob didn't expect. McCaw had spoken to his brother, John, about the franchise, and John, a minority shareholder of the Seattle Mariners baseball team, expressed interest. When Bob learned that, he set up a meeting among John, Colangelo, and Griffiths. When the negotiations concluded, the McCaws had spent much more than Bob ever anticipated, making an investment that gave them a 60 percent interest in the basketball team, the basketball arena, and the Vancouver Canucks hockey team. The Griffiths family had been farther behind the financial eight ball than even Bob suspected.

Three months later, the Vancouver Grizzlies, carrying a price tag of $125 million, became the NBA's twenty-ninth franchise, contingent upon final review and ratification by the league. The mere formality made Bob ecstatic. It had taken him thirteen years, a humiliating episode with Nelson Skalbania, and a major rescue of Arthur Griffiths Jr. to get a team placed in Vancouver.

But Bob had barely finished his victory cigar when elation turned to despair. Vancouver's new owners, Vancouver Basketball Management, Inc., refused to pay the remaining portion of the commission — more than $500,000 — still due Bob Walsh Enterprises, arguing that not all "pre-conditions" of the franchise had been satisfied. Once the franchise had been formally ratified, then Vancouver would pay.

As far as Bob was concerned, he, Bernie Russi, and BWE had delivered the franchise. And he knew the remaining formalities might take several months, months BWE didn't have. BWE's anticipated commission had already been allocated to other projects, and without it the company faced trouble. Bob made several attempts to set up meetings with Vancouver's owners, but got rebuffed. He came to suspect they didn't care that BWE had patiently waited for the

Griffiths family to solve a series of family estate issues, or that BWE had produced the critical investors, or that Bob had lobbied the NBA on Vancouver's behalf up to and through the favorable vote by the NBA Board of Governors.

When several BWE board members finally met with the new Vancouver officials, they refused BWE's proposal that Vancouver pay BWE in installments. In fact, they made it clear they didn't want to discuss the issue anymore.

The Other Gerber Baby

Bob was the first person who was there to comfort me when my brother died and he was standing by my side when I got married. That's the kind of guy Bob is. He's there when you need him to be.

— Steve Raible, news anchor, KIRO-TV, Seattle, Washington

*M*Most early prospecting by Bob Walsh Enterprises in the former Soviet Union proved more creative than successful. The company abandoned some investments as impractical, several for a lack of capital, and others for reasons that fell under the umbrella category of risk versus reward, lumber among them. At first flush, and even after a prolonged look, the idea of importing lumber from Russian forests to the Pacific Northwest seemed to hold considerable merit. The math worked so well that BWE even entered into an agreement to supply Contract Lumber of Portland, Oregon, with thirty containers of timber. The deal spiraled into scrap for a lot of reasons — diseased trees, falling prices, BWE's inability to acquire a consistent grade of product, the Russians' inability to obtain licenses and permits — and in hindsight BWE considered itself fortunate to get out while the getting was good. Conversely, BWE plunged into pharmaceuticals while the getting in was good.

Pharmaceuticals presented an interesting series of opportunities and constraints. While Walsh Pharma had been one of the first Western companies of its kind to open in Moscow, it faced stiff competition from several major brands, especially Centrum, produced by Lederle in the USA, and a half-dozen other low-cost producers in Russia and Eastern Europe. Although Walsh Pharma priced its products reasonably, the fate of BWE's investment in large part hinged on Russia's free-market reforms. Extensive unemployment, poor living standards, inflation, and political instability all had the potential to blow Walsh Pharma apart. BWE couldn't forecast what direction the Russian government might take, had no way to predict whether Russia's legal and regulatory systems would remain intact, and had no defense against Russia's draconian business laws and taxation systems.

Milana and Timmy Walsh

And any significant devaluation of the ruble had the potential to sink the company overnight.

While the pharmaceutical market remained unsaturated and vast — Russia and other former Soviet republics had populations of 148 million and 290 million, respectively — Russians had never been educated in the use of pharmaceuticals. While Americans took vitamins as dietary supplements, Russians took them only when they became ill, and then mainly in the winter. Consequently, BWE had to spend heavily to create brand awareness. It also had to stay on-target, flexible, and proprietary with its product line.

That was just one reason BWE abandoned its fledgling aspirin business. Bayer, which dominated the market, owned the trademark name "aspirin," and objected to BWE's use of it. Rather than engage in an expensive haggle over the issue with Bayer's lawyers, BWE instead turned its focus to developing a line of homeopathic products to complement its vitamin offerings.

Four different manufacturers churned out BWE vitamins and homeopathic remedies — Botanical Laboratories in Ferndale, Washington; Magno-Humphries in Tigard, Oregon; Halls Laboratories of Portland, Oregon; and ViTech in Kent, Washington — and BWE distributed them through a network built by Sergey Volkov. BWE also assigned Portland, Oregon-native Kristin Hayden the responsibility of promoting Walsh Pharma products in Moscow, her efforts to include direct mailings, radio and television campaigns, and point-of-sale posters. Through Bob Walsh's contacts, *Walsh Polyvit* became the "Official Vitamin" of the Russian and Georgian Olympic teams.

Витаминный комплекс для детей до 3-х лет **Polyvit®Baby.** Содержит все основные витамины, так необходимые Вашему малышу. Состав комплекса разработан на основе рекомендаций Совета по пищевым продуктам и питанию Национальной Академии Наук США. **Polyvit®Baby** одобрен Министерством Здравоохранения России.

Another Gerber Baby: Timmy Walsh, pictured on the Polyvit Baby box

In its first eighteen months, Walsh Pharma soared to $1.2 million in sales, then more than matched that figure over the next eight months. Within twenty-six months after the launch of *Walsh Polyvit*, BWE had started to receive product inquiries and orders from St. Petersburg, the Ukraine, Belarus, Latvia, the Volga basin, the Urals, northwest Russia, Kazakhstan, Georgia, Armenia, Azerbaijan, and Turkey.

Walsh Pharma grew so fast that it attracted suitors of its own. Suramed, a Swiss-based pharmaceutical distributor, asked BWE to become an investor in a chain of Russian pharmacies. That didn't fly — Suramed spent too much money on fancy cars and other trappings for its executives to suit BWE's board — and neither did a potential offer from the Disney Investment Group. So BWE stayed its original course of creating brand awareness and expanding its line of vitamins and homeopathics.

Walsh Polyvit, an adult-oriented general multivitamin, competed directly with Centrum and Unicap. *Polyvit Jr.* tablets came in different colors and animal shapes to make them appealing to children. *Polyvit Baby*, the first vitamin for infants actively marketed in the former Soviet Union, was a liquid product administered with a dropper. *Polyvit Nova Vita*, a mineral tablet, had been formulated to meet the special needs of pregnant women. *Polyvit Geriatric*, a general multivitamin for senior citizens, quickly became the market leader over *Geriatric Pharmatone*, a Swiss-made product.

BWE marketed its own homeopathic remedies under the "Bioline" label: *Bioline Pain, Bioline Fever, Bioline Insomnia*, and *Bioline Allergy*.

BWE planned to triple the number of Walsh Pharma products within five years, establish a proprietary distribution system called "Walsh Russia," and explore the possibility of an Initial Public Offering. With an IPO, BWE's board of directors believed they could push Walsh Pharma profits beyond their wildest original expectations. But Walsh Pharma would always remain a business with a personal touch.

A few months after Milana Walsh gave birth to Timothy Koulagin Walsh in Seattle's Swedish Hospital, his father, fifty-four-year-old Bob Walsh, snapped his photograph. That photograph was reproduced on thousands of boxes of *Polyvit Baby*, almost instantly transforming blonde-haired, blue-eyed, chubby-cheeked Timmy into one of the most famous faces in the former Soviet Union. In fact, within a year of his birth, Timmy Walsh had become the Russian equivalent of the Gerber Baby.

The Greatest Of Ease

Bob is such a big-hearted person. He can't say no. When he sees some problems he wants to help. His heart will not let him say no.

— Nana Bagdavadze, artist, Seattle, Washington

While there is nothing in his early archives that adequately explains Bob Walsh's obsession with things that fly, there is a cache of evidence that Bob spent much of his professional career associating himself with airborne objects. He took flying lessons in Boston, once nearly crashing his plane in what Bob always described as the most harrowing moment of his life. Later, he tramped the skies on commercial jets — Bob had one of the top twenty mileage totals in the history of United Airlines — to such an extent that he may have been the only individual west of the 100th meridian with a frequent flyer card on Turkish Airlines. Then, of course, he brokered the first meeting between the Blue Angels and the Soviet cosmonauts, made diplomatic arrangements for a spectacular air show at the

University of Washington's Husky Stadium, and involved himself in the Europe-America 500 Space Flight, which set some sort of standard for outlandish publicity stunts.

Bob's interest in flying things may or may not account for his equal passion for circuses. But if it does, it explains a lot since the marquee actors of the Moscow Circus happened to be a collection of trapeze artists. Bob first spotted The Flying Cranes in Moscow before the 1990 Goodwill Games. Witnessing their breathtaking wizardry, he knew he had to book the act into Seattle. So the Flying Cranes came to town when the Moscow Circus toured North America in 1988, and made return engagements in 1989 and 1990. The Seattle Organizing Committee profited almost criminally the first two times the Moscow Circus played Seattle, but Bob Walsh & Associates practically went out of business when the 1990 tour got reduced to a veritable peep show by a once-in-a-century snowstorm. Bob had always wanted to try the circus again. Promoted properly and absent unforeseen natural calamity, the Moscow Circus presented a potential financial bonanza.

The board of directors at Bob Walsh Enterprises thrilled over the notion of extracting cash from the Moscow Circus's fourth American tour in six years, but was sufficiently wary of disaster, natural or otherwise, that it instructed Bob to locate sponsors or co-presenters to limit BWE's financial exposure. With that marching order, Bob pursued a Moscow Circus booking with his usual breakneck abandon.

The circus had been one of Russia's greatest cultural traditions ever since its introduction to the court of Catherine the Great. The first of more than seventy permanent circus buildings in Russia opened in St. Petersburg in 1877. After Lenin nationalized the circus in 1919, transforming it into a state-sanctioned entertainment, the first professional circus school opened in the late 1920s.

Many Russian circus students learned their craft at the Government College of the Circus Arts during a difficult four-year curriculum that included ballet, pantomime, juggling, trapeze, high wire, tumbling, and gymnastics. Students studied general circus disciplines the first year, specialized in one the second year, and spent their final two years perfecting an act. Each year more than 100 million Russians attended shows produced by the country's 130 touring circuses, which Russians considered on a par with ballet, opera, and theater. Russians even held circus performers in the same esteem as cosmonauts and Olympians, and the stories they enacted on — and high above — the distinctively Russian one-ring stage symbolized the most important folk legends, proverbs, and patriotic ideals Russia had to offer.

Bob had a personal interest in the Moscow Circus, two of its star performers having become close friends. Bob met Misha Kalinin, an equilibrist, during the 1990 Moscow Circus. Among his other seemingly impossible feats, Misha could contort his body and execute complicated maneuvers while standing on his hands. His performance usually ended in a see-it-to-believe-it moment when he supported his entire body on one hand while playing a trumpet in the other. When the Soviet Union disappeared, Misha and his wife, Larissa, moved to the United States and, ultimately, into the home of Bob and Milana Walsh, becoming extended houseguests as Misha toured the country with the circus and Larissa awaited the birth of her first child.

Misha Kalinin (standing on hand) performs with "Spellbound" in Las Vegas

Bob's other Moscow Circus friend, Vilen Golovko Jr., whom everyone called "Willie," starred on the flying trapeze. Because the Moscow Circus had been such a popular tradition in Russia for so long — it held a loftier position than television — Russia produced many circus families, and even family dynasties. Willie, who had performed in the 1988 and 1990 editions of the circus and during the Opening Ceremony of the 1986 and 1990 Goodwill Games, hailed from one of those dynasties. His father had been a trapeze artist and, after retiring, encouraged Willie to follow in his footsteps and create an act of his own.

Willie sought out Pyotr Maistrenko, a technical genius in the circus world, to help him create an entirely new kind of trapeze act. Maistrenko drew upon his own memories of the Great Patriotic War, in which he had lost four family members, to inspire it. When Maistrenko heard Rasul Gamzatov's haunting ballad, "The Flying Cranes," a story about fallen war heroes whose souls rose from the battlefield in the form of flying cranes, he knew he had his theme: The trapeze flyers, performing to the music of Wagner and Stravinsky, would soar through the air in white costumes. Lighted by a series of strobes and seen through a scrim of green smoke, they would evoke the drama of battle, each one eventually falling into the net. The act symbolized Maistrenko's belief that mankind either flew — or crashed — as a flock.

The Flying Cranes made the cover of the New York Times Sunday Magazine

After director Valentin Gneuschev joined Maistrenko on the project, they synchronized the dramatic elements of story, light, and soaring movement that they believed would set The Flying Cranes apart from all other trapeze acts. Willie became the key component, the "catcher" who hung suspended from bended knees far above the ring, and in whose hands the other flyers entrusted their necks. It was a position for which Willie came physically well suited. A Soviet army veteran, Willie had broad shoulders, a barrel chest, and a linebacker's forearms. With his long, dark hair combed straight back and tied in a small ponytail, he looked like the Russian equivalent of Steven Segal.

After recruiting several male members of The Flying Cranes from Moscow's circus colleges, Willie was especially eager that the one woman needed for the act be absolutely perfect. He found precisely the woman when Lena, a gymnast and dancer who had twice been offered a position with the Bolshoi Ballet, auditioned. She not only got the job, she became Willie's wife.

When the Flying Cranes made their Moscow debut in 1985, they had a show of equal parts power, bravado, and art. They had not only mastered the difficult quadruple somersault, they were close to becoming the first group in the 140-year history of the trapeze to perform a backward quintuple somersault. By 1990, the Flying Cranes had become the most accomplished aerialists in the world, providing a fitting finale to a Moscow Circus that also included innovative jugglers and dancing bears, brilliant clowns and mimes, and thundering horseback riders. The famous American choreographer, Jerome Robbins, frequently watched the Flying Cranes perform. Actress Katherine Hepburn saw the Flying Cranes five times during one of their American tours.

Bob Walsh, who had obtained a portion of the West Coast rights to produce the Moscow Circus, projected that Bob Walsh Enterprises could net more than $150,000 in each of the four venues he booked: Portland, Vancouver, Phoenix, and Tacoma. But his anticipated profit proved to be a financial mirage. Despite considerable marketing efforts, the circus failed to attract capacity crowds, and utterly bombed in Tacoma, where problems with Ticketmaster's telephone system thwarted callers from ordering tickets.

While Bob Walsh Enterprises hoped to generate enough cash from the Moscow Circus to fund other foreign and domestic projects, the company instead suffered a setback of more than $200,000. And when all Moscow Circus revenues had been allocated, BWE found itself with a cash balance of exactly $144. Irritated, but unruffled, Bob again began pounding the telephones, confident he could stoke some new projects to life.

Igniting The Torch

You have to understand what Bob does. Unless you have seen it, you can't comprehend it. I don't think there's anybody else in America who does what Bob does.

> – Dave Syferd, former CEO,
>   Bob Walsh Enterprises,
>   Seattle, Washington

𝓑 Bob Walsh shifted professional gears as often as Doppler issued storm warnings. One addition to Bob's catalog of surprises that especially startled Don Nielsen, the man tending the books at Bob Walsh Enterprises, evolved from a junket Bob took to the NCAA Final Four in Charlotte, North Carolina, with Jack McMillan, one of the principal executives at the Nordstrom department store chain. As a post-tournament sidelight, Bob and Jack flew to Norfolk, Virginia, where McMillan had business at the future site of the MacArthur Center, a mall whose owners sought an upscale anchor tenant. While McMillan inspected the place, Bob made a couple of telephone calls, arranged a meeting with Robert Southwick, Norfolk's director of economic development, and came away with an assignment to produce a report assessing Norfolk's chances of landing an NBA franchise. Bob's ability to uncover economic opportunity in any place and circumstance never failed to amaze the staid and conservative Nielsen.

At the time of that excursion, McMillan had just agreed to chair the Sports and Events Council, the same organization that had throttled Bob's event business, nearly sending him to bankruptcy. For purely financial reasons, McMillan had never been entirely comfortable with the manner in which Bob had been shelved by Chamber of Commerce President George Duff. Not only had his ouster of Bob sabotaged McMillan, who had a sizeable investment in Bob Walsh Enterprises, the Council had floundered without Bob's diplomatic expertise and sports contacts.

The Council had failed to attract any sporting events of consequence to the city, specifically flopping with the U.S. Olympic Gymnastics Trials and U.S. Olympic Swimming and Diving Trials. It had made a comically stumbling run at a Major League Soccer franchise, been passed over for five consecutive editions of the Final Four, and created high-profile enemies at USA Swimming and USA Track and Field.

In the Council's defense, since Bob had almost single-handedly captured a string of Final Fours, the NBA All-Star Game, and Goodwill Games, more than eighty sports councils had sprouted into existence, the majority enjoying far greater funding than Seattle's. Still, the Sports Council had no one, administratively or on its board, who could work diplomatic angles well enough to make the difference in a bid process.

Steve Morris, president of the Seattle-King County Convention and Visitors Bureau, later put his finger on the Sports Council's problem.

"What it never figured out how to do, what it never had the resources to do, was go get major events," Morris recalled. "Every time money had to be raised to bid on something, everybody in the boardroom looked at the ceiling and quickly scurried out of there because they didn't want to be asked for a check. It took an entrepreneur to do major events, and that was Bob. He was a master at it."

To rectify the problem, McMillan recruited Bob to work on the Sports Council's behalf, which Bob initially recoiled from doing. He still harbored resentment against the Council for a series of perceived injustices and had just launched into a new batch of time-consuming projects. Bob was trying to help Alexander Ratner, a former Goodwill Games colleague, build a Moscow-to-Maui travel business, and he had started exploring the possibility of brokering an NBA franchise into Mexico City. In concert with BWE Vice President Gretchen Nelson, Bob had also become involved in the promotion of CARE International's fiftieth anniversary celebration and had agreed to pursue a Major League Baseball franchise on behalf of Vancouver. On top of all that, Bob had become a New York consultant for the 1998 Goodwill Games and was seeking ways to economically assist the Republic of Georgia through the auspices of the Walsh International Relief Fund.

But Jack McMillan had always been a friend. He was also an investor and board member of Bob Walsh Enterprises, and Bob, who had eminent respect for him, couldn't turn him down. So first they targeted the Olympic Sports Festival, an event run by the United States Olympic Committee to showcase the nation's top young hopefuls in a wide range of summer and winter sports. To assess Seattle's chances of receiving the bid, Bob contacted Harvey Schiller, the USOC's executive director, who not only told Bob that Seattle had a good chance of claiming the bid over Phoenix, Richmond, and Dallas, but encouraged a future bid by Seattle for the Summer Olympic Games.

Taking that cue, Bob approached several of his contacts at the Port of Seattle. Within a month, the Port had assembled a consortium of Vancouver, B.C., businessmen to join Seattle in a dual-city bid for the 2004 Games. And within a matter of weeks, Bob had become fully engaged in the event business again, pitching the "Cascadia Olympics" on behalf of the Cascadia Games Exploratory Committee.

Although no two cities had ever collaborated on a bid for the Summer Olympics, a regionalized Games seemed to Bob and other members of the consortium to be a progressive solution to the staggering costs, environmental impacts, and colossal disruptions associated with staging such a spectacle. Bob also figured that with Vancouver hosting 50 percent of the action and bearing half the costs, the likely negative perception that the Games would overwhelm public resources would not become an issue.

He figured wrong.

In an editorial haymaker, *The Seattle Times* reduced the Cascadia Olympics to a "pipe dream," and to an extent they were. In order for Seattle and Vancouver to win an Olympic bid, the International Olympic Committee would have to amend its charter since the

IOC awarded the Summer Olympics to cities, not countries. And while the USOC encouraged a future Seattle bid for the Olympics, it would not support a bid for 2004, which was too close to the 2002 Winter Olympics in Salt Lake City.

Although the Cascadia Olympics died unlamented, Bob did not abandon his personal pipe dream of pursuing an Olympic bid on Seattle's behalf. In case the *Times* had forgotten, Seattle's most enduring symbol had also been called a pipe dream. In 1959, when Seattle businessman Eddie Carlson sat in a coffee shop and sketched on a paper placemat what seemed to be a monument to those spinning plate routines once so popular on *The Ed Sullivan Show*, no one could guess the Space Needle would soon become a civic icon. So Bob, ever the optimist, scheduled trips to IOC strongholds in Paris and Lausanne, Switzerland, to learn the politics and formalities of the Olympic bid process.

"When Bob, Jack McMillan, and I got to Paris," recalled Dave Syferd, a marketing maven who had joined the board of directors at Bob Walsh Enterprises, "McMillan and I figured we had appointments set up, that there was a plan. But there wasn't. Bob's plan was that we would sit in the lobby of this big exposition hall and grab who we could. It was the most bizarre strategy I'd ever seen."

McMillan was more than incredulous; he was appalled.

"What do you mean we don't have any meetings set up?" Jack demanded of Bob. "We fly all the way from Seattle to Paris with no meetings? We're not going to get a thing accomplished."

"Don't worry about it," Bob told him.

"Jack McMillan was the kind of guy who would have had everything greased," Morris explained later. "His attitude was, 'What do you mean we're going to work the lobby? What the heck are we, prostitutes?'"

But Bob understood the value of being visible and accessible. As he worked the lobby, people from all over the world stopped to talk to him. Bob, Jack, and Dave departed Paris having seen exactly the people they had to see and learning precisely what had to be done. And when the Summer Games Organizing Committee officially came into existence three months later, it retained Bob Walsh Enterprises to develop a bid for the 2008 Olympics. The contract mandated that Bob both lobby USOC and IOC members and help fashion bids for several amateur athletic events which would showcase Seattle to Olympic officials.

Bob soon had Seattle in the running for the McDonald's America Cup Gymnastics Championships and the U.S. Olympic Cycling Trials. But his work on those bids got quickly sidetracked when he received an intriguing offer from Eduard Shevardnadze. The Georgian president wanted Bob to start playing Monopoly in Tbilisi with real buildings.

Third World Thrills

Bob has a heart of gold and showers his gift of unselfish giving on the people around the world.

> *– Blair Farrington, Blair Farrington Productions, Las Vegas, Nevada*

*N*o longer shattered by gunfire, the city wheezed in a melee of traffic — foot and auto — and all the new outdoor bistros on Rustaveli Avenue gave Tbilisi, Georgia, an almost festive air. Hundreds of small kiosks, offering Bjormi mineral water, Samgori ice cream, Marlboro cigarettes, and French perfume, remained open after dark, unheard of even a year earlier. Market shelves sagged with Snapple, Post cereals, Mars bars, and Coca Cola. The foreign investors — Kodak, Calvin Klein, and Sony — that had once been so opposed to venturing into the city for fear of anarchy, now looked at it as a blooming vineyard of opportunity.

Georgia still suffered ethnic conflicts, but general mayhem had vanished, making Eduard Shevardnadze's efforts seem almost magical. In the four years since a bloody drama played out in Tbilisi's theater and government districts, Shevardnadze had initiated big-bang democratic and economic reforms, stabilized the currency, and largely eliminated the Mafia. Young visionaries and economists had been elected to Parliament and more than 1,200 businesses privatized. Shevardnadze had established a National Security Council, created the offices of Prosecutor General and Mayor of Tbilisi, and proposed an avalanche of legislation — bills against monopolies and corruption, bills on consumer rights, bills aimed at creating sound political and economic policies. With the support of the World Bank and International Monetary Fund, Shevardnadze had done exactly as the West had hoped he would: begin to create a democracy from the rubble of Communism.

The road to a true free market absent turmoil and corruption remained long and daunting. Georgia had an appalling unemployment rate, no coherent industrial policy, low tax revenues, no significant foreign trade, mounting foreign debt, and a per capita income of less than $20 per month. Rail links to Russia and Armenia stood severed. Sputtering energy supplies crippled industries, giving ammunition to Shevardnadze's critics, who complained he ran the country like a private duchy, muzzled dissent, and used an attempt on his life as a pretext for arresting and imprisoning political opponents without fair trials.

Shevardnadze had been scheduled to attend the signing of a new Georgian State Constitution. As his car neared the Parliament building, a man in an adjacent apartment detonated a remote-control bomb, instantly setting Shevardnadze's vehicle ablaze and shattering its windows. Shevardnadze emerged from the car reeling, bleeding, and subsequently complaining that the Russians had masterminded the attack. If nothing else, the incident crystallized public support for the controversial leader, whose new policies and programs soon had foreigners pouring money into the Georgian economy.

A German group opened a travel agency, British investors built a microbrewery, Turks explored investments in transportation, banking, and agriculture. John Kluge's Metromedia Corporation examined joint ventures in communications and cable television. Westinghouse Electric eyed the possibility of becoming the centerpiece of Georgia's efforts to revive its power generation resources. Sea-Land prepared a comprehensive feasibility study aimed at developing container systems at Georgian ports. Shell Oil locked its sights on the Black Sea coast. And Bob Walsh deliberated over a windfall of potential projects in real estate and dairy processing.

In the months following delivery of the last Boeing relief supplies to Tbilisi, Bob frequented Georgian ministries that managed the country's agricultural, transportation, health, and energy departments, and toured several Hawaii-like resorts on the Black Sea. The Georgians wanted to modernize the country's infrastructure, making Bob one of the focal points for bringing in millions of investment dollars. Bob required little prodding, having believed in Georgia's commercial potential for years. He had twice attempted to set up wine export businesses with Georgian entrepreneurs, tried to open a pharmacy in Tbilisi, and even signed Georgia's national singing and dance ensemble to a contract to tour the United States. But

Bob Walsh with Georgian partner Kakha Gvelesiani

all of his efforts had been thwarted by a lack of cash, Georgia's civil war, and the country's more pressing humanitarian needs. Those problems, in Bob's view, had started to fade. Once high-risk territory, Georgia brimmed with promise.

Together with Sara Benveniste, a new BWE employee who had graduated from the Jackson School of International Studies at the University of Washington, Bob looked into redeveloping the Port of Poti on the Black Sea with new container terminals, oil refineries, or food distribution warehouses. Georgia's Ministry of Health pitched Bob and Sara on the possibility of developing thirty pieces of real estate, some on the Black Sea, several in or near Tbilisi, with hospitals, clinics, spas, and resorts. When word of Bob's interest in those properties leaked, other cash-strapped Georgians approached him offering additional opportunities.

Kakha Gvelesiani and George Tavadze became two of the first. Confined to a wheelchair since taking a bullet in the spine during the siege that toppled Zviad Gamsakhurdia, Gvelesiani had started to develop an Expo Center that he hoped to turn into the Georgian equivalent of a small American mall. A squat, engaging man with a quick wit, Tavadaze operated an insurance business. Gvelesiani and Tavadze served on a commercial task force Shevardnadze had assembled to locate and attract Western investment. They touted Bob and Sara on a number of potential joint ventures, including one with Tbilisi's most profitable ice cream factory, Samgori.

Bob's confidence in Georgia, and Sara's as well, received bolstering not only from the positive political and economic changes taking place in the country, but from their conversations with a young diplomat at Georgia's new Embassy in Washington, D.C. George Makharadze promoted Georgian business opportunities to potential United States investors. He had been especially helpful in showing Bob and Sara the significance of the pipelines that would one day send oil from Baku, Azerbaijan, across Georgia to Black Sea ports, pointing out how those pipelines would become a focal point of U.S. interest.

In all, Georgians presented Bob and Sara with the chance to develop eighty pieces of property, including the thirty controlled by the Ministry of Health. The best included a once-grand hotel that was now just a shell, gutted and bullet-ridden. But it stood directly across from Parliament. A former resort on Tbilisi's Holy Mountain, Mtatsminda, had been looted and left in ruins during the civil war. An office building near the Kura River had been abandoned, half-built. Two vacant lots in the center of Tbilisi stood overgrown with weeds.

Despite Bob and Sara's pleadings, the board of directors at Bob Walsh Enterprises exhibited little interest in the Georgian real estate opportunities. Having heard Bob gush for years about Georgia's potential, most board members had become immune to what they perceived as another epidemic of Bob hyperbole. Only Jack McMillan, Ed Hewson, and Ruth McIntrye, Bob's first wife and a recent addition to BWE's board, would even entertain the possibility that Georgia had enough democratic structures in place to guarantee favorable treatment of Western investment.

To weaken board resistance, Bob resorted to what might be called his Emerald City offensive. Years earlier, when Seattleites had rejected the nickname "Emerald City," Bob had turned to national sportscasters of his acquaintance, convincing them to open their network telecasts with the greeting "Welcome to the Emerald City." The nickname stuck after outsiders endorsed it, in fact so well that more than 200 Seattle-area businesses eventually got named or renamed to include "The Emerald City" moniker, Bob's personal favorite being "The Emerald City's Loveliest Ladies," a damn fine escort service. So Bob reasoned that if outsiders endorsed the Tbilisi opportunities to BWE's board members, perhaps they would take them seriously.

The independent verification Bob sought careened into his life by chance when, on an airplane from Boston to New York, he was spotted by fellow Seattle resident Larry Snyder, who knew a bit about Bob's activities through a mutual acquaintance, former Bob Walsh & Associates president Kimberly Brown. The managing director of STAMCO (Short Term Assets Management Company), a firm that invested pension funds, Snyder introduced himself and asked Bob if he wanted to share a taxi into mid-Manhattan.

Bob had gone east on mainly painful business — to bury his mother. Funeral services had been held in Seattle, where Betty spent the last years of her life, and only Ruth McIntyre, Bob's sister, Toni, her children, Bill Russell, Freddie Mae Gautier, and a few others attended. Bob then took Betty's cremains to Boston, stopping first in Washington, D.C., where several State Department functionaries sat with mouths agape after Bob placed Betty's urn on a table during a meeting. The next day, Bob arrived in Boston to lay Betty next to Matt. The night before the burial, Bob took Betty's urn bar hopping to all of Betty's favorite watering holes. In each, Bob placed her urn on a bar stool and ordered her a double scotch. Bob and Betty's urn wound up at the Parker House, closing down the joint. After Betty's burial, he departed for New York, encountering Synder.

During the cab ride into Manhattan, Bob told Larry about the ongoing activities at Bob Walsh Enterprises. Its Product Division (Walsh Pharma) sold vitamins, its Sports and Events Division bid for major athletic competitions, and its Consulting Division had recently entertained various marketing proposals from a communications company (US West), a restaurant chain (Planet Hollywood), a charitable organization (The Mike Utely Foundation), a champagne distributor (Korbel), and a Cadillac dealership (Frederick). BWE also had two new divisions: the Video Production Unit, to capture income from broadcast rights associated with the sports and cultural events produced by BWE, and Walsh Main Events, which offered tickets, lodging, and travel to corporate groups wanting to attend major sports events.

Bob also explained to Snyder that BWE had geared up for the bid on the 2008 Summer Olympics by hiring Dave Syferd, the former chairman of a marketing firm, as its new CEO, and Steve Penny, executive director of USA Cycling, to manage the Olympic effort on a daily basis. Bob, Dave, and Steve had not only secured a variety of events to supplement the Olympic bid, including the U.S. Olympic Cycling Trials, they had acquired the rights to the Seattle leg of the 1996 U.S. Olympic Torch Relay.

Snyder found that Bob's projects and prospects in Georgia and the former Soviet Union intrigued him most. Eager to learn more, Snyder accompanied Bob to Georgia five weeks later, afterward agreeing to act as the outside influence with BWE's board Bob thought he needed.

"What Bob has developed," Snyder later told the board, "is unique. The vitamins and Georgia business opportunities are two of the best I have seen in twenty years. If Bob takes advantage of it, he could end up making a ton of money."

Largely because of Snyder's endorsement, BWE's board determined to seek $3 million through a stock offering. The cash would enable Walsh Pharma to purchase more product, add distributors, and create advertising campaigns. But one obstacle blocked the Georgian projects — a problem that could not be solved unless the Georgian Parliament changed some of its laws on foreign investment that affected real estate leases.

Unbelievably, Bob got the Georgians to change the most significant of those laws within two days.

"Can you imagine a private citizen changing a law in this country?" Snyder later marveled. "And that's nothing compared to doing it in a foreign country. It was amazing."

Location, Location, Location

Bob was one of the first Americans to recognize the economic importance of the Silk Road and the role the oil pipelines would play in our part of the world.

– Vaso Margvelashvili, resident, Tbilisi, Georgia

Framed by birch trees, and elegant in a grand European sort of way, the Hotel Tbilisi stood vacant at 13 Rustaveli Avenue, absent windows, missing its guts, its face ravaged by thousands of bullet holes. For symbolic and political reasons, no downtown reclamation project in Georgia had a higher priority with Eduard Shevardnadze than the restoration of that forlorn shell. So when the president summoned Bob Walsh to his office on the fourth floor of the Government House one afternoon, he made Bob promise that the Hotel Tbilisi would become his top Georgian project.

Constructed in 1911 in the classical Italianate style favored throughout Europe in the early twentieth century, the Hotel Tbilisi rose six stories and displayed a magnificent baroque façade that, in spite of the bullet holes, retained its period detail. Situated on the corner of Joriashvili Street and Rustaveli Avenue in the heart of Tbilisi's business, commercial, theater, and administrative districts, the hotel featured easy proximity to shops, restaurants, the national opera and ballet, Parliament, City Hall, and foreign embassies. Although all that remained of its 226 rooms was dangling rebar, blackened walls, and a foundation ruptured during the 1988 Armenian earthquake, it didn't

The Hotel Tbilisi in the midst of reconstruction

take much imagination for Bob to envision the equivalent of New York's Park Hyatt or Washington, D.C.'s St. Regis one day gracing the corner of Joriashvili and Rustaveli. Nor did it take much creativity to comprehend the role that a re-furbished Hotel Tbilisi could play in a region where a new oil pipeline would soon come under construction.

Shevardnadze had thrown his support behind the refurbishing of an existing pipeline that ran from Baku, Azerbaijan, across Georgia, to the Port of Supsa on the Black Sea coast. When completed, the pipeline would provide Georgia with new oil transit revenues. Tbilisi would argu-ably become the leading business and trading center in the Caucasus and Central Asia, and the Hotel Tbilisi would command the center of action. It would cater to the oil men who came to spend money, to investors on the prowl for projects, and to diplomats who sought to talk policy with Shevardnadze's government. Bob became so convinced he had a winner that he got in touch with Jurgen Bartels, president of Seattle-based Westin Hotels and Resorts, which operated properties in thirty-eight countries. A European, Bartels had developed The Radisson in Moscow, and Bob knew he would appreciate the Hotel Tbilisi's potential. After Westin's European Project Manager, Herman Uscategui, inspected the property, Bartels committed Westin as the hotel operator, even taking an equity position in the proposed "Westin Tbilisi."

Bob had originally been enlightened about eighty pieces of Georgian real estate, including thirty controlled by the Ministry of Health. Bob Walsh Enterprises selected six, targeting each for redevelopment in what amounted to the largest commercial privatization endeavor ever undertaken in the Republic of Georgia. For each project, Bob Walsh Enterprises established a joint stock company in which BWE secured rent-free, ninety-nine-year leases. BWE owned 60 percent of each company, the Georgians 40 percent.

The Tbilisi Hotel Joint Stock Company became a partnership between BWE and a Georgian entity, the Tbilisi City Company. BWE agreed to contribute $102,000 to launch reconstruction of the hotel, with initial emphasis on restoring the façade and locating investors who could provide $25 million to cover reconstruction costs. BWE wanted to create a five-star establishment, built to Western standards.

The Mtatsminda Plateau Company became the second BWE-Tbilisi City Company partnership. The plan involved renovation of the stunning but badly damaged structure on the top of Tbilisi's Holy Mountain. Wrapped in a giant colonnade which supported open-air terraces around three sides of the building, each with panoramic views of all

Mtatsminda Plateau, below and left of the TV tower

Tbilisi, the Caucasus Mountains, and Kura River, the Mtatsminda property stood 2,187 feet above sea level and looked more like a memorial than the abandoned restaurant and reception center it once had been. Before the civil war, the Mtatsminda property had been one of the top tourist attractions in Georgia, attracting thousands of people daily in the summer months. Accessible both by automobile and funicular railway, it had all the makings of a restaurant, reception center, nightclub, or possibly a casino. The surrounding 126 acres could accommodate a small hotel, a private residential area, or a family entertainment center.

The Tbilisi Real Estate Company, the third BWE-Tbilisi City Company partnership, included premier properties in or near the center of the city. Although not as visibly appealing as the Westin Tbilisi or Mtatsminda Plateau, two vacant lots, one on Rustaveli Avenue across the street from Parliament, the other at Freedom Square, offered ideal future sites for office buildings, retail, or residential facilities. A third property, located on a large lot on the Kura River, contained a partially constructed seven-story building, work on which had been abandoned during the civil war.

BWE's fourth joint stock company, with Samgori Ltd., called for Bob Walsh Enterprises to have an ownership interest in and operational control over Samgori, Tbilisi's most profitable ice cream plant. Although Samgori, a name that in Georgian means "three mountains," had been the market leader in Georgia, its plant needed modern equipment and Western management expertise. BWE agreed to contribute $1.5 million to the venture.

In addition to its partnerships with the Tbilisi City Company and Samgori Ltd., Bob Walsh Enterprises signed a letter of intent with the Ministry of Health to create joint stock companies that would eventually own and control the Ministry's thirty properties. When those partnerships were created, BWE would contribute $25 million over a ten-year period toward development costs.

BWE celebrated the signing of the joint ventures at a reception hosted by Georgian Prime Minister Niko Lekishvili and Badri Shoshitaishvili, the mayor of Tbilisi, who proposed a toast.

"We are many times grateful," the mayor said to Bob, "to have you as our new partner. Because now you are one of us."

The Pumpkin Princess

We brought Bob in on this deal because he could have the kind of conversations with the Russians no one else could have. Bob is all about a culture of personal relationships, and that is how you do business in Russia.

> *— Ted Bristol, Vice President,*
> *Sagamore Associates,*
> *Washington, D.C.*

On a map of the South Pacific, trace a line from Hawaii to Tahiti, skip past Samoa and Bora Bora and veer southeast over Pago Pago. There, just west of where the International Dateline meets the Tropic of Cancer, sits the Kingdom of Tonga, an archipelago containing 172 islands. The landmass is less than half the size of Rhode Island, and Tonga's population — 105,000 — would just about fill the Rose Bowl. A tropical paradise, Tonga is also a tempest of bizarre customs — locals frequently decorate graves with beer bottles — and strange natural phenomena, such as the bats with fox-like heads that cling to Casuarinas trees and are hunted — and devoured — only by members of the Royal House of Tonga.

Tonga is the only South Pacific island chain never to be colonized, although it has had its share of interlopers, first the Dutch, then the English, and more recently an infestation of Mormons. Tonga is also the first nation in the world to greet the new day. Because of its position thirteen hours ahead of Greenwich Mean Time, the Tonga Visitors Bureau promotes the Polynesian kingdom officially as "The Land Where Time Begins," and unofficially with this slogan: "Do It The Tongan Way – Tomorrow."

Not much happens on Tonga, but when news is made it almost always involves King Taufa'ahau Tupou IV, a descendant of cannibal chiefs, and a man whose persona is a testimony to eccentric enthusiasms. King Tupou traverses his kingdom either in his Royal Chair, carried by an overly burdened phalanx of barefoot guards, or in his Royal Winnebago. He is officially recognized as the world's heaviest monarch at 350 pounds, but that was before the Royal Diet. King Tupou got fat — he required two seats at St. Paul's Cathedral in London for the wedding of Charles and Diana — mainly by becoming a one-man Burger King, and then spent several years trying to lose weight through a regimen of power walking, bicycle exercise, and a healthier diet, which reportedly included feasting on fox bats, roasted.

King Tupou might also be the world's quirkiest monarch, a reputation he carved during several abortive attempts to improve Tonga's economy. Tonga produces coconut, copra, bananas, vanilla beans, cocoa, coffee, ginger, and black pepper, but its economy is — or was for a while, anyway — precariously dependent on the cultivation of pumpkins. King Tupou acted out several lame but colorful inspirations in an attempt to diversify Tonga's financial base, and was himself inspired by a succession of dreamers and con men who breezed into Tonga and bent the King's royal ear.

One of the King's schemes involved his willingness to permit a stash of U.S. nuclear waste to be dumped into Tonga's pristine waters, a notion that set off an environmental typhoon. The King next offered to dispose of thirty million used tires from Washington State, figuring he could use them to fire a Tongan generator. That prompted a high-decibel howl from Earth Day holdovers. For one fruitless interlude, King Tupou tried to harness wave energy from the Pacific Ocean. During an even fruitier interlude, he hatched plans to make Tonga a world leader in computers.

When crude oil bubbled to the surface of the sea around the main Tongan island of Tongatapu, it appeared King Tupou would sit astride a throne of oil for decades. It didn't happen. After the oil men plugged the wells and departed, a newspaper headline in Western Samoa preened, "For Tonga, It's Back To Coconuts." Not quite. King Tupou cleared away thousands of palms, intent on turning Tonga into a giant pumpkin patch to supply an insatiable demand from Japan. Good idea, but not good enough. So Tonga attempted to sell domain names on the Internet, charging $100 to register "dot to" designations after all the good "dot com" ones were gone.

The King's curious machinations reached their apex, or their nadir, when he approved a quixotic plot designed to make Tonga a major player in space. Tongans thought it uproarious. The nation had only 5,000 radios, 4,000 telephones, yams larger than Tonga's entire hard-drive capacity, no building taller than a coconut palm, and an average per capital income of $2,000. But King Tupou never joked about his undertakings, and this one started to unfold when two San Diego entrepreneurs dreamed of relocating to a tropical island.

Jerry Fletcher had been a Navy Seal, and Dr. Matt Nilson had retired from Intelsat, a consortium that provided much of the world's international satellite communications. Nilson had made money in cellular telephones and figured he could make even more by supplying satellite services in the largely uncovered Asia-Pacific sector. But to enter the satellite business, he needed to furnish an application on behalf of a sovereign nation to Geneva's International Telecommunications Union, which handled that sort of thing.

When Fletcher wandered into Tonga, setting himself up as a Budweiser distributor, he befriended a local named Kelepi Tupou, who introduced him to King Tupou's only daughter, Her Royal Highness Princess Salote Mafile'o Pilolevu Tuita. When Nilson arrived, Fletcher introduced him to the Pumpkin Princess, at which point Nilson told the Pumpkin Princess about his idea: There, up in the sky, on a geostationary arc 36,000 kilometers above the equator, loomed a gold mine. Sovereign nations such as Tonga could reserve slots along the band at no cost. With those slots, and with satellite rental agreements, Tonga could provide TV, phone, and data service to customers throughout Asia and the South Pacific. Nilson advised that the Pumpkin Princess lay claim to sixteen orbital parking places. Intrigued, she took Nilson to meet King Tupou. Setting aside his passion for pumpkins, King Tupou authorized Nilson to establish "Friendly Islands Satellite Communications Inc.," doing business as "Tongasat." The Pumpkin Princess named herself chairman, Nilson managing director, and personally took a 60 percent cut of the action.

After Nilson made applications for the sixteen orbital slots, a dozen countries, including the United States, complained that Tonga's applications were grossly out of proportion to the country's telecommunications needs. The international bellyaching had no effect. Tongasat received six of the sixteen positions in March, 1991, and a seventh slot a year later, making Tonga the sixth most prolific acquirer of orbital rights in the world. With that, Tongasat had set itself up to lease the slots to satellite operators.

Nilson then contacted a lawyer, Carl Hilliard, who contacted two investors in Fort Wayne, Indiana, Jim Simon and Michael Sternberg. Together, they formed Rimsat, Ltd., in the offshore tax haven of the Federation of St. Christopher and Nevis in the British West Indies. Nilson first leased three Tongastat orbital slots to Rimsat, and a month later Rimsat officials ventured to Russia to acquire some satellites. Rimsat's ensuing $138 million deal with the Russian trade organization Informcosmos called for the Russians to lease seven satellites to Rimsat, with options on dozens of others.

Only one problem: Rimsat had started with $1.8 million in seed capital, supplemented by $1.7 million from the sale of nonvoting Rimsat stock. Thus, when Rimsat signed its $138 million contract with the Russians, it had capital of approximately 1 percent of its liabilities. Nilson prevented this celestial house of cards from crashing by flying to Kuala Lumpur, Malaysia. The deep pockets there belonged to Tajudin Ramli, chairman of Malaysian Airline System. Nilson sweet talked the Malaysian into forking over $38,395,238 in exchange for 50 percent of Rimsat's voting shares and 45 percent of the company.

Eighteen months after Rimsat's formation, "Rimsat I" flew into space and parked in a Tongasat orbital slot to serve Sun TV of Madras, India, Reuters Television of London, AsiaNet, and Domsat of the Philippines. Launched a year later, "Rimsat II" had customers as diverse as Asian Television of Bombay, India, and EMTV of Hong Kong.

Then the entire galactic show started to unravel. Rimsat axed Hilliard as its legal counsel, slapping him with a malpractice suit. Hilliard and Nilson convinced the High Court of Justice in the Federation of St. Christopher and Nevus to place Rimsat in receivership with Hilliard at the controls. Rimsat hurled back a contempt action. The Malaysian billionaire filed a $130 million racketeering suit against Sternberg, Simon, Hilliard, Nilson, and the Pumpkin Princess. The Russian Space Agency confiscated Rimsat's satellites, turned off a transponder serving millions of U.S. taxi-driver wannabes in India, and threatened countless others in Malaysia and Papua New Guinea with an imminent interruption of *Gilligan's Island* reruns. Rimsat promptly hired a universe of lawyers, who cranked out gushers of scandalously priced paperwork. The mess finally landed in U.S. Bankruptcy Court, which the Russians refused to recognize. In frustration, Rimsat shareholders turned to Sagamore Associates, hiring the Washington, D.C., firm to persuade the U.S. government to pressure the Russian government to return the satellites. Shortly thereafter, the following article appeared in *Satellite News*.

Rimsat, Russians, and Mediator
Intensify Talks To End Dispute

One of the most encouraging developments is the entrance of unofficial mediator Bob Walsh of Seattle, who has long-standing relationships with Russian officials, to try resolving the clash and lift Rimsat out of bankruptcy proceedings. Walsh, an organizer of the 1990 Goodwill Games held in Seattle between the United States and Russia, was scheduled to meet Friday with Yuli Vorongsov, the Russian ambassador to the United States. Walsh traveled to Moscow and met with officials of the Russian Space Agency and Informcosmos for sixteen to eighteen hours in attempt to settle the conflict and save the company.

Bob usually took odd projects to Sagamore CEO David Gogol. This time Gogol, representing Rimsat's Class C shareholders, ticketed Bob for a seat in the theater of the absurd. Gogol had certified himself an expert in unraveling complex governmental problems, but the Rimsat fiasco had degenerated into a mess requiring unique intervention. Gogol's main problem became how to enforce the contract between Rimsat and the Russians. Gogol fashioned an argument that the Rimsat-Russian dispute had ceased to be a squabble between commercial enterprises and had escalated into an imbroglio involving nations that demanded intrusion by the U.S. government. Gogol mobilized Indiana's congressional delegation, U.S. departments of State and Commerce, and Vice President Al Gore's office. He wanted to impart a message to the Russians that the theft of the satellites would scare away American investment in Russia, and he had some leverage: The Russians wanted more licenses from Americans to launch Russian satellites on Russian rockets. But Gogol couldn't get reliable information from the Russians, largely negating that leverage. Too many people with palms itching for grease now stood between the Russian Space Agency and the Rimsat investors he represented.

But Gogol had a trump card. Bob Walsh knew his way around Russia. He operated a vitamin business there, had done humanitarian work there, and had contacts inside the Russian Space Agency from the Europe-America 500 Space Flight project. Bob, Gogol figured, could get to the right players in Russia and reopen dialogue.

Bob came to the project with plenty on his plate. Together with BWE's Sara Benveniste, he had been working to secure a Seattle operation for Djondi Maridashvili, a Georgian gymnastics champion who had been paralyzed after falling awkwardly during a tumbling routine. Bob had also been preparing a bid for the 1999 World Track & Field Championships and jetting all over Europe lobbying International Olympic Committee delegates as part of his pursuit of the Summer Olympic Games.

But Bob couldn't say no to David Gogol. So he looked over his assignment, trying to reduce the stalemate to a comprehensible picture. It wasn't pretty: Multiple lawsuits in several legal jurisdictions. An angry Malaysian billionaire. A King who ate fox bats. A conniving Pumpkin Princess. Several Dagwood Bumstead attorneys. A bankruptcy judge who didn't know what to do. This looked to Bob like it would be in court forever. And even if all parties wanted to settle, which he soon recognized they did not, none of the attorneys had any financial incentive to settle.

In the employ of the U.S. Bankruptcy Court, Bob flew to Fort Wayne, Indiana, to meet with Rimsat investors and attorneys, jetted to Washington, D.C., for a conference at the Russian Embassy, and then went to Moscow for a summit at the Russian Space Agency. While Bob started the project believing the Russians had committed a dastardly act of thievery, he soon came to the conclusion the real fault was not in Russia but in Fort Wayne, and to a lesser extent with the Malaysian billionaire and the Pumpkin Princess. And all the American lawyers exacerbated the situation with a Grand Coulee of legal sludge. To make certain he had made a correct assessment, Bob revisited all the major players, including Michael Tupalov, the managing director of InformCosmoConsult, which represented Informcosmos. Bob even booked a flight to Tonga to consult with the King, but the meeting failed to materialize. As far as Bob could determine, the case boiled down to the fact that the Russians would no longer negotiate with — or even talk to — anyone at Rimsat. That was made dramatically clear to BWE's Kristin Hayden when she, Bob, and some Rimsat attorneys attended a meeting at the Russian Space Agency.

"These other Americans were threatening to sue the Russians," Kristin explained later. "It was laughable because the laws were changing on a daily basis. Bob understood where the Russians were coming from. In talking to the head of the Russian Space Agency, Bob tried to find out about the guy's family. His mother was ill, and Bob offered to fly her to America for medical help. The Americans were talking about suing, and Bob was talking about helping the guy's mother. Those Americans were getting nowhere and Bob was getting everywhere."

Bob figured that the only way out of the mess was to replace the Rimsat crowd with new investors and start all over again. Both the Bankruptcy Court and Russian Ambassador Yuri Vorongsov supported Bob's proposal that he attempt to locate new investors who could settle with Rimsat and cut a new deal with the Russians.

Bob thought perhaps Ted Turner might become one of those new investors, but Turner showed little interest. However, Bill Gates of Microsoft and Craig McCaw, a brother to Bruce and John McCaw, expressed considerable interest after Bob and BWE CEO Dave Syferd briefed their underlings about the project's potential. Gates and McCaw owned a company called Teledesic, which had been plotting one of the grandest industrial undertakings of the century. They desired to create an Internet in the sky, strewing space with nearly 900 broadband satellites capable of delivering vast amounts of digital data to any location, no matter how remote. Teledesic had been trying to forge a global partnership of service providers and manufacturers, and the Russians were clearly major players. With several hundred satellites to launch, Teledesic would almost certainly become a large user of Russian launch capacity. Bob's plan, hatched in conjunction with Michael Tupalov of InformCosmosConsult, involved getting some money out of Teledesic and forming a new company with the Russians. Rimsat would keep only a small percentage, but its debts would disappear. It all looked doable until the Russians thwarted that plan by demanding a 51 percent interest in any new company. But even if the Russians hadn't thwarted it, Bob could not find a way to make the slavering American lawyers go away.

After trustee Paul Underwood assured Bob that all legal actions would be put on hold, Bob relayed that news to the Russians. But almost immediately, rival attorneys representing various factions in the case undercut those assurances. For example, Bob scheduled a trustee-approved conference in Washington, D.C., with Hilliard. But the night before the meeting, an order came from a Rimsat attorney to cancel it. Bob subsequently discovered that Hilliard had been subpoenaed by an attorney representing Rimsat creditors, and that additional subpoenas had been served on Joseph Krabacher, an attorney representing the Russians and the Pumpkin Princess. The fallout from those subpoenas ultimately blew apart settlement negotiations.

Bob finally removed himself from the affair because he couldn't maintain credibility with the Russians and because the American side could not stay on the same page of the agenda for more than a minute and a half. It especially galled Bob that every time he made a bit of progress with the Russians, Krabacher intruded, or the guys from Fort Wayne flew to Moscow and created chaos behind the scenes.

By the time the saga played out, the only people who made money were the lawyers and the Pumpkin Princess, who squirreled away a reported fortune of $25 million while leaving her government and fellow Tongans to subsist on pumpkins. The Pumpkin Princess's greed so enraged her brother, Crown Prince Tupouto'a, that he hauled her into court. She retaliated with an injunction against him and the Tongan government to prevent their interference in her operation.

After Matt Nilson, who dreamed up the whole thing, left Tonga, he married a Filipino satellite engineer and moved to Manila. Bob Walsh Enterprises, meanwhile, received a $120,000 consulting fee for Bob's involvement in the project. That not only covered BWE's $42,000 loss on the Europe-America 500 Space Flight, it meant that Bob's various space adventures resulted in an overall profit of $78,000, give or take a pumpkin.

Tobacco Road

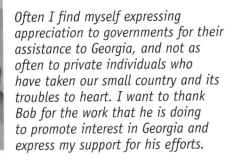

Often I find myself expressing appreciation to governments for their assistance to Georgia, and not as often to private individuals who have taken our small country and its troubles to heart. I want to thank Bob for the work that he is doing to promote interest in Georgia and express my support for his efforts.

– Eduard Shevardnadze, President, former Soviet republic of Georgia

Near midnight on January 3, 1997, a Ford Taurus traveling eighty miles per hour burst into DuPont Circle, one of Washington, D.C.'s busiest intersections. The man behind the wheel, in his mid-thirties, had thinning, dark hair, wore horn-rimmed glasses, and had the air of an academic. He had recently received a degree in international business from Harvard University and worked at the Georgian Embassy as its Deputy Chief of Mission. According to more than 150 testimonials subsequently issued on his behalf, he possessed the talent, character, energy, and leadership skills to rise quickly into political prominence. Some of his colleagues thought he might become Georgia's next ambassador to the United States, perhaps a member of the Georgian Parliament, or possibly Georgia's next president. The young diplomat driving the 1997 Ford Taurus was George Makharadze, and he had everything going for him when he reached DuPont Circle that night — except a .15 blood-alcohol level.

Roaring down a service road in the 1600 block of Connecticut Avenue NW, the Taurus rear-ended a Nissan parked at a stoplight. The impact sent the Nissan hurtling into the air, whereupon it careened off the roof of a 1982 Volkswagen coupe and ricocheted into a Saturn. After rear-ending the Nissan, the Taurus struck a Chevrolet Capri taxi cab before coming to rest against a light pole.

Makharadze, who had spent much of the evening enjoying dinner and wine with friends at a nearby Greek restaurant, spent the early hours of January 4 considering the consequences of convictions on charges of aggravated assault and manslaughter. An ebullient six-teen-year-old Brazilian girl, Joviane Waltrick, had been sitting in the Volkswagen coupe when the Nissan crushed it. Waltrick died from what a ten-page affidavit in support of Makharadze's arrest warrant called "massive trauma to the head and torso."

The doctrine of diplomatic immunity can be traced to ancient kings, who sometimes put foreign messengers to death for bearing bad news. The 1961 Vienna Convention on Diplomatic Relations and the 1963 Vienna Convention on Consular Relations codified modern diplomatic and consular practices, including diplomatic immunity. It came down to this: A host nation may expel a foreign diplomat, but cannot institute legal action against or incarcerate the individual without permission from the offender's government — no matter how serious the crime.

George Makharadze enjoyed diplomatic immunity. But within days of the chain-reaction crash, his crime had escalated into an international news event replete with predictable political fallout. U.S. Congressman David Dreier, a Republican from Claremont, California, drafted legislation aimed at reforming the system of diplomatic immunity to ensure that diplomats who committed real crimes paid for them. Viviane Wagner, the dead teenager's mother, fueled much of the public furor by pressuring the governments of the United States and Georgia to ignore Makharadze's diplomatic status and hold him accountable for his actions. Wagner conducted vigils at the flower-strewn site of the accident, passing out leaflets that urged authorities to press charges against Makharadze. Mothers Against Drunk Driving, the National Organization For Victims Assistance, and several other groups soon rallied behind her campaign, "Justice For

418

Joviane," compelling the Clinton Administration to request that the Republic of Georgia waive Makharadze's diplomatic immunity.

His inflammatory arrest report demanded action. "Upon approaching the defendant," it stated, "the officer immediately smelled a strong odor of alcohol on his person. As the defendant exited his vehicle, the officer noted the defendant was unsteady on his feet to the extent that he had to place his hand on his car in order to keep his balance. The defendant belligerently responded that he was a diplomat who enjoyed full diplomatic immunity and threatened to drive away."

Makharadze's driving record damned him further. Nine months earlier, Makharadze had been clocked at ninety on an interstate roadway near Richmond, Virginia, where the posted limit was sixty-five. Police cited him for speeding, reckless driving, and suspicion of operating a vehicle under the influence of alcohol. Claiming diplomatic immunity, Makharadze avoided a DUI charge. Four months later, police again stopped Makharadze for driving the wrong way down a one-way section of 41st Street in Washington, D.C., near Wisconsin Avenue. The investigating officer, who suspected Makharadze of drunken driving, reported that the diplomat nearly hit his police cruiser. The officer released Makharadze after the Georgian again claimed diplomatic immunity.

Senator Judd Gregg, a New Hampshire Republican, joined a legion of U.S. politicians determined to make Makharadze a poster child for the accumulated frustrations over diplomats who drove while intoxicated and got away with it, who racked up hundreds of thousands of dollars in parking tickets and got away with it, and who were caught shoplifting and got away with it. Only a week before Makharadze's accident, diplomats from Russia and Belarus scuffled with New York City police officers who tried to arrest them on suspicion of drunken driving. The diplomats displayed their identifications and walked. Gregg argued that the United States should withhold $30 million in federal aid to Georgia unless it handed over Makharadze.

Georgia could have followed Zaire's lead. A year earlier, Zaire's ambassador to France had been responsible for an automobile accident that claimed the lives of two thirteen-year-old boys. The Zairean government ignored demands by the French — and the thousands of protestors who marched on the French Riviera — that it waive diplomatic immunity and recalled its ambassador. Georgian President Eduard Shevardnadze could have done the same with Makharadze, his friend and advisor. Shevardnadze had personally selected Makharadze to become one of the first Georgians to attend a special school of international business at Harvard, with the hope that others would follow and return to their homeland with the knowledge and skills to further Georgia's push to democracy. But confronted by the egregious nature of Makharadze's offense, his prior driving record, and considering the potential loss of foreign aid, Shevardnadze had little choice but to sacrifice his Deputy Chief of Mission. Six weeks after the accident, Shevardnadze assured the U.S. State Department that Georgia would not block the efforts of the U.S. Justice Department to prosecute the young diplomat.

Makharadze had been willing to plead guilty to a charge of negligent homicide, which carried a maximum term of five years in prison. But once the Georgian government surrendered his right of immunity, the Justice Department started to prosecute on charges of multiple aggravated assault and involuntary manslaughter, felonies in the District of Columbia.

Two months later, and almost in a daze, Makharadze walked into Room 201 of the District of Columbia Superior Court. The spectator gallery, which seated eighty people, overflowed, and included Viviane Wagner, her husband, and two sons. When Makharadze saw her, he begged in a quavering voice for forgiveness. Wagner, already seeking $15 million in wrongful death damages from Makharadze, the Republic of Georgia, the Ford Motor Company, and the Greek restaurant where Makharadze drank before the accident, wept when Makharadze's words tumbled out.

"I only wish I could undo what I have done," he stammered. "I can only pray and ask forgiveness from the victims, their families, my country, and this country. It's very difficult, Mrs. Wagner. I want you to know how difficult the pain is. For the rest of my life, I pray for Joviane. Every day I will pray. I'm sorry. I'm sorry. Only you have the power to forgive."

Makharadze's attorneys, Lawrence Barcella Jr. and Kirby D. Behre, described the Georgian diplomat as a caring professional whose conduct on the evening of January 3, 1997, had been an aberration. They also argued that the volatile nature of the case prevented Makharadze from receiving a fair hearing "in the media and in the minds of most Americans," maintaining that Makharadze had become a symbol for the anger Americans held for out-of-control diplomats.

But Assistant U.S. Attorney Katherine Winfree demanded a sentence ranging from ten to thirty years. "We are satisfied," she stated, "that his conduct rose to the level of second-degree murder." Another U.S. attorney described Makharadze as a "street hoodlum."

Unmoved by remonstrances from Makharadze's attorneys, and aware that punishment for the crimes to which Makharadze had confessed typically ranged from probation to four years, Judge Harold L. Cushenberry gave Makharadze seven to twenty-one years. Guards took him directly to jail.

Makaradze's sentence stunned and saddened Bob Walsh and Sara Benveniste, both of whom considered Makharadze a personal friend as well as a professional colleague. Bob and Sara had met Makharadze at the Georgian Embassy in Washington, D.C. several times prior to the accident to discuss Georgian business opportunities, coming away impressed with the diplomat's engaging personality and professional credentials.

After receiving his sentence, Makharadze entered a Washington D.C., jail, where he spent most of his time in solitary confinement. That actually pleased Makharadze since most of his fellow inmates were killers.

"The jail was very cold," Makharadze admitted later. "There was always water on the floor. There were no books, no newspapers. The only thing I had was a Bible. There were frequent riots and I was forced to walk the line between siding with the inmates and trying not to get into further trouble."

Makharadze mainly worried about his parents. They lived in Tbilisi, Georgia, and neither was able to travel to the United States to visit. Makharadze feared he would never see them again.

"I did have a few visitors," Makharadze explained later. "The mother of the poor girl came to the jail. The first time, all she could do was cry. She was really upset. The next couple of times she came we started to talk."

Viviane Wagner also brought her other children to see Makharadze, who arranged through a friend, Mamuka Tsereteli, executive director of the America-Georgia Business Development Council, for an artist in Tbilisi to paint an icon for the grief-stricken family.

"Fortunately," recalled Makharadze, "we could establish a relation. It was not easy. But we communicated."

After Makharadze completed seven months in solitary, federal authorities transported him by bus to Butner, North

Carolina, a small tobacco town that looks like everyone in it has given up.

One Friday afternoon in mid-1998, Bob Walsh threaded a rented Honda Accord through downtown Butner, took a right at the only BP station for miles, and drove twenty minutes through a forest, finally confronting a wide valley that included a hoosegow for every stripe of hooligan: state and federal penitentiaries, youth detention centers, detox facilities. The most prominent inmate in the Butner complex had to be Jonathan Pollard, convicted of giving Israel top-secret U.S. military intelligence and diplomatic codes and providing Israeli intelligence with the names of important American agents inside the former Soviet Union. A number of key CIA operatives in the Eastern Bloc had reportedly been executed as a result of Pollard's spying, the apparent reason he had been given a life sentence.

Vincente Gigante, reputed boss of New York's Genovese crime family and a man dubbed the "oddfather" for his habit of walking down New York streets in his bathrobe and pajamas, also occupied a cell somewhere in Butner. Gigante had been cleared of seven counts of murder, but convicted of racketeering and two murder conspiracies. Sol Wachtler, New York's former chief judge, had also been tossed in stir somewhere in Butner after pleading guilty to threatening to kidnap the daughter of an ex-lover.

Bob located the building that housed Makharadze behind four rows of chain-link fence that bristled with barbed wire. It had taken two months for the U.S. government and Georgian Embassy to complete a background check and approve Bob's application to visit Makharadze. Once inside the prison, Bob filled out a confetti of forms before receiving an escort through a series of electronically monitored gates. Bob could not take his wallet, credit cards, or hotel key past those gates. Security guards permitted him to carry $20 in ones and fives, a package of unopened cigarettes, but no lighters or matches.

The guard who processed Bob's admission seemed to be in his mid-thirties. A talkative man, he had been working in the Butner facility for less than a year after transferring from another federal lockup in Virginia.

"Do you know George Makharadze?" Bob asked him.

"A little," the guard replied. "George is one of the nicest guys in this prison. Everybody here thinks he got screwed because his was such a high-profile case. I've known guys who did the same thing he did and didn't do anywhere near the jail time. All the guys feel sorry for him. What he did was wrong, but the system wasn't fair."

Another guard led Bob down a dim hallway, through a door, and into a brightly lit cafeteria adjacent to a small courtyard. Five minutes later, Makharadze entered, wearing brown khaki pants and Nike shoes. They hugged briefly, then sat down to talk.

"You've lost weight," Bob commented.

"Forty pounds," Makharadze shrugged.

"How is this place?" asked Bob. "Are you all right?"

"Better than in D.C. It's clean. We get three meals a day. We can watch TV two hours a day. Some of the inmates are working on college degrees. I spend a lot of time in the library. But it's prison. The experience has made me stronger. If it hadn't been for the fact the girl died, this would have been a great learning experience. I only wish I could undo what I have done. Fortunately, there is much support from my friends."

"Do you get many visitors?"

"Some, a few. My sister has been here, not my parents. The girl's mother has visited twice. She made these steps and that's good. She is going back to Brazil. But I want to stay in contact with her. Tell me, are you going to Tbilisi soon?"

"In a couple of months."

"How is business?"

Bob explained that the Seattle Bid Committee had shelved plans to pursue the 2008 Olympics and would make a bid for the 2012 Games instead. Bob Walsh Enterprises had also completed the sale of $2 million in stock and received $5.5 million from a large investor. As part of that investment, BWE had formed an off-shore corporation in the British Virgin Islands called Bob Walsh Enterprises International. BWEI had assumed operation of the four joint-stock companies that had originally been formed between BWE and its Georgian partners, the Tbilisi City Company and Samgori Ltd. BWEI had committed up to $1 million to develop the Westin Tbilisi.

"How is the hotel?" Makharadze asked. "Any progress?"

"Slow," said Bob. "We've had some problems I'm sure you know about. Work on the façade is just about complete. The Westin logo is already up."

The main problem, Bob told Makharadze, involved several families that squatted in shacks on property near the rear of the hotel. They needed to be relocated before major construction could commence, but had refused to move, causing dozens of delays. On a more positive note, all the debris had been removed from the interior of the hotel, and sixty people worked at the site full-time. No progress had been made at the Mtatsminda Plateau, or with any of the other properties except the ice cream plant, where BWEI had just installed some new equipment.

"That's about it," Bob said. "But I could spend all day talking about the problems."

"Be patient," Makharadze advised Bob. "There are all these new ways of doing things in Georgia, but the old residue systems remain in place."

Bob would soon discover how troublesome they could be.

Bewitched In Babylon

I haven't had many jobs, but working with Bob was definitely an experience. I have never met anyone else exactly like him.

> – Kimberly Brown, former president,
> Bob Walsh & Associates,
> Seattle, Washington

*I*n his more fanciful moments, Bob Walsh envisioned the Tbilisi Westin filled to capacity with oil barons and world tourists, and the abandoned, three-story structure atop Mtatsminda Plateau restored to its former grandeur, booked with galas and receptions. To make his reveries a reality, Bob escorted a parade of speculators through Georgia: the president of the Federal Reserve Bank of the Middle East, the director of Visa International, a cornucopia of U.S. and European financial barons, and anyone else who had a heartbeat and a checkbook. The itinerary for each tour always included meetings with government officials. Each meeting called for a subsequent feast, and each feast called for the wine.

In Georgia, most things call for the wine. One night, Bob's son, Timmy, awoke from a sound sleep and slipped out of his room at the Krtsanisi Government Residence in Tbilisi. When, five minutes later, Bob discovered Timmy missing, he raised the alarm. Several of the women who

work in the residence started checking empty rooms, while others frantically raced down hallways, calling Timmy's name. When they couldn't find him, they summoned Eduard Shevardnadze's soldiers, who burst into the building brandishing assault rifles, and scoured it as if a diplomat had been abducted. Five minutes later, someone located Timmy sitting sleepy-eyed and unharmed on a stair on a far side of the residence. The Krtsanisi women flailed their arms, cried with joy, and babbled

One of Eduard Shevardnadze's soldiers, with Toni, Bob, and Timmy Walsh

about miracles, invoking the name of God.

The commotion done, one of Bob's traveling companions started to return to his room, passing en route a doorway in which a Georgian man, Krtsanisi's cook, stood gesticulating wildly, flapping his large, white apron, and yelping things in Georgian. The cook wanted Bob's friend to follow him into to a kitchen, which he did, at which point the wigged-out cook popped corks on several bottles of wine. The cook then started to propose toast after toast, saying things Bob's friend couldn't understand. What Bob's friend could comprehend — a raised glass is difficult to misinterpret — was that the cook wanted him to participate in the spirit of the occasion, whatever it was. But it had to be something big because the cook had finally uncorked twenty bottles of wine.

After the wine was gone from the fourth toast and still eighteen bottles remained, Bob's friend tried — unsuccessfully — to tell the cook he was all toasted out. The cook wouldn't hear of it, even taking great umbrage, and poured more wine as Bob's friend recalled the inscription on the Georgian Horn: *He who drinks me to the bottom owns me.* At that point, a frail Georgian woman named Maya came by and smiled. Her black hair usually tied in a bun, Maya ran the cleaning and cooking operations at Krtsanisi. She understood — and spoke — some English.

"What's happening here?" Bob's friend asked.

"Drink more," she said.

"What's with this cook? Why are we toasting."

"He's celebrating the return of Timmy."

"But Timmy's okay."

"That's why he's celebrating."

"Isn't twenty bottles of wine a bit much to celebrate Timmy's return?"

"He also wishes to celebrate all the children of the world."

"Mother of God."

And the cook went about doing this as if Timmy and all the children of the world had been rescued after a week on a mountain top, barely surviving packs of wolves and wild dogs.

"The cook is pretty worked up," Bob's friend told Maya.

"This cook here, he wants to share with you all this wine," Maya said, pointing at the remaining eighteen bottles. "Then he wants you to eat that basket of food over there, and take this other basket of food back to your room. And please have some of this bread. It is something he believes should be done for Bob and his son, who was lost, but now has been found."

The curiosities of the Georgian mind, including the stratagems they employ to see them through one more day, are not known in America. Somehow, though, Bob had become so attuned to them that a Georgian cook stood ready to consume a veritable vineyard in the interest of Bob's and Timmy's well-being. All of the investors Bob brought to Georgia saw that this was true. And when they departed for home, they did so thunderstruck at the friendships Bob had developed in a country so far from his own, from maids to celebratory cooks to Eduard Shevardnadze.

"It was quite remarkable," recalled Nick Imperato, head of Stanford University's prestigious think tank, The Hoover Institute. "What I saw when I went to Tbilisi with Bob was that he had developed connections in Georgia that only government-appointed emissaries or CEOs of major corporations should have."

Another time, when a car carrying Bob and one of his entourages pulled up at Shevardnadze's gated compound, a soldier wearing a dark blue beret and holding an AK-47 assault rifle leaned into the window to check identifications. Informed by a Georgian chauffeur named Merab Papava that Bob was in the car, the soldier, a cigarette lodged over his ear, replied that he didn't know a Bob Walsh.

"Five million people in Georgia know who Bob Walsh is!" barked Merab. "If you don't know who the hell Bob is that's your own damn fault!"

The mystified guard stammered and fumbled, quickly opening the huge iron gate to Shevardnadze's sanctuary.

"Stupid fool!" yelled Merab, tearing off up the driveway.

Since Bob Walsh Enterprises International possessed some of the most prized development projects in Georgia, Bob suspected Western investors would swarm all over them. The Tbilisi Westin had a chance to become the grandest hotel between the Black and Caspian seas, and the Mtatsminda Plateau a hit with tourists. The vacant lots at Rustaveli 7 and Freedom Square easily ranked as the best undeveloped sites in the city, and BWEI had the political connections, if not the cash, to bring each of its projects — and dozens of others — to fruition. In Bob's mind, that Georgia also presented itself as a beguiling Eden of spectacular landscapes, old stone churches, grape arbors, and open-air cafes, only sweetened the sales pitch.

But the majority of speculators didn't view Georgia through the optimistic lenses Bob did, Tbilisi's seductive wiles unable to disguise so many obvious problems, especially with its infrastructure. In addition to Georgia's own troubles, its neighbors coped constantly with turbulence: Chechnya at bloody odds with Russia to the north, the Armenia-Azerbaijan dispute unresolved to the south. And for all of his political clout, Shevardnadze's authority realistically remained limited to slightly more than half of Georgia's territory as a result of separatist movements, especially in Abkhazia, supported by Russia. The Russians had made their intentions clear: They would continue to sow chaos in the Caucasus in part to extend their sphere of political influence, in part to quash plans for a new oil pipeline slated to snake across Georgia from its source on the Caspian Sea to the Turkish port of Ceyhan. So while Georgia appeared ripe to Bob for commercial plucking, it seemed to many investors who performed due diligence to be one hair-trigger finger away from anarchy.

The various assassination attempts on Shevardnadze exacerbated apprehension. The first, in August of 1995, had left the president dazed, cut, and bruised after a car bomb exploded near his motorcade in the courtyard of the Parliament building. The second occurred on Vakhtang Gorgasali Street, one of the routes Shevardnadze took from his office to his residence, when the presidential motorcade was attacked with anti-tank grenade launchers, killing one of his bodyguards and wounding two others, including his personal physician. Shevardnadze survived only because he rode in an armored vehicle.

In the aftermath of that attempt, Georgian Prosecutor General Dzhamlet Babilashvili announced the arrest of ten individuals for their alleged roles in the assault. However, a day later, four United Nations Mission observers, monitoring developments in breakaway Abkhazia, got snatched by a previously unknown character named Gocha Esebua. What happened next could have plotted a sleazy Italian movie. As Esebua bargained his captives through the media for the release of the individuals held in connection with the assassination attempt, a permanent feast went on inside the house where the hostages had been detained. Throughout their term of bondage, hostages gulped wine with hostage-takers and cheered Winter Olympics hockey games on satellite TV.

Russia's political, economic, and criminal turmoil also adversely affected investor attitudes about Georgia, since most investors had only a muddled grasp of politics and geography and tended to lump Russia's problems with Georgia's. Georgia suffered further from reports that its economy had become irrevocably dependent on corruption, and from speculation over what manner of chaos might ensue if Shevardnadze died or was ousted. The potential for criminal peril also permeated conversation, heightened by a continual flow of negative news reports.

U.S. News & World Report carried an account about the American owner of the Radisson Hotel in Moscow who had been assassinated after a falling out with his Russian partners. *Spin* described the growing popularity and distribution of dangerous new drugs throughout the former Soviet Union, including the synthetic amphetamine "vint." Containing a noxious brew of chemicals, including gasoline, vint produced a high that lasted for three days. Both *Time* and *Newsweek* ran frightening reports about the gun-toting bandits of the Russian Mafia, which so effectively blended financial wizardry with bone-crunching muscle that not only had it become a state within a state, but the illegitimate successor to the Communist Party.

After the Soviet Union collapsed, Russia and other republics rushed to embrace Western investors, few offering sweeter come-ons than Georgia, where some romances flourished. But most did not. Wente Brothers of Napa Valley, California, for example, invested $1.5 million in a privatized winery in Tbilisi through a joint venture called "Sameba" and lost its proverbial shirt. The Georgians didn't understand, or wouldn't adhere to, Western business practices, preferring to operate through a Communist-residue combination of cronyism and double-dealing.

Early on, even Bob grew frustrated with his Georgian projects. BWEI sank hundreds of thousands of dollars into pre-construction work at the site of the Tbilisi Westin, but constant delays plagued the project. So did battles with the Tbilisi mayor's office, most stemming from corpulent Vice Mayor Zaza Shengelia, a recycled Communist who tried to camouflage his ignorance of schedules, contracts, and accounting with transparent bluster and table-pounding truculence.

Then the Starwood Corporation swallowed Westin Hotels and Resorts, ending Westin's involvement with the Hotel Tbilisi, and forcing BWEI to locate a new hotel operator. Through skillful negotiation by BWEI's Lloyd Stafford, the Marriott Corporation agreed to replace Westin. But when the squatters in the rear of the hotel still declined monetary offers to budge, Marriott and BWEI had no choice but to scale down the project. Instead of reconstructing the Marriott Tbilisi into a 250-room hotel, as originally planned, BWEI and Marriott agreed to build two hotels, a 125-room Marriott Tbilisi and a 125-room Marriott Courtyard across town.

Every project found some sort of financial or political snag. The Mtatsminda Plateau redevelopment got bogged down in ownership disputes, and the joint venture with Samgori, the dairy processing plant, collapsed due to a partnership squabble, as did a similar and subsequent venture with Tbilmargarini. BWEI finally settled into an arrangement with Sante, renaming the company "Sante Walsh Products." Sante produced ice cream, a seasonal product in Georgia consumed primarily in summer months. To balance out the business, BWEI invested heavily to modernize the Sante plant and make it possible for Sante to churn out an array of dairy products and confections, including many that didn't require refrigeration. Although sales looked promising after Sante rolled out its first ice cream bars, the company ran into disputes with Sante officials over operational and management procedures.

The persistent snafus at the hotel, Mtatsminda, and Sante Walsh might have been more palatable if the Russian ruble hadn't collapsed. When that carnage ceased, most experts agreed that if a similar currency devaluation had occurred in America, it would have wiped out eighteen companies the size of General Motors. The ruble devaluation in Russia not only hit Walsh Pharma hard, it had a nasty ripple effect in other former Soviet republics that played into investor worries that Georgia was not the place in which to sink a substantial amount of cash.

During dozens of trips to Tbilisi, Bob tried to show investors it was possible to make money there. But no matter how many he marched through the city, he could not get one to make the kind of financial commitment that would put his projects over the top. Investors had too many concerns that behind the façade of a beguiling Eden lurked unscrupulous freebooters and corrupt officials. True or not, speculation begat belief and fear. So one after the other, tepid tycoons listened to Georgian songs, drank the wine, heard Bob's pleadings, and dropped away, concluding that investing in Georgia was just too dicey.

"Bob had a chance to make a positive impact in that society," remembered Roger Reynolds, an analyst for Coldstream Capital Management, a Bellevue, Washington, investment advisory firm that managed stock and bond portfolios. "I didn't know how he was going to do it. But for all of the problems he faced, I was putting my money on him."

The Torch Is Passed

*Bob and I used to have breakfast
every Saturday morning for years.
He couldn't tell me anything I didn't
already know. But at least he was
a good listener.*

*– Stanley Kramer, film producer,
Beverly Hills, California*

*B*ob Walsh and Kathy Scanlan had
always made an intriguing odd couple. They
had always been so different in the way they
approached projects — she with a brilliance
for detail, he with the touch of an alchemist
— that it was sometimes difficult to imagine they had ever functioned successfully
as a team. But their professional relationship worked because they respected each
other's strengths more than they lamented
each other's limitations. Recognizing his
own in the matter of the 2012 Summer
Olympic Games, Bob sought out Kathy to
ride herd over the most critical aspect of the
bid process.

In the four years Bob had chased
his Olympic dream, the Seattle Bid Committee had conducted more than 100 lobbying efforts with International Olympic

Committee and United States Olympic Committee members, raised and spent more than $1.2 million of Boeing, Seafirst, Microsoft, and Holland America money, almost abandoned the pursuit altogether, and nearly gone broke. Except for his insider dealings with the IOC and USOC, Bob stayed in the shadows, content, if not entirely satisfied, with letting first Dave Syferd and later Clark Kokich serve as voices of the bid effort. Both had been capable; more important, neither carried the baggage that Bob forever lugged after his controversial acquisition of the Goodwill Games. In fact, even after all these years, the big brokers of Seattle business still viewed Bob, and viewed him somewhat unfairly, as the personification of Code Blue.

Behind the scenes, in places where the media couldn't poke, Bob's persistent efforts on Seattle's behalf had placed the city in excellent position to claim the United States bid for the 2012 Games, a fact not only acknowledged to Bob, Syferd, and Kokich by IOC and USOC members, but reported in several newspapers, including *The Washington Post*. In an article rating the prospects of the nine candidate cities, *The Post* cited Seattle as "the bid to beat." The Seattle Bid Committee now only needed a favorable technical resolution from the Seattle City Council, one place in which Kathy Scanlan could succeed where Bob could not.

Kathy Scanlan

Kathy had criss-crossed the map since the Goodwill Games, first as an administrator with the Seattle SuperSonics, and then as executive director of the World University Games in Buffalo, New York. After returning to Seattle, Kathy had formed Scanlan, Sorensen, and Potter, Inc., with two Goodwill colleagues, Jennifer Potter and Gretchen Sorensen. The consulting firm's clientele included World Cup USA, the City of Seattle, The Business Alliance Against Poverty, the Seattle Aquarium, and the American Zoo Association, but the business had apparently not entirely satisfied Kathy's ambitions.

Bob caught up with Kathy in Indianapolis, where she directed USA Gymnastics, the federation that governed the sport's national, international, and Olympic efforts. To induce Kathy back to Seattle to massage city bureaucrats, Bob had worked out an employment plan for her with the Seattle-King County Convention and Visitors Bureau: Kathy would become president of the Seattle Bid Committee and build on the efforts of Bob, Syferd, Kokich, and Steve Penny, who had done the bulk of the organizing work on several pre-Olympic events, including the 1996 Olympic Torch Relay.

Kathy faced a major timing problem. The USOC needed to know in a matter of months which cities would officially declare their candidacy for the 2012 Games. That barely gave Kathy enough time to settle her affairs in Indianapolis, return to Seattle, and organize a team, much less fashion an argument for why Seattle should engage itself in an Olympic bid. Kathy counted on confronting the same objections — squawks about traffic, noise, education, parks, and potholes — that had marked her earlier tenure with the Seattle Organizing Committee, but she soon discovered several new dynamics had come into play. Where Ted Turner and the Soviet Union had been the villains in early Goodwill Games planning, the International Olympic Committee now sported the prominent black hat, having come to be viewed as a cabal of opportunistic vultures who ran vast extortion schemes on any city stupid enough, or naïve enough, to curry its favor.

Seattle's political and sporting environment had also changed. Since the conclusion of the Goodwill Games, the city had developed a new — and profound — distaste for any sporting venture that might require use of public funds. Area voters had resoundingly rejected an opportunity to build the Seattle Mariners a new $400 million playpen. Ignoring the results of the ballot box, the Washington State Legislature had flamboozled the citizenry into footing the bill anyway with an add-on to the sales tax. Equally onerous, a new football stadium had gone on the drawing board, slated to replace the Kingdome. It would be financed in part by $300 million from the civic exchequer at a time when the Kingdome's substantial debts had yet to be retired.

The anti-sporting sentiment became palpably hostile and ran along these lines: Seattle did not need to mortgage its future to the International Olympic Committee, or take on what surely would become a gargantuan public works project, or validate itself by bidding on the Olympic Games.

"Seattle has really come of age," argued Seattle political consultant Bob Gogerty. "Hosting the Olympics is for cities that want to be somebody."

As Seattle City Councilman Nick Licata framed the debate over the city's opposition to the Olympics, Joni Balter of *The Seattle Times* summarized it best: "The Olympics will overwhelm the agenda for years," she wrote, adding, "There is honor in passing on this enormously complicated extravaganza."

Galvanized by an e-mail avalanche urging City Hall to declare the Olympics the wrong way to address Seattle's problems, Licata decreed that no one on the Seattle Bid Committee had articulated one iota of good reasoning for pursuing an event that would probably cost $2 billion, drain money from education, and probably throttle salmon restoration in Puget Sound. Licata and his supporters grew especially terrified that Seattle would be asked to indemnify the Olympics against any losses or lawsuits in the event the city landed the Games.

A16 Seattle Post-Intelligencer • Thursday, November 19, 1998

Seattle Post-Intelligencer

Voice of the Northwest since 1863

J.D. Alexander *Editor and Publisher*
John Currie *Business Manager*
Joann Byrd *Editorial Page Editor*

Kenneth F. Bunting *Managing Editor*
Chris A. Beringer, Janet E. Grimley, Neal Pattison *Assistant Managing Editors*

A Hearst Newspaper

Olympic bid ploy is flawed, foolish

The attempt by the Seattle Olympic Bid Committee to make an end run around the Seattle City Council to gain an endorsement from the Puget Sound Regional Council for its bid to host the summer Games in 2012 is a flawed, inflammatory strategy.

Whether to endorse such a bid is Seattle's decision to make, not the Regional Council's. The committee's ploy is guaranteed to anger people. The question of whether to bring the Olympics here is contentious enough without adding in such highhanded shenanigans.

From the outset, the committee expected Seattle to be the host-city candidate in the application for the Games. But the City Council voted not to support such a bid. So it's a pathetically transparent move to now propose that the Puget Sound Regional Council can credibly override the City Council and commit Seattle to host the Games.

The low-profile Puget Sound Regional Council, a four-county transportation and growth-management planning agency, is composed of elected officials from cities, counties and ports.

Even though members of our state's congressional delegation have signed a letter to the Regional Council asking it to endorse the bid, this body is not a legitimate substitute for the City Council.

We remain convinced that the City Council was too hasty in turning its back on the Olympics. Panicked by a perfectly predictable outpouring of opposition from naysayers, it said no before the facts were in. The council would be wise to explore the matter much further.

We welcome the support of the congressional delegation for the bid. But the fundamental problem that rightly gave pause to Seattle City Council members remains unanswered even if the Puget Sound Regional Council were to endorse the bid: Who indemnifies taxpayers against losses?

Surely the Puget Sound Regional Council does not propose to expose taxpayers to a risk the City Council refused to accept. Yet taxpayer money may be on the line regardless of which governing body approves the bid.

We believe Seattle should not give up on the Olympics until it has been clearly demonstrated that it's a losing proposition for taxpayers. That has yet to be demonstrated. Meanwhile, the Puget Sound Regional Council should mind its own business and not attempt to usurp the city's authority in a matter of bringing the Olympics to Seattle.

The Olympic effort didn't receive support from Seattle's morning newspaper

Kathy Scanlan had no mind to ask the city for an unqualified endorsement of the Olympic bid effort. She desired to ask only for the opportunity to work with governments, business leaders, and citizens groups to develop a plan for the bid process. That plan would be put to a public vote, taxpayers deciding its fate. If it passed, a bid would be pursued. If it failed, only the Seattle Bid Committee would lose any money.

Kathy argued that the Summer Olympics would inject $2 billion into the economy, not drain $2 billion out of it, and create lasting improvements in housing, education, arts, and neighborhoods. Where Licata and Balter stood ready to defend the civic garrison against one more traffic jam, Scanlan countered that Olympic cities historically experienced less, not more, traffic. More important, she believed, the private funds the Games would generate from sponsorships, TV rights, and ticket sales would help address regional transportation needs, especially light rail. Atlanta, the 1996 Olympic venue, had built seven miles of rapid transit track and new stations, twelve new miles of highway, and made major improvements at Hartsfield International Airport, all with private or federal dollars. No new stadiums would have to be built for a Seattle Olympics. The biggest facilities requirement would be housing that, after the Games, could provide affordable neighborhood alternatives to address a growing population.

Played out in newspaper forums, on TV shows, in focus groups, and in public hearings, the debate stormed for months, finally coming down to a make all or break all appearance by the Seattle Bid Committee before the Seattle City Council, which had to determine only whether a study of an Olympic bid was in the city's best interests.

Panicked by a perfectly predictable outpouring of opposition, and perhaps reacting to an unfolding scandal involving Salt Lake City Olympic boosters and bribe takers in the International Olympic Committee, the Seattle City Council said no by a vote of 8-1. It would not permit an evaluation, much less allow the electorate to vote on one.

"I was flabbergasted the Council nixed it so fast," recalled Steve Morris, president of the Seattle-King County Convention and Visitors Bureau. "We took a front-running position on a multibillion dollar event that could have been ours and said we don't give a shit and we don't want it. In fact, hell no, we really don't want it."

Several Seattle Bid Committee employees lamented the six-month lag between the time Bob recruited Kathy and when she officially became president. Perhaps if Kathy had come on board earlier, they felt, the outcome might have been different. Then again, given the quality of opposition, maybe it would have been exactly the same.

"Kathy had no chance," Jennifer Potter later conceded. "With enough time, Kathy could have pulled that bid together. At least it was sudden death, not protracted death."

Bob vented for weeks, his mood alternating between sullen despair and animated disgust. Joni Balter's negative editorials annoyed him. He became angry with the dogmatic Shelly Yapp, an early Goodwill Games administrator, when she blurted, "It was a good idea to turn down the Olympics. We would have paid through the nose." He grew exasperated at the Seattle business establishment. If Bob didn't go through proper channels, he received a figurative flogging. If he did, he barely got a hearing. It dismayed Bob that Kathy had hired Gretchen Sorensen, once part of the Seattle Organizing Committee, to lead the lobbying effort with the Seattle City Council. And it mystified him when the usually savvy Bob Gogerty said, "Hosting the Olympics is for cities that want to be somebody." New York, Los Angeles, Washington, D.C., San Francisco, Beijing, Sydney, Cape Town, Rome, Paris, Istanbul, Athens, and Moscow had all mounted Olympic bids. Weren't they somebody?

It further inflamed Bob that Olympic objectors didn't seem to realize the stakes involved. A city that won an Olympic bid qualified for hundreds of millions of federal dollars. A city that pursued a bid could expect to be inundated by all manner of smaller athletic competitions, such as track, gymnastic, and swimming meets, as well as by athletic conferences and conventions that filled hotel rooms and occupied exhibition space.

Bob found himself more distressed than angry that he'd spent four years first believing that he could, and then convinced that he would, win the U.S. bid for the Summer Olympic Games. As he soaked up the setback, something really bad happened.

The Fugitive

*Bob is one of the few people I know
who is sincerely committed to
the success of others.*

*— Jim Baumann, The Follett Corporation,
Chicago, Illinois*

*A*s Bob Walsh strode through his office one morning, pondering another passel of project possibilities, he received a frightening telephone call. The man who seized Bob's ear refused to identify himself, but insisted he was not a crank. And then the caller told Bob to brace himself: Through reliable sources, he had learned that Bob had been targeted for elimination by the Russian Mafia. With an urgent tone to his voice, the man added that he didn't know why and didn't know when, giving Bob pause to speculate wildly about how. In addition to the several articles Bob had read about the hitmen of the Russian Mafia, he had anecdotal evidence from an ex-FBI man of his acquaintance that they left horrific signatures. Sometimes, they cut off fingertips to thwart identification of the corpse. Occasionally they yanked out all the teeth to render dental records useless. Some victims wound up in rivers. And some showed up only as a head encased in a plastic bag. The mysterious informant told Bob he was sorry. Then he hung up abruptly, leaving Bob to fight off a surge of nausea. Bob quickly dialed up his ex-FBI friend.

"I just got a terrible phone call," blurted Bob, all rubbery.

"And?"

"This guy, he didn't say who he was, just told me the Russian Mafia is after me."

"God, are you sure?"

"Well, I don't know. That's what he said."

"What did you do to the Russian Mafia?"

"Nothing as far as I know."

"Is this guy reliable?"

"I don't know."

"Bob, I think maybe you ought to get away for a while."

Considering the cold efficiency of the Russian Mafia, and figuring this was not a moment in which he could afford to be sanguine, Bob quickly packed some things, raced to the airport, and boarded a plane for Maui. When he arrived at his condo at the Lahaina Shores Beach Resort, Bob called his office and learned that *The Seattle Times* had been trying to reach him.

"What did they want?" Bob asked.

"They wanted us to confirm that you're dead," a secretary replied.

"What?"

"They said they've got a report out of Moscow that an American businessman named Bob Walsh was found shot."

Bob spent the next several days trying to determine why he had been fingered for erasure by the Russian Mafia and who had been the source behind the bizarre story of his death. Did another Bob Walsh exist? There couldn't be another American businessman named Bob Walsh who traveled to Moscow. Could there? Were the two situations related? Bob had no clue. He did know that thousands of Russians had relocated to the Seattle area over the last several years, but he had become acquainted with just a handful of them, none dangerous as far as he could tell. Some suspicious-looking Russians frequented restaurants near the Westin Hotel on the northern edge of downtown, jabbering into cell phones for hours on end. Bob suspected that most belonged to a ring of car thieves. But he didn't know any of those guys personally, although it was clear from the way they stared at Bob that they knew who he was. Bob had a hard time convincing himself that he was of any interest to them, or any other Russians in Seattle. He hadn't done business with any Russians lately and almost never associated with them. That included Nina, his first Russian wife and Milana Walsh, who had filed for divorce. Bob knew that neither had anything to do with the Russian Mafia.

Bob had spent every possible minute he could with his son, Timmy, even taking him to Tbilisi so many times, including nine trips through Istanbul, that Timmy became an Executive Premier on United Airlines by the time he was three years old. Among other things, their junkets convinced several of Bob's Tbilisi friends that what Bob needed was a Georgian wife.

The Tbilisi mayor's office assumed the responsibility of orchestrating the recruitment pro-

Timmy Walsh in Tbilisi, Georgia

cess, putting out the word that it sought matrimonial candidates for a high-profile American businessman. Applications poured in and the mayor's underlings interviewed dozens of candidates for Bob to accept or reject on his subsequent visits.

Oblivious to the matchmaking, Bob didn't catch the drift of what was going on for quite a while. When Bob attended a meeting, friends or associates casually introduced him to one or two women who appeared for reasons unannounced, or seemingly no reason at all. When Bob accepted dinner invitations, his hosts invariably seated him next to stray females. Bob met a stash of Georgian women in this fashion, most of whom pawed after Bob or fawned over Timmy. One exotic-looking woman, whose hair tumbled down her shoulders in an enchanting cascade of red, and who seemed to have been sewn into her sheath dress, put such a gleam in Bob's eye during a dinner party that he entertained the thought of inviting her to the United States. But Bob resisted the temptation, recognizing that if he indulged even half of his fantasies he could wind up getting sold for scrap. While Bob's friends encouraged his domesticity, another situation solidified Bob's resolve to lay socially low, underscoring as it did the perils of wanton behavior.

It involved one of Bob's best friends whom Bob believed to be happily married. But then Bob's friend confessed that he'd carried on a long dalliance with a former girlfriend, herself married. They had met at business conventions four or five times a year, but their affair had taken a gruesome turn, owing to a series of lurid letters. Apparently, the cheating wife loved to receive letters rife with scarlet passages that outlined in blushing detail what manner of adventures Bob's friend planned for her the next time they met. The woman had saved dozens of these missives in a drawer in her desk office. Her husband had found them.

"How bad are they?" Bob asked.

"Terrible. If my wife ever finds out, that's the end of our marriage."

The wronged husband had plotted a perfect revenge. He had called Bob's friend and, in a friendly tone of voice, requested his FAX number. A few minutes later, Bob's friend received copies of the incriminating documents and a follow-up telephone call.

"He asked me if I got the FAX. I told him yes. And then he told me that he had my wife's FAX number at work. He said he wanted me to go to bed every night wondering when he was going to send these letters to her."

"Has he sent anything yet?"

"No. But he keeps calling to remind me he still has the letters and my wife's FAX number."

"How long as this been going on?"

"Three years. This guy has been *torturing* me for three years. I can't sleep at night. I've lost about thirty pounds. A while back, he didn't call for a few months and I thought it was over. But then I came home and he'd left a message on our answering machine."

"Jeez, it'd be better if he just beat you up or burned down your house and got it over with."

Bob didn't know which was worse: a vengeful husband bent on torture or the Russian mob. Bob explored every avenue he could think of trying to find out why the Russian Mafia wanted to snuff him, but couldn't, finally deciding after a fitful stretch in Hawaii that if the mob really had plans for him there was nothing he could do. Bob had no luck, either, locating the source of the story about his death. *The Seattle Times* refused to divulge it.

Bob's personal melodramas at least came to something of a satisfactory conclusion when a Seattle judge made his split from Milana official.

"Congratulations," the judge announced as Bob prepared to leave the courtroom. "You are now divorced. It's nice to do business with a Seattle living legend."

The Art
Of Survival

It's difficult to get Georgians to understand how business is done. Georgians would prefer to do a deal and then toast for days over it. The day in and day out of business is difficult for them.

    *– Dick Nelson, Board of Directors,
      Bob Walsh Enterprises,
      Seattle, Washington*

Kristin Hayden originally wanted nothing to do with Tbilisi, Georgia. After two intense years in Moscow, she could not imagine ever again living in the former Soviet Union. Kristin desired to move to Western Europe where life was not as draining, where the juxtaposition of luxury and scarcity did not coexist so dramatically. But Bob Walsh courted Kristin hard, first in Paris, then in London, finally in the United States. Kristin might have been more inclined to refuse Bob's plea to relocate to Tbilisi had she not run out of options. Her job-hunting had reached a dead end, and European work permits had become difficult to obtain. So Kristin reluctantly agreed to try Tbilisi for a while, assured by Bob that she soon would be seduced by its blandishments.

Reared in Portland, Oregon, Kristin received early programming for a long whirl of international travel. Her father, Bill, had been an exchange student in Chile; her mother, Dorothy, an exchange student in Japan. Kristin had studied in South Africa as a Rotary Scholar and later as an exchange student at the Aviation Institute in Moscow just about the time Mikhail Gorbachev got deposed, and just as the city became flush with protest and discontent over seventy years of broken Communist promises. She departed before the entire house of cards tumbled.

Graduating with honors from Macalester College, a liberal arts school in St. Paul, Minnesota, Kristin emerged proficient in the Russian language and received her introduction to the discordant world of Bob Walsh during the Europe-America 500 Space Flight, working as a freelance translator. Two years later, she joined Bob Walsh Enterprises, then spent the next two in Moscow, flourishing and burning herself out in the employ of Walsh Pharma.

To rekindle her energy, Kristin quit and moved to Paris, where, for a year, she studied French, played the saxophone in a band, frequented cafes and cabarets, fell in love, and had the time of her life. Then she swept into London, got a job with a Russian-related Non Government Organization, and resigned after a year for the lack of a challenge. Returning to the United States, Kristin got bored all over again. She hankered for Western Europe, but found that her only viable alternative was Bob's invitation to represent Bob Walsh Enterprises International in Tbilisi.

Bob needed someone there he could trust, someone who shared passion for his projects, who was intelligent, independent, and comfortable with cultural diversity. For a long while that someone had been Sara Benveniste, a spontaneous spirit who embraced adventures the same way Bob did. Bob and Sara had spent several years working the Tbilisi real estate and ice cream projects, nursing them through a succession of successes, pains, and frustrations. Sara had done great work in a variety of projects, including arranging treatment in Seattle for Eduard Shevardnadze's personal physician, Merab Bokhua. Dr. Bokhua had been standing next to Shevardnadze in downtown Tbilisi when assassins tried to take out the Georgian leader and had suffered damage to his inner ear. Through all the projects, Bob and Sara had become great friends, and he tried to talk her out of leaving the company. But Sara had a mind to study medicine. So when she departed, Bob seized on Kristin.

Like Sara, Kristin radiated energy and flamboyance. She also possessed a philosophic disposition and was neither ruffled by Bob's professional eccentricities nor put off by his private melodramas. In

fact, Kristin had as much fascination for Bob's foibles as she did for his remarkable people skills. After a few months in Tbilisi, Kristin understood exactly why Bob found Georgia so alluring. As the western portal of the Great Silk Road and the newest conduit of

Kristin Hayden, left, and Sara Benveniste

Caspian oil to world markets, Georgia had become a strategic gateway of energy and trade routes linking East and West. With a vibrant, free-market economy, Georgia had a chance to become a stabilizing force in an unstable region. The Georgian government had affirmed its western orientation by regular passage of legislation aimed at economic, legal, and fiscal policy reform. But Kristin also saw why Georgia was such a hard sell to outsiders. Despite the Georgians' considerable efforts to establish a democracy, massive external debt and little internal income withered the economy. Living standards remained low. Health care and education did not receive sufficient human or monetary resources. Prolonged electrical blackouts made winters almost unbearable. Eight years after the collapse of the Soviet Union, Georgia remained a testimony to how messy the dissolution of an empire could be. But Kristin also recognized that even one significant investor could make a substantial impact in the country if that investor had the patience to accept the vagaries of Georgian business and the tolerance it required for Eduard Shevardnadze to institute his reforms.

The president worked hard at them. Among other things, he established a "Corruption Research Center" to investigate hundreds of cases that clogged Georgian courts and bogged down parliamentary affairs, perpetually keeping the Georgian treasury in a state of impoverishment. Shevardnadze also tossed aside cabinet members and impeached dozens of ministers in communication, energy, and finance after their actions revealed "power abuse in order to fulfill their personal interests." Shevardnadze once even forced the resignation of most of the country's 350 judges after determining they were ignorant of the law.

It tore at Bob's heart to watch how hard Georgians struggled to survive. Since the government did not have sufficient resources to pay police, for example, the police were forced to extract their wages from motorists in catch-as-catch-can fashion. The police often parked on the side of the road waiting for any car that did not contain diplomats, government workers, or foreigners. Nailed with a trumped-up charge, the driver had a choice: give the officer a tribute — perhaps one or two lari, worth about fifty cents each — or receive a traffic ticket, which could include the loss of a driver's license and a fine of ten to fifteen lari. It wasn't much of a choice.

As Kristin rode with her driver, Merab Papava, a police officer signaled Merab to stop. Lathered at the injustice of it, Merab jumped out of his car and yelled at the police officer.

"You took a wrong turn," said the cop.

"No, no. There was no way," said Merab.

"Couldn't you just give me a little something?"

"No, I can't."

"Not even just a little something?"

"No!" shouted Merab, who got back in his car and drove away.

One day a group of Bob's traveling companions rode in a van that police stopped for seemingly no reason. If the van hadn't contained Americans, it would have required a bribe for the police to let it proceed.

"How much would it cost?" asked one of the van's occupants, Larry Coffman, a marketing expert from Woodinville, Washington.

A translator named Paata Enukidze answered.

"Depends on what you did wrong."

"Give me an example."

"It costs two lari if you did nothing wrong. If you did something wrong and were not drunk, then it's three lari. If you're drunk, it's four lari. And if you're really drunk, that's five lari."

"Jesus," said Coffman.

Tax collectors sported some of Tbilisi's greasiest palms. Since almost no Georgian companies paid their fair share of taxes, the government collected scant revenues, could not establish a sufficient state budget, and had little money available to pay salaries for vital services, such as police. Georgian tax collectors preferred doing business with tax delinquents since it was difficult to elicit bribes from companies that subscribed to the letter of the law, such as Bob Walsh Enterprises International. The Tbilisi Marriott, for example, drew a rash of tax collectors, who spent days going through BWEI's paperwork, searching for transgressions. They could find nothing wrong.

"It frustrated them," Kristin explained later, "that we paid all our taxes."

Customs agents offered almost as much trouble as tax collectors. Bob once took a contingent of tourists to Tbilisi. While he swept a circuit of government offices, some of the tourists explored the city, purchasing dozens of souvenirs, mostly the small statues, scarves, oil paintings, and ornate Georgian daggers available at street kiosks. When it came time to leave Tbilisi, the tourists learned that their purchases had to be cleared through customs, and that the expedient way to do it was for a customs agent to drop by their lodgings and conduct an examination before the contingent left for the airport. The agent first had to photograph each item separately, for which there was a fee. But, for a minor tribute, the agent would photograph several items at once. The agent then declared that the purchases qualified as "antiquities," for which there was a hefty tax. But, with a little grease, the purchases would be reclassified as trinkets and taxed at a lower rate. The agent, Bob believed, could not be accused of a moral shortcoming as much as he could be accused of practicing survival.

Tbilisi presented a contradictory sight. Georgians had nice apartments, cell phones, CD players, radios, cars, food, wine, and cigarettes, but most had no money. And for those who had no money, it was amazing how well they dressed. Many Georgians relied on relatives and extended family to survive. One of Bob's partners, George Tavadze, supported five families of relatives on his BWEI salary. What Georgians couldn't buy they bartered, and what they couldn't barter they borrowed.

Compared to most of her Georgian friends, Kristin lived a privileged existence. The average Georgian didn't work and spent a lot of time hanging out. The average Georgian developed creative methods to live a tolerable life, but worried a lot and complained a lot. The average Georgian developed remarkable resiliency and waited for things to change.

Bob knew they would. For him, it came down to a simple matter of belief.

Salute To Yesterday

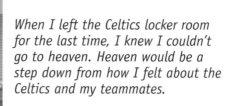

When I left the Celtics locker room for the last time, I knew I couldn't go to heaven. Heaven would be a step down from how I felt about the Celtics and my teammates.

> – Bill Russell, member, eleven NBA
> championship teams,
> Seattle, Washington

*F*ew sporting tributes ever attracted a more luminous assembly of athletic and entertainment icons than the May 26, 1999, gala at Boston's FleetCenter. The honoree, Bill Russell, had just been named *Sports Illustrated's* choice as "Team Athlete of the Twentieth Century," and was about to become the first member of the Boston Celtics to have his jersey number (6) reretired. NBA legends Kareem Abdul-Jabbar, Larry Bird, Bob Cousy, John Havlicek, Oscar Robertson, and Wilt Chamberlain had come to fete Russell, along with a crop of celebrities that included Muhammad Ali, Jim Brown, Hank Aaron, Aretha Franklin, Johnny Mathis, George Plimpton, and Rachel Robinson, the widow of baseball great Jackie Robinson.

Entertainer Bill Cosby, a Russell friend and admirer, served as master of ceremonies.

Russell had never been inside the FleetCenter, a new arena that replaced the old Boston Garden, where Russell had carved his incomparable Hall of Fame career, and where his first retirement ceremony had occurred in 1972. Russell had been celebrated privately that time only by his former coach, Red Auerbach, and a handful of ex-teammates. At Russell's request, no fans had been permitted to attend. But this time, thousands turned out, occupying every seat in the FleetCenter not claimed by the likes of K.C. Jones, Bryant Gumbel, Tom Brokaw, or Bill Walton.

Bob Walsh and Bill Russell

Nostalgic and proud of his friend, Bob Walsh took a seat near the head table next to Wally Walker, a long-ago client, a long-time friend, and now the president of the Seattle SuperSonics. As Bob watched Russell cackle and grin, banter with Cosby and hug Auerbach, he couldn't help but recall many of his earliest memories of Russell here in Boston, their long association at KABC in Los Angeles, and the years they spent together building the Seattle SuperSonics. Bob's entire life had changed as a result of his association with Russell, and in many ways Russell's had changed because of his friendship with Bob. As Bob watched his friend, the thought struck him that the years had mellowed Russell in a wonderful way. Bob also thought about something else Russell had once told him, something especially appropriate given the glitz of Russell's present circumstance. Russell had frequently said that he came from a place so mean that it was years before he knew that "mother" was just one word. And now, Bob mused, his old friend had been declared the greatest team player of the twentieth century, the subject of video tributes from Elgin Baylor, Magic Johnson, Michael Jordan, Kevin McHale, Jerry West, Bill Bradley, Lenny Wilkens, and President Bill Clinton.

Aside from Russell's daughter, all of the banquet speakers — except one — had been famous athletes or entertainers, which made the other exception, a dark-eyed man with thinning hair in his mid-fifties, seem curiously out of his element. Aside from Bob and a couple of others, no one in the audience recognized him. He had never played organized basketball, nor

The Celtics retired Russell's jersey again on May 26, 1999

had he coached it. He had no professional connection to Russell, and only a slight personal one. He had met Russell just once, two years earlier. The dark-eyed man had not witnessed any of the 143 combats between Russell and Chamberlain. In fact, Russell had been long retired before the mysterious gentleman had ever seen a Russell rebound, a Russell block, or a Russell hook on a highlight reel. For much of his life, he did not know what Russell even looked like. But he had an admiration for, and an attachment to, Russell that was perhaps more personally profound than any of the others in the FleetCenter. Russell stood as the primary reason this dark-eyed man had become who he

450

was. And so he had flown to Boston from Washington, D.C., where he worked out of a suite of offices in a red-brick building on New Hampshire Avenue, to participate in the most splendid athletic tribute anyone in Boston had ever seen.

Nervous and perspiring, even a little intimidated, the dark-eyed man prepared to step to the podium. In other settings, before people with far different interests and tastes, he had often spoken of struggles, frequently saying things like, "Piece by piece, we are creating the democratic structures. Our key message is that democracy should be a way of life. But democracy is not an easy way to live. It's messy and noisy. And you need to accommodate yourself to it. But at the same time, democracy is not the enemy. Democracy is law and order. So we are moving in that direction, to educate our people. And we are moving to reform our economy. But it is all a very slow process, and this is a transition period."

Those kind of speeches came easily for the dark-eyed man. But this speech in the FleetCenter made him apprehensive. He had so much to say about Bill Russell, but had only been granted five minutes and had never faced so many glittering heroes and celebrities. He had prepared carefully, writing and rewriting the text of his talk to make it just right. While he spoke English superbly, he coated it with Georgian, and sometimes English words spoken by Georgians came out with unintended meanings. He did not want to innocently say, for example, "I *blame* Bill Russell, who *poisoned* me into becoming an admirer of this wonderful country," when what he really meant was, "I *credit* Bill Russell, who *influenced* me into becoming an admirer of this wonderful country." He labored hard so that he could convey precisely what Bill Russell had meant to him.

When his turn at the podium arrived, the man introduced himself as Tedo Japaridze, and then he started to talk about his youth. He had been born, he explained, in a place called Tbilisi, Georgia, in the former Soviet Union. Georgia, he went on to say, was an ancient land of myths and legends made famous by Greek mythology. In this unfamiliar Georgia, Jason and the Argonauts sought the Golden Fleece and Zeus chained Prometheus to a mountain. And then Tedo Japaridze told the audience about how, as a young man, he had watched his father listen intently to strange radio transmissions from the Voice of America. Some of those transmissions had featured the exploits of a tall, skinny, American basketball star named Bill Russell. Tedo Japaridze added with great flourish that he had been afraid Soviet authorities would

451

discover that he listened to foreign broadcasts — it was a high crime — but that, like his father, he had been unable to pull himself away from the mesmerizing accounts of Russell's feats on the court. Russell had almost personally destroyed the great Soviet national team at the 1956 Olympic Games in Melbourne, and then he had gone on to wage tremendous battles with Chamberlain while starring for the Boston Celtics. Tedo Japaridze had listened to all of it.

Now hanging on his tale, the audience listened as Tedo Japaridze described how he had done exactly as generations of American youngsters had done — imitate his hero. After listening to Voice of America transmissions, he had gone to the streets of Tbilisi and played basketball, pretending to be Bill Russell, only imagining what Russell must really look like. Georgia did not have television in those years, and so the words from the Voice of America and an active imagination provided Tedo Japaridze his only clues.

Tedo Japaridze loved to tell stories, a passion he inherited from his father, and as a boy he had regaled his Georgian friends with many stories about Bill Russell — how high he jumped, how he blocked shots, how he battled the famous Chamberlain. And then Tedo Japaridze said:

"The most fascinating story about Bill Russell belongs to a friend of mine, who told me once, 'Bill Russell reached the basket with his foot!' And I said, 'Are you crazy?' But this friend, he insisted it was true and this became one of the biggest legends about Bill Russell, that he could reach the basket with his foot."

L to R: Tedo Japaridze, Bill Russell, Bob Walsh, and Tamaz Chikhladze

Tedo Japardize explained to the FleetCenter audience that from that day forward Bill Russell had become ingrained in his imagination, and that his interest in Russell inspired him to learn more about America and democratic institutions.

"I started reading books," Tedo Japaridze said. "I read Mark Twain, O'Henry, James Fenimore Cooper, Jack London. I started researching facts about America, its history, culture, and music and, of course, its people. I became a fan of jazz, although this was also forbidden. And the person who provoked my professional interest toward your country happened to be Bill Russell. And later, I broadened my knowledge about America — its political systems and institutions, its market economy, and the fundamental values on which America is based. And always, Bill Russell was permanently with me, pushing me, even without knowing how deeply he influenced me."

Tedo Japaridze had subsequently graduated from college and learned to speak English. He took advanced courses in Moscow, studying the American presidency, absorbing everything he could about the United States at the Canadian-American Institute, a top think tank. And then, when the Soviet Union broke apart, he had come to America where, after some years, he had finally met his hero, Bill Russell. The introduction occurred in a hotel room in Cleveland, Ohio, during NBA All-Star Weekend, the same weekend the National Basketball Association presented and honored the fifty greatest players in its history.

Tedo Japaridze had met Russell through Bob Walsh, who had known Russell since the late 1960s. Tedo had befriended Bob a few years earlier when Bob's business and humanitarian interests took him to Georgia. Bob and Tedo now attended many special basketball events together — NBA All-Star games, Final Fours — and when Bob had learned of Tedo's story about Russell, he had wanted Russell to hear it. So Bob had introduced perhaps two of his most disparate friends, and Russell had loved what he heard.

"When I finally met my legend I almost died!" Tedo told the FleetCenter audience. "Here I am, in front of this incredible person, and he has no idea about this crazy Georgian kid who imitated him. I crunched down! I wanted to say something but I didn't know what to say and so I started telling him a story. And I said, 'Mr. Russell, you know, I was a child and I listened to these Voice of America transmissions. And they tell these stories about the Olympic Games and NBA. And before that, I had gotten some other stories from my father's friends who used to be members of our international team.' And then I started telling Bill Russell about how famous he was in Georgia and recalled how I and my friends had made up many legends about him.

"'Legends?' Russell inquired.

"'Yes, legends, fairytales.'"

"'What kind of fairytales?'

"'You know, there are many, but the most popular fairytale is that you were able to reach with your foot to the basket.'

"'Young man, that's not a fairytale. It's true.'

"Bill Russell tells me he has been high jumper and he can do this! Again, I almost died! So after this I went back to Georgia. I take my son and we go to the mountains for a week, but how can you hide in Georgia? Friends learn you are there. And I saw my friends, who are fifty years old now, and more. One is the state minister. Others are members of Parliament, others artists and doctors. They still lived with legends about Bill Russell, and some of them still believed this fantastic story about him. But I said to them, 'This legend about Bill Russell reaching the basket with his foot is true.' So Bill Russell destroyed my legends, because these stories which we used to create and still believed — they were true!"

Tedo Japaridze told the FleetCenter crowd that it was a simple but wonderful coincidence that today, May 26, was Georgia's Independence Day, and there could be no more appropriate day to be here, in Boston, honoring a man who had awakened his interest in the United States.

"Thank you for this incredible opportunity," Tedo said, looking at Russell. "You are the greatest ambassador of basketball."

As he left the podium, the Honorable Tedo Japaridze, Georgia's ambassador to the United States, received a standing ovation.

Peace Offerings

Timmy Walsh is popular in Georgia even with President Shevardnadze, who spoke of Timmy in a speech in Washington, D.C., at the NATO meetings. My request is that Timmy serve as "Honorary Ambassador" for the Peace Conference. He already has helped bridge the gap between children around the world.

> *– Tedo Japaridze, Georgian Ambassador*
> *to the United States,*
> *Washington, D.C.*

*H*e entered the conference chamber through a rear door wearing a light blue suit and red silk tie, wisps of unruly white hair sprouting above a face tempered by seven decades of unfathomable experience. Commanding his sanctum, Eduard Amvrosiyevich Shevardnadze paused, nodding with a faint smile as his fierce, hazel eyes ferreted over the several Americans who stood waiting to shake his hand. If this day was typical, Shevardnadze had assumed a seat in an armored Mercedes Benz, a gift from the German government, shortly after 8 a.m. and embarked on a twelve-minute, high-speed ride to his office in downtown Tbilisi. He would remain there until well after 10 p.m. before returning to a hillside residence guarded by soldiers ever ready to call down the furies at the least whiff of trouble. A workaholic, Shevardnadze rarely varied his routine, nor did he ever leave Georgia for more than three or four days at a time, lest the country fracture in his absence.

Bob Walsh marveled at Shevardnadze's grit. A man of great personal charm and unsparing ruthlessness, Shevardnadze had endured a civil war and dodged nineteen recorded assassination plots, including two full-fledged attempts, during a decade in the Machiavellian warren of Georgian politics. Shevardnadze had long ago developed a rat's sense of when to strike and when to retreat, but Bob still wondered how the man coped with so many problems. For all of Shevardnadze's efforts, Georgia's democratic institutions remained weak and flimsy. And yet, either through guile, or the force of his personality, or both, Shevardnadze had managed to keep propped up what most observers in the West saw as an irrational house of political cards. Bob's respect for Shevardnadze's efforts had prompted him to prevail upon U.S. Congressman Norm Dicks of Washington State to nominate the Georgian president for the Nobel Peace Prize. In Bob's opinion, no one deserved it more. Any leader with less resolve than Shevardnadze would have been dead a long time ago, or looking for a place to hide.

This was not the first time Bob had speculated over how Shevardnadze governed in an atmosphere of such ancient vendettas and historical paranoias, in a region in which a well-placed bribe seldom escaped an open palm. Shevardnadze's own country was tough enough to deal with, but his neighborhood sometimes made the Balkans seem like Disneyland. Georgia enjoyed decent relations with Azerbaijan, its neighbor to the east, but Georgians generally loathed Armenia, their neighbor to the south. The Azeris had warred with Armenia over Armenia's occupation of Nagorno-Karabakh, an ethnically steaming enclave on the Azeri-Armenian border. Christian Armenia detested mainly Muslim Azerbaijan, irrationally convinced, among other things, that the Azeris had set off the 1988 Armenian earthquake with an underground nuclear test.

Northeast of Azerbaijan, Kazakhstan had fallen under the spell of president Nursultan Nazarabyev, who had also made himself head of Kazakhstan's Supreme Court, granted himself the power to dissolve the Kazakh parliament at will, and placed his daughter and son-in-law in charge of the Kazakh media to ensure there would never be any mention of the country's mined roads, environmental poisoning, and appalling human rights record. Next door to Kazakhstan, Uzbekistan president Islam Karimov had become a "person of interest" to Amnesty International, Human Rights Watch, and the United Nations Torture Committee for a rash of political executions. Next door to Uzbekistan, Turkmenistan seemed to exist at the whim of Saparamurad Niyazov, a cartoon dictator who lived in the capital city of Ashkhabad

Bob Walsh and Eduard Shevardnadze greet Kakha Gvelesiani in Shevardnadze's office

in a place locally described as the "pink pleasure palace." After declaring his "genetic right" to rule Turkmenistan for life, Mr. Niyazov changed his name to Saparamurad Turkmenbashi ("Chief of all Turkmen"), outlawed all political parties except his own, and erected, on top of the Arch of Neutrality that rises from a downtown plaza, a 120-foot gold-plated statue of himself that rotates to follow the sun. Turkmenbashi's photograph — he leers with the proprietary grin of a whorehouse owner — appeared on Turkmenistan currency, the manat, and adorned banners that streamed from every public building. Turkmenbashi had not only renamed a Caspian Sea port city after himself, changing Krasnovodsk into "Turkmenbashi," he had named a meteorite in his honor after it smashed into the northern part of the country. Despite the exotic trappings with which he surrounded himself, Turkmenbashi presided over a calamity: Turkmenistan had the highest mortality rate, the highest unemployment rate, and the lowest literacy rate among the fifteen former Soviet republics.

The root of the chaos enveloping Shevardnadze went far deeper than the neighborhood tyrants who posed as democratically elected presidents. It started with Russia's insistence on controlling the flow of oil and natural gas through a multi-veined network of pipelines from the Caspian Sea so that it could extend its sphere of influence to the

Balkans, Mediterranean, and Middle East. Russia had attacked Chechnya in 1994 largely to ensure control of a pipeline from Baku, via Grozny, the Chechen capital, to the Russian city of Tikhoretsk. Russia had supported the Abkhazian uprising in Georgia to scuttle Georgia's plans to serve as a transit corridor for Caspian oil and gain control over the long Black Sea coastline. And Russia, refusing to be evicted, maintained military bases in Georgia to protect that interest.

To achieve its political and economic ends, Russia hounded Shevardnadze unmercifully. Shevardnadze believed the first assassination attempt on his life, a car bombing that forced him to wear a hearing aid ever after, occurred in part because he refused to cancel a pipeline project beneficial to Georgia. Russia capriciously cut off natural gas supplies to Georgia to undermine Shevardnadze's power base inside his own borders, a strategy that had the desired effect. Hundreds of people had recently taken to Tbilisi streets to protest the city's ongoing electricity shortages, many clamoring for Shevardnadze to resign if he could not guarantee uninterrupted power.

Russia constantly sought to undermine Shevardnadze in less obvious ways. It exempted residents in Abkhazia and Ossetia, two autonomous republics, from visa requirements imposed on other Georgian residents to create cracks in Shevardnadze's credibility. The Russians also concocted a clever story that Chechen rebels had started to operate in Georgian territory. By making that claim, the Russians laid a foundation for justifying their own military intervention in Georgia. The Russians even resorted to dirty tricks. Once, Shevardnadze had been flying home from a meeting in Turkey when his pilot told him that the two Georgian Air Force jets that normally escorted his plane to guard against airborne attack were nowhere to be seen. Only later did Shevardnadze discover the jets could not fly because sand had been poured into their engines. Shevardnadze blamed the Russians.

Bob couldn't help but feel perplexed over the degree to which the Russians meddled in Georgia's affairs when the Russians couldn't resolve the messes they had made inside their own borders. The average Russian male now had a life expectancy of just fifty-seven years, down from sixty-two in 1985, when Russians first heard the word *perestroika*. True, Russians had been terrorized by plagues, famines, environmental catastrophes, sieges, schisms, purges, and nuclear meltdowns, but many of their own problems were self-inflicted. One in particular represented lunacy unique to Russia. In fact, nothing in Bob's mind so eloquently symbolized Russia's inability to help itself as its failure to find lyrics to go with Mikhail Glinka's "Patriotic Song," Russia's national anthem — but not for a lack of trying. Russia adopted Glinka's 1833 composition as its anthem following the collapse of the Soviet Union. Over the next decade, dozens of poets, composers, and high government commissions proposed hundreds of different texts. But the Russian government could not agree on a final version, leaving, among other things, its Olympic athletes with no words to sing on victory podiums. The issue had been studied by Russia's State Duma, the lower house of Parliament, the Ministry of Culture, and Vladimir Putin's administration, and still no one could come up with precisely the right words.

Unfortunately, Russia stood equally inept when big events cleaved the nation. The submarine Kursk had gone down a few months earlier in the Barents Sea, kindling an old Soviet habit. President Vladimir Putin remained silent for five days — Gorbachev waited eighteen days in 1986 before acknowledging the Chernobyl disaster — before publicly addressing the fate of the 118-man crew apparently doomed to the deep. During the crisis, as relatives of the sailors waited news of their fathers, sons, and brothers, Putin hectored, bullied, and resisted all international offers of help. Instead, he vacationed on the Black Sea, named ambassadors to Chile and Jamaica, and even sent birthday greetings to an actress. Although Putin proclaimed his government capable of handling the Kursk disaster, it bungled the situation majestically. And the real reason, Bob suspected, was that the Russians probably had nuclear weapons aboard the submarine that they wanted to keep secret. Either that, or Putin did not want the woeful condition of the sub exposed to the world.

"Nice to see you again, Mr. President," Bob said.

"Welcome," Shevardnadze said through his interpreter, wrapping his massive arms around Bob, the bear hug almost swallowing him.

Shevardnadze didn't have to be informed about the reason for Bob's visit. He had already endorsed Bob's newest project in a letter Bob carried with him. It said:

Mr. Bob Walsh, Chairman
Organizing Committee of the International Peace Forum

I was pleased to hear that the National Peace Foundation and Bob Walsh Enterprises, in cooperation with the Georgian Youth

Foundation, are organizing an International Peace Festival to focus on alternatives to violence. You and your organizations have made important contributions to peace building, democracy, and economic development in our region. With your help, we have kept the Southern Caucasus from becoming another Balkans. I want to ask you to continue working on this initiative and inviting the people of good will to join in this great peace building enterprise.

Sincerely,

Eduard Shevardnadze

Introduced to the Peace Festival by Mamuka Tsereteli, the executive director of the America-Georgia Business Development Council, Bob had subsequently been asked by Stephen P. Strickland of the sponsoring National Peace Foundation, a Washington, D.C-based organization that carried out conflict resolution programs in the United States and at the international level, to chair the Festival's steering committee.

At first, and mainly because he had become so occupied with the rearing of his son, Timmy, Bob had been reluctant to get involved. But the more he thought about it, the more convinced he became that the Peace Festival, designed to promote political, social, and economic stability in Georgia, Armenia, and Azerbaijan, could play an important role in the future of the Caucasus. It also had the potential, Bob recognized, to become the most significant project of his career, especially considering the high-stakes oil game going on in the region and the critical part Georgia played in it. So Bob had agreed to throw his professional efforts into the Festival, and the steering committee had emerged with a list of people it hoped would serve on an advisory board: former Secretary of State James Baker, Archbishop Desmond Tutu, ex-President Jimmy Carter, the Dalai Lama, philanthropist George Soros, and Ted Turner of Time Warner.

To clarify how the Peace Festival ought to be structured, Bob had turned to Jarlath Hume, with whom he had organized the 1990 Goodwill Games. Jarlath prepared a paper outlining potential themes, advising that Bob consider organizing a series of forums and lectures that examined conflict points around the globe — India and Pakistan, South Africa, Northern Ireland, North Korea — with the goal of developing practical ways to manage and resolve conflicts.

As Bob explained to Shevardnadze, the Festival would be held in Tbilisi over the course of a week and unite world leaders, Nobel Peace laureates, and student ambassadors for a series of discussions on topics important to the Caucasus, including business and social development, and especially conflict resolution. During the Festival, Tbilisi would also host international film and arts festivals, several musical concerts, and a sporting event. Many of the important Festival guests would stay at the soon-to-open Tbilisi Marriott.

"In addition," Bob advised Shevardnadze, "I've started to compile a list of special people I'd like to invite. All of them have taken notable actions in the name of peace building. They would provide Festival-goers with great examples of how individual efforts on behalf of peace building can make a positive difference."

The first name on Bob's list: Lynne Cox, the marathon swimmer from California. Cox's successful crossing of the Bering Strait had helped knock down a border between the United States and former Soviet Union that had stood for forty years. Cox had completed several other peace-building swims since the Bering Strait, her last major efforts occurring in 1994 when she navigated part of the Red Sea between Egypt and Israel, and then opened a border on the Jordan River between Israel and Jordan. Cox had also worked for several years hoping to get approval to perform a series of swims in the conflict-prone states in the former Yugoslavia.

Bob wanted to invite Jim Whittaker, who had orchestrated the 1990 International Peace Climb of Mount Everest, and Gary Furlong, a Seattle attorney who had led a team of physicians and medical personnel into Armenia following the 1988 earthquake. Furlong had recently become president of the Seattle-Tashkent (Uzbekistan) Sister City Committee.

"We believe," Bob told Shevardnadze, "that we have created the framework for a very successful Festival."

In order for Bob to pull it off, he needed Shevardnadze's continued diplomatic support, similar endorsements from the governments of Azerbaijan and Armenia, and $6 million in funding he hoped to acquire largely from the international oil companies headquartered in the Azeri capital of Baku. As he had with the Goodwill Games, Bob also required seed money from the United States government and told Shevardnadze he felt reasonably confident he could get it.

After Bob left Shevardnadze's office, he placed two telephone calls, the first to David Gogol at Sagamore Associates in Washington,

D.C. Bob required Gogol's help in crafting the federal funding request. The second call went to Tedo Japaridze, the Georgian ambassador to the United States who held the key to U.S. government funding: an introduction to a former chairman of the Joint Chiefs of Staff. If Bob could sway the decorated general, the Peace Festival had a chance.

From The Cradle

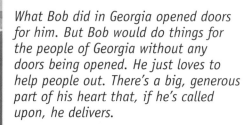

What Bob did in Georgia opened doors for him. But Bob would do things for the people of Georgia without any doors being opened. He just loves to help people out. There's a big, generous part of his heart that, if he's called upon, he delivers.

– Gretchen Nelson, former employee,
Bob Walsh Enterprises,
Seattle, Washington

*A*fter they exhausted every natural and surgical option available and nothing worked, Paul Schulte and Nancy Welts of Seattle, Washington, started to seriously consider the possibility of adoption. They especially had their hearts set on a little girl and entertained the notion of looking toward China for one until Nancy encountered a friend of hers. Suzanne Lavendar reminded Nancy that Bob Walsh had helped facilitate a couple of adoptions in Russia, and also had, in concert with Dr. Robert Day, the lead administrator at the Fred Hutchinson Cancer Research Center, once explored the idea of opening an adoption agency in Moscow. It hadn't worked out, but Dr. Day had adopted two little Russian girls. Another of Bob's former colleagues, Jim Sheldon, who had served the Seattle Organizing Committee as its vice president of sports during the Goodwill Games, had also adopted in Russia, receiving two boys. They had come from different Moscow orphanages and, remarkably, had turned out to be brothers.

Both Suzanne and Nancy had lengthy ties to Bob. Suzanne toiled for two years at Bob Walsh Enterprises in the early 1990s as a project director, her most vivid experience the Europe-America 500 Space Flight. Nancy knew Bob through her brother, Rick Welts, one of Bob's first employees at Bob Walsh & Associates, and also through her own work as the one-time director of public relations for the Seattle SuperSonics. Intrigued by the possibility that Bob could make the adoption process a personal experience, rather than the bureaucratic one she knew she would endure if she went through an agency, Nancy set up an appointment.

"My ties now are in Georgia," Bob advised her. "They're the greatest people in the world. I'd like to see if we couldn't help you find a Georgian child."

Most individuals who sought to adopt in the former Soviet Union utilized such services as Adoptive Families of America or the National Adoption Information Clearinghouse, agencies that ran prospective parents through a gauntlet of expensive and time-consuming hoops. The document-gathering process alone gobbled up six months, and then it often took a year or more for a child to become available. In addition to paying agency fees ranging from $15,000 to $50,000, adoptive parents could count on spending thousands of dollars in cash on facilitators, drivers, translators, and local bureaucrats who might gum the works without the proper incentive.

Georgia enforced stricter out-of-country adoption requirements than any former Soviet republic because First Lady Nanuli Shevardnadze had made the issue her personal crusade. During a speech at the United Nations a year before Nancy consulted Bob, Mrs. Shevardnadze delivered a rabid denunciation of "selling our children abroad." Undaunted by Mrs. Shevardnadze's rhetoric, Bob telephoned Nelly Saroyan in Tbilisi, requesting her assistance.

Bob and Nelly had once collaborated on securing an eye operation for a ten-year-old Tbilisi girl, Ia Mirotadze, and orchestrated a series of Boeing relief flights to assist victims of Georgia's civil strife. Bob knew that if anyone could make a Georgian adoption happen, Nelly could. And Nelly launched her inquiries by stalking the Georgian ministries of education, health, and internal affairs, where she discovered that Paul and Nancy's sole hope of adoption was to secure a humanitarian exception, which meant a child who required medical attention not readily available in Georgia.

Over the next few weeks, Paul and Nancy gathered up and sent to Nelly all their tax returns, health certificates, photographs, and personal biographies. A few weeks after that, Nelly called, summoning them to Tbilisi, where they arrived, Bob in tow. They had no idea what to expect, but what happened first unnerved them. During a walk near Eduard Shevardnadze's personal residence, Nelly launched into a monolog about infants who suffered physical and mental disabilities, obliquely suggesting that Paul and Nancy consider adopting an impaired or disadvantaged child. Neither had come prepared to deal with such a scenario, nor

Nancy Welts, left, and Nelly Saroyan in Tbilisi, Georgia

could they determine whether Nelly was priming them to make such a decision. But they didn't have to wait long to find out.

Three days later, Paul, Nancy, Bob, and Nelly entered Nanuli Shevardnadze's office. A large, imposing woman, reportedly given to bouts of severe depression, Mrs. Shevardnadze had a reputation for being tough and professional — tougher, some believed, than her famous husband. After Paul, Nancy, Bob, and Nelly had been introduced to a retinue of Mrs. Shevardnadze's functionaries, the First Lady and Bob chatted about the status of the Tbilisi Marriott and Mtatsminda Plateau projects, their conversation segueing after several minutes into the business at hand.

"Who are these people you brought with you?" Mrs. Shevardnadze asked, with Nelly translating.

Bob knew that Mrs. Shevardnadze knew exactly who Paul and Nancy were and precisely why they were there.

"Mrs. Shevardnadze," Bob explained, "these are the people I've been telling you about. They are here seeking to adopt a child.

They've sent in all their paperwork. You have background information on them."

Mrs. Shevardnadze considered Bob's statement.

"You seem like a nice couple," she said at last. "But we don't allow these kind of adoptions. We love our children and don't give them up easily. You should know that I've spoken about this at the United Nations. There are 15,000 Georgian couples that want to adopt children. We love our children, and we're not going to let them go."

As Nancy welled with tears and gripped Paul's left hand, he leaned toward to Nelly.

"What's transpiring here?"

"Don't say anything."

"If, however," Mrs. Shevardnadze continued, "you want to come and live in Georgia we could probably work something out. We also have a number of children who are mentally or physically damaged. You can have all you want of those to take home with you."

Mrs. Shevardnadze then suggested that Paul and Nancy visit Tbilisi's largest orphanage. One boy there, she said, had no arms or legs. Another child suffered from mental retardation. And a little girl with developmental problems had been placed in the orphanage. She might interest them.

The meeting lasted just over an hour, leaving Paul and Nancy deflated and believing that adopting a healthy child was out of the question. When they reached the street outside Mrs. Shevardnadze's office, Paul turned to Bob.

"Well, I guess that's it."

"Maybe not."

"The president's wife just said no."

"Well, let's wait and see."

"There's one child at the orphanage," interjected Nelly, "that isn't too bad."

Nancy had been intrigued by Mrs. Shevardnadze's reference to the little girl who apparently had developmental problems. But she didn't want to get her hopes up.

"I don't think I'm up for this," Paul said.

"You should go to the hospital," suggested Nelly.

"Nelly, this isn't what we signed up for. We aren't doing anything humanitarian here. We are hoping to get a healthy girl. It doesn't matter what flavor. I don't know about going to the orphanage. I don't think I want to put Nancy through that. Do you really think we should go?"

"You must go."

When Bob left for another meeting across town, Nelly, Paul, and Nancy drove to the Ministry of Education to secure some paperwork, then arrived at Tbilisi's Children's Experimental Hospital about an hour later. Paul had heard accounts of the grim archipelago of orphanages in the former Soviet Union. Many had been identified by organizations such as Human Rights Watch as little more than bleak warehouses in which children were exposed to cruelty and neglect, in which some infants were fed and changed but received no stimulation, while others were left to lie half-naked in their own filth. Most orphans, considered defective whether they were nor not, received no education and minimal health care.

The Children's Experimental Hospital fortunately failed to live up to Paul and Nancy's grim expectations. The nurses seemed attentive and caring. And while the orphanage itself appeared to Paul like something out of 1920, it was clean and brightly lit. Nancy noticed the bassinets and pink and blue color scheme.

"They have a ward of children here who are mentally damaged," Nelly explained. "They want you to look at these children."

"I don't think I can do it," Nancy said.

"Well," said Paul, "you wait here and I'll go."

The ward contained about a dozen infants, most suffering from cerebral palsy and Down's syndrome, all lying in cribs with vacuous stares. Paul didn't know quite what to do, how he was supposed to react, or whether the nurses were gauging his reaction to the infants presented to him.

After Paul and Nelly rejoined Nancy, Nelly advised them that the hospital had another ward filled with children who had physical impairments.

"You should also see these children," said Nelly.

Nancy remained outside while Paul observed one little boy who had no arms or legs. Several children essentially had flippers for arms, and some appeared to be afflicted with spina bifida.

The third ward contained a dozen to fifteen children. One child had only one arm. Another boy apparently couldn't hear, and another couldn't see. As Paul surveyed this group, almost certain there was no child here he wanted to adopt, his eyes suddenly riveted on the center of the room where a large playpen held seven or eight children. There, in the middle of them, a little girl seemed curiously out of place. She appeared to be about seven months old and didn't have much hair, but she had bright blue eyes that twinkled. Unlike the other children, she smiled and, Paul noticed, reacted to movement and noise.

"This one is not too bad," one of the nurses told Paul.

After the nurses got the little girl dressed and brought her out to show Nancy, they explained that the child had been born to a young Georgian woman who had abandoned her. The nurses also said the little girl had a litany of things wrong with her internally, including developmental and motor skills problems, but hastened to add that the problems could probably be corrected in the United States. Georgia, the nurses added, did not have the resources or medical competency to help the little girl.

Neither Paul nor Nancy could see anything visibly wrong with her. Paul waved a finger in front of her eyes and she quickly followed it. She laughed easily, seemed to have a gregarious personality, and appeared completely healthy.

"She was adorable," Paul would recount later. "She had this internal spirit that would not be denied. When we looked at her we couldn't believe what the nurses told us. But, of course, we couldn't be certain since her problems were supposedly internal. As we looked at her we thought an adoption might work, or it might not work. We didn't know."

Nancy couldn't bring herself to hold the little girl, afraid that she might become too attached. Then one of the nurses produced a document, written in Georgian, and asked Paul and Nancy to sign it. They declined, needing more time to think about what they had witnessed in the fifteen minutes they had just spent in Tbilisi's largest orphanage.

"She's not too bad," one of the nurses repeated. "She might not be here when you come back."

En route home, during a layover in London, Paul and Nancy located an Internet café where they started to research the medical problems the nurses had ascribed to the little girl with the bright, blue eyes. Paul thought, but did not immediately confide to Nancy, that he did not believe the adoption would take place. Despite the little girl's outward appearance, it seemed too risky. Nancy thought, but did not immediately confide to Paul, that they had to adopt the little girl despite all the things the nurses had told them.

Paul and Nancy subsequently consulted a pediatrician and related what they knew about the little girl's alleged medical condition. When the doctor alleviated their concerns, essentially telling them that in his opinion the little girl had been misdiagnosed, they made the decision to adopt. Nancy had already been mulling over names, and particularly favored "Lexie," short for Alexandra.

A week later, having been summoned again by Nelly, Paul arrived in Tbilisi for the purpose of appearing before a tribunal of three Georgian judges, all women, to explain why he wanted to adopt and why he believed he and Nancy made suitable parents. Paul was told that if the adoption were granted, he would have to wait two weeks before it became final to allow time for anyone to come forward to object. Paul planned to return to Seattle after his court appearance, then fly back to Tbilisi with Nancy to collect Lexie if no complications developed. But as Paul prepared to face the court, he discovered complications had already surfaced. One of the three judges had expressed adamant opposition to the adoption.

"At first, she was a most terrible woman," Nelly explained later. "She just said no, no, no. And she didn't say why. But when she was told about the baby's medical condition she was willing to do it and happy to do it."

Paul then learned through Nelly that two other women, women Paul never met, had also expressed misgivings about the adoption. Fortunately, neither came forward to object officially. The best Paul could figure was that they either opposed the adoption on moral grounds — many Georgians considered it the equivalent of buying and selling babies — or had considered trying to position themselves to make a few dollars on the transaction. Such a maneuver wouldn't have surprised him. One of the men affiliated with Lexie's orphanage, who couldn't have earned more than a few hundred lari a week, drove a $40,000 SUV.

Following Paul's appearance before the tribunal, and after he and Nelly surmounted a flood of procedural roadblocks, the court approved the adoption. But then a new complication developed when Eduard Shevardnadze's government suddenly became embroiled in a military crisis. Led by Akaki Eliava, a former supporter of Zviad Gamsakhurdia, renegade army troops seized tanks on the outskirts of Kutaisi, the capital city of Imereti, a province that in the sixth century B.C. had been the heart of the Kingdom of Colchis. Eliava's forces kidnapped Georgian Security Minister Djmemal Gakhokidze, two generals, and Shevardnadze's personal representative in the district. Three soldiers died in an exchange of gunfire. Later that evening, the very evening the adoption was approved, Paul watched Shevardnadze go ballistic on television about the infamy of the military uprising.

The situation sufficiently rattled Nelly, who feared that a state of emergency might be declared, that she made an instant decision.

"I think you should take Lexie home with you now," she told Paul.

"How? We have to wait two weeks and I can't stay here that whole time. I have to go home."

"No, I think you should stay. Let me see what I can do to accelerate the program so you can take Lexie home right now."

Among other things, they had to obtain a passport for Lexie, but a clerk at the United States Embassy balked at issuing one on the spot. Nelly, clearly wanting to strangle the woman, managed to prevail. Then they went to the Russian Embassy to acquire visas that would permit them to enter Moscow, from which Paul intended to fly to the United States with Lexie. But the Russian they encountered insisted it would take two weeks to process the visas, sending Nelly into another paroxysm of table pounding.

Paul had rarely witnessed such a determined woman and did not yet understand that when Nelly Saroyan got it in her mind to do something, seas figuratively parted. Once, when British Airways misplaced a piece of Tbilisi-bound luggage that belonged to one of Bob's traveling companions, Nelly made several British air officials rue the day their mothers evicted them.

"We must have the visas today," Nelly insisted to the clerk.

"Two weeks," replied the Russian, equally determined.

"No, today!"

Nelly knew how to take matters into her own hands. She barged into an embassy office, telling its befuddled occupant that she had to have a visa immediately and wouldn't take no for an answer.

"If you did that in America," Paul told her, "they would throw you out."

"It's the only way to get things done," Nelly replied. "It's the way the KGB used to do things."

Paul got his visa, but not before he paid nearly five times the ordinary cost of one, about $40. That done, Paul, Nelly, and Lexie cleared Georgian customs and flew to Moscow, registering at The Radisson Hotel. Paul quickly ventured to the United States Embassy, where he confronted a Marine guard stationed behind bullet-proof glass. Paul picked up the telephone and informed the guard he desired to process a foreign adoption.

The Marine tapped his keyboard for a few minutes, finally looking up.

"Sorry, you're not in the computer. You haven't completed the prerequisites for immigration. You will not be cleared and you will not take this child to the United States."

Paul and Nancy had furnished Nelly all the paperwork she requested to satisfy adoption requirements in Georgia. But they hadn't filled out the necessary federal paperwork that would allow Lexie to enter the United States, nor had they completed a mandatory home study, or fulfilled all Washington State requirements. As Paul stood there helplessly, trying to figure out what to do next, a State Department official joined the Marine. After quizzing Paul for a few minutes, he shook his head.

Paul Schulte with daughter "Lexie"

"We can't let you through," he told Paul. "You take her back to Georgia and get your paperwork completed. Then you can come back and we will process you through."

"How long will this take?"

"Probably six months."

"Six months? I've got to take her now."

With Paul having brought Lexie this far, he didn't want to return to the United States without her. Neither did he want to send Lexie back to Georgia with Nelly. Given the political climate there, and fearful that the two women Nelly had mentioned might object to the adoption, he suspected he might never see Lexie again. But the United States Embassy would not let him proceed. On top of that, his Russian visa was only good for a few days, he still worried that if Lexie didn't receive medical attention her development might be impaired, and he had come down with a severe case of the flu. He returned to The Raddison and called Nancy, then Bob.

"We got big problems here," he told him. "They are telling me to send Lexie and Nelly back to Georgia and for me to come to the United States. What should I do?"

"Don't do anything. Just hunker down."

Paul and Nelly hunkered. When Paul's visa expired, he didn't dare leave The Radisson. When he applied for, and received, a visa extension, he was informed he would not receive another one and to prepare to leave for the United States without Lexie. After a few days of getting nowhere at the Embassy, where Paul was constantly told no, come back, or wait, and in the middle of running up an $8,000 hotel tab, Paul felt like giving up. He had almost come to the conclusion he would not be able to get Lexie into the United States, at least not this time around, and maybe not ever.

"Don't worry about it," said Nelly, who burned up the telephone lines to Tbilisi, commanding each person she spoke with to conduct prayer vigils so the situation would be resolved favorably.

"Everyone prayed," Nelly later admitted. "Many people around the world prayed for this."

Paul could not be convinced prayer was the entire answer. The only way for Lexie to be cleared to enter the United States was if the State Department granted a "humanitarian parole," the basis for which was that she required immediate medical attention. The State Department had not been eager to do that, nor had the Immigration and Naturalization Service. While Paul waited for any positive development, he took Lexie for a physical exam and had her fingerprints recorded, both mandatory procedures.

"If you had gone through an agency and then paid your $25,000," one official told Paul, "you would have been routed right through."

What Paul didn't know was that Bob had started the routing

Nelly Saroyan and "Lexie" in Tbilisi, Georgia

472

process on his end. He had telephoned the office of Washington State Senator Slade Gorton, successfully persuading him to write letters of support to the State Department and INS. He had called David Gogol at Sagamore Associates, who assigned one of his operatives, Bernard Toon, to elicit the support of Washington State's congressional delegation.

More important, Bob had outlined the situation for Dick Smith, the Northwest's regional director of U.S. Customs and Immigration. Smith had played a key role in the security effort during the Goodwill Games, helped clear the way for Bob's first Russian wife, Nina, to enter the United States from Vancouver, and worked with Bob on security issues during the Europe-America 500 Space Flight.

When Bob called, Smith happened to be in Denver attending a conference, which turned out to be stroke of superb timing. Smith corralled some of his influential associates, including a key official based in Rome who handled customs issues in Russia and Eastern Europe, and convinced them that, despite the extraordinary circumstances, this adoption would not start a precedent and would allow the baby to receive the medical care she apparently required. He also said he would accept personal responsibility. Given Smith's credibility in the customs business, his colleagues decided to go along with it.

Nancy worked her own angles. Although told by a woman at a Seattle adoption agency that, under current circumstances, Lexie would never be permitted to fly from Moscow to the United States, Nancy refused to take no for an answer. She telephoned Washington State senators Gorton and Patty Murray, also securing a letter of support from Gorton. And then she walked that letter to U.S. Customs and Immigration in downtown Seattle, hoping to hand it off to Smith. But with Smith in Denver, she instead spoke to his assistant, Bob Coleman, who heard her out and promised to do whatever he could.

Nancy and Bob Coleman remained in contact throughout the following week. During one telephone call, he told her the case had three possible outcomes. The State Department would say no, it would decide not to decide, or it would grant Lexie a humanitarian parole.

"Two of the three are not in your favor," Coleman told Nancy.

Nine days after he arrived in Moscow, and on the day he was scheduled to return to the United States, Paul returned to the U.S. Embassy. He only had a few hours remaining before his flight left for America, and he still didn't know what was going to happen. After

473

Paul shuffled around the Embassy for nearly three hours, seemingly getting nowhere again, an official approached him.

"Go over to INS right now."

Paul walked across the hall, past the Marine guard, and stood in front of window No. 7. The curtain rose. A woman looked at Paul, quickly signed a piece of paper, and shoved it under the glass in Paul's direction.

"Go!" she said.

"What do you mean, go?"

"Leave right now."

Paul stared down at the piece of paper. The humanitarian parole had been granted.

"You better get to the airport right now," the woman repeated.

Paul bolted the Embassy, collected Nelly and Lexie, and raced toward the Moscow airport. When he arrived at the Delta counter, the Russian manning the desk told him that he hadn't yet paid for his ticket.

"But I have," protested Paul. "We paid $1,900 for a one-way ticket."

"The ticket is not paid for," replied the Russian firmly.

"This ticket was paid for in the United States and he's not going to pay for another one," Nelly excoriated him.

Nelly prevailed and Paul secured his ticket. But then he discovered he needed another document processed and soon found himself confronting a mid-level bureaucrat, who took Paul's paperwork and disappeared for forty-five minutes. When he returned, he remonstrated Paul.

"You should have been here three hours before the flight," he said. "You weren't here soon enough."

"I've got to go," Paul argued. "You won't let me stay. I've got this little girl. I've got to get on this airplane."

The Russian told Nelly that this new piece of documentation required a fee. When Paul checked his pockets, he discovered he had $300.

"It will cost $290," the Russian announced conveniently.

After the Russian took the money and walked into an inner office, Paul asked Nelly to go to the gate and hold the plane. After waiting for several agonizing minutes, Paul pushed a bell. The Russian finally returned and handed Paul a piece of paper.

"Go!" he commanded.

Holding Lexie, Paul dashed to the gate, relieved that Nelly had held the plane following a commotion with the gate attendant. He kissed Nelly goodbye and boarded the flight.

Later, after Paul and Nancy had Lexie examined, they learned that she had no physical problems of consequence, leaving both counting their blessings and recognizing that the unconventional adoption had occurred only because of Bob's friendship with Nelly, Bob's relationship with the Shevardnadzes, and his long association with Dick Smith. Paul and Nancy also came to understand that if they had followed procedures correctly, they probably would not have gotten Lexie. Doing it Bob and Nelly's way, the serendipitous approach, turned out to be exactly right.

Alexandra Saroyan Welts Schulte

Paul and Nancy named their new daughter Alexandra Saroyan Welts Schulte. It delighted Nelly Saroyan, enduring another winter in Tbilisi without electricity. Nelly still had a long wait for the miracle that would fix that.

Millennium Without Lights

I traveled with Bob to Tbilisi. It was a delightful and rare experience to see the respect and genuine feeling the Georgians had for Bob.

> — Tom Jernstedt, National Collegiate Athletic Association, Indianapolis, Indiana

*B*ob Walsh's fifty-fifth trip to Tbilisi, Georgia shook him up more than any he had taken there since civil war racked the republic. He couldn't encamp in his usual lodgings, the Krtsanisi Government Residence; it had no heat or electricity, the Russians having cut off Georgia's natural gas supplies. He couldn't venture out in the evenings to socialize with friends; the streets had suddenly turned dangerous. Even when Bob left the Metechi Palace Hotel during daylight hours, he felt comfortable doing so only in the company of bodyguards. Kidnappings and muggings had escalated in inverse proportion to Georgia's standard of living, which had dropped every year since the late-1990s, when euphoria over Eduard Shevardnadze's political and social reforms reached its peak. But each winter since, there had been a little less electricity than the winter before. Each year there had been more unemployment, and law-abiding Georgians had become less hopeful about their futures. Bob could see why. They had waited ten years for democracy to take root and their lives to improve, but things were worse now than they had been just two years earlier. But Bob remained the optimist. He had witnessed the shootings in Tbilisi nearly a decade earlier, and watched refugees stream into the city after starving in the mountains. The current situation bore no resemblance to that.

"This country still has all the economic and tourist potential I always thought it had," Bob had told Kristin Hayden. "Transition periods are always difficult. But I believe in Georgia and its future. Things will be better again. I will always come back here."

It was odd, Bob thought, how little Americans knew about the ramifications of the Soviet collapse, or how difficult the transition to democracy had been on former Soviet citizens. But then, it didn't surprise him much, either. Americans had, of course, cheered when all the walls tumbled, but the story had quickly given way to new and more enticing headlines. In the interim, enough Russians had immigrated legally to the United States to repopulate cities the size of Seattle or Phoenix. And the number of Russians who had entered America illegally probably stood at triple that. The Seattle metropolitan area alone had become home to more than 100,000 Russians, most of whom had likely never even heard of the place before the 1990 Goodwill Games. New York, Dallas, Las Vegas, and Reno contained significant new enclaves of Russians, and more than 3,000 Russians reportedly drove taxi cabs in Los Angeles, which also had a radio station that broadcast Dodgers games in Russian.

A couple of Bob's Russian friends now worked casino showrooms in Nevada and toured with Ringling Brothers. Misha Kalinin and his wife, Larissa, had relocated to America when Misha's stint with the Moscow Circus ended. After living with Bob and Milana Walsh for a year, they had settled first in Las Vegas, finally purchasing a home in the suburb of Henderson. An aerialist, Misha labored for a time in a show called *Spellbound* at Harrah's, then joined Ringling Brothers. Vilen "Willie" Golovko, the star of The Flying Cranes, moved his family to an apartment near Reno, where he found casino work before also going on tour with Ringling Brothers. Willie's apartment complex teemed with Russians.

Of the hundreds of thousands of Russians who swarmed — legally and illegally — into the United States after the end of the Cold War, none, as far as Bob knew, received a more dramatic introduction to America than Elana Arustamova. The daughter of two doctors, Elana departed Moscow for Seattle on August 13, 1991, in the company of several Soviet pilots who planned to participate in an air show at Payne Field in Everett, a city north of Seattle. Representing a new Russian sports marketing company, Elana intended to spend ten days in the Pacific Northwest before flying to Portugal to attend a basketball tournament. Five days after arriving in Everett, Elana found herself at a reception when a reporter approached her.

"What do you think of the situation in Russia?" he asked.

"I assume you mean all the changes, *perestroika* and all that," Elana began.

"No, not that," the reporter interrupted. "What do you think about what's happening with Gorbachev?"

"What about Gorbachev?"

"You know, the coup."

"Coup? What is 'coup'?"

"It's on CNN."

Elana located a television set.

"Suddenly," she admitted later, "my legs were absolutely shot."

Elana had planned to return to Moscow following her brief excursion to Portugal, but Gorbachev's house arrest changed everything. When Elana called home, her friends advised she not return for a while. The situation, they said, had turned too dangerous. Elana had arrived in the United States with enough money and clothes to sustain herself for two weeks. She still had an apartment, a car, and a husband in Moscow. By the time she saw him and Moscow again after nearly three years she would be divorced and Moscow would be transformed into a menagerie of convenience stores, strip malls, strip joints, fast-food outlets, gigantic billboards, neon signs, discos, coffee shops, boutiques, night clubs, vagrants, panhandlers, and drug dealers.

"It was unbelievable," Elana told Bob later. "I leave the Soviet Union, and when I finally go back I see Joe Camel next to the Kremlin."

Elana proved herself a survivor. After working as a translator during the Europe-America 500 Space Flight — her introduction to Bob Walsh — she found employment with a fishing company that did business in the former Soviet Union. A couple of years later, she

478

landed a job with a foundation that promoted Russian-American business opportunities.

"Of course, I am glad I came to America," Elana said later. "But things have not gone so well for the people I left behind."

Elana's parents, for example, had worked all their lives as doctors. Expecting to receive pensions from the Soviet government when they retired, they were instead cast aside after Communism crumbled, useless to anyone in the New Russia and too old to do anything about it.

"Neither of my parents has enough money to live on," Elana explained later. "My mother, who worked for thirty-seven years, makes $18 a month with her pension and is lucky if she gets paid. She spends all day going from one store to another trying to find food, trying to find the best deals. I bought her a condominium near the Volga River and that's where she lives. What she is going through is very unfair. She feels robbed. In the Soviet era she would have been paid and wouldn't have to worry about anything. There are a lot people like her, a lot of people who wish Communism would come back. What has happened to people in Russia is very sad."

"In first years of *perestroika*, Russian people were crazy for freedom," Willie Golovko told Bob one afternoon before Bob watched Willie perform with The Flying Cranes at the Reno Hilton. "Now freedom, but different problems. For some, life is better in Russia. For most, no. Ten percent of people have big money, 90 percent have no money. Before, in Soviet Union, everybody had some money, free medical, no worries. Now it's all worries, no money, no fun. It's same future for everybody."

Bob first met Sergei Sviridov during a meeting in which he introduced mountain climber Jim Whittaker to members of the USSR State Sports Committee. After the breakup, Sergei joined the Russian Olympic Committee. Sergei had been born in Crimea, which Nikita Khrushchev made part of the Ukraine in 1953.

"So when the Soviet Union split apart," Sergei recalled, "I worked in Moscow, but suddenly my parents and brother were living in a foreign country. When I want to go see them, I must go through customs to a place I was born. It's unnatural. Before all of this, we had one president, now we have fifteen. Before there was one ambassador to the United States, now there are fifteen. This has been disaster. Why should you destroy something, then rebuild it again? In America, people look at former Soviet Union and think it was great that it broke apart.

I think it's a crime. Maybe for American government it is better, but for people who live there it is not better. The whole world is opening borders and we closed them. This is stupid."

"The breakup is the worst thing that could have happened," reflected Alexander Kozlovsky, the former deputy of the USSR State Sports Committee who became vice president of the Russian Olympic Committee. "It's tragic what has happened in my country. The old way was better."

During his days at the USSR State Sports Committee, Kozlovsky frequently employed Helen Shiskana to perform translating services, sometimes assigning her to Bob Walsh.

"I hated Communism," Helen told Bob. "And fortunately life has turned out fantastic for me. From a material point of view, I'm definitely not begging. But if I didn't help my parents, they wouldn't make ends meet. People who are forty are kicked out on the streets. People who are older, well, our government hopes they will die from hunger or illness so they won't have to pay the bloody pension. In the Soviet Union we had poverty, but this new kind of poverty makes my blood boil and heart ache. But what can you do? Eighty percent of the country doesn't get paid for months. When the free market came people reeled with joy. But what happened

Helen Shiskana

was, we got this democracy and then had to pay with all kinds of shit."

"In the short run, it all seems so negative," added Irina Kibina, a translator during the Europe-America 500 Space Flight who later became deputy mayor of the Novgorod City Duma. "I'm still optimistic about the future. But unfortunately, before that, we must suffer because the country made a lot of mistakes, and many of the mistakes were paved by big blood. Our society was not ready for these changes."

"In my country," said Kakha Gvelesiani, who runs an Expo Center in Tbilisi, Georgia, "we have 55,000 doctors and Georgia needs 7,000 or 8,000. The mentalities of people are still not commercialized. At the same time, our government is not ready to solve the social problems. The United States built its society over lots of years. In former Soviet Union, republics were economically tied with each other. After the Soviet Union was destroyed, all economies of these states were destroyed. Society did not develop naturally. Many people have nothing to do, nowhere to go. But Georgia is still much more advanced than most places."

Vaso Margvelashvili, who introduced Bob to Georgia, could not find permanent work after the breakup or the training to prepare him to flourish in a free-market economy. Georgia could offer him little. It could not offer much to Nelly Saroyan, either. Nelly still lives in the same seventh-floor apartment, still hauls buckets of water up the stairs to fill her sink, bathtub, and toilet, and continues to live without electricity much of the winter. Nelly would like to move to the United States, but does not know how and is likely to stay tethered to her circumstances.

One Sunday afternoon, feeling sad over the daily plight of his Georgian friends, Bob traveled to the outskirts of Tbilisi in the company of Kristin Hayden and Aimee Shoemaker of Bob Walsh Enterprises to attend the funeral of Tengiz Chkonia, once head of Foreign Affairs at Georgia's Ministry of Health. Bob had been apprised of Chkonia's death by his son, David, a young man Bob hadn't heard from in a long time and, in fact, barely knew.

Some years earlier, Tengiz had asked if Bob would arrange financial assistance so that David could be educated in the United States. Bob agreed, taking care of David's enrollment at Earlham College in Richmond, Indiana, and personally paying a portion of his tuition. Bob also personally paid for Anna Kozlovsky, a daughter of Alexander Kozlovsky, and Iralki Tskhadadze, a Georgian, to study at Seattle University.

When Bob, Kristin, and Aimee arrived at the cemetery, built on terraced steps near a small church, they walked up a dirt mound where a couple of hundred mourners, including several high-ranking Georgian officials, had gathered around Tengiz's widow. When Bob approached to offer condolences, the widow burst into a crying jag that stunned Kristin and Aimee.

"When the widow saw Bob," Aimee said later, "she grabbed him and just wouldn't let go. She thanked him repeatedly for all that he had done for her son and her family and for coming to the funeral. She was really visibly affected by his presence. It obviously meant so much to her that Bob was there."

"The scene brought tears to my eyes," recalled Kristin. "It was just such a touching moment and so representative of what Bob had done in Georgia over all those years. Everybody there was struck by it."

That night, Bob, Kristin, and Aimee attended a *supra*, a traditional Georgian feast that also served, in this instance, as a wake. When Tengiz's widow spotted Bob sitting at one of the five rows of tables, she again lost emotional control and clutched at him, thanking him profusely. Her reaction convinced Kristin and Aimee that Bob's legacy in Georgia rested not in hotels or other commercial

Aimee Shoemaker, left, and Kristin Hayden

endeavors. They saw it summarized in the appreciative face of a Georgian widow.

At another *supra* Bob and Kristin attended, Bob briefly left the room. When he returned, he asked Kristin, who always took care of passports and cash, if she had any money.

"I need $100," said Bob.

"For what? What do you need $100 for?"

"Just give me $100."

During a brief interrogation, Kristin learned that Bob wanted to give the money to an old woman Bob had just met. She cleaned toilets and, Kristin suspected, probably made no more than ten lari, or $5, a month.

"It's too much," Kristin argued. "Way too much. This woman doesn't even know who you are. And you'll never even see her again. Stop throwing money around."

As Bob protested, Kristin recalled a passage written by the Dalai Lama. It said something to the effect that it is easy to spoil friends and the people you love, but true kindness sometimes demands the spoiling of strangers.

Bob finally got his way, and as he left the *supra* that night, he said goodbye to the old Georgian cleaning woman, who stood speechless at the sudden gift of one hundred American dollars from a complete stranger.

Full Circle

*I'm not a hero worshipper, but I like
people who can make things happen.
I really admire Bob and his hudspah
in seeing where he wants to go
and not paying much allegiance
to anybody except the guys who
are going to get him there.*

> – Larry Coffman, editor & publisher,
> MARKETING,
> Woodinville, Washington

Bob Walsh never stopped puzzling
over Gene Fisher's odd disappearance in
the aftermath of the Goodwill Games. Bob
had attempted to track Gene down several
times over several years, but every lead hit
a dead end, leaving Bob to conclude that
either Gene didn't want to be found, or that
he had met with an accident. Neither proved
to be the case and, in fact, Gene's MIA status turned out to be ridiculously easy to explain. Bob finally fleshed out the story by
contacting Tom Jensen, who had been one
of Gene's closest friends.

"Let's find out what happened to
him once and for all," Bob told Jensen.

Jensen went to the Social Security
Administration, requesting that it sleuth
through its records. Within a week, Jensen
discovered that Gene had not only not gone

L to R: Lili Rtskhiladze, Nana Bagdavadze, Bob Walsh, Bernie Russi,
Julie Russi, and Gene Fisher

very far, but that he practically lived within walking distance of Bob's offices in downtown Seattle.

Gene had, he explained of his unrepentant wanderlust, relocated to Reno in the aftermath of the Games, obviously without leaving a trail. Then, with no fanfare, he had quietly returned to Seattle a year or so later, eventually going to work for a firm that managed medical and pension trust accounts. He had maintained a low profile for no particular reason, and had not communicated with anyone from the old Seattle Organizing Committee, also for no particular reason. But that, of course, had Bob and the few SOC holdovers he still talked to convinced that Gene had vanished off the planet.

Once they reunited, Bob determined to never again lose track of his former Goodwill comrade, quickly arranging to bring Gene in on a project Bob had been trying to launch since 1992.

While touring Tbilisi in the company of Seattle talk show host Dave Ross, Bob had signed an agreement to produce a series of United States performances for a group of young Georgian singers. With Tbilisi embroiled in civil war, nothing had come of it. Bob had signed a second agreement two years later with Georgia's famed national singing and dancing ensemble, to stage a half-dozen U.S. shows. That hadn't worked, either. Bob's third agreement with the group in the summer of 1997 also failed to materialize, but his fourth attempt paid dividends. A seventy-two member ensemble that bore only slight resemblance to such ethnic companies as "Riverdance" and "Tango Argentino," the Georgians would appear in nine United States cities, including Seattle, Pasadena, New York, Chicago, and Washington, D.C. Bob wanted Gene, who had organized numerous exchanges between the U.S. and USSR prior to the Goodwill Games, to help Aimee Shoemaker of Bob Walsh Enterprises coordinate some of the tour's logistics.

Gene took Bob up on his offer, his intrigue stemming not so much from doing the troupe's bookings as his fascination over the manner in which Bob had parlayed the Goodwill Games into a kaleidoscope of international activity. It boggled Gene, for example, that Bob's seemingly inconsequential gift of vitamins to Gosteleradio and USSR State Sports Committee officials prior to the Games had resulted in a pharmaceutical company. Walsh Pharma, which had soared to number three in the Russian marketplace before crashing along with the ruble, had made a substantial turnaround, orders picking up so dramatically that plans had been formulated to take Walsh Pharma into Azerbaijan, Uzbekistan, and Turkey.

It further amazed Gene that Bob now had his name attached to a dairy processing plant, Sante Walsh Products, and that two of his real estate projects stood on the verge

Bob and Timmy Walsh in Maui

486

of completion. Both the Tbilisi Marriott, once a blackened shell, and the Tbilisi Courtyard Marriott, going up on a vacant lot near Freedom Square, would open within a few months. Bob had not only kept his promise to Eduard Shevardnadze, the investors in Bob Walsh Enterprises had reaped a veritable windfall in the bargain, many receiving 30 percent profits on their investment.

Nothing Bob had done since the Games surprised Gene more than the fact that Timmy Walsh, about to start to first grade, had become the paramount project in Bob's life. The Bob Walsh that Gene Fisher had worked with before and during the Goodwill Games had gallivanted all over the world, work consuming his life. This Bob Walsh had become the quintessential single parent, timing his still-frequent travels to coincide with weekends when Milana Walsh had custody of Timmy, while relying on Kristin Hayden in Tbilisi and Aimee Shoemaker, Andy Keehn, and Hannah McIntosh at BWE's offices in Seattle to make certain that business, now largely centered around the Peace Festival, got accomplished.

"Bob took the role of responsible parent very seriously," Gene explained later. "This was an aspect of his character I never would have imagined when we worked together. I just had not seen that in him. I thought, 'Wow!'"

As Bob and Gene got reacquainted, spending a succession of Sunday mornings rehashing stories at Seattle's Sixth Avenue Bar & Grill, they talked as much about their time apart as their time together, Gene initially filling Bob in on the few highlights of his self-imposed exile. Because he had removed himself from Bob's loop, Gene had been unaware that Bob and Kathy Scanlan had spent the better part of a year pursuing a bid for the Olympic Games, or that Kathy now ran Seattle's new Music Experience Project for Microsoft billionaire Paul Allen. Neither did Gene realize that Jarlath Hume, the cofounder of the Goodwill Games, had organized a successful series of arts fairs in Seattle, or that he had business interests in the Russian Far East. Gene had been unaware of it all: The space shot, the relief flights to Georgia, the Vancouver Grizzlies — it had taken a year for BWE to finally receive its commission — and even Bob's relationship with George Makharadze. The former diplomat had just recently departed Butner, North Carolina, and returned to Georgia, where he had been placed in a minimum-security jail to serve out the remainder of his sentence for killing Joviane Waltrick in a drunk-driving accident.

Gene had a special interest in hearing Bob's updates about the medical cases he and Bob had brought to successful conclusions, and it delighted him to learn that, on the occasion of Bob's fifty-ninth birthday, several of his Georgian friends had thrown him a huge party in Tbilisi. More than 200 people attended, the highlight of the feast occurring late in the evening when the tamada, Vaho Tskhadadze, launched into one of his innumerable toasts. As Vaho spoke, all the Georgians turned their heads toward the rear of the room where, next to each other, sat Zizi Bagdavadze and Kakha Merabishvili, both perfect pictures of health.

Following her bone barrow transplant, Zizi had made several follow-up visits to the Fred Hutchinson Cancer Research Center, the doctors finding no trace of cancer. Zizi lived in Tbilisi, had become a mother, and worked at the Academy of Art. Kakha, nineteen years old when he entered Seattle's Providence Hospital, had never experienced another sick day after Dr. Peter Mansfield left him lying, pink instead of blue, on an operating table eleven years earlier. Kakha now worked for a Georgian television station. He had a wife and had just recently become a first-time father. The best part of the birthday party, at least as far as Bob was concerned, occurred when Zizi and Kakha strode to the center of the room and danced to wild applause. Everyone at the party knew the story about how they had been saved, and several Georgians raised toasts to their American doctors, especially Lester Sauvage, Peter Mansfield, Bob Day, and Rainier Storb.

None of Bob's post-Goodwill projects surprised Gene less than the Peace Festival, another testimony, Gene believed, to Bob's ability to facilitate a vision through a congealing of major players. Bob had gone hard after Ted Turner, hoping to elicit his financial support. But other projects occupied Turner's attention, including Bo Derek, whom he had taken up with after shedding Jane Fonda, and a potential television deal in Russia with Bob Wussler, whom he had taken up with again after Time Warner had shed Turner from its board of directors.

Although Bob had been unable to recruit Turner, he had still assembled an impressive list of Peace Festival supporters. The advisory board included Jim Baumann, president and CEO of the Follett Corporation, with whom Bob had once attempted to create the "Spirit of America Games." It also included former U.S. Senator Dale Bumpers, U.S. Congressman Norm Dicks, the Rev. Theodore Hesburgh, president emeritus of the University of Notre Dame, and Archbishop Desmond Tutu, the 1984 Nobel Peace prize winner. Bob's most recent additions to the board were Bill Russell and Carla Stovall, the attorney general of the state of Kansas and a rising star in the Republican Party. Bob had also attracted the support of someone who had great clout with the United States government, General John Shalikashvili, the former chairman of the Joint Chiefs of Staff.

When Georgian Ambassador Tedo Japaridze made the introduction, Bob immediately sized up General Shalikashvili as one of the more impressive men he had ever encountered. A native of Warsaw, Poland, General Shalikashvili had held staff and command positions in Alaska, Germany, Italy, Vietnam, and Korea. In April of 1991, he had commanded "Operation Provide Comfort," a relief mission that returned hundreds of thousands of Kurdish refugees to Northern Iraq following the Persian Gulf War. Shalikashvili had then served as Supreme Allied Commander in Europe before President Bill Clinton appointed him the thirteenth chairman of the Joint Chiefs of Staff, making General Shalikashvili the linear descendant of Omar Bradley, Maxwell Taylor, and Colin Powell. After serving as the principal military advisor to the President and National Security Council, General Shalikashvili had retired, moving to southwest Washington State.

Bob and Jim Baumann had explained the particulars of the Peace Festival to General Shalikashvili in Seattle's Westin Hotel. A week later, after General Shalikashvili had run a security check on Bob, he had agreed to not only endorse the Festival, but endorse it personally to members of Congress, including Alaska's Ted Stevens, the head of the Senate Appropriations Committee.

Armed with a proposal drawn up by David Gogol and Ted Bristol at Sagamore Associates, General Shalikashvili had pitched the Festival so successfully to Stevens that Bob had received a federal grant of $945,000. The funding would not only jump-start the Festival, it would serve as an official endorsement of the Festival by the U.S. government, which Bob figured to use to secure diplomatic and additional financial support from the Azeri and Armenian governments and the oil companies headquartered in Central Asia, Bob's next stop.

But the day before Bob departed, he received an alarming telephone call from Vaso Margvelashvili in Tbilisi.

Life In
The Projects

With Bob, there was always a bigger good. Unlike an ambassador, he's a grass roots guy who has worked his way up through diplomatic levels. Bob got to the top people by building blocks from the bottom up.

— Mike Scallon, Board of Directors,
1990 Goodwill Games,
Seattle, Washington

*A*As British Airways 6723 streaked over the peaks of the Caucasus Mountains, en route to Baku, Azerbaijan, Bob Walsh tossed aside the in-flight magazine, hoisted himself out of seat 2A, strode to the rear of the cabin, and stood for a long time peering out a window, caught up in a reel of reflections over what had been a chaotic couple of months. Georgia's national singing and dancing ensemble, Erisioni, had just returned to Tbilisi after completing its first tour of the United States to largely outstanding reviews. *The New York Times, The Los Angeles Times*, and *The Orange County Register*, in particular, had lavished high praise upon the troupe, which didn't surprise Bob in the least. He'd been enchanted by the company several times. The surprise occurred when ten members of the cast, sans

Erisioni received rave reviews during its first U.S. tour

passports, defected as the singers and dancers boarded the plane in New York for their return to Tbilisi.

Despite the brief hassle that created, it pleased Bob the Georgian singers and dancers had finally toured America. For one thing, their performances had reunited him with Blair Farrington, the Las Vegas entertainment impresario with whom he had once collaborated on arguably the most amusing farce in the history of Bob Walsh Enterprises, The Seattle Seahawks Tenth Anniversary Celebration. With Erisioni gamboling across the country, Bob had sought out Farrington in the hope that Farrington might find use for Erisioni in one of his upcoming productions. While that possibility remained under discussion, Farrington had politely but adamantly dismissed the opportunity to reminisce over the long-ago Seahawk fiasco, when a dozen corpulent members of the Mount Baptist Zion Choir got stuck in an elevator at the Seattle Opera House.

The last couple of months had also brought Andrew Card flitting across Bob's radar screen. With the George W. Bush administration taking tax cut proposals to Congress, Bush's new White House Chief of Staff had been attracting the attention of Beltway TV pundits, his talk show appearances reminding Bob of his long-ago meetings with Card during planning sessions for the Goodwill Games. Card had directed the White House Task Force that coordinated the federal government's involvement in the Games.

Card was just one of several individuals who had recently popped up out of Bob's past. Law enforcement authorities in Texas had unearthed the bones of atheist Madalyn Murray O'Hair, which solved the mystery of her four-year disappearance and took Bob back to his days at WNAC in Boston when he had recruited O'Hair for a series of radio interviews, often just before or after Richard Cardinal Cushing, a booking juxtaposition that still amused Bob. He had also been reminded of Francis Gary Powers, the late U-2 pilot and good friend whom he had employed briefly at KABC in Los Angeles. His son, Francis Gary Powers Jr., had appeared on a C-Span interview touting the new Cold War Museum in Washington, D.C. Another KABC colleague, Maureen Reagan, had generated a few headlines for, unfortunately, developing cancer. Bob had sent her flowers. TV sportscaster Matt Millen, a client of Bob's when Millen starred for the Oakland Raiders, had been hired as president and CEO of the Detroit Lions, giving Bob pause to calculate that his commission would have been $150,000 on Millen's $3 million annual salary if he had remained Millen's agent.

Bob had also spent time ruminating over Kenny O'Donnell, John F. Kennedy's former appointment secretary. Long dead, O'Donnell had become the lead character in a movie titled *Thirteen Days*, Kevin Costner starring as O'Donnell. Bob had frequently enjoyed O'Donnell's company, both while working on his advisory committee when he sought the Massachusetts gubernatorial nomination, and later in Los Angeles when O'Donnell stumped there on behalf of Robert Kennedy.

Stanley Kramer's death at age eighty-seven had also touched off a wave of nostalgia. Bob had spent several years representing the film director's business interests in Seattle, a job highlighted by his weekly breakfasts with Kramer. Bob still had copies of all of Kramer's old *Seattle Times* columns filed away in his office, and a copy of the contract Kramer signed authorizing Bob to represent him. Bob had always admired Kramer's intellect, his movies, especially *High Noon* and *Judgment At Nuremberg*, and his stories, particularly the ones with Spencer Tracy and Katharine Hepburn.

As Bob reflected over ghosts from his past, his eye caught a glint of sunlight. Through the tiny aperture of British Airways 6723, he could barely make out the northeastern shore of the Caspian Sea, a mislabeled saltwater lake so vast — 750 miles long, 200 miles wide, 149,200 square miles in all — that it could contain all five of the Great Lakes with room left over for the Mojave Desert, New Jersey, Hawaii,

Connecticut, Los Angeles, and Manhattan. According to the article Bob had finished a few minutes earlier, the Caspian, along with the Black and Mediterranean seas, stood as remnants of a once-great ocean called the Sea of Tethys, which existed in the Triassic Period before the Alps, Himalayas, and Caucasus rose. But the Caspian's modern notoriety stemmed from the prize it contained. Bob hadn't known that texts predating the time of Christ had made reference to it, or that armies of Alexander the Great had made use of the methane gas that leaked through Caspian soil. Neither had Bob been aware that Zoroaster had been inspired by the Caspian basin's eternal flames to create a religion of fire worshipping, nor that Azerbaijan's oil had been alluded to by Marco Polo and obsessed over by Cyrus The Great, Genghis Kahn, Tamerlane, and Peter the Great.

When Robert and Ludwig Nobel arrived on the southwestern shore of the Caspian in 1873, they established the Nobel Brothers Extracting Partnership, which transformed Baku, Azerbaijan, into the first

mecca of the oil industry and later provided Alfred Nobel with seed money to launch the Nobel Prizes. The Rothchilds subsequently added to their swelling fortune by bankrolling a rail link between Baku and the Black Sea a quarter of a century before the Soviets used Baku's oil to fund their social-

Baku, Azerbaijan: The first mecca of the oil industry

ist revolution. A quarter of a century after that, Adolf Hitler tried unsuccessfully to capture Baku, believing that its oil held the key to defeating Russia in the Great Patriotic War. The Soviets had invented off-shore drilling near Baku in the war's aftermath, but when the Soviet Union rotted away, dozens of international oil companies swooped into the city, determined to lay claim to its riches.

Nobody really knew how much oil was there. According to the article, as much as 200 billion barrels, equivalent to the combined deposits of Iraq and Iran, or the North Sea, might lie hidden beneath the Caspian seabed. The oil money had just started to flow, Heydar Aliyev serving as gatekeeper to Baku's riches.

The president of Azerbaijan had been a KGB general and Politburo member under Leonid Brezhnev and Mikhail Gorbachev, but had been ousted by Gorbachev for engaging in excessive corruption. After the breakup of the Soviet Union, Aliyev returned to his native Azerbaijan, grasped power through a military coup, and got himself elected president by a comfortable 98.5 percent of the vote. Like most rulers in Central Asia and the Caucasus, Aliyev had turned into more monarch than president, and ran his country like a private fiefdom. After his most recent election, which Human Rights Watch called "blatantly unfair," Aliyev had declared his intention to rule Azerbaijan for life, appointing his son, Ilham Aliyev, head of the state-owned Azerbaijan International Oil Company, which effectively permitted Aliyev and his clan to personally profit from the country's vast oil and gas resources. Surviving four coup attempts during his decade in power, Aliyev had also managed to transform himself into a living icon, in part by plastering his profile and proverbs on rugs, roads, and buildings all over the country, in part by constructing two museums to glorify his life's alleged accomplishments, and in part by playing hardball with his political opponents, most of whom were wanted, exiled, jailed, or dead. Unlike Eduard Shevardnadze in Georgia, who had at least attempted to democratize his country, Aliyev had done nothing in Azerbaijan except line his pockets while most of the country went to rack and ruin.

If it were true, as some archeological discoveries suggested, that the Biblical Garden of Eden may have been located in Azerbaijan, also the setting for the new James Bond movie, *The World Is Not Enough*, Aliyev had certainly bungled God's handiwork. Azerbaijan ranked number one in the world in refugees — one in every seven residents had been classified as internally displaced — and fourth in corruption. Azerbaijan was so corrupt, in fact, that the police had dispensed with the pretense of fabricating traffic violations and now openly asked motorists for presents. Worse, Azerbaijan drove out investment faster than it attracted it. More than 110 Turkish companies had packed their bags and fled Azerbaijan in the preceding year, citing corruption as the major cause. Sixty European companies had evacuated for the same reason. Several foreign airlines had also bolted Baku, including Royal Dutch Airlines, UAE's Emirates Airlines, and Austrian Air. Even Pakistani Air had pulled out, the equivalent of the devil fleeing hell because of excessive heat.

Actually, Aliyev didn't so much operate a monarchy as he did a kleptocracy. It had become impossible to open or operate a business in Baku without paying a bribe to the government. Customs officials at Bina Airport had been bought off so expertly and extravagantly that the Azeri government lost a reported $200 million annually in cigarette import taxes and untold additional millions in uncollected taxes on spirits, sugar, flour, and fruit juices. Due to constant theft in the energy sector, Azerbaijan had been forced to briefly cut off electricity. Azerbaijan had even been reduced to importing oil, a stunning development since Azerbaijan sat astride one of the greatest oil repositories on earth, tantamount to Alaska importing snow.

In advance of his flight to Baku, Bob had printed out a series of Internet stories about the so-called Republic of Azerbaijan, the headlines leaving little doubt in Bob's mind that he was about to enter one of the more screwed up places on the planet.

Azerbaijani Minister Under Fire Over Dubious Hotel Deal (Agence France-Presse)

Azerbaijan's Economic Upturn Blighted by Corruption (Agence France-Presse)

Corruption Causes Foreign Businesses To Leave Azerbaijan (Azadlyg)

No Rule Of Law In Azerbaijan (Human Rights Watch)

Azerbaijan Takes Last Place In CIS By Crimes Per Every 100 Persons (AzadInform)

Latest Survey On Bribery Ranks Azerbaijan, Indonesia, Nigeria Worst (Dow Jones)

Azerbaijan's Aliyev Slams Bina Airport Corruption (Reuters)

Price-Fixing Of Cigarette Imports Damages Azeri Economy (Zerkalo)

Ancient Fish Of Caviar Trade Now Face Smugglers, Oil Drills (Christian Science Monitor)

Despite the incriminating text beneath those headlines, Bob looked forward to a possible meeting Heydar Aliyev, clasping a perverse fascination for Third World hobgoblins in the first place, and hoping the Azeri president would bless the Peace Festival in the second place. Bob required the support of Aliyev's government before he could successfully persuade the consortium of Baku oil companies to help underwrite the $6 million event. If he got both, the Festival would take place in nine months — unless, of course, current events in Tbilisi blew the show apart.

And that had been the subject of Vaso Margvelashvili's call to Bob before he embarked for Baku. The Georgian newspaper *Rezonansi* had printed a spate of stunning articles characterizing Bob as a corrupt businessman, a spy working on behalf of Russia, a thief who had absconded with international aid earmarked for Georgia, and an embezzler who had misappropriated Peace Festival funds. The newspaper carried statements made by representatives of the Georgian Youth Foundation, a Peace Festival participant, accusing Bob of turning the Festival into a political and commercial spectacle, accusing Georgian ambassador Tedo Japaridze of working as a Russian agent, and calling into question the business ethics of Kristin Hayden, who had been laboring on Festival business in Tbilisi. Another Tbilisi newspaper, *The Georgian Times*, editorialized that *Rezonansi's* stories "may be followed by a political scandal of international proportions."

Bob recognized *The Georgian Times'* apocalyptic spin for the hooey it was. And he would have had difficulty believing he'd been the target of such journalistic bilge had it not been for the fact the source of the articles was Irakli Kakabadze. He worked for the National Peace Foundation and Bob had pegged him, even before the articles, as certifiably crazy. Still, Kakabadze's ravings had resulted in *Rezonansi* asserting that organizing activities for the Peace Festival had not occurred in a timely fashion when they had been underway for more than a year. They had resulted in a claim that Bob had abandoned the original focus of the Festival — conflict resolution — when $710,000 had been budgeted for it. The paper had accused Bob of diverting funds from the Georgian Youth Foundation to pay for his personal travel expenses when, first, Bob paid his own expenses and, second, the Georgian Youth Foundation had not contributed a lari to the Festival. Everything *Rezonansi* published had been a lie.

Bob found it particularly bizarre to read in *Rezonansi* that he had been appointed "Supervisor of U.S. Congress Support To Georgia" when such a position did not exist in the U.S. government. Supposedly, Bob had used Festival funds to support his nomination of Eduard Shevardnadze for the Nobel Peace Prize when, in fact, the nomination had gone through U.S. Congressman Norm Dicks and had not required any fee.

It rankled Bob that *Rezonansi* published such fiction, especially since he and his shareholders had invested $17 million in Georgia, had made commitments to spend an additional $60 million, and that their investments had resulted in more than 400 new jobs for Georgians. *Rezonansi's* stories more than rankled Shevardnadze, who thundered for ten minutes from his pulpit in front of the Foreign Investment Commission about the outrageousness of *Rezonansi's* articles while simultaneously portraying Bob as a flag-waving Georgian.

Bob could have dismissed *Rezonansi's* stories as a predictable consequence of a free press not yet having become a responsible one, but too many people had been bouncing off walls. Vaso Margvelashvili and Nelly Saroyan had risen publicly to Bob's defense, and Lili Rtskhiladze, the mother of Zizi and Nana Bagdavadze, had taken to the warpath. In Washington, D.C., ambassador Tedo Japaridze had spoken animatedly of heads rolling. Bob had also received telephone calls from the U.S. State Department, the American Embassy in Georgia, the America-Georgia Business Development Council, and the National Peace Foundation. While the articles had been wholly without merit, they had, Bob realized, the potential to make the oil companies and other sponsors flee the controversy. Shevardnadze's alarm stemmed from the potential of those articles to drive Bob and his investors out of Georgia and dissuade other American companies from investing in it as well.

As Bob stood staring out the window, mulling over the fact that, of the 1,800 miles of international borders in the Caucasus, only nine separating Azerbaijan and Turkey were friendly, he wondered what he had gotten himself into, whether the Peace Festival had been such a good idea, whether he ought to file a lawsuit against *Rezonansi* as a purely symbolic protest, and whether the pleasure he'd experienced in Georgia compensated for the current mess. He felt relieved, though, that both Bill Taylor and Ted Kiem of the U.S. State Department and General John Shalikashvili had worked so hard to stabilize the Caucasus. Without their efforts, peace in the region would have been even more difficult to maintain.

A few minutes later, after the stewardess requested that he return to his seat, Bob received one unsettling answer as he engaged an American who lived and worked in Baku.

"Why are you going to Baku?" the man asked.

"We're organizing a Peace Festival."

"A Peace Festival?"

Bob briefly explained the concept, mentioning that he had appointments with representatives of several oil companies, another with Zurab Gumberidze, Georgia's ambassador to Azerbaijan, and that he hoped to be granted an audience with Azeri President Heydar Aliyev.

"Good luck," the man from Baku said. "You should know that in this part of the world there have been eight wars and twenty-seven attempted coups in the last nine years. You might be organizing the only Peace Festival in history where a war broke out."

Epilogue

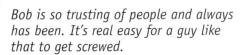

Bob is so trusting of people and always has been. It's real easy for a guy like that to get screwed.

*– Dave Watkins, TEAM Watkins,
Seattle, Washington*

The highway from Bina International Airport to downtown Baku, Azerbaijan, runs past an arid, alkaline tableland, from which a blur of black derricks rise against every horizon, and throughout which the tang of diesel oil and tar pungently scents the air. More potholes than pavement, the road is lined for miles by mud-and-reed hovels that house many of the nation's million refugees. In front of them, old men peddle potatoes and watermelons out of the trunks of rusted cars, while old women offer cheap scarves and prayer beads. Younger men squat on alternating street corners, idly smoking the day away. Halfway from Bina to Baku, a public market situated beneath a misaligned, corrugated roof offers lamb, nuts, lemons, and cabbages that seemingly could rust an iron stomach. The squalor is incredible. These Bakhuvians have nothing to do and no hope except the occasional largess of international relief agencies. Ironically, they live within walking distance of a Klondike of riches.

Eventually, the road to Baku smoothes out and starts to sport the ubiquitous Marlboro, Coca Cola, and Joe Camel logos that signal entry into the heart of the city. A dusty, Silk Road way station during the period of Communist stagnation, Baku has become a post-Soviet Margaritaville of incongruous grime and glitter. Even as the homeless loiter near abandoned brown and gray buildings, a few of them built by German prisoners during World War II, women encrusted in jewels strut down nearby leafy boulevards, oblivious to the surrounding impoverishment, while BMWs and Volvos from Dubai joust for room with battered Ladas, and a tiny donkey pulls a cart past a smattering of the only ATM machines between China and Turkey.

Once a fortress, old Baku is a labyrinth of isthmian alleys, caravansaries, and small mosques, much of it encircled by grandiose limestone villas built a hundred years ago. Part of the Old Town features slaughter-in-the-street markets and much of it operates on a kiosk economy. Overlaying old Baku, boomtown Baku is a spectacle of hard hats and hard currency where the national flower is the satellite dish. All the big oil players are here: Amaco, Shell, British Petroleum, Pennzoil, Elf, Statoil, Lukoil, Itochu, Agip, and along with them the smorgasbord of geologists, engineers, roustabouts, bankers, rock singers, and women of liberal virtue who have come conniving after a share of the same nascent boom, 100 billion barrels of oil, maybe 200 billion, the largest pool on earth after the Persian Gulf.

Against a backdrop of Baku's ancient decay, the oil money has built the Lord Nelson Pub in the new Hyatt Regency Hotel, where dark-suited, dark-eyed men swill cocktails in the company of British Airways stewardesses and young, lithe Azeri women looking for passports out of town. Oil money has also transformed "Oilmen's Boulevard," Neftchilar Prospekti, into a series of Yeves Rocher boutiques, discos, and theme restaurants. At the Ragin' Cajun, a couple of hundred American ex-pats party to the dawn. At Cidir and other joints, belly dancers from Istanbul and Russian chanteuses gyrate and croon cares away.

Bob Walsh encamped at the five-star Park Hyatt Hotel, a well-appointed marble and crystal testimony to Baku's petrodollars. The hotel is so spotless that one afternoon an oblivious guest nearly knocked himself senseless when he strode into a plate-glass window, mistaking it for an open archway. The Park Hyatt presents an attentive staff, most of them young, attractive Azeri women who reflect the Persian, Russian, and Turkish influences of a region unhappily positioned halfway between Russia and the Middle East.

Bob and Kristin Hayden had just spent three days making the rounds of Baku's government offices, meeting with Azerbaijan's Minister of Foreign Affairs, and Zurab Gumberidze, the Georgian ambassador to Azerbaijan who had personally shuttled them to meetings in his black luxury automobile. Bob and Kristin had also conferred with representatives of several oil companies, whisked through the American Chamber of Commerce, the offices of World Vision, and spent an afternoon attending a reception at the American Embassy, where Azeri President Heydar Aliyev delivered one of his interminably tedious speeches. They also sat entranced another day as the Park Hyatt's owner, Paulo Parvis, delivered a blistering denunciation of members of the U.S. Congress who sold their souls to corporations in exchange for campaign contributions.

"People say we are corrupt," Parvis said pointedly to Bob. "Your own U.S. Congress is as corrupt as any country over here."

The U.S. Congress aside, Bob felt good about his trip to Baku, confident that with a little more effort he would ultimately receive the support he required to stage the $6 million Peace Festival. Bob also felt that that once he doused the tempest in Tbilisi sparked by the falsified articles in the *Rezonansi* newspaper, he would be able to pull off the Fesitval to everyone's satisfaction. Then he would head to Hawaii for a long vacation, remembering to not invite any stray Russian translators. Bob yearned to make his life a lot less complicated. But complications trailed Bob the way the dust cloud stalks Pig Pen.

One afternoon after lunch at the Park Hyatt, one of Bob's traveling companions struck up a conversation with an Azeri woman who, according to the metallic tag on her neatly pressed white blouse, was named Sabina. She worked as a hostess in the hotel restaurant, appeared to be about thirty years old, had waist-length reddish hair, black eyebrows, and green opaline eyes. Sabina looked like the Azeri equivalent of Ann-Margret and was the kind of woman most men mentally stripped to the skin.

When Bob's companion queried her, Sabina explained that her father was part Iranian, part Turkish. Her mother, now deceased, had been Russian. Sabina worked three days a week at the Park Hyatt and sometimes picked up odd jobs as an interpreter at the oil conferences routinely held in Baku.

"How do you like Baku?" Bob's companion asked Sabina.

"I like it," Sabina said, her English excellent. "I was born in Naqadeh, a small town south of Urmia in West Azerbaijan Province. Of course, now Baku is my home. But there are so many problems. I would give anything if I could visit America."

"Maybe one day you will."

"This man I've seen you with, what is his name?"

"Which man? There have been several."

"That one," Sabina said, pointing through the restaurant's doors toward the hotel lobby, her eyes suddenly bright with mercenary glitter. "I see that he signs all the checks. Maybe he is the one who will help me. I will ask him about America."

Sabina broke into a smile, gave her long, dark red hair a seductive shake, and started in his direction, seemingly determined to make a major project out of Bob Walsh.

Afterword

Bob is one of the kindest, caring people I've ever met. On the other hand, you just never know what Bob is going to do next.

*— Freddie Mae Gautier,
Seattle, Washington*

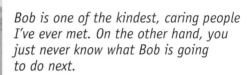

Bob abandoned work on the Peace Festival five months after his trip to Baku when it became clear to him that too many political problems existed for the Festival to proceed. The Russians opposed the Festival, which ran philosophically contrary to Russia's desire to keep the Caucasus in a constant state of turbulence. Bob could not convince government officials from Azerbaijan or Armenia to put aside their differences long enough to talk to each other in Tbilisi. That left Baku's oil companies disinclined to provide financial support for the Festival.

The Georgian Youth Foundation, again illustrating that Georgia isn't so much a crossroads between East and West as it is a permanent fault line, promised to disrupt Bob's planning efforts on the Festival unless given a measure of control over the $945,000 Bob had secured from the U.S. government. And finally, Bob pulled out after he received a telephone call from Nelly Saroyan informing him that his longtime friend, Vaso Margvelashvili, had been beaten up on a Tbilisi street. Vaso had suffered severe head injuries that required surgery. Apparently, he had been whacked either with a pipe or the butt end of a rifle, opening a huge gash in his skull. Although Vaso did not know what provoked the attack, Bob felt it might have had something to do with Vaso's public defense of Bob against the scurrilous Georgian newspaper attacks. Then again, Vaso's beating might have been a random event.

Bob volunteered to spirit Vaso out of Georgia and pay for his operation. And while he was at it, Bob decided to recall Kristin Hayden from Tbilisi as well. With no Peace Festival to keep her occupied, he didn't need her there anymore.

"Even without the Peace Festival," Bob told Gene Fisher, "we've still got a lot of great projects in Georgia. And one of these days, people will discover what a great place Georgia really is."

"So what's next?"

"Time to add to the program," Bob said. "Time to add another country."

"Another country?"

Bob had always harbored designs on doing something big in Argentina.

Acknowledgements

A book as diverse as this one requires the help of many friends and colleagues. I would like to thank my editor Vicki McCown, whose expertise improved the manuscript immeasurably. The good parts are hers, any mistakes all mine. I would like to thank my publisher, Sheryn Hara, who cracks an encouraging whip, and Scott Fisher for his brilliance at graphic design. I am especially grateful to Larry Coffman, Gene Fisher, Kristin Hayden, Bernie Russi, Gene Pfeifer, Ruth McIntyre, Jim Baumann, and Sara Benveniste for the guidance and advice they offered, and grateful, as well, for the long hours Roger Allan, Elana Arustamova, David Gogol, Bill Hahn, Bob Henabery, Jarlath Hume, Tedo Japaridze, Andy Keehn, Hannah McIntosh, Jack McMillan, Ed Parks, Nelly Saroyan, and

Aimee Shoemaker gave to the project. I would further like to thank Richard Blackwell, Lynne Cox, Bill Russell, Gary Furlong, Dianne Roberts, Paul Schulte, Ted Turner, Rick Welts, Nancy Welts, and Jim Whittaker for telling such wonderful stories. Thanks to Misha and Larissa Kalinin, Willie Golovko, Irina Kibina, Alexander Kozlovsky, Helen Shiskana, Sergei Sviridov, and Sergey Volkov for their insights about Russia and the former Soviet Union, and to Nana Bagdavadze, Zizi Bagdavadze, Tina Kuratashvili, George Makaradze, Vaso Margvelashvili, Kakha and Margo Merabishvili, Lili Rtskhiladze, and Mamuka Tsereteli for their enlightenments about the Republic of Georgia. Five doctors — Robert Day, Roy Farrell, Peter Mansfield, Rainier Storb, and Lester Sauvage — also provided extremely helpful information, as did Bob Agnew, Kimberly Brown, Don Fair, Don Horowitz, Tom Jernstedt, Doug Jewett, Tom and Sharon Lovejoy, Toshi Moriguchi, Steve Morris, Karl Moynes, Dick Nelson, Gretchen Nelson, Don Nielsen, Ed Parks, Nicole Preveaux, Steve Raible, Dave Ross, Mike Scallon, Kathy Scanlan, Bill Sears, Dick Smith, Jennifer Stroud, Dave Syferd, Wally Walker, Toni Walsh, Dave Watkins, and Bob and Valerie Yurina. I would also like to single out several others for their support, including Kenneth Ballenger, Tom Jensen, Bruce Nordstrom, Charles Parris, David Raith, Gail Scott, and Lynn Wingard. Special thanks to Arthur Gorlick for providing his Goodwill Games archives, to *Post-Intelligencer* columnist Art Thiel for his analytical and emotional support, to Dan Waggoner for his expert suggestions, to Ron Studham for keeping meticulous notes about the history of Bob Walsh Enterprises, to the former employees of Bob Walsh & Associates, to the numerous individuals who consented to be interviewed, to the staffs at the University of Washington's Suzzalo Library, *Seattle Post-Intelligencer*, and *The Seattle Times*, and to the attentive crew at Seattle's Sixth Avenue Bar & Grill for keeping the coffee cups filled.

BIBLIOGRAPHY

BOOKS

Allen, Steve. Hi-Ho Steverino!, Barricade Books, 1992

Allenov, Mikhail M., et al. Moscow: Treasures and Traditions, Smithsonian Institution & USSR Ministry of Culture, 1990

Andrew, Christopher; Gordievsky, Oleg. KGB: The Inside Story, Harper Collins, 1990

Ascherson, Neal. The Black Sea, Hill and Wang, 1995

Avakian, Arra S. Armenia: A Journey Through History, Electric Press, 1998

Bank, Ted, Editor. Readings in Anthropology: People of the Bering Sea, Irvington Publishing, 1971

Barker, Adele Marie, Editor. Consuming Russia, Duke University Press, 1999

Barrett, Don. Los Angeles Radio People, Volume 2, 1957-97, db Marketing Company, 1997

Batalden, Stephen K.; Sandra L. The Newly Independent States of Eurasia, Oryz, 1993

Binyon, Michael. Life In Russia, Pantheon Books, 1983

Blackwell, Richard. Mr. Blackwell: From Rags To Bitches, General Publishing Group., Los Angeles, 1995

Blum, Dieter. The Land and People of the Soviet Union, Harry N. Abrams Inc., New York, 1980

Bogart, Leo. Premises for Propaganda: The United States Information Agency's Operating Assumptions in the Cold War, Free Press, 1976

Bokeria, Giga; Targamadze, Givi; Ramishvili, Levan. Georgian Media in the 90s: A Step To Liberty. United Nations Development Program, 1997

Brundy, Yitzhaka. Reinventing Russia, Harvard University Press, 1998

Byman, Jeremy. Ted Turner: Cable Television Tycoon (Makers of the Media), Morgan Reynolds, 1998

Can, Turhan. Istanbul: Gate To The Orient, Touristic Publishing Service, LTD, 1997

Carlson, Don; Comstock, Craig. Citizen Summitry, Jeremy P. Tarcher., Inc., 1985

Carlson, Althea. Riding A White Horse: Ted Turner's Goodwill Games and Other Crusades, Episcopal Press, 1998

Chalmers, David Mark. Hooded Americanism: The History of the Ku Klux Klan, Duke University Press, 1987

Coburn, Broughton; Cahill, Tim; Breashers, David. Everest: Mountain Without Mercy, National Geographic Society, 1997

Coppieters, Bruno, Editor. Contested Borders of the Caucasus, VUB University Press, 1996

Dabars, Zita. The Russian Way, Passport Books, 1997

Darchiasvili, David, et al. Elections In Georgia, The Caucasian Institute For Peace, Democracy and Development, 1995

Dezell, Maureen. Irish America, Doubleday, 2000

Dourglishvili, Nino. Social Change and the Georgian Family, United Nations Development Program, 1997

Dubrovin, M., Editor. A Book of English and Russian Proverbs and Sayings, "Prosvesheniye," 1993

Ekedahl, Carolyn McGiffert; Goodman, Melvin. The Wars of Eduard Shevardnadze, Penn State University Press, 1997

Elliott, Mark. Azerbaijan With Georgia, Trail Blazer Publications, 1999

507

Engelstein, Laura; Sandler, Stephanie. Self & Story in Russian History, Cornell University Press, 2000

Engholm, Christopher; Miller, Chris; Manning, Maurie. The Armenian Earthquake, Lucent Books, 1989

English, Robert; Halperin, Jonathan. Beyond the Kremlin, Transaction Books, 1987

Epstein, Edward Jay. The Secret History of Armand Hammer, Random House, 1996

Fainsod, Merle. How Russia Is Ruled, Harvard University Press, 1963

Filene, Peter G. American Views of Soviet Russia, Dorsey Press, 1968

Franzusoff, Victor. Talking to the Russians: Glimpses of History by a Voice of America Pioneer, Fithian Press, 1998

Freemantle, Brian. KGB, Holt, Rinehart and Winston, 1982

Freeze, Gregory. Russia: A History, Oxford University Press, 1997

Friedman, Thomas L. The Lexus and the Olive Tree, Farrar, Straus and Giroux, 1999

Gachechiladze, Revaz. Population Migration in Georgia and its Socio-Economic Consequences, United Nations Development Program, 1997

Geifman, Anna. Entangled In Terror, Scholarly Resources Inc., 2000

Goldberg, Robert; Goldberg, Gerald Jay. Citizen Turner, Harcourt, Brace and Company, 1995

Goldstein, Darra. The Georgian Feast: The Vibrant Culture and Savory Food of the Republic of Georgia, University of California Press, 1999

Gogol, Nikolai. Dead Souls, Penguin Classics, 1961

Gorbachev, Mikhail. Gorbachev: On My Country and the World, Columbia University Press, 1999

Halberstam, David. The Fifties, Ballantine Books, 1993

Halperin, Charles. Russia and the Golden Horde, Indiana University Press, 1987

Hammer, Armand. Hammer: G.P. Putnam's Sons, 1987

Hayes, Harold, Editor. Smiling Through The Apocalypse, Delta Books, 1971

Johnson, Gary K., Editor. NCAA Basketball's Finest, National Collegiate Athletic Association, 1991

Kaplan, Robert D. Eastward To Tartary, Random House, 2000

Keegan, John. The Second World War, Penguin, 1989

Kennan, George. The Decision To Intervene: Soviet-American Relations 1917-1920, Princeton University Press, 1958

Khmaladze, Vakhtang. Local Self-Government in Georgia: Its Past, Its Present and Tendency. United Nations Development Program, 1997

Klose, Kevin. Russia and the Russians, W.W. Norton & Company, 1984

Knight, Amy. Beria: Stalin's First Lieutenant, Princeton University Press, 1993

Knight, Amy. Spies Without Cloaks, Princeton University Press, 1996

Kon, Igor; Riordan, James. Sex and Russian Society, Indiana University Press, 1993

Lamb, Brian. BOOKNOTES Life Stories, Three Rivers Press, 1999

Landro, Laura. Survival: Taking Control of Your Fight Against Cancer, Simon & Schuster, 1998

Landrum, Gene. Profile of Power, Gene N. Landrum, 1996

Laqueur, Walter. The Long Road To Freedom: Russia and Glasnost, Collier Books, 1989

Laufer, Peter. Inside Talk Radio: America's Voice or Just Hot Air?, Birch Lane Books, 1995

Laughlin, William S. Aleuts, Survivors of the Bering Land Bridge, Holt Rinehart
    & Winston, 1997
Lehtmets, Ann; Hoile, Douglas. Sentence: Siberia, Wakefield Press, 1994
Lenin, V.I. What Is To Be Done?, International Publishers, 1969
Lordkipanidze, Miriam. Essays on Georgian History, Metsniereba, 1994
Loughlin, Thomas; Ohtani, Kiyotaka; Editors. Dynamics of the Bering Sea,
    University of Alaska, 1999
Lowe, Janet. Ted Turner Speaks: Insight From the World's Greatest Maverick,
    John Wiley & Sons, 1999
Marrin, Albert. Stalin, Viking Penguin, New York, 1988
McNeal, Robert H. Stalin: Man and Ruler, New York University Press, 1988
Medvedev, Roy. Post-Soviet Russia, Columbia University Press, 2000
Metreveli, Roin. Tbilisi, Publisher's International, 1999
Mouravi-Tarkhan, George. Poverty in a Transitional Society: Georgia, United
    Nations Development Program, 1998
Moynahan, Brian. The Russian Century, Random House, 1994
Murray, William J. My Life Without God, Thomas Nelson Publishers, 1982
O'Connor, Thomas H. The Boston Irish, Back Bay Books, 1995
Otfinoski, Steven. Joseph Stalin: Russia's Last Czar, Millbrook Press, 1993
Perry, John Curtis; Pleshakov, Constantine. The Flight of the Romanovs, Basic
    Books, 1989
Philbin, Regis. I'm Only One Man!, Hyperion, New York City, 1995
Rancour-Laferriere, Daniel. The Slave Soul of Russia, New York University
    Press, 1995
Reddaway, Peter. Uncensored Russia, American Heritage Press, 1972
Remnick, David. Lenin's Tomb, Random House, 1993
Richmond, Yale. U.S.-Soviet Exchanges, 1958-1986: Who Wins?, Westview
    Press, 1987
Roberts, Elizabeth. Xenophobe's Guide To The Russians, Ravette Publishing, 1994
Rogers, Mary; Streissguth, Tom; Sexton, Colleen. Georgia Then & Now, Lerner
    Publications Company, 1993
Rosen, Roger. Georgia: A Sovereign Country Of The Caucasus, Odyssey
    Publications, 1999
Russell, Bill; McSweeny, William. Go Up For Glory, Coward-McCann, Inc., New
    York City, 1966
Russell, Bill; Branch, Taylor. Second Wind: The Memoirs of an Opinionated Man,
    Random House, 1979
Sakharov, Andre. Moscow and Beyond 1986 to 1989, Alfred A. Knopf, New
    York, 1991
Scaduto, Guiliano. The Voice of America, American Literary Press, 1999
Scott, Gini Graham. Can We Talk?, Insight Books, 1996
Shaffer, Marianne; Santos, George. Bone Marrow Transplants: A Guide For Cancer
    Patients and Their Families, Taylor Publishing, 1994
Shevardnadze, Eduard. Letters From Georgia, DEMOCRACY AND
    REVIVAL, 1994
Shevchenko, Arkady N. Breaking Moscow, Alfred A. Knopf, 1985
Shipler, David K. Russia: Broken Idols, Solemn Dreams, Times Books, 1983
Shoemaker, M. Wesley. Russian & Eurasian States, Stryker-Post, 1997
Shulman, Holly Cowan. The Voice of America: Propaganda and Democracy,
    1941-45, University of Wisconsin Press, 1991
Smith, Hedrick. The Russians, Ballantine Books, 1976

Smith, Hedrick. The New Russians, Avon Books, 1990, 1991
Solzhenitsyn, Aleksandr. The Gulag Archipelago, Volume I, Westview Press, 1998
Solzhenitsyn, Aleksandr. The Gulag Archipelago, Volume II, Westview Press, 1998
Solzhenitsyn, Aleksandr. The Gulag Archipelago, Volume III, Westview
      Press, 1998
Spoto, Donald. The Dark Side of Genius, Little, Brown and Company, 1983
Styron, William. Darkness Visible: A Memoir of Madness, Random House, 1990
Suny, Ronald Grigor. Revenge of the Past, Stanford University Press, 1993
Talbott, Strobe. Khrushchev Remembers: The Last Testament, Little, Brown, 1974
Twining, David T. The New Eurasia, Praeger, 1993
Ulam, Adam. The Bolsheviks, Harvard University Press, 1998
Unsworth, Walt. Everest: A Mountaineering History, Mountaineers Books, 2000
Urdang, B. The Armenian Earthquake Disaster, Sphinx Press, 1989
Ushakova, Alexander A. In The Gunsight of the KGB, Alfred A. Knopf, 1989
Van Der Rhoer, Edward. The Shadow Network, Charles Scribner's Sons, 1983
Vasquez, John A. Beyond Confrontation, University of Michigan Press, 1995
Vitale, Dick; Douchant, Mike. Tourney Time, Masters Press, 1993
Wade, Wyn Craig. The Fiery Cross, Oxford University Press, 1998
Wallechinsky, David; Wallace, Irving. The People's Almanac, Doubleday &
      Company, 1975
Wallechinsky, David; Wallace, Irving. The People's Almanac #2, Bantam
      Books, 1978
Warner, Gale; Shuman, Michael. Pathfinders in Soviet-American Relations,
      Continuum Books, 1987
Watson, Emmett: My Life In Print, Lesser Seattle Publishing, 1993
West, Frederick Hadleigh; West, Constance, et al. American Beginnings: The
      Prehistory and Palaeoecology of Beringia, University of Chicago
      Press, 1996
Whittaker, Jim. A Life On The Edge, The Mountaineers, 1999
Whittemore, Hank. CNN: The Inside Story, Little, Brown and Company, 1990
Wilkens, Lenny; Pluto, Terry. Unguarded: My Forty Years Surviving In The NBA,
      Simon & Schuster, 2000
Wright, Peter. Spy Catcher, Viking Penguin Inc., 1987
Yost, Graham. The KGB, Facts on File, 1989
Zbarsky, Ilya; Hutchinson, Samuel. Lenin's Embalmers, The Harvill Press, 1997

CONTRIBUTORS

Robert T. Agnew (Seattle, Wash.), **Mike Alderson** (Seattle, Wash.), **Roger Allan** (Lebanon, N.H.), **Elana Arustamova** (Seattle, Wash.), **Bob Arthur** (Albuquerque, N.M.), **Nana Bagdavadze** (Seattle, Wash.), **Zizi Bagdavadze** (Tbilisi, Georgia), **Joni Balter** (Seattle, Wash.), **Sara Benveniste** (Seattle, Wash.), **Richard (Mr.) Blackwell** (Los Angeles, Calif.), **Peter Bloomquist** (Seattle, Wash.), **Amy Boisjolie** (Bothell, Wash.), **Fred Brack** (Seattle, Wash.), **Herb Bridge** (Seattle, Wash.), **Ted Bristol** (Washington, D.C.), **Kimberly Brown** (Bainbridge Island, Wash.), **Emory Bundy** (Seattle, Wash.), **John Burnham** (Tbilisi, Georgia), **Andrew Caldwell** (Seattle, Wash.), **Michael Chalabi** (Baku, Azerbaijan), **Tamila Chantladze** (Tbilisi, Georgia), **Soso Charkviani** (Tbilisi, Georgia), **Yoko Chiba** (London, England), **Jamal Chkvaseli** (Tbilisi, Georgia), **Julia Church** (Washington, D.C.), **Paula Clarkson** (Seattle, Wash.), **Larry Coffman** (Woodinville, Wash.), **Patsy Collins** (Seattle, Wash.), **William Harrison Courtney** (Tbilisi, Georgia), **Lynne Cox** (Los Alamitos, Calif.), **Ian Curtis** (Baku, Azerbaijan), **Dato Datoshvili** (Tbilisi, Georgia), **Dr. Robert Day** (Seattle, Wash.), **Amy Denman** (Tbilisi, Georgia), **Zina Diakonidze** (Tbilisi, Georgia), **Marisa DiGiacomo** (Seattle, Wash.), **Don Ellis** (Cape Cod, Mass.), **Paata Enukidze** (Tbilisi, Georgia), **Don Fair** (Bellevue, Wash.), **Ramzi Faras** (Nicosia, Cyprus), **Dr. Roy Farrell** (Seattle, Wash.), **Blair Farrington** (Las Vegas, Nev.), **Gene Fisher** (Seattle, Wash.), **Gary Furlong** (Seattle, Wash.), **Freddie Mae Gautier** (Seattle, Wash.), **Nino Gerkeuli** (Tbilisi, Georgia), **Jonelle Glosch** (Baku, Azerbaijan), **Michael Giorgadze** (Tbilisi, Georgia), **David Gogol** (Washington, D.C.), **Svetlana Golovko** (New York City, N.Y.), **Vilen V. Golovko** (Reno, Nev.), **Rusiko Gorgiladve** (Tbilisi, Georgia), **Arthur Gorlick** (Seattle, Wash.), **Dr. Zurab Gumberidze** (Baku, Azerbaijan), **Katharine Guroff** (Bethesda, Md.) **Kakha Gvelesiani** (Tbilisi, Georgia), **Bill Hahn** (Boston, Mass.), **Kristin Hayden** (Tbilisi, Georgia), **Bob Henabery** (Sterling, Va.), **Ian Henry** (Seattle, Wash.), **Nicholas Hintibidze** (Seattle, Wash.), **Givi Homeriki** (Tbilisi, Georgia), **Don Horowitz** (Seattle, Wash.), **Jim Host** (Lexington, Ky.), **Jarlath Hume** (Seattle, Wash.), **Nick Imperato** (Palo Alto, Calif.), **Maka Janikashvili** (Tbilisi, Georgia), **Tedo Japaridze** (Washington, D.C.), **Tom Jernstedt** (Indianapolis, Ind.), **Doug Jewett** (Seattle, Wash.), **Larissa Kalinin** (Las Vegas, Nev.), **Misha Kalinin** (Las Vegas, Nev.), **Kaka Kavtuashvili** (Tbilisi, Georgia), **Carol Keaton** (Seattle, Wash.), **Andy Keehn** (Seattle, Wash.), **Vladimir Khatin** (Las Vegas, Nev.), **Irina Kibina** (Novgorod, Russia), **Vitali Klochko** (Las Vegas, Nev.), **Alexander Kozlovsky** (Moscow, Russia), **Ressan Kontselidze** (Tbilisi, Georgia), **Tina Kuratashvili** (Seattle, Wash.), **Rex Lardner** (Chicago, Ill.), **Suzanne Lavender** (Seattle, Wash.), **Chris Lootz** (Boston, Mass.), **Sandi Lootz** (Boston, Mass.), **Sharon Lovejoy** (Bellevue, Wash.), **Tom Lovejoy** (Bellevue, Wash), **George Makharadze** (Butner, N.C.), **Dr. Peter Mansfield** (Seattle, Wash.), **Vaso Margvelashvili** (Tbilisi, Georgia), **Terry Mark** (Seattle, Wash.), **Bruce Marr** (Reno, Nev.), **Carmen Matthews** (Seattle, Wash.), **Brian P. McCarthy** (Chicago, Ill.), **Bruce McCaw** (Kirkland, Wash.), **Hannah McIntosh** (Seattle, Wash.), **Ruth McIntyre** (Seattle, Wash.), **Jack McMillan** (Seattle, Wash.), **Robert McMillen** (Seattle, Wash.), **Kakha Merabishvili** (Tbilisi, Georgia), **Margo Merabishvili** (Tbilisi, Georgia), **Ia Mirotadze** (Tbilisi, Georgia), **Ian H. Moncaster** (Seattle, Wash.), **Toshi Moriguchi** (Seattle, Wash.), **Steve Morris** (Seattle, Wash.), **Karl Moynes** (Portland, Ore.), **Gretchen Nelson** (Seattle, Wash.), **Richard Nelson** (Seattle, Wash.), **Don Nielsen** (Seattle, Wash.), **Merab Papava** (Tbilisi, Georgia), **Manana Papinaghvili** (Tbilisi, Georgia), **Ed Parks** (Seattle, Wash.), **Maya Patarashvili** (Tbilisi, Georgia), **Palmer Payne** (Booth Bay Harbor, M.I.), **Steve Penny** (Indianapolis, Ind.), **Anna Petrachenkova** (Las Vegas, Nev.), **Eugene Pfeifer** (Seattle, Wash.), **Jennifer Potter** (Seattle, Wash.), **Nicole Preveaux** (Seattle, Wash.), **Steve Raible** (Seattle, Wash.), **Molly Raymond** (Washington, D.C.), **Philip Remler** (Tbilisi, Georgia), **Dianne Roberts** (Port Townsend, Wash.), **Dave Ross** (Seattle, Wash.), **Bill Russell** (Mercer Island, Wash.), **Bernie Russi** (Seattle, Wash.), **Lili Rtskhiladze** (Tbilisi, Georgia), **Ayoub-Farid M Saab** (Nicosia, Cyprus), **Ed Salazar** (Moscow, Russia), **Nelly Sarayon** (Tbilisi,

Georgia), **Dr. Lester Sauvage Sr.** (Seattle, Wash.), **Mike Scallon** (Seattle, Wash.), **Kathy Scanlan** (Seattle, Wash.), **Paul Schulte** (Seattle, Wash.), **Bob Scott** (Miami, Fla.), **Bill Sears** (Seattle, Wash.), **Dave Syferd** (Seattle, Wash.), **Kindle Shaw** (Seattle, Wash.), **Elizabeth W. Shelton** (Baku, Azerbaijan), **Eduard Shevardnadze** (Tbilisi, Georgia), **Helen Shiskana** (Moscow, Russia), **Aimee Shoemaker** (Seattle, Wash), **Kitty Sigua** (Tbilisi, Georgia), **Dick Smith** (Seattle, Wash.), **Jack Smith** (Seattle, Wash.), **Larry Snyder** (Seattle, Wash.), **Robert Spencer** (Los Angeles, Calif.), **Lela Sulikachvili** (Tbilisi, Georgia), **Vladimir Stepania** (Seattle, Wash.), **Dr. Rainier Storb** (Seattle, Wash.), **Rev. William Sullivan** (Seattle, Wash.), **Sergei Sviridov** (Moscow, Russia), **Virginia Swanson** (Seattle, Wash.), **Jim Talbot** (Seattle, Wash.), **George Tavadze** (Tbilisi, Georgia), **Art Thiel** (Seattle, Wash.), **John Thompson** (Everett, Wash.), **Mamuka Tsereteli** (Washington, D.C.), **Maya Tsintsadze** (Tbilisi, Georgia), **Vakho Tskhadadze** (Tbilisi, Georgia), **Giorgi Tsomaia** (Tbilisi, Georgia), **Ted Turner** (Atlanta, Ga.), **Perry Ury** (Hartford, Conn.), **Sergey Volkov** (Seattle, Wash.), **Wally Walker** (Seattle, Wash.), **Bob Walsh** (Seattle, Wash.), **Toni Walsh** (Seattle, Wash.), **Dave Watkins** (Seattle, Wash.), **Emmett Watson** (Seattle, Wash.), **Lea Watson** (Seattle, Wash.), **Nancy Welts** (Seattle, Wash.), **Rick Welts** (Los Angeles, Calif.), **Jim Whittaker** (Port Townsend, Wash.), **Lenny Wilkens** (Seattle, Wash.), **Lynn Wingard** (Federal Way, Wash.), **Tom Wingard** (Federal Way, Wash.), **Shelly Yapp** (Seattle, Wash.), **Bob Yurina** (Seattle, Wash.), **Valerie Yurina** (Seattle, Wash.).

PHOTO CREDITS

Roger Allan Collection, 43, 46, 50; **Richard Blackwell Collection**, 59, 68; **Dr. Robert Day Collection**, 185; **Blair Farrington Collection**, 108; **Gary Furlong Collection**, 238; **Bill Hahn Collection**, 44, 45, 48, 51, 54; **Don Horowitz Collection**, 228; **Tom Jernstedt Collection**, 476; **Sharon Lovejoy Collection**, 114, 119, 180, 198, 318, 320, 324, 328, 407, 445, 482, 484; **Jack McMillan Collection**, 330; **Dick Nelson Collection**, 443; **Ed Parks Collection**, 259, 305; **Nicole Preveaux Collection**, i; **David Raith Collection**, 195; **Bernie Russi Collection**, 42; **Sagamore Associates**, 27, 171, 409; **Dr. Lester Sauvage Collection**, 201; **Paul Schulte-Nancy Welts Collection**, 475; **Corky Trewin Collection**, 10, 18, 19, 20, 22, 23, 24, 30, 34, 98, 100, 101,102, 107, 191, 192, 206, 208, 232, 233, 281, 352; **Seattle Organizing Committee**, 190, 225, 236, 240, 247, 278, 279, 433; **Wally Walker Collection**, 317; **Bob Walsh Enterprises**, viii, 3, 14, 29, 39, 40, 53, 56, 61, 62, 63, 64, 65, 70, 72, 74, 78, 81, 87, 89, 90, 91, 99, 105, 117, 118, 122, 135, 142, 145, 148, 149, 151, 170, 175, 181, 183, 217, 220, 224, 251, 254, 256, 257, 265, 266, 272, 286, 289, 290, 291, 292, 295, 299, 301, 302, 303, 310, 332, 333, 340, 341, 342, 345, 346, 348, 349, 358, 364, 366, 369, 371, 374, 375, 376, 380, 385, 386, 389, 394, 399, 401, 405, 406, 417, 425, 426, 432, 438, 440, 448, 449, 450, 452, 455, 457, 465, 471, 472, 480, 485, 486, 490, 491, 499, 503 ; **Toni Walsh Collection**, 35, 213, 350, 463; **Jim Whittaker Collection**, 262, 263, 264, 271;

INDEX

Index

Order Form

Qty.	Title	US Price	Can. Price	Total
	Who The Hell Is Bob? **by Steve Rudman** **Hard Bound Edition**	**$27.95**	**$35.95**	
	Soft Bound Edition	**$21.95**	**$28.95**	
	Shipping and Handling Add $3.50 for orders in the US/Add $7.50 for Global Priority			
	Sales tax (WA state residents only, add 8.6%)			
	Total enclosed			

Telephone Orders:
Call 1-800-461-1931
Have your VISA or
MasterCard ready.

Fax Orders:
425-398-1380
Fill out this order form and fax.

Postal Orders:
Hara Publishing
P.O. Box 19732
Seattle, WA 98109

E-mail Orders:
harapub@foxinternet.net

Method of Payment:

☐   Check or Money Order

☐   **VISA**

☐   **MasterCard**

Expiration Date: _____

Card #: _____

Signature: _____

Name _____
Address _____
City _____ **State** _____ **ZIP** _____
Phone (**)** _____ **Fax (**   **)** _____
E-mail _____

Quantity discounts are available.
Call 425-398-3679 for more information.
Thank you for your order!